CW01509582

The Removal of Confusion

The Removal of Confusion

Concerning the Flood of the Saintly Seal Aḥmad al-Tijānī

A Translation of

Kāshif al-Ilbās ʿan Fayḍa al-Khatm Abī al-ʿAbbās

by

Shaykh al-Islam
Al-Ḥājj Ibrāhīm b. ʿAbd-Allāh Niasse

Biography of Author by Sayyid ʿAlī Cisse

Introduction by Shaykh Ḥasan b. ʿAlī Cisse

Ḥadīth Analysis by Shaykh Tijānī b. ʿAlī Cisse

Translation by
Zachary Wright, Muhtar Holland and Abdullahi El-Okene

2010

First published in 2010 by
Fons Vitae
49 Mockingbird Valley Drive
Louisville, KY 40207
http://www.fonsvitae.com
Email: fonsvitaeky@aol.com

© Copyright Fons Vitae 2010

Library of Congress Control Number: 2009935222
ISBN 9781891785474

No part of this book may be reproduced
in any form without prior permission of
the publishers. All rights reserved.

Printed and bound in Malaysia

Contents

Appendices

Acknowledgements

All thanks and praise is to Allah, the First, the Last. Success in this endeavor is by His Grace alone, all mistakes are from our own ignorance and egos. Working on this manuscript has been a tremendous blessing for all those concerned. We can only pray that with our meager efforts we manage to transmit a small portion of the force and clarity of the original Arabic text.

The English translation of the *Kāshif* would not have been realized without the support and encouragement of the late Shaykh Ḥasan Cisse and his brother and successor, Shaykh Tijānī Cisse, may Allah be pleased with them both. It was they who entrusted the completion of this translation, first to Abdullahi El-Okene, and lastly to Zachary Wright. A first draft of excerpts of the work was realized through the efforts of Kamal Husayni, who first commissioned Muhtar Holland to translate the book. Special thanks are also due to M. D. Yusuf and Dawud Jeffries for their support in the final printing of this translation.

The final product found here benefitted from the insights and hard work of countless others: Fakhruddin Owaisi (South Africa), Saʿad Abū Bakr al-Maidugari (Nigeria), and Najmirah Abdullah (Senegal/South Africa) for translation advice; and Ashaki Taha-Cisse, Yahya Weldon, and Yusuf Hilliard for editing assistance. Appreciation is also due to Professors Rüdiger Seesemann (Northwestern) and Ousmane Kane (Columbia) for their comments, corrections, and advice on the manuscript.

Proceeds from the sale of this book are donated to the ongoing construction of the Grand Mosque in Medina-Baye Kaolack, Senegal, first established by Shaykh Ibrāhīm Niasse in 1937.

May Allah accept our efforts

Background to the Text

The *Kāshif al-ilbās* is the magnum opus of twentieth-century West Africa's greatest Muslim leader, Shaykh al-Islam Ibrāhīm ʿAbd-Allāh Niasse (1900–1975). No Sufi master can be reduced to a single text, and the mass following of Shaykh Ibrāhīm, described as the largest single Muslim movement in modern West Africa,[1] most certainly found its primary inspiration in the brilliant career and spiritual zeal of the Shaykh rather than written words. This analysis of what is, arguably, the most significant Arabic text of twentieth-century West Africa cannot escape the essential paradox of Sufi writing, namely, the difficulty of putting the ineffable experience of God into words. The *Kāshif* repeatedly insists that the communication of experiential spiritual knowledge (*maʿrifa*)—the key concept on which Shaykh Ibrāhīm's movement was predicated and the subject that occupies the largest portion of the *Kāshif*—is beyond words. The Shaykh writes of spiritual experience or "taste" (*dhawq*): "It cannot be acquired through talking or written texts, but can only be received directly from the people of spiritual experience (*ahl al-adhwāq*)."

While some recent academic research has rightly devalued the role of texts in the transmission of Sufi knowledge,[2] none can deny the continued relevance of studying the writings of prominent Sufis. Sadly, serious textual consideration of West African Sufism has been stifled by lingering colonial prejudice of a supposedly unlearned, localized *Islam Noir* ("Negro Islam"). Time and again, received knowledge concerning African Muslims' lack of scholarly qualifications has substituted for actual study of their teachings

1 Mervyn Hiskett, *The Development of Islam in West Africa* (London: Longman, 1984), p. 287.

2 Proceedings from the workshop, "Sufi Texts, Sufi Contexts," Institute for the Study of Islamic Thought in Africa (ISITA), Northwestern University (28–29 May 2007), particularly the presentations of Carl Ernst, Valerie Hoffman, and Rüdiger Seesemann.

and writings. West African Arabic writings deserve a closer look. This translation is a significant step forward in understanding Islamic religiosity on the African continent.

Understanding the contents of the *Kāshif al-ilbās* requires some background of the life and mission of its author.[3] Shaykh Ibrāhīm was a Muslim scholar and sage of the Tijāniyya Sufi order.[4] The Tijāniyya has spread to all corners of the Muslim world since Shaykh Aḥmad al-Tijānī (d. 1815, Fes) established the confraternity in North Africa in the late eighteenth century. Many eminent scholars have emerged from among the Tijāniyya in the last two centuries, but none has been as successful in propagating the Order as Shaykh Ibrāhīm. It is currently estimated that those owing their initiation into the Tijāniyya to Shaykh Ibrāhīm number around one hundred million and make up more than half of all the Tijānīs in the world.[5]

Shaykh Ibrāhīm explained his historical mission in spreading Islam and the Tijāniyya throughout West Africa and beyond as being endowed with *al-Fayḍa al-Tijāniyya*, the "Tijānī Flood" predicted by Shaykh Aḥmad al-Tijānī that would occasion people entering the Tijānī spiritual path group upon group. If *fayḍa* was the doctrine, the distinguishing practice of Shaykh Ibrāhīm's movement was *tarbiya*, or spiritual training. Through *tarbiya*, aspirants transcended the confines of their ego-selves and "tasted" the directly-experienced knowledge, or gnosis (*maʿrifa*), of God. Certainly this practice was not new within Sufism or the Tijāniyya itself, but Shaykh Ibrāhīm's ability to help millions attain the highly valued spiritual illumination (*fatḥ*) was surely unprecedented. Of course, there is much more to the story of Shaykh Ibrāhīm—his ground-breaking legal rulings, his creation of a grass-roots pan-African and pan-Islamic movement, his world travels and close relations with some of the most renowned revolutionary leaders

3 For more information on the life and thought of Shaykh Ibrāhīm Niasse, see Rüdiger Seesemann, *The Divine Flood: Ibrāhīm Niasse and the Roots of a Twentieth-century Sufi Revival* (Oxford University Press, forthcoming); Joseph Hill, "Divine Knowledge and Islamic Authority: Religious Specialization among Disciples of Baay Ñas" (Ph.D. thesis, Yale University, 2007); Andre Brigaglia, "The *Fayda* Tijaniyya of Ibrāhīm Nyass: Genesis and Implications of a Sufi Doctrine," in *Islam et Sociétés au sud du Sahara* 14–15 (2001); Ousmane Kane, "Shaykh al-Islam al-Hajj Ibrāhīm Niasse," in Robinson and Triaud (eds.), *Le Temps des Marabouts, Itinéraires et stratéfies islamiques en Afrique occidentale française v. 1880–1960* (Paris: Karthala, 2000); Mervyn Hiskett, "The Community of Grace and its Opponents, the Rejecters," in *African Language Studies* 17 (1980).

4 For more on the Tijāniyya, see Zachary Wright, *On the Path of the Prophet: Shaykh Ahmad Tijani and the Tariqa Muhammadiyya* (Atlanta: AAII, 2005); Triaud and Robinson (eds.), *La Tijaniyya, Une Confrérie musulmane à la conquête de l'Afrique* (Paris: Karthala, 2000); Abdelaziz Benabdallah, *La Tijania: une Voie Spirituelle et Sociale* (Marrakesh: Al Quobba Zarqua, 1998); and Jamil Abun-Nasr, *The Tijaniyya, A Sufi Order in the Modern World* (London: Oxford University Press, 1965).

5 Statistics presented by Shaykh Ḥasan Cisse at the International Tijani Forum in Fes, Morocco, 28 June 2007.

(Kwame Nkrumah, Sekou Touré and Gamal Abdel Nasser for example) of his time—but this concept of a flood of gnosis, spiritual illumination for all who desired it, was the key to understanding the Shaykh's life and mission.

The *Kāshif al-ilbās*, written early in the Shaykh's career in 1931–1932, is primarily a justification for the transmission of the experiential knowledge (*maʿrifa*) of God on a widespread scale. The self's complete immersion and annihilation in the divine Essence, which Sufism has long maintained is essential for true knowledge of God, is a concept that has been fraught with tension throughout Islamic history, both among the detractors of Sufism and among Sufis themselves. The aspirant who becomes "enraptured" in God may behave as one absent from his senses or he may make extraordinary spiritual claims. The *Kāshif* thus presents the means of attaining gnosis (*maʿrifa*) and the results of such knowledge for its possessor; in the process differentiating false pretentions from sincere expression, delusion from real experience, heresy from Islamic orthodoxy.

Divine gnosis and the possibility of its mass transmission through the Tijānī *fayḍa* was certainly one of the issues current in early twentieth-century West Africa, and is *the* the key issue of the *Kāshif*. But it was not the only matter of dispute to which Shaykh Ibrāhīm was responding in his work. Around the time the *Kāshif* was written, there seems to have been a lively debate in Senegal over whether it was possible to "see" God. This debate erupted in a series of polemical exchanges immediately after the *Kāshif*'s writing between the followers of Shaykh Ibrāhīm and Aḥmad Dem (d. 1973), a Fulani scholar living in Sokone, Senegal.[6] Other issues with an immediate historical context include the emphasis on public recitation of Sufi litanies. This was, no doubt, a response to the century-old dispute between scholars of the Tijānī and Qādirī Sufi orders in northern Nigeria and elsewhere, over whether Sufis should recite their liturgies silently or out loud in public. Other questions emerged with the triumph of Sufi leaders over traditional forms of authority in West African society in the early twentieth century. For example, what was the spiritual identity and social role of women in the new religious order of the Sufi shaykhs? To these questions, Shaykh Ibrāhīm devoted separate sections of the *Kāshif*. Other subjects addressed in the work confront some of the most contentious issues still facing Muslims today: the orthodoxy of Sufism and its practices, the untenability of continued racial and cultural prejudices, the nature of religious authority and the ethics of disagreement between Muslims.

---

6 Aḥmad Dem's polemical work against the possibility of "seeing" God was entitled *Tanbīḥ al-aghbiyāʾ*. It produced immediate refutations from ʿUthmān Ndiaye, whose work was entitled *Sawārim al-ḥaqq*, and from ʿAlī Cisse, whose work was entitled *Mikhzam li abāṭil Aḥmad Dem*. For the specifics of this debate, see chapter three ("Seeing God") of Seesemann's *The Divine Flood*. I am indebted to Seesemann for providing me an advance copy of this and other chapters.

Conventions of writing change with the times, and Sufi literature is no exception. For one familiar with the genre of Islamic scholarly prose since the eighteenth-century, it is not surprising to find that roughly half of the *Kāshif* consists of citations from prior works. The source analyses conducted on important Sufi works in the region immediately prior to the *Kāshif*—on Ibn al-Mubārak al-Lamaṭī's *Ibrīz* (written 1719, Morocco) and ʿUmar al-Fūtī Tal's *Rimāḥ* (written 1844, Senegal) by Bernd Radtke,[7] and on Mālik Sy's *Ifḥām al-munkir al-jānī* (written 1921, Senegal) by Ravane Mbaye[8]—permit a useful comparison to Shaykh Ibrāhīm's citation from previous sources. According to Radtke, the *Ibrīz* contains 270 citations from 139 different books, with most sources used not more than once or twice. The *Rimāḥ* contains about 640 citations from 123 sources, with most citations (two-thirds) coming from nine authors (with eighteen to ninety-eight citations from each). Mbaye did not keep track of the number of citations in the *Ifḥām*, but he estimates more than 200 sources,[9] while six works are cited more frequently (between four and thirty citations from each). In the *Kāshif*, Shaykh Ibrāhīm uses 271 citations from 112 different works. There are eighteen works which Shaykh Ibrāhīm cites more frequently: between four and seventeen times each.

A closer look at the main sources used in each of the three seminal Tijānī works—the *Rimāḥ*, the *Ifḥām*, and the *Kāshif*—reveal a diverse group of sources for Tijānī writers in West Africa. Of the main sources listed by Radtke for al-Ḥājj ʿUmar, Mbaye for al-Ḥājj Mālik and ourselves for Shaykh Ibrāhīm, the only work cited more than four times by all three writers is the primary text of the Tijāniyya: ʿAlī Harāzim al-Barāda's *Jawāhir al-maʿānī*. Shaykh Ibrāhīm shares al-Ḥājj ʿUmar's frequent recourse to the works of ʿAbd al-Wahhāb al-Shaʿrānī (d. 1565, Egypt), Aḥmad Zarrūq (d. 1493, Libya), Ibn ʿAṭāʾ Allāh (d. 1309, Alexandria), and Ibn al-Mubārak al-Lamaṭī's *Ibrīz*. Shaykh Ibrāhīm also shares al-Ḥājj Mālik's predilection for the nineteenth-century Moroccan Tijānī scholar Ibn al-Sāʾiḥ's *Bughya al-mustafīd* and the eighteenth-century Turkish Sufi exegete Ismāʿīl al-Ḥaqqī's *Rūḥ al-bayān*. To this list of distinguished Sufi writers, Shaykh

---

7 Bernd Radtke, "Ibriziana: Themes and Sources of a Seminal Sufi Work," *Sudanic Africa* 7 (1996); and Radtke, "Studies on the Sources of the *Kitab Rimah Hizb al-Rahim* of al-Hajj ʿUmar 6 (1995).

8 Ravane Mbaye, *Le Grand Savant El Hadji Malick Sy, Pensée et Action, tome troisième: Ifham al-Munkir al-Jani, Réduction au silence du dénégateur* (Beirut: Dar Albouraq, 2003).

9 This number may be inflated, as an examination of Mbaye's "Index of works cited" for the *Ifḥām* reveals that Mbaye neglects to distinguish between works cited by Sy directly and works referenced by authors whom Sy cites. For example, Shaykh Ibrāhīm Niasse may cite from Shaʿrānī, who in turn cites from a work of Ibn al-ʿArabī. In such a case, our list of the sources in the *Kāshif* would not include the work of Ibn al-ʿArabī, only the work of Shaʿrānī.

Ibrāhīm adds frequent use (four or more citations each) of the writings of the Malian Qādirī Shaykh Mukhtār Kuntī (d. 1811), Ibn al-ʿArabī al-Ḥātimī, Abū Ḥāmid al-Ghazālī (d. 1111, Baghdad), the Moroccan Shādhilī scholar Ibn ʿAjība (d. 1809), the Moroccan Tijānī Shaykh Aḥmad Sukayrij (d. 1949), the Persian Sufi al-Qusharyī (d. 1072), the Indian scholar Aḥmad al-Ṣāwī (d. 1825), the Mauritanian Shādhilī master Muḥammad al-Yadālī (d. 1753), and the writings of al-Ḥājj ʿUmar himself.

Radtke's observation on the diversity of subject matters these works draw from is certainly confirmed by examining an overview of the sources used in *Kāshif*. Like Lamaṭī and al-Ḥājj ʿUmar, Shaykh Ibrāhīm cites works of exegesis (*tafsīr*),[10] prophetic traditions (*ḥadīth*),[11] jurisprudence (*fiqh*),[12] theology (*ʿaqīda*),[13] grammar (*naḥw*),[14] religious principles (*uṣūl*)[15] and history/ biography (*sīra*),[16] as well as works of Sufism. The geographical diversity of sources also deserves notice: authors from India, Persia, Turkey, the Arab Middle East, and Morocco are cited alongside authors from West Africa. The diversity of subjects and geography demonstrate definitively

10 Most notably the *Tafsīr al-Jalālayn* of Jalāl al-Dīn al-Suyūṭī and Jalāl al-Dīn al-Maḥallī (along with the commentary of Aḥmad al-Ṣāwī on the margins), the *Jawāhir al-ḥisān* of ʿAbd al-Raḥmān al-Thaʿālibī (d. 1471), *Rūḥ al-bayān* of Ismāʿīl al-Ḥaqqī, the *Tafsīr al-kabīr* of Fakhr al-Dīn al-Rāzī (d. 1210), the *Baḥr al-ʿulūm* of Abū Layth al-Samarqandi, and the *Taʾwīlāt al-najmiyya* of ʿAlāʾ al-Dawla al-Simnānī (thirteenth century, Persia).

11 Aside from the six *Sunan* of Bukhārī, Muslim, Abū Dāwūd, Tirmidhī, Ibn Majā, and Nasāʾī; these include the *Musnad* of Aḥmad b. Ḥanbal, the *Muwaṭṭāʾ* of Imam Mālik, the *Shifāʾ* of Qāḍī ʿĪyāḍ, *Kitāb al-adhkār* of Nawawī, the *Sunan al-kubrā* of Bayhaqī, *al-Maqāṣid al-ḥasana* of Sakhāwī (d. 1497, Egypt), the *Fatḥ al-Bārī* of Ibn Ḥajar al-ʿAsqalānī (d. 1448, Egypt), *al-Fatawa al-ḥadīthiyya* of Ibn Ḥajar al-Haytamī al-Makkī (d. 1556, Mecca) and other classical works of prophetic traditions.

12 These are, predictably, mostly of the Mālikī school (*madhhab*), such as the *Risāla* of Qayrawānī (d. 996, Fes), the *Mukhtaṣar* of Khalīl, or the *Bidaya al-mujtahid* of Ibn Rushd. But there are a few notable exceptions, such as the Shāfiʿī scholar ʿAbd al-Mālik al-Juwaynī (known as Imam al-Ḥaramayn, d. 1085, Hijaz) and Imam Badr al-Dīn al-Zarkashī al-Shāfiʿī (d. 1392).

13 Such works include important works of the Ashʿarī school, such as the *Sharḥ al-mawāqif* of ʿAlī b. Muḥammad al-Jurjānī (d. 1413), the *Idāʾa al-dujanna* of al-Maqqārī (d. 1632, Tlemcen/Damascus), and *al-Durr al-thamīn wa al-mawrid al-maʿin* of al-Mayyāra (d. 1662, Fes).

14 Among the works cited in this category are *al-Qāmūs al-muḥīt* by Abū al-Ṭahir b. Ibrāhīm Majd al-Dīn al-Fayruz Abadi (d. 1414, Shiraz/Mecca) and its commentary *Tāj al-ʿarūs min jawāhir al-qāmūs* by Murtaḍā al-Zabīdī (d. 1790, India/Egypt).

15 An example would be the *al-Asrār al-ʿaqliyya* by the Egyptian Shāfiʿī scholar Taqiyy al-Dīn al-Maqtaraḥ (d. 1215).

16 Such works would include the comprehensive history of the early Muslim community by Ṭabarānī, or the historical compilation of legal opinions in the Maghrib, the *Miʿyār* of al-Wānsharīsī

that West African Muslim writers participated in global Muslim currents of scholarly exchange.

The *Kāshif* thus deftly weaves together the writings of the past Sufi masters. This format was, of course, not lost on Shaykh Ibrāhīm himself, who describes his own work as one that "collects the cream of the books authored on this discipline (of Sufism)." It was a style well received by his contemporaries. In the section of commendation of the *Kāshif*, Shaykh Ibrāhīm includes the praise poetry of a number of scholars from Mauritania associated with the heritage of Muḥammad al-Ḥāfiẓ al-Shinqīṭī (d. 1830), who first introduced the Tijāniyya south of the Sahara. The Shaykh writes:

> I have presented my work entitled *Kāshif al-ilbās* to a community among the people of my age, the people of explanation (*ḥall*), joining (*ʿaqd*) and scholarly criticism in the sciences of the sacred law and the divine Reality. They are the masters of creation and leaders of the distinguished folk of the sufi path. All of them, praise be to Allah, praised me for this work and wrote a commendation. So I wanted to include here their commendations and testimonies in order that the fair-minded person would know that this book contains nothing other than a collection (*jamʿ*), so the words in it are the words of the scholars (*ʿulamāʾ*), and the doctrine on which it is built is the doctrine of the bosom-friends.

This ability to gather the knowledge of earlier scholars was thus considered an important testimony to a shaykh's scholarly credentials. Certainly the work played a role in the submission of many within the Idaw ʿAlī scholarly tribe to Shaykh Ibrāhīm beginning in the 1930s. It is likewise related that when Shaykh Ibrāhīm first visited Nigeria in 1945, he took with him four copies of the *Kāshif*, which he left with the *ʿulamāʾ* in the city of Kano, one of the most renowned centers of Muslim scholarship in all of Africa. After reading the book, the Kano scholars testified that such a work, which gathers so much knowledge together in one place, was an occurrence they thought relegated to the scholars of Islam's golden ages.[17]

This is not to say that the *Kāshif* contains nothing original. In his analysis of the sources for al-Ḥājj ʿUmar's *Rimāḥ*, Radtke rightly draws

17 Interview with Shaykh Tijānī ʿAlī Cisse, Medina-Baye, Kaolack, Senegal, June 2009. Rüdiger Seesemann reports a similar version of events from Barham Diop, the traveling companion of Shaykh Ibrāhīm: "On his departure from Kano, Shaykh Ibrāhīm left behind a few copies of *Kāshif al-ilbās*. Later the book found its way into the hands of a few religious scholars, who assumed that the author had lived in Senegal a long time ago—until ʿAlī Cisse and Abū Bakr Serigne Mbaye (Niasse) made a stopover in Kano on their way to the Hijaz. The scholars of Kano were stunned by their visitors: 'Where are you from?'—'Senegal.' Then the scholars asked whether they had heard about a saint called Ibrāhīm Niasse, who had lived in Senegal a long time ago. 'He is alive, he is still in Senegal. This is his brother.'"

the reader's attention beyond the author's incorporation of so many other sources, to focus instead on *how* the author uses his sources. The *Kāshif* of course also contains a good deal of the author's own prose and poetry. But the methodology the Shaykh uses in citing from other works deserves a closer look. Generally speaking, Shaykh Ibrāhīm presents a series of citations on a given subject, usually interspersed with his own comments. He concludes by including what Shaykh Aḥmad al-Tijānī (d. 1815), the founder of the Tijāniyya Sufi order, has himself said concerning the subject in question. The significance of this straightforward approach should not go unnoticed. In fact, Shaykh Ibrāhīm says in the text: "Whoever examines it (the *Kāshif*) closely and judges it fairly will know for certain that this compilation was authored by Shaykh al-Tijānī with his own hand." The guiding spiritual presence of Shaykh Aḥmad al-Tijānī aside, Shaykh Ibrāhīm's methodology in selecting and ordering citations seems to be a conscious effort to demonstrate the dialectic between the Tijāniyya and earlier Sufi traditions, thereby giving fresh perspective to Shaykh al-Tijānī's own words. Moreover, Shaykh Ibrāhīm hoped that such fresh perspective would benefit and unite his Tijānī readership, praying in the book's conclusion that Allah would "make it a source of discernment for the Spiritual Path and its people, stringing them together (like pearls) in the company of the Noble Seal (al-Tijānī)."

The claim that Shaykh al-Tijānī is the real author of the *Kāshif* of course has broader implications than just putting the Shaykh's words in dialogue with other Sufi traditions. In fact, the *Kāshif*, like many other Sufi texts, has its own reputation for saintly blessing (*baraka*), simply as a physical object. Shaykh Ibrāhīm writes: "May Allah put tremendous blessing (*baraka*) in it, to the extent that it may bless any place it is found." Today, many followers of Shaykh Ibrāhīm carry the book with them when they travel just to have the blessing of it in their possession wherever they go.[18]

Standards of Muslim sainthood and saintly blessing—where personal agency is often obscured with reference to God, the Prophet Muḥammad, or a previous saint—should not prevent the reader from grasping the unprecedented or original quality of Shaykh Ibrāhīm's *Kāshif al-ilbās*. The *Kāshif* argues in a nutshell that acquiring the experiential knowledge of God (*maʿrifa*) is the essential purpose of human existence, and that a "flood" has come within the ranks of the Tijāniyya to spread the Sufi path of the Seal of Saints, Shaykh Aḥmad al-Tijānī; thereby reconnecting Muslims to the Divine in a time of ignorance and distance from God. Even if the *Kāshif* is filled largely with a collection of the "cream" of past Sufi writings, Shaykh Ibrāhīm's essential argument is extraordinarily bold and unprecedented. His frequent warnings in the text not to reject the pronouncements of God's saints are an indication that he was aware of this. The result of this

18 Interview with Shaykh Tijānī ʿAlī Cisse, Medina-Baye, Kaolack, Senegal, June 2009.

masterful blend of the Sufi tradition, in which the concept of a flood of gnosis is fully justified, was no less than the foundation for one of the greatest Sufi movements in modern times. The significance of the *Kāshif* in the development of modern West African Muslim religious identity, and the religiosity of Shaykh Ibrāhīm's followers elsewhere around the world, cannot be underestimated.

Whatever the blessing or lofty purpose of a Sufi text, the reader of the *Kāshif* should not forget the suspicion with which Sufis have generally treated writing. "Secrets are in the hearts of the distinguished folk (*rijāl*), not in the bellies of books," Shaykh Ibrāhīm Niasse was fond of saying.[19] Indeed, very particular circumstances inspire a Sufi master such as Shaykh Ibrāhīm to write in the first place, and most Sufi shaykhs left no writings at all. The purpose of Sufi texts is to respond to particular issues at hand, not to serve as the means of actually transmitting the knowledge of God or the means of purifying the ego-self (*nafs*). These essential aims of Sufism are meant to be transmitted from spiritual master to disciple in the absence of texts. The *Kāshif* was written to make space for the emergence of the Tijānī Flood, not to actually initiate aspirants into the knowledge of God brought by this Flood. Sufi texts remain important sources for study not because they contain the actual practices of people, but because they help establish a conceptual space within which practice unfolds. Careful consideration of works such as *Kāshif al-ilbās* is a prerequisite to the serious discussion of Islam in West Africa.

Zachary Wright

Medina-Baye, Kaolack, Senegal
June 2009 (Rajab 1430)

19 Interview with Shaykh Ḥasan Cisse, Lagos, Nigeria, February 2006.

Note on Translation

This translation is based on the most recent Arabic publication of the *Kāshif al-ilbās*, edited by Shaykh Tijānī b. ʿAlī Cisse (Cairo: al-Sharkat al-Dawliyya lī al-Ṭibāʿa, 2001). There are several reasons for using this particular printing over earlier publications of the work (beginning in 1951). Shaykh Tijānī Cisse's 2001 edition is much more than a reprinting of earlier publications. It is based on the earliest available manuscripts of the original text. Moreover, Shaykh Tijānī conducted an extensive analysis of the prophetic traditions cited by Shaykh Ibrāhīm Niasse. It is related that one scholar of al-Azhar (Egypt), upon seeing the work of Shaykh al-Tijānī in this regard, remarked that this effort alone would fulfill the requirements for a Ph.D. in *ḥadīth* studies from that prestigious institution.

Shaykh al-Tijānī's footnotes to the 2001 Arabic edition include chapter and page number references to specific collections of *ḥadīth*, as well as alternative narrations of the tradition in question. Unfortunately, this translation cannot hope to reproduce this extensive technical analysis of the prophetic traditions cited in the text, but we have made use of his work to indicate the general source of the *ḥadīth* in question.

We also have made every attempt to identify the authors and texts cited by Shaykh Ibrāhīm. The Arabic text assumes a degree of familiarity with the Islamic scholarly tradition that cannot be taken for granted among an English readership. For works or personalities which Shaykh Ibrāhīm mentions more than once, only the first reference is footnoted. Otherwise, a reference list of sources is available at the end of this book: the reader is encouraged to return there should he/she forget a reference that has already been mentioned. The same is true for Arabic words which appear in the translation: a glossary of Arabic terms is included in the back should the reader be unable recall an Arabic word earlier defined. Honorary titles are a common occurrence in Arabic texts and need not distract the reader from recognizing names. The titles are not usually part of the name itself and the same personality may be referred to with different titles: shaykh (spiritual guide, scholar), Sayyid (master, descendant of the Prophet, ﷺ), imam (prayer leader), or Sīdī (an abbreviated form of Sayyid). The traditional blessings on the prophets, the Prophet Muḥammad, and his companions are defined in the table below.

Knowledge of the Arabic language is not sufficient to translate a work of this kind. This translation benefits from the knowledgeable shaykhs who continue to teach and transmit the *Kāshif al-ilbās* to committed students. In many cases, knowledge of the context of the text is indispensable to understanding the Arabic itself. An immediate example is the translation of the book's title. Although *ilbās* literally translates as "clothing" or "garb," the meaning intended by Shaykh Ibrāhīm, as many scholars confirm, was actually *iltibās*, meaning "confusion" or "ambiguity."

As scholars of linguistics have rightly concluded, there is no truly authoritative translation: every translation is but an interpretation made by the translator. In many cases, Shaykh Ibrāhīm quotes from works that have already been translated into English. Just as we have translated these passages independently of previous translations, qualified independent or alternative translations of the *Kāshif* can only add to a more complete portrait of the author's original meaning.

Arabic glyph	English meaning	Usage
عز وجل	Mighty and Majestic is He	on mention of God
عليه السلام	Peace be upon him	on mention of a prophet
عليهم السلام	Peace be upon them	on mention of more than one prophet
ﷺ	May the peace and blessings of God be upon him	on mention of the Prophet Muḥammad, and on occasion following the mention of other prophets
رضي الله عنه	May God be pleased with him	on mention of a companion of the Prophet Muḥammad
رضي الله عنها	May God be pleased with her	on mention of a female companion of the Prophet Muḥammad
رضي الله عنهم	May God be pleased with them	on mention of several companions of the Prophet Muḥammad

Biography of Authors

Shaykh Ibrāhīm Niasse (b. 1900, Tayba Niassene, Senegal; d. 1975, London)
The "Bringer of the Tijānī Flood" (Ṣāḥib al-Fayḍa al-Tijāniyya), Shaykh Ibrāhīm became widely recognized as one the preeminent Muslim scholars and the leading authority of the Tijāniyya Sufi order of his age. He traveled widely, becoming known as "Shaykh al-Islām" for his comprehensive mastery of the Islamic sciences. His success in spreading Islam and the Tijāniyya on the African continent was unprecedented.

Sayyid ʿAlī Cisse (b. 1906, Diossong, Senegal; d. 1982, Medina-Baye Kaolack, Senegal)
Sayyid ʿAlī, a descendent of one of the oldest scholarly families in West Africa, became the closest disciple and spiritual inheritor (*khalīfa*) of Shaykh Ibrāhīm. He wrote several books besides the *tarjama* (biography) of the Shaykh in the beginning of the *Kāshif*. He married Shaykh Ibrāhīm's eldest daughter, Fāṭima Zahra Niasse; and their sons have since emerged as some of the primary spokesmen for the following of Shaykh Ibrāhīm.

Shaykh Ḥasan Cisse (b. 1945, Medina-Baye Kaolack; d. 2008, Medina-Baye Kaolack, Senegal)
The Imam designated by Shaykh Ibrāhīm to succeed Sayyid ʿAlī, Shaykh Ḥasan became the preeminent representative of the "Tijānī Flood" in recent years. He spread Islam and the Tijāniyya in America and South Africa and numerous other lands. He founded a humanitarian NGO, the African American Islamic Institute (AAII), to promote cultural exchange and fulfill educational and health-care needs. He studied in Senegal, Mauritania, and Egypt, and was awarded an honorary doctorate from al-Azhar University in Cairo.

Shaykh Tijānī Cisse (b. 1955, Medina-Baye Kaolack)

The second son of Sayyid ʿAlī Cisse and Fāṭima Zahra Niasse, Shaykh al-Tijānī (also spelled Cheikh Tidiane) succeeded his elder brother as the Imam of the Grand Mosque in Medina-Baye and President of the AAII in 2008. As a student at al-Azhar University, he specialized in *ḥadīth* studies. He has since edited and printed many books of Shaykh Ibrāhīm and other Tijānī scholars. Shaykh al-Tijānī was the last student taught by Shaykh Ibrāhīm, the last to receive unlimited authorization (*ijāza muṭlaqa*) in the Islamic sciences from his father Sayyid ʿAlī, and the closest companion of Shaykh Ḥasan.

Zachary Wright

A graduate student in African History at Northwestern University (Chicago), Zachary is also the author of *On the Path of the Prophet: Shaykh Ahmad Tijani and the Tariqa Muhammadiyya* (AAII Publishing, 2005). He has been blessed to maintain close contact with the community of Shaykh Ibrāhīm Niasse for the last twelve years, and to have studied with Shaykh Ḥasan and Shaykh Tijānī Cisse.

Muhtar Holland

Muhtar Holland has published numerous works and translations, the most recent being a translation of Imam al-Tirmidhī's *al-Shamāʾil* (Fons Vitae & Muslim Literary Society, forthcoming). He has worked as Senior Research Fellow at the Islamic Foundation in England and the Director of the Nur al-Islam Translation Center in New York.

Abdullahi El-Okene

Abdullahi El-Okene is a professor of Engineering at Ahmadu Bello University in Zaria, Nigeria. He received his instruction in the Islamic sciences in Nigeria, and later spent a good deal of time in the companionship of Shaykh Ḥasan Cisse, being entrusted by him with several Arabic-English translation projects. He is the Chairman of the International Organization of the Tijaniyyah Brotherhood based in Nigeria, and several other Islamic organizations.

Arabic Transliteration Key

Arabic letter	Transliteration	Phonetic equivalent
ا	ā	talk
ب	b	boy
ت	t	table
ث	th	bath
ج	j	joy
ح	ḥ	-
خ	kh	-
د	d	day
ذ	dh	then
ر	r	run
ز	z	zebra
س	s	sun
ش	sh	shine
ص	ṣ	-
ض	ḍ	-
ط	ṭ	-
ظ	ẓ	-
ع	ʿ	-
غ	gh	-
ف	f	feast
ق	q	-
ك	k	key
ل	l	love
م	m	mother
ن	n	none
ه	h	health
و	w/ū	weather/food
ي	y/ī	yes/street
ء	ʾ	(glottal stop)
ة	-	(silent)/hat
َ	a	bag
	i	big
ُ	u	bug

Introduction to the 2001 Arabic Edition by Shaykh Ḥasan Cisse

In the Name of Allah, the Compassionate, the Merciful

Praise be to Allah, the First, the Last, the Manifest, the Hidden; who said, *Will they not meditate on the Qurʾān, or are there locks on their hearts?* (Qurʾān, 47:24). And He said, *He gives wisdom to whomsoever He pleases; and whoever is given wisdom, has truly been given abundant good* (2:269). What passes the lips derives merely from the throat, and above every scholar is someone more knowledgeable.

Blessings and Peace on the Radiant Light, the Lightning Flash, the Fountainhead of divine Effulgence; he who has acquired Allah's Magnificent Light, our Master Muḥammad, the Opener of what was closed, the Seal of what has passed, the Helper of Truth by the Truth, the Guide to Your Straight Path, and on his family, may this prayer be equal to his worth, and to the greatness of his extent in space and time. It was he ﷺ who said, "Relate from me, even if one verse." And he said, "Let the one present inform the one absent, for perhaps the one informed (in my absence) will comprehend more than the one hearing (directly from me)."

The subject of Sufism is bound inextricably to Allah. It begins with Him, ends with Him, and returns to Him, may He be Glorified and Exalted. The Sufis are the elite of Allah's servants. They are the guardians of His religion and His community, the ones upholding His Book and His sacred law in every time and every place. Their words, their actions, their movements and rest, their knowledge, their overflowing bounties, their righteous deeds and their spiritual stations are all for the sake of Allah and to Him do they return. Allah, Glorified and Exalted is He, is their Trainer, their Teacher, their Guide and their Director to the balanced, straight path. It is this divine connection in which all of them are found: joined in earnestness, love, intimacy, proximity, and absorption in the divine Essence of Allah, Holy and Exalted is He. The Sufi has become the Qurʾānic verse, *Wheresoever you turn is the Countenance of Allah* (2:115): not seeing anything except Him. It has been said, "Sufism is when the Real makes you die to yourself, and brings you back to life because of Him." Once our master, teacher, and patron, Abū al-ʿAbbās al-Tijānī ☙, was asked about the true nature of Sufism. He responded, "Know that Sufism is obeying the commands and avoiding the prohibitions, externally and internally, in a way that pleases Him, not in a way that pleases you."

We are not here today for the purpose of defending the Sufis. Allah is the One defending them. He, may He be praised and exalted, said: *Surely Allah is the Defender of those who believe* (22:38). The defense of the Sufis is thus to remain innocent of anything that contravenes the sacred law. Then they become worthy of the statement of Shaykh Aḥmad al-Tijānī: "If you hear something related from me, weigh it on the scale of the sacred law. What balances, take it; what does not, leave it." What can be added to the truth but misguidance? So we invite the weighing of the entirety of the Shaykh's companions and beloved ones, both the common folk and the elite, on this scale.

What great, glad tidings is this reprinting of the book, *The Removal of Confusion concerning the Flood of the Saintly Seal Aḥmad al-Tijānī*, after a complete redaction from its original manuscript. In truth, this book deserves to be inscribed in golden ink due to what is contained herein by way of religious sciences, secrets, overflowing bounties, and illuminations. May Allah be well-pleased with the author, for by this summary he has brought benefit to the servants in all lands. He has collected in this work everything that had been separated and dispersed in previous books of the Sufis. Indeed, he has gathered the cream of these works concerning the science of Sufism. The author said that whoever examines this book closely, and with fairness, will know for certain that this work was in actuality authored by Shaykh Aḥmad al-Tijānī himself. May Allah be pleased with him, and allow us to benefit from him.

Before concluding, I wish to thank my dear brother, the distinguished master, Shaykh Tijānī ʿAlī Cisse, who expended great effort to accomplish this pious work and praiseworthy endeavor. He reprinted this book after a complete redaction. He also identified the prophetic traditions cited in the work using the great *ḥadīth* collections of Imam al-Bukhārī, Muslim, Tirmidhī, Abū Dāwūd, Ibn Māja, al-Nasāʾī, and others. In all, the sources for this work include more than thirty collections of prophetic traditions, such as the commentary on (Ghazālī's) *Iḥyāʾ ʿulūm al-dīn* (Murtaḍā al-Zabīdī's) *Ittiḥāf al-sāda al-muttaqīn*. This work facilitates the accomplished reader to find the relevant *ḥadīth* himself or an alternative narration.

Allah is the Guarantor of success. We ask Him, Glorious and Exalted is He, to purify this work for the sake of His Noble Countenance. May

He regard it with pleasure and acceptance, and may it be an acceptable service (*khidma*) for our honorable patron, shaykh and means of access to Allah, the Shaykh of Islam and spiritual guide for humanity, the pole of right guidance and succor of the servants, Shaykh Ibrāhīm b. al-Ḥājj ʿAbd-Allāh al-Tijānī. May Allah be pleased with him and his father, Amen. Surely He is the One who Hears, the Close, the One who Answers prayers.

Biography of the Author, Shaykh Ibrāhīm Niasse

By Shaykh ʿAlī b. Sayyid al-Ḥasan Cisse

In the Name of Allah, the Compassionate, the Merciful. May Allah bestow blessings upon the secret of the divine Essence, he through whom the divine Names and Attributes are elucidated, our master Muḥammad, the best of creation. And on his family and companions, may Allah grant fountains of grace (*faḍl*) and overflowing bounties (*fuyūḍāt*).

This is only a small portion of the author's biography, may Allah be pleased with him.

He is a Shaykh in all the degrees and ramifications of the rank. He is the mouthpiece of his time, the light of his age, unique of his kind, the focus of Allah's attention among His creation. He is the open doorway for anyone who wishes to enter the Holy Presence. The age knows no equal in knowledge and religious piety. He is the Shaykh for the training of spiritual aspirants, the repository of learning for the rightly-guided, and the seal of those who have attained certain knowledge (*al-muḥaqqiqīn*) in the fourteenth century of the Islamic era. He is the splendor of the nights and the days. He is the authorative source (*ḥujja*) of the distinguished gnostics (*al-ʿārifīn*), the blazing pride of the Muḥammadan community. He is the champion the Ṭarīqa Aḥmadiyya Ibrāhīmiyya Ḥanīfiyya (Tijāniyya), for he is the elite of its most distinguished men. He is the rising sun of the religious and gnostic sciences, the confluence of discernment, insight, and gnosis. He is the impregnable fortress, the lofty mountain cave. He is the pearl in the crown worn by the noble champions of Truth. He bears the precious necklace from the saintly poles (*aqṭāb*); he lifts the flag of noble virtues among the human race. He brings together the knowledge of the previous scholars: knowledge that had been dispersed and separated, from the time after the foundation of this Muslim community until recent times. He is endowed with a beautiful, pleasant character, and with the sanctified qualities of the Prophet Muḥammad ﷺ.

From the favor from the Most Bountifully Generous (*al-Karīm*), the Ever-Giving (*al-Wahhāb*), he mastered the sacred sciences and the gnostic understandings of the Compassionate Lord to a degree impossible to describe by even the most eloquent and profuse tongue. He has no like and no equal in the present or the future. By means of the Muḥammadan inheritance and the spiritual training of the Seal of Saints, Aḥmad al-Tijānī, he ascended the peaks of honor, purity and perfection. He was crowned with resplendent jewels. He is possessed of subtle instruction, weighty knowledge and precise explanations.

This is our Shaykh, our means of access to Allah, the incomparable saintly pole, the great preeminent gnostic sage, Shaykh Ibrāhīm b. al-Ḥājj ʿAbd-Allāh al-Tijānī b. Sayyid Muḥammad b. Madamba b. Bakr b. Muḥammad al-Amin b. Samba b. al-Riḍā. May Allah be well pleased with them all, and may He enable us and our loved ones to benefit by him. Amen.

Upbringing of the Shaykh

He was born after the afternoon prayer on Thursday, in the middle of Rajab in the year 1320 (A.H.),[20] in Ṭayba, a village built by his father ﷺ. The fact that this Imam, the Bosom-Friend (*al-Khalīl*)[21] of majestic prestige, was born in Ṭayba—which means "delightful goodness"—is sufficient proof for the appropriateness of the town's name.

He grew up in the care of his father, modeling his decency, righteousness, devoutness, valor, chastity, propriety, and piety. He studied the Qurʾān under his father and memorized it perfectly in the *Warsh*-style of recitation as taught by Imam Nāfiʿ.[22] It is reported that he was eager to be of service as an adolescent, and signs of nobility had already become apparent in him in his youth.

After memorizing the Qurʾān, he devoted himself earnestly to the study of the formal Islamic sciences in both their literal and implied meanings. He succeeded in acquiring knowledge and understanding, reaching the

20 Corresponding to 17 October 1902. The actual year of the Shaykh's birth was 1318 (8 November 1900), according to a note the Shaykh himself wrote (1934–1935). The note is cited in Muḥammad b. Iktush, *Min akhbār al-Shaykh Ibrāhīm* (p. 26); a copy of the original is also in the possession of Rüdiger Seesemann.

21 Al-Khalīl is the name Islamic tradition gives to Prophet Ibrāhīm.

22 According to *ḥadīth* (in *Ṣaḥīḥ al-Bukhārī*), the Qurʾān has seven different styles of reading, the two most famous being *hafs* and *warsh*. *Warsh* reciters trace their school through Imam Nāfiʿ, a teacher of Qurʾān recitation (*tajwīd*) in Medina, Arabia. His student, Abū Saʿīd ʿUthmān b. Saʿīd al-Miṣrī (d. 197/812), nicknamed "Warsh" because of his light complexion, brought the style of recitation to Egypt. The *Warsh* style remains the most common recitation in North and West Africa.

desired goals and purpose. Indeed, he learned the sciences exhaustively and mastered all their disciplines, distinguishing himself in a very short period of time. So Allah appointed him as a mercy for His servants and as a benefit for both the ancestors and the contemporaries.

In all of this, his education was personally undertaken by his father, a man of famous reputation and firmly established qualifications. Praise be to Allah, he received from him the precious gems of beneficial learning, the gifts of the secrets (*asrār*), the remembrances (*adhkār*) and the sacred law (*sharīʿa*).

Then Allah granted him complete spiritual illumination (*fatḥ*), presenting him with sciences bestowed by divine grace. So he excelled in them as well. He did not study these sciences under any human being: he was taught only by the One who is All-Knowing, by means of divine inspiration (*ilhām*). He remained unceasingly devoted to the acquisition and provision of beneficial knowledge, until many seekers of sacred learning were attracted to him. Students derived benefit from his school (*madrasa*), and righteous erudite scholars received training at his hand, as evidenced and confirmed by the people of discernment and perception. His blessing thus spread to all the brethren, and his degree was exalted above all peers.

Affiliation with the Tijāniyya Sufi Path

He received the Tijāniyya Order from the unique figure of his epoch, the proof of the people of his era, the copious well of Tijānī litanies (*awrād*) and secrets, and the assembly point of its lights and remembrances (*adhkār*): his Shaykh and father, the erudite scholar, the wise exemplar, the undoubted deputy (*khalīfa*) of Shaykh al-Tijānī and the bearer of his flag in the western lands, al-Ḥājj ʿAbd-Allāh b. Sayyid Muḥammad. He was indeed the Shaykh, the Imam, one of the eminent saints, who combined in his person the sacred law (*sharīʿa*) and divine Reality (*ḥaqīqa*) and so became the guide of the Sufi way. May the Most Generous Lord never cease exalting him to the most praiseworthy station (*al-maqām al-aḥmad*).

After receiving the Ṭarīqa, a great yearning entered the young Shaykh's perfected, lofty, serene, and well-pleasing soul.[23] His lofty spiritual aspiration (*himma*) was awakened anew, and with such force that it would have demolished the unshakable mountains had it been directed towards them. It led him to harvest the fruits of divine sciences (*al-ʿulūm al-ḥaqqaniyya*), heavenly experiences (*al-adhwāq al-malakūtiyya*) and angelic secrets (*al-asrār al-jabarūtiyya*), to a point that no one before or after him could aspire. How splendid are these verses of the eloquent orator, erudite scholar and excellent poet, in which he eulogizes this Shaykh:

---

23 Shaykh ʿAlī Cisse's use of words such as *al-nafs al-kāmila* and *al-nafs al-marḍiya* convey the meaning that Shaykh Ibrāhīm had, at this early stage, completed the purification of the soul (*tazkiya al-nafs*) central in Sufi doctrine.

The famous pole (*quṭb*) of the Tijāniyya, its crown and Imam
And his predecesors were (also) its crowns.

Owner of the highest rank, unreachable
By the gnostics, whatever the exalted nature of their gnosis.

By him, the sacred law has had its reputation enhanced
By him the divine Reality has had its stature elevated.

But for him, both of them would have been barren shells
Their pillars in ruins.

So he then embarked on the task of benefitting the people with the sciences of divine bestowal and experiential knowledge of the Lord. He devoted himself to this task morning and evening, day and night.

Knowledge and Character

As for his grasp of the Qurʾān and the Sunna, his good manners, education, guidance, linguistic fluency, eloquence, and proficiency, he feasted on these sciences and monopolized them. Trying to match his mastery of them would be like seating an uninvited guest at the table where he dines. The learned and cultured men of his time, near and far, testified to his learning. When he spoke, the eloquent Arabs would fall on their knees in front of him, raising their heads and lending him their ears. He commanded all the sciences, both transmitted and rationally deduced. He would decipher their meanings as he saw fit, extracting the pearls from their treasure-troves on the spur of the moment. As for his knowledge of the divine realities (*al-ḥaqāʾiq al-rabbāniyya*), the sacred gnostic sciences (*al-maʿārif al-qudsiyya*) and the spiritual states pertaining to the Essential Being (*al-aḥwāl al-dhātiyya*): he was their standard-bearer, the key to their doors, their beacon (*mishkāt*), their lamp (*miṣbāḥ*) and their lantern (*zujāja*).[24]

He was copiously endowed with excellent merits and virtues. Neither the pen nor the tongue can describe the extent of such glorious qualities or the abundance of his benefit for his Lord's creatures. From his bounty, good conduct, and generosity, he tenderly provided for those in need, like a mother nursing her child; continuously struggling to please the Kind and Beneficent Lord. Those whom he nurtured attained (spiritual) maturity always in love of his nurturing. So his reputation soared and his mention spread to the farthest horizons.

---

24 The reference here is to the Qurʾān (24:35), *Allah is the Light of the heavens and the earth. The similitude of His Light is as a niche (mishkāt), wherein is a lamp (miṣbāḥ). The lamp in a glass (zujāja), the glass is, as it were, a glittering star... Mishkāt* is here translated as "beacon" to reflect what most Qurʾān interpreters understand to mean the place wherein a lamp is placed to give off more light (for which "niche" is only a partial translation). See Edward Lane, *Arabic Lexicon*, p. 1590.

The triumphant banner of virtue was firmly planted at his feet, without dispute or dissension. In every single moment, he never ceased bestowing moral excellence, blessings, and the overflowing surplus of his bounty. His grace, noble generosity and beneficence were showered everywhere. His excellent qualities are beyond enumeration, and no record could contain a complete list of his merits even if all the world's pens were used until they snapped on their scrolls.

Writings

As for the excellence of his poetry and prose, his mastery of the skills of rhetoric and explanation, and his eloquent use of the pen and the tongue, Saḥbān and Ḥassān could not have matched him![25] He is the author of numerous literary compositions, as well as many reports, informative responses and useful notes, in which he reconciles the differences in the texts of the Imams who are reliable sources of guidance. His literary works include the following:[26]

Kāshif al-ilbās ᶜan fayḍa al-khatm Abī al-ᶜAbbās [The removal of confusion concerning the flood of the saintly seal Abū al-ᶜAbbās (Aḥmad al-Tijānī);

Masarra al-majāmiᶜ fī masāʾil al-jāmiᶜ [The charm of compositions, concerning the issues relating to the congregational mosque];

al-Khamr al-ḥalāl: fī madḥ Sayyid al-Rijāl [The lawful wine, in praise of the leader of men];

Taysīr al-wuṣūl ilā ḥaḍra al-Rasūl [The facilitation of attainment to the presence of the Messenger];

Ṭīb al-anfās fī madāʾiḥ al-khatm Abī al-ᶜAbbās [The perfume of breaths in praises of the seal Abū al-ᶜAbbas];

Rawḍ al-muḥibbīn fī madḥ al-ᶜārifīn [The garden of the lovers, in praise of the gnostic sages];

al-Nūr al-rabbānī fī madḥ al-Sayyid Aḥmad al-Tijānī [The divine light in praise of Sayyid Aḥmad al-Tijānī];

Rūḥ al-adab limā ḥawā min ḥikam wa adab [The spirit of good morals, and what it contains of wisdom and manners];

---

25 Saḥban and Ḥassān were famous for their eloquence and their eulogies in the time of the Prophet.

26 Other important works were written after Shaykh ᶜAlī Cisse wrote this introduction. For a complete list of Shaykh Ibrāhīm's writings, see Ousmane Kane, John Hunwick and Rüdiger Seesemann, "Senegambia I: The Niassene Tradition," in Hunwick (ed.), *Arabic Literature of Africa*, vol. 4, *The Writings of Western Sudanic Africa* (Leiden: Brill, 2003), p. 279–301.

Nūr al-baṣar fī madḥ Sayyid al-Bashar [Light of the eye in praise of the master of humankind];

al-Sirr al-akbar wa al-kibrīt al-aḥmar [The greatest secret and the red sulfur];

Tuḥfa al-aṭfāl fī ḥaqā'iq al-afʿāl fī al-ṣarf [The children's gift, concerning the real meanings of verbs in conjugation];

al-Fayḍ al-Aḥmadī fī al-mawlid al-Muḥammadī [The Aḥmadan bounty concerning the Muḥammadan birthday];

Tabṣira al-anām fī jawāz ru'ya al-Bārī fī al-yaqẓa wa al-manām [The enlightenment of humanity: concerning the permissibility of the vision of the Creator while awake or asleep]; and

Rūḥ al-ḥubb fī madḥ al-quṭb [The spirit of love in celebration of the saintly pole].

Bringer of the Flood *(fayḍa)*

Allah established him as a spring (*manhal*) for the spiritual wayfarers, one who provides hope for aspirants and seekers, help for those in need, support for the destitute, and nourishment for the starving. Allah endowed him with the Flood (*fayḍa*) mentioned by the Hidden pole, the renowned Muḥammadan Seal, our Shaykh and our assistance, the owner of the effusion (*fayḍ*), our master Aḥmad b. Muḥammad al-Tijānī. And this *fayḍa* has spread and continued without interruption, for its occurrence comes near the End of Time. At his hand, thousands upon thousands attained to the perfection of experientially-witnessed gnosis (*al-maʿrifa al-ʿayāniyya al-shahūdiyya*). Many, both White and Black, would come to him each day in droves from all regions of the earth to enter into our Tijāniyya Order, the repository of divine favor and gifts of gnosis. No one who received from him this prodigious litany (*wird*) failed to gain from it the benefit of divine aid and access to the realms of gnosis. As the most excellent poet has written:

> O the best of those at whose door is found waiting the excellent ones;
> Their own retinues vie with each other to visit him
>
> Indeed, the success of the creation is found in visiting you
> And in neglecting visiting you is its deprivation
>
> By your fragrance the creation achieves (its needs)
> And white people have followed the black in visiting you.
>
> You have lightened the dreariness of your disciples' journey
> No longer do they dread its boulders and rocks
>
> You are the Imam, the leader of the way, its physician

The skilled guide of the path, its Luqmān,[27] its Sultan

Indeed, you are its Tubba,[28] its Caesar,
Its Anūshirwān,[29] its Negus,[30] and its Khāqān.[31]

Indeed, in this time, Shaykh Ibrāhīm is the one who carries the burdens of spiritual training according to the prophetic Muḥammadan inheritance. It is he who bears the flag of spiritual elevation according to the most praiseworthy Abrahamic model (*al-tarqiyya al-aḥmadiyya al-ibrāhīmiyya*). He is the sanctuary of secrets (*asrār*), spiritual experience (*adhwāq*), lights (*anwār*), states (*aḥwāl*), stations (*maqāmāt*), and manifestations of the Seal of Sainthood (*al-tajalliyāt al-khatmiyya*).

These words should be clear to you, as testimony has been provided by some of the leading descendents of our distinguished preeminent shaykhs. These men, who are the foundation of the Spiritual Path, have come to him in order to join his company, obtain his guidance, cling to the hem of his robes, and receive the Tijānī litany (*wird*). Such noble descendents include

27 The Prophet Luqmān was attributed with great wisdom. See Qur'ān, 31:12–13.

28 Tubba was the name given to the ancient kings of Arabia based in Yemen.

29 Khusru Anūshirwān (r. 531–79 C.E.) reigned during the golden age of Sāsānian civilization in Persia. He was known as "Anushirwān the Just." Under his leadership Persian culture spread to the Far East, and scholars from around the world came to study at the universities he established.

30 Negus simply means "King" in Amharic and other languages common to Ethiopia. Islamic tradition tells of a particularly just Negus (named Ashama) ruling Abyssinia (Ethiopia) at the time of the Prophet Muḥammad, who accepted Muslims fleeing persecution in Mecca and converted to Islam in secret. When the Negus died, the Prophet led his community in a funeral prayer for him.

31 Khāqān, also spelled Khakhan or Khagan, the "Khan of Khans" or "Great Khan," was a title used by Chinese emperors as well as other peoples of the Far East.

those of Shaykh Muḥammad al-Ḥāfiẓ,[32] Sayyid Muḥamdi,[33] Shaykh Mawlūd Fāl,[34] Shaykh Muḥammad ʿĀl[35] and of Shaykh Muḥammad al-Ḥanaf.[36]

Shaykh Ibrāhīm gave them the best of spiritual trainings (*tarbiya*), guided them on the straightest of ways and paths, and presented them to their Lord in the best of conditions. So they entered the fortress of His domain, drunk on the wine of the divine Presence, extinct to their own existence and remaining in the world only because of Him. Congratulations are due to these outstanding masters, and still more congratulations, since they were related to the shaykhs of this Shaykh, the magnanimous director, trainer, and promoter. Yet their filial relationship to the previous shaykhs did not prevent them from reaching the perfect figure of the age. They deserve congratulations, because it is filial relationship to the shaykhs that has obstructed and impeded many of our contemporaries, like others among the people of ancient times.

O Allah! Remove the obstacle from us, and relieve us of attachments and impediments, just as You have done for those You have blessed with understanding, the people of veracity and certitude. Promote us at all times to the highest stations of direct knowledge (*maʿrifa*) of You. Grant every success to those who join this Shaykh, befriend him, and believe him, or those who recognize him, submit to him, and do not disobey him. Let the news be repeated and broadcast in all the regions of the earth, making it known that he has no peer in spiritual training (*tarbiya*) and guiding people toward the Sublime Sacred Presence.

---

32 Shaykh Muḥammad al-Ḥāfiẓ b. al-Mukhtār b. al-Ḥabīb al-Shinqīṭī (1759–1830), mentioned in the text as "our Shaykh and our means of access to Allah … by whose hand the Ṭarīqa has spread in the lands of the far west." Shaykh al-Ḥāfiẓ was of the Idaw ʿAlī people in Mauritania. He visited Shaykh Aḥmad al-Tijānī in Fes in from 1800 to 1804/5 and was the first to bring the Tijāniyya Order into Mauritania, from where it later spread to the rest of West Africa.

33 Shaykh Muḥamdi b. ʿAbd-Allāh al-ʿAlawī (known as "Baddi") was the inheritor (*khalīfa*) and son-in-law of Shaykh Muḥammad al-Ḥāfiẓ and the author of his most comprehensive biography, *Nuzha al-mustamʿ wa al-lafiz fī manāqib al-Shaykh Muḥammad al-Ḥāfiẓ* (written in 1832).

34 Shaykh Mawlūd Fāl was initiated into the Tijāniyya by Muḥammad al-Ḥāfiẓ, and later traveled to Fes, Morocco, to have his initiation renewed by the main *zāwiya* there just after the passing of Shaykh Aḥmad al-Tijānī in 1815. Mawlud Fal traveled widely throughout West Africa and left many propagators of the Order in regions such as Futa Jallon, northern Nigeria, and Sudan.

35 Muḥammad ʿĀl b. al-Fatḥ was a renowned Tijānī shaykh of the Ḥāfiẓiyya legacy. According to Shaykh Tijānī ʿAlī Cisse (interview, Medina Baye Senegal, October 2008), Shaykh Ibrāhīm Niasse sent Muḥammad ʿĀl to Shaykh Aḥmad Sukayrij when the latter requested someone who could write Arabic very well.

36 Muḥammad al-Ḥanaf was also a prominent Tijānī shaykh of the Idaw ʿAlī people in nineteenth-century Mauritania. His grandson became Shaykh Ibrāhīm's follower.

Time swore that it would surely bring us the like of him.
You have falsified your oath, O Time, so make amends!

How excellent is the one who said in praise of him:

A Shaykh, who when he gives spiritual instruction, is as Aḥmad
And if he should speak, it is only with the greatest intelligence and prudence.

The following verses were composed in his honor by his brother-in-spirit and his brother-by-birth, the meticulous erudite scholar and brilliant poet, the knowledgeable one of Allah, al-Ḥājj Muḥammad Zaynab,[37] the son of Shaykh al-Ḥājj ʿAbd-Allāh ﷺ.

You must know that the Imam has provided
A copious flood (*fayḍ*) of that which benefits the servants,

At the hands of the intermediary to (Shaykh Aḥmad) al-Tijānī,
In showers filled with radiant lights and knowledge.

So any one among you who loves his Lord
Will find him pleasing as a Shaykh, quenching your thirst in his river.

Loving one's Lord is evidenced by loving him
And hatred of Him is likewise evidenced by hating him.

He inherited the secret of our Shaykh al-Tijānī
From his ancestor, the best of the people of ʿAdnān.[38]

He renewed the religion soon after it had fallen into oblivion,
As well as the Sunna of the Chosen One among the people of Muḍar.[39]

He repaired the Path of our Shaykh al-Tijānī
In our country, when the structures had collapsed.

He restored the Path of our Hidden Shaykh,
After it had been sold for properties and chattels.

He rebuilt each part of the Path's edifice that had fallen into disrepair
Which had floundered in desolation, like knowledge of the classical sciences.

Allah appointed him for the benefit of His creatures,

---

37 Muḥammad Zaynab was considered one of the most knowledgeable of the community around al-Ḥājj ʿAbd-Allāh, training many of Shaykh Ibrāhīm's early followers in the classical Islamic sciences.

38 ʿAdnān was a descendent of Prophet Ismāʿīl through his son Kedar. The Banū, or tribe or people, of ʿAdnān are the ʿAdnānī Arabs tracing descent through Prophet Ibrāhīm. The "best of the Banū ʿAdnān" refers to the Prophet Muḥammad.

39 The Banū Muḍar, one of two branches of the ʿAdānī tribe of northern Arabia, trace descent from Muḍar, who descended from Nizār, a son of ʿAdnān.

> And he has banished every deadly peril with the truth.

And the Poet continued:

> You must be utterly devoted to him if you seek him,
> And you must abandon every distraction altogether.
>
> Indeed the chains of transmission (*salāsil*) from the Shaykhs
> Have been superseded by him, together with the snares.
>
> He has provided spiritual training for the aspirant in a beautiful manner
> Similar to our Shaykh al-Tijānī, the giver of gracious favors.
>
> By him the eyes of the sleepers have been awakened;
> And by him the hearts of the heedless have been enlightened.
>
> In every affair, the Imam has based his actions
> On the Remembrance (*dhikr*)[40] and the Sunna
>
> So you must surrender to him, O Shaykhs of the age;
> Unless you have reverted to the utmost state of detestation.
>
> Because in esoteric knowledge he is an Ibrāhīm;
> A prodigious expert in this Spiritual Path.
>
> We therefore bear witness to his superiority;
> For we are among his children in respect (to knowledge) of the Truth.

And the Poet continued:

> In his presence, O seeker, you will surely be educated well
> He will provide you with useful instruction.
>
> Often he has trained shaykhs who had deviated
> From the course of right guidance, but then were guided.
>
> He has come with the correct method of spiritual training (*tarbiya*)
> From among the explicitly established practices.
>
> His aspiration (*himma*) uplifts the condition of the one who seeks his Lord
> So keep him company if you wish to achieve the goal.

There is more of this poem, for it is very lengthy.

Personal Attributes

As for his modesty and the beauty of his relations with the creation, he had no equal in readiness to pardon or forgive. He had no equal in generosity, patience, fairness, restraint, dignity, loving affection, trustworthiness, service, fidelity, sympathy, and good manners in relation to every creature of

40 Here meaning the Qur'ān.

Allah. He had no equal in his loyal adherence to the Sunna of the Prophet, the Best of Creatures and the Secret of Wisdom. Of such virtues, he was the pole (*quṭb*) of their temple (*miḥrāb*), the key to their doors.

It should not be necessary to describe the beauty and purity of his outward appearance; just as his inner being received the perfection of the divine Essence, so his outer was endowed with divine Beauty. May Allah not deprive us of the pleasure of witnessing him and consorting with him, in both the world of sense and signification. From his light, his beauty, and the cheerfulness of his face, the radiant full-moon derives brilliance in the pitch-black night.

His ability to relate on good terms with his fellow creatures, to give every creditor his rightful due and every shareholder his rightful share, and to model himself on the characteristics of his Lord—the Creator, the All-Generous, the Ever-Giving, the Guide, the Kind, and the Compassionate—dazzled the minds of the well-versed masters. He observed the stipulations concerning the Hereafter with regard to close relatives and strangers, and he was always protective of the rights of beloved friends. He attained to the utmost degree in humility, submissiveness, abstinence, and repentant devotion to Allah, in private and in public. He entrusted his affairs completely to Allah, with the best thoughts of Him, and was completely indifferent to anything other than Him; until he was recognized by the elite and the common folk, the near and the far.

With regard to the love of Allah's Messenger and the people of his household, Allah favored him with a station that had never been achieved and never aspired to. That has been expressed in verse by the poet and marvel of the time, the famous erudite scholar and judge, Muḥammad ᶜAbd-Allāh b. Muṣṭafa al-ᶜAlawī:

May Allah reward Ibrāhīm for providing benefit
To the lowliest and the highest in relation to him

You see them spending time in his home;
And establishing a residence during that sojourn.

For there they have no fear of thirst, nor of hunger;
And they fear no annoyance from him, nor any loathing.

Nor are they afraid of any humiliation or contempt;
Nor are they afraid of disappointment or anything else.

And the poet continued:

Among the proofs of Deputyship (*khilāfa*), he bears a sign
From Allah, not hidden from those who pay attention.

Upon his face is a light from Allah, shining brightly;
Allah prohibited everything from him except completeness and perfection.

He is well acquainted with two servants of Allah[41]
How marvelous is their excellence and his, an abundant spring

For in the flood (*fayḍa*) of gnosis (*ᶜirfān*), the later generations
Resemble the earlier ones in beneficial knowledge.

As for his generosity, his beneficence, the abundance of his plentiful gifts, his divine endowment, his liberality, and his munificence: they are like the ocean and the pouring rain that would leave Ḥātim[42] consigned to oblivion. May the shawls of gratitude for him never cease to be spread out, and may his exploits never cease to be recounted and remembered.

Founding of Medina

In the beginning of his career, he lived in his father's home in Kaolack (Senegal). Allah supported him with the assistance of those near to him. People started coming to him from various lands, for Allah gave him what He had not given to any of his people before him. So the place became cramped for him, because of the multitude of followers clinging to him. He founded a new city outside of Kaolack, called *Madīna al-jadīd* [the new city], and this is where the incomparable pole (*al-quṭb al-farīd*) came to reside. In this place, he built a center of religious devotion (*zāwiya*) founded on the blessed day of Monday, in the middle of the sacred month of *Dhū al-Qaᶜda* in the year 1349 (A.H.).[43] He completed it in a space of time that was unusually short for the construction of such a building, but its owner was for Allah and Allah was for him, so nothing else need be said! It was made habitable by the performance of the five ritual prayers, the recital of the daily congregational litany (*waẓīfa*) of the Tijāniyya Order, and the remembrance of Allah, day and night, at all times, individually and in congregation. It became famous among the people as the refuge of those who remember Allah (*zāwiya ahl al-dhikr*).

Is not the mosque of Ibrāhīm founded on piety (*taqwā*)?
No sinful speech or idle talk is found in your land

The companionship of Abū al-ᶜAbbās (al-Tijānī) is found in your circle
You attained the loftiest status and the highest rank

The religion's propagation is found within your circle
What good fortune for the one whose name is found therein

And from this takes inspiration
Indeed, he will see in this circle the balanced refuge for the religion.

---

41 The "two servants" are likely the Prophet Muḥammad and Shaykh Aḥmad al-Tijānī.

42 Ḥātim, a member of the tribe of Tayy, was renowned for boundless generosity.

43 Corresponding to 4 April 1931.

I have now relinquished control of the reins, in despair of catching up with one tenth of one tenth of his perfections, his exploits, his glorious deeds, and the nobility of his character. But if someone contemplates the sparkling pearls of his being, and the marvelous benefits that accumulated in him, his eye will recognize the signs that point to his superiority and his preeminence. I am one of those who bear witness to this.

> O son of the noble ones, will you not draw near and carefully consider
> What has been related to you? For there is no observer like one who listens.

His Noble Parents

As for his father ﵁ he was the proof of Islam and the lamplight of the darkness, the guardian of the sacred law, the reviver of this spiritual path after the extinction of its lights, and the re-builder of its structure and its minaret after the collapse of its foundation. He was the most pious exemplar, the most prudent in judgment, the brave hero, the one who reunited that which had been scattered and dispersed. He was the master among the preeminent men of this ideal spiritual path, the greatest Shaykh, the most famous great saint, the orthodox Sufi, our Shaykh and our master, al-Ḥājj ʿAbd-Allāh b. al-Sayyid Muḥammad. This Shaykh was a renowned commentator on all the sciences, including the branches and the roots, especially the Qurʾān and the prophetic traditions. I came across a document concerning his biography, in which the writer says that this father had explained the Qurʾān to certain men of distinction more than one hundred times. The document also said that he had performed the Pilgrimage and visited the tomb of the Prophet ﷺ, that he had exerted himself with great endeavor for the sake of Allah, and that he had awakened the eyes of the sleepers. From the blessed grace of this venerable master, we have received every benefit, bounty and good fortune; may Allah grant him a good reward on our behalf. His exploits, his strength in the religion, his abstinence, and his piety are too profuse to be accounted for. May Allah enable us and all our loved ones to derive real benefit from him, and may He shower his blessings and his fragrant perfumes upon us until the Day of Judgment. Amen, O Lord of All the Worlds.

As for his mother, may Allah be well pleased with her, she is the precious unique pearl and the priceless jewel. She is righteous, pious, ascetic, virtuous, noble, and attentive to the Lordly rights in her spiritual state and her speech. She is devoted to the conduct and practices prescribed by the Sunna, to righteous deeds and meritorious actions worthy of praise. She is endowed with abundant blessing and shining lights, firmly rooted, fully capable, possessed with real certainty, one who has taken hold of the strong rope; our mother ʿĀʾisha bint Ibrāhīm. From the moment when Allah placed her under the care of al-Ḥājj ʿAbd-Allāh, she never ceased to be attentive to his good pleasure, exerting herself strenuously in obedience to him. She never did anything that would anger him or hurt him, or anything that would trouble his mind or the minds of the relatives and neighbors, and she never raised her voice above his voice. She used to treat him graciously in every way, making every effort to please him, and never opposing him in anything whatsoever. Whenever he gave her an instruction, she promptly complied. Her relationship with him never ceased to be like this, until he departed from this worldly abode to the residence on high, well pleased with her and grateful for her earnest endeavor. Testimony to that has been given on her behalf by the elite and the common folk, by friends and enemies alike. She is still living at the present time. May Allah grant us the joy of her prolonged life.

I have been informed by someone in whose word I trust—the honorable master and great scholarly gnostic, my master and my intimate friend, Abū Bakr b. Shaykh al-Ḥājj ᶜAbd-Allāh,[44]—that this mother informed him that she had the following experience: In the first month of her pregnancy with this Shaykh, she saw herself in a dream, in which she seemed to be standing on something and there was a deep well beneath her. The moon suddenly split from the direction of the East and fell upon her. She was afraid for herself and extremely scared, and in the morning she came to the father of this Shaykh and told him the story. Her husband warned her to say nothing about it and keep it a secret saying, "You must never talk to anyone about that again."

She had also informed Abū Bakr that when she gave birth to the child, the father summoned her and asked her, "Have you any hopeful expectation for this son of yours?" She said: "I said 'Yes!'" He then asked her, "And what have you hoped for him?" She replied, "I hope for the best for him, and that he will be noble, virtuous and pious, if Allah wills!" The father said to her, "Yes, I have also hoped for that, and know it will come to be true if Allah prolongs his life and grants us the joy of his survival."

I have also been informed by a trustworthy source that al-Ḥājj ᶜAbd-Allāh said of ᶜĀʾisha that she would certainly give birth to a son who would inherit from him a complete and perfect inheritance. He said, "If not, that will never again be possible for anyone, because there was no one superior to her among the women of bygone times." Indeed, all words and paper are not sufficient to record her virtues, excellent merits, piety, beneficence, and good-natured treatment of every creature of Allah, Exalted is He.

We have reported here only as much as time has allowed due to the absence of leisure. It has been arranged with sensitivity, for fear of long-windedness and as a precaution against that which wearies the minds. But what we have concealed, in relation to what we have reported, is like a drop

44 Also known as Baye Mbaye (1903–73), he was the youngest son of al-Ḥājj ᶜAbd-Allāh Niasse and one of the earliest disciples of Shaykh Ibrāhīm.

of water in relation to the ocean, for we have been keen to preserve the secrets and to make them inaccessible to strangers. We beseech Allah to assist us at some other time in the composition of a separate literary work, devoted to the glorious exploits of this Shaykh and the special qualities by which Allah has distinguished him among those who share his lineage and the people of his era. This is not, for Allah, any hard task.

By the Presences of Prophethood and Sainthood, I beseech Allah that we, and all our loved ones and our brethren, derive benefit from this Shaykh; a benefit that is both special and universal, enduring for all eternity. May his fragrant perfumes and his blessings return to us, and may the oceans of his overflowing grace (*fuyūḍāt*) and support (*amdādāt*) overwhelm us. Amen, O Lord of all the worlds!

I completed this short biography in the town of Kaolack on Wednesday, the nineteenth of the sacred month of Dhū al-Ḥijja, in the year 1352.[45] May Allah cause our city to prosper and may He keep it safe. Amen. I am the poor one in need of Allah, Exalted is He. I beseech Allah the Master to grant me perfect purity and the spiritual elevation of the ranks of noble ones.

ʿAlī Cisse b. Sayyid al-Ḥasan b. ʿAndal b. Sayyid Ibrāhīm, may Allah be well pleased with them all

45 Corresponding to 4 April 1934.

Author's Foreword

In the Name of Allah, the Compassionate, the Merciful

Praise be to Allah, the Lord of all the worlds, the Compassionate, the Merciful, the Master of the Day of Judgment. Praise to Him who overwhelmed His saints in seas of lights, who favored them with the purity of the spiritual states and the secrets, who busied them with His remembrance in the evening and the early morning, who gathered them under the wing of the Chosen Beloved (Muḥammad). Praise be to Him who made Himself known to the saints, so they came to know Him directly and thus departed from the sphere of ignorance and denial. Praise be to Him who chose them for His service, His love and the fellowship of His righteous bosom-friends. Praise be to Him who attracted them to the presence of His Holiness, so they were enraptured in the contemplation of divine Majesty and the witnessing of divine Beauty, and so became wholly immersed in beholding the divine Perfection.

May blessing and peace be upon the supreme means of access to Allah, the truest source of intimate knowledge; the one to whom the perfection of the Essence was revealed, so he became the focal point of the Names and the Attributes: our master Muḥammad ﷺ. And peace be upon his family and his companions, the rightly guided; and the successive generations, and all those who follow them in spiritual excellence until the Day of Judgment. And special salutations to (Shaykh Aḥmad al-Tijānī), his grandson and the inheritor of his secrets; the helper of the saintly poles (*aqṭāb*), the saints (*awliyāʾ*) and the gnostic sages (*ʿārifīn*); the support of the great ones, the righteous, the martyrs, the saintly-substitutes (*budalāʾ*) and the champions of the Truth.

The following remarks are offered by the poor servant in dire need of the mercy of his Compassionate Master, the oblivious one who readily admits his ignorance and his shortcoming, Ibrāhīm, the son of Shaykh al-Ḥājj ʿAbd-Allāh. By the gracious favor of his Master, may he never cease to be enraptured in the Beauty of His Majesty!

Since ignorance, stupidity, envy and stubbornness have become widespread in these lands of ours, negative criticism is frequently leveled at the people of the Tijānī Flood (*ahl al-Fayḍa al-Tijāniyya*), alleging that they have corrupted the spiritual path. This is nothing but the denial of their own Shaykh (Aḥmad al-Tijānī), who, out of the gracious favor of the Compassionate Lord, has been our guide and support since the appearance of this Muḥammadan-Aḥmadan-Abrahamic, Rightly-Guided Tijānī Flood (*al-Fayḍa al-Tijāniyya al-Aḥmadiyya al-Muḥammadiyya al-Ibrāhīmiyya al-Ḥanīfiyya*). I therefore ignored this ignorance for a very long time, even when they came up with preposterous defamations on account of my being aligned with the Tijānī Flood. May Allah protect us from being like those whose fields of pasture resemble the barren wastelands. Afraid of my lower self (*nafs*) and the rejection of my Muslim brethren, I made myself content with the defense provided by the Holy Presence (*ḥaḍra al-quds*), for indeed this Presence defends itself and those who have faith in it. May Allah include us among His servants who rely on Him alone.

This continued for a long period of time, and they continued engaging themselves in negative criticism, falsehood, and slander. Finally, it occurred to me that I should collect something from the speeches of the venerable Imams, concerning the explanation of the doctrines of the saintly servants of Allah. I therefore sought help from Allah the Exalted and embarked on the composition of this blessed book, obtaining support from the abundant grace of the venerable sun of the religion, our master Shaykh al-Tijānī, the owner of the firmly established station. Refuting them is indeed a rejoinder on behalf of this Shaykh al-Tijānī, the Seal of the Saints, since he is the master (*ṣāḥib*) of the Tijānī Flood and the one who bestows it upon his companions, by means of his ancestor, the Prophet ﷺ, who received it from the Presence of the Lord of lords. So this work became obligatory on me, since I am a servant (*khadīm*) of that majestic dignitary (al-Tijānī).

I have arranged the contents of this work into a general introduction and three sections, each with three chapters; followed by a general conclusion. The introduction deals with the correct interpretation of Shaykh al-Zarrūq's statement—on the authority of his Shaykh al-Ḥaḍramī—concerning the cessation of spiritual training (*tarbiya*). The first section addresses three issues: 1) the reality of Sufism and sources for teaching the liturgical remembrances (*adhkār*); 2) the excellence of the liturgical remembrance and its being the most direct path to Allah; and 3) the congregational remembrance and Qurʾān recitation. The second section treats the following issues: 1) the Tijānī flood and what its owner (al-Tijānī) said about it; 2) the orthodox foundation of the sciences of spiritual experience (*ʿulūm al-adhwāq*); and 3) the sphere of spiritual training (*tarbiya*) in the Tijāniyya Order. The third section contains the following chapters: 1) a warning against criticism of one's Muslim brethren, and those for whom such criticism is permissible; 2) the necessity of seeking a shaykh who is capable of spiritual training, his character, and the spiritual state of the disciple; and 3) the veracity of the visionary experiences of the people of spiritual distinction, and what the scholars have said about seeing the Essential Being (*dhāt*) of the Exalted and Glorious Creator. The conclusion deals with our own confidence in and reliance on the sciences and secrets of the spiritual path of Shaykh al-Tijānī, the Seal of the Saints.

I beseech Allah, with the tongue of humility and the speech of self-effacement, that my book may be sincerely devoted to His Noble Countenance, and that it may benefit me and be of benefit to my believing brethren until the Day of Judgment. I have given it the title: *The Removal of Confusion Concerning the Flood of the Saintly Seal Aḥmad al-Tijānī*. Now let us embark on the intended purpose with the assistance of the Glorified divine Sovereign. And all success is achieved with the help of Allah, for He is the Guide by His grace to the straight path.

General Introduction

According to Sīdī (Aḥmad) Zarrūq,[1] in the book *Taʾsīs al-qawāʾid*: "Our Shaykh Abū al-ʿAbbās al-Ḥaḍramī ﷺ said: 'Spiritual training (*tarbiya*) in the technical sense has ceased to be practiced, and all that remains is training by spiritual zeal (*himma*) and state (*ḥāl*). So it is incumbent on you to follow the Qurʾān and the Sunna, without addition or subtraction.'" The rest of this quotation will be presented later. But let us say here that this statement, made in the ninth century after the Hijra (sixteenth century of the Common Era), should not be understood, especially by the one deprived of spiritual experience and gnosis, as meaning that spiritual training has ceased absolutely. Neither Zarrūq nor his Shaykh al-Ḥaḍramī meant this. The actual meaning intended was explained by the erudite scholar Ibn ʿAjība[2] in his *Īqāẓ al-himam*:

---

1 Sīdī Aḥmad Zarrūq al-Burnūsī al-Fāsī (d. 1493) was a North African scholarly Sufi who stressed the proper balance between the sacred law (*sharīʿa*) and Sufism. He spent many years in Cairo, where he studied under Muḥammad al-Sakhawī, the student of Ibn Ḥajar al-ʿAsqalānī. His primary spiritual guide in Cairo was Aḥmad b. ʿUqba al-Ḥaḍramī (d. 1489), a saint with both Shādhilī and Qādiri Sufi affiliation, who was originally from Yemen but who had settled in Cairo. Zarrūq himself eventually settled in Libya. Like his Shaykh Ḥaḍramī, Zarrūq's exact Sufi affliliations are ambiguous, seemingly a mixture of the Shādhiliyya, Qādiriyya, and Suhrawardiyya lines of transmission and practices. He authored numerous works on jurisprudence, prophetic traditions, supplications and Sufism. The work cited here is one of his more important on the subject of Sufism: *Taʾsīs al-qawāʾid wa al-usūl wa taḥṣīl al-fawāʾid li-dhawī al-wuṣūl fī al-taṣawwuf*. For more on Shaykh Aḥmad Zarrūq, see Scott Kugle, *Rebel between Spirit and Law: Aḥmad Zarruq, Sainthood, and Authority in Islam* (Bloomington: Indiana University Press, 2006); and Ali Fahmi Khashim, *Zarruq, the Sufi: A Guide in the Way and a Leader to the Truth, a Biographical and Critical Study of a Mystic from North Africa* (London: Outline Series, 1976); and Zaineb Istrabadi, *The Principles of Sufism (Qawāʾid al-Taṣawwuf): An Annotated Translation with Introduction* (Ph.D. thesis, Indiana University, 1988).

2 Aḥmad Ibn ʿAjība (d. 1809) was a prominent scholar of the Shādhiliyya Sufi order in Morocco. His commentary on the *Kitāb al-ḥikam* by Ibn ʿAṭāʾ Allāh (d. 1309, Alexandria), entitled *Īqāẓ al-himam*, is considered one of the best of many such commentaries, and it is widely known in West Africa. His autobiography has been translated: *The*

Some might hold to the literal meaning of al-Ḥaḍramī's words: "Spiritual training in the technical sense has ceased to be practiced, and all that remains is training by spiritual zeal and state. So it is incumbent on you to follow the Qurʾān and the Sunna." My response to this is as follows: Ḥaḍramī did not mean to say that the cessation of spiritual training will last for all eternity. Far be it from Ḥaḍramī to pass such judgment on Allah and limit His Power! What he meant was that there were many impostors and pretenders in his time, so he warned his contemporaries to beware of them. The high erudition of al-Ḥaḍramī and Zarrūq is inconsistent with the literal meaning of their words. Even if they are held to the literal meaning, that spiritual training had ceased for all eternity, they are surely not infallible. Every statement, theirs included, is subject to evaluation, except for the statement of our Prophet ﷺ. Indeed, following the time of al-Ḥaḍramī, an innumerable number of distinguished Sufi scholars have been carrying out orthodox spiritual training by means of spiritual states (*ḥāl*), spoken words (*maqāl*), and zeal (*himma*). They also exist in this time of ours, famous like radiant beacons. Allah has guided many of the creation with their assistance, and with their help He has taught the saints what no one knows, except those whom Allah has blessed.

Ibn ʿAjība's explanation is proven by the appearance of Shaykh Aḥmad al-Tijānī, the Seal of Saints and the standard-bearer of spiritual training well after the ninth-century statements of al-Ḥaḍramī and his student. Shaykh al-Tijānī's role as a spiritual trainer cannot be doubted by anyone endowed with the slightest faith in and submission to him. The same is true of Shaykh al-Sayyid al-Mukhtār al-Kuntī,[3] as well as the perfected ones who were trained by such men, and thereby attained to the highest rank of those shaykhs providing spiritual training (*tarbiya*) and elevation (*tarqiya*).

The erudite scholar and knowledgeable one of Allah, Sīdī ʿUbayda b. Muḥammad al-Ṣaghīr,[4] the author of *Mīzāb al-raḥma*, had this to say in

---

Autobiography (Fahrasa) of a Moroccan Sufi: Aḥmad ibn ʿAjiba, by Jean-Louis Michon and David Streight (Louisville, KY: Fons Vitae, 1999).

3 Al-Mukhtār al-Kuntī (d. 1811), described by Shaykh Ibrāhīm elsewhere in the text as "the shaykh of shaykhs, the renowned scholar and divine gnostic," was one of the most important Qādiri shaykhs and scholars in eighteenth-century West Africa. He lived in Timbuktu, Mali, but revived the Qādiriyya Sufi order throughout West Africa, becoming the shaykh of Usman dan Fodio (d. 1817), the founder of the Sokoto Caliphate based in northern Nigeria, as well as several Mauritanian branches of the Qādiriyya. His most important work was *al-Kawkab al-waqqād fī faḍl dhikr al-mashāʾikh wa ḥaqāʾiq*. For more on Kuntī, see Aziz Batran, *The Qadiryya Brotherhood in West Africa and the Western Sahara: The Life and Times of Shaykh al-Mukhtar al-Kunti, (1729–1811)* (Rabat: Université Mohammed V, 2001).

4 ʿUbayda b. Muḥammad al-Ṣaghīr was a nineteenth-century Mauritanian scholar of the Ḥāfiẓiyya Tijānī legacy. His primary work, *Mīzāb al-raḥma fī al-tarbiya bi*

honor of Shaykh al-Tijānī, may Allah be well pleased with him, and may He enable us to benefit by him:

> Without seclusion (*khalwa*) he gave spiritual training, while others trained by seclusion
> So what a difference there is between the two Yazīds in style![5]

According to Sayyid al-ʿArabī b. al-Sāʾiḥ ﷺ:[6]

> Our goal in spiritual training within this sufi path is to be free from the necessity of seclusion (*khalwa*), withdrawal from the people, and other such practices involving extreme severity with the self (*nafs*). We insist that spiritual training from the beginning must be carried out in accordance with the method of the righteous early believers (*al-salaf al-ṣāliḥ*). This original method is the way of thankfulness (*ṭarīqa al-shukr*), happiness with the Glorious Benefactor and spiritual discipline of the heart (*al-riyāḍa al-qalbiyya*). This is opposed to the other method, invented by those who came after the first three centuries of Islam, adopted as a technique to meet the difficulties of the time. This method entails strenuous exertion, physical suffering and discipline of the body. The difference between the two methods is that the first is directed at (purifying) the hearts, while the second is directed against the physical body.
>
> Indeed, the crucial factor in attaining to the Presence of Allah the Exalted is the purification of the heart. What purifies or corrupts the heart is in accordance with the immaculate sacred law and the enlightened prophetic tradition. The heart is not necessarily purified by oppressing the self with asceticism, dietary restriction, shabby clothing, or continuous physical discomfort; unless one attends to the conditions of the heart.
>
> Those who came after the first three centuries of Islam chose to implement the second method due to the multiplicity of lustful desires and the development of (misguided) opinions. They resorted to this in order to purify and improve the ego-self, and to illuminate the heart and rid it of lusts. But they were careful not to exaggerate (in their

---

al-ṭarīqa al-Tijāniyya, is considered a synthesis of the teachings of Muḥammad al-Ḥāfiẓ al-Shinqīṭī. The book, written in 1851, details a process of spiritual training (*tarbiya*) based on the principle of gratitude (*shukr*) passing through the three stations of *islām*, *īmān*, and *iḥsān*.

5 This is an idiomatic phrase in Arabic simply meaning there is a great disparity between the two things mentioned.

6 Muḥammad al-ʿArabī b. al-Sāʾiḥ (d. 1892, Rabat) was one of the most celebrated Tijānī scholars of the nineteenth century. His work, *Bughya al-mustafīd*, is one of the primary works of the Order. Among his other writings is *al-Jawāb al-shāfī*, which is the source for this citation in question. For more on his life and work, see Abdelaziz Benabdallah, *Le Soufisme Afro-Maghrebin aux XIX et XXème Siècles (Rabat, 1995).*

> practices), to go beyond the limit of conventional observance, or to transgress into heretical innovation.

According to Shaykh Abū ʿAbd-Allāh b. ʿAbbād:[7]

> It is a heretical innovation to attempt to purify the soul (*nafs*) by isolation, the restriction of diet to herbs and bran, and the endurance of excessive asceticism and poverty, without attention to the states of the heart. Emphasis should be on what endows the heart with commendable traits, and what removes from it blameworthy traits. Groups of people have mistakenly practiced exercises of physical deprivation, strenuously exerting themselves, with no intention of sincere devotion to their Lord. The result was only the confusion of their minds and the depletion of their physical strength. They obtained no profit from their actions. All this was due to their ignorance of the prophetic Sunna and practice of the early righteous believers (*al-salaf al-ṣāliḥ*).

The abundantly-gifted Sayyid al-ʿArabī also said in his book *al-Jawāb al-shāfi*:

> Praise be to Allah, there are many who carry the burdens of training in our spiritual path (*ṭarīqa*). No country and no time have been devoid of them since the demise of our master, the Shaykh (al-Tijānī) ﵁. In fact, a number of them emerged in the Shaykh's lifetime, although they did not make a public display of this because of the rule of the age. They were detected only by those for whom Allah the Almighty has foreordained the opportunity to benefit from them. They remained hidden because of what they gained through the blessed grace of their teacher: the state of perfection called "jealous guardianship of Allah's secrets" (*al-ghayra ʿala Allāh*). This state of concealment of one's secret thoughts and innermost feelings comprises the general behavior of the hidden and innocent Malamatiyya.[8] So their real qualities are unknown, for they show no sign to indicate that they are endowed with Allah's providential care. They blend in with the common people

---

7 Abū ʿAbd-Allāh b. ʿAbbād al-Rundī (d. 1390) was born in Ronda, Andalusia, and later settled in Fes, Morocco; where he led the Friday prayer in the Qarawiyyin mosque. He was a renowned shaykh of the Shādhiliyya order, and authored the first commentary on the *Ḥikam* of Ibn ʿAṭāʾ Allāh, entitled *Ghayth al-mawāhib al-ʿalīyya*, which is also known as *al-Tanbīh*. He also authored two collections of letters. For more on his life and works, see John Renard (trans.), *Ibn ʿAbbad of Ronda: Letters on the Sufi Path* (New York: Paulist Press, 1986).

8 The Malamatiyya were Sufis that invite public reproach by pretending to be engaged in reprehensible behavior. This was a means of hiding their real spiritual position and purifying their ego-selves. Later Sufis justified the appellation "Malamati" for a person of high spiritual state who blended with the ordinary Muslims, not distinguishing himself by public displays of piety beyond that normally practiced by the Muslim community.

in their external behavior and ordinary religious devotions, and thus are not usually recognized as the people of Allah's special favor. This is a position in which Allah the Exalted established them, adorning them with excellent merit, whether they are aware of it or not.

Sayyid al-ʿArabī also said, as recorded in *al-Bughyat* (*al-mustafīd*):

To summarize the matter: among the unique individuals of this Muḥammadan spiritual path (*al-Ṭarīqa al-Muḥammadiyya*), there exist people qualified to provide spiritual training. They do so by means of the litany (*wird*) and other remembrances of the Tijāniyya, in accordance with the stipulations regarding this established by the Shaykh on the basis of what he received from the Prophet ﷺ. This method was taught the Shaykh by the Prophet ﷺ for the people of the spiritual path, so it is a guarantee of secret knowledge, benefits, and blessings. There is no possibility of departing from what the Prophet ﷺ has granted, and on which he has fixed his guarantee. The extent of our explanation on this is sufficient here, and Allah is the Custodian of enabling grace and guidance.

Our Shaykh and means of access to our Lord, Shaykh Aḥmad al-Tijānī, Seal of the Saints ؓ, has demonstrated that among the people of his spiritual path are the masters of spiritual training (*mashāʾikh al-tarbiya*). This is indicated by his authentic statements recorded in the *Jāmiʿ*:[9]

(He said) "If Allah grants illumination (*fatḥ*) to my companions, the one among them who sits in my presence, in the town where I am, will fear his own destruction (*halāk*)." One of his companions asked him, "Is this from you, or from Allah?" To this he replied, "It is from Allah, without my having a choice in the matter." He mentioned this on the second Sunday of the sacred month of Shaʿban, in the year 1223 of the Hijra (1808 C.E.). Then he said on the next Monday: "The fear that was mentioned is for the one among my companions who has been authorized with the power of divine disposition (*taṣarruf*), and to provide his fellow creatures with spiritual training (*tarbiya*)."

The complete statement of Sīdī Zarrūq in *Taʾsīs al-qawāʾid*, partially quoted earlier, reads as follows:

We conclude with the statement of our Shaykh Abū al-ʿAbbās al-Ḥaḍramī ؓ: "Spiritual training (*tarbiya*) in the technical sense has ceased to be practiced, and all that remains is training by spiritual zeal (*himma*) and state (*ḥāl*). So it is incumbent on you to follow the

---

9 The *Kitāb al-jāmiʿ li al-ʿulūm al-fāʾida min biḥār al-quṭb al-maktūm* is one of the primary sources of the Tijānī order, written during the founder's lifetime in 1808. Its author was Muḥammad b. al-Mishrī, a prominent Sufi and scholar from Constantine, Algeria. Unlike the *Jawāhir al-maʿānī*, the work has never been published.

Qurʾān and the Sunna, without addition or subtraction. This applies to one's dealing with the Real (*al-Ḥaqq*), with one's own self (*nafs*), and with the creation.

"Three things must be observed in one's relationship to the Real: the performance of obligatory duties, the avoidance of forbidden things, and the submission to the rule of the sacred law.

"Three things also must be observed in dealing with one's ego-self (*nafs*): moderation, refraining from exciting it, guarding against its mischievous impulses toward (arbitrary) attraction and repulsion, acceptance and rejection, approach and retreat.

"There are also three things to observe in one's relationship with the creation: providing their rightful dues, withholding oneself from their possessions, and eschewing that which disturbs their hearts, except in the unavoidable case of genuine necessity.

"The aspirant (*murīd*) is doomed to destruction and failure if he should manifest any of the following: ostentation; a desire to influence the general administration of affairs; taking it on himself to correct the reprehensible behavior of the general public; preoccupation with holy war (*jihād*), while neglecting other virtues; wanting to monopolize all merits for himself; seeking out the imperfections of his fellow brothers; preoccupation with warning others; acting on hearsay; participating in social gatherings with neither the intention to learn nor to teach; mixing with worldly leaders under the pretext of religious devotion; preoccupation with subtle intricacies (of the religion), rather than actual practice to rectify his faults; undertaking spiritual training (*tarbiya*) without authorization (*taqdīm*) from a shaykh, imam or scholar; following any and every person, the one speaking truth and the one speaking falsehood, without distinguishing their spiritual states; looking down on those connected to Allah, and assuming their insincerity because of what he sees in them; fondness for special permissions and ambiguous interpretations; preferring the esoteric (*bāṭin*) to the apparent (*ẓāhir*), or remaining content with the apparent without reference to the esoteric, or concluding something from one incompatible with the other; being satisfied with knowledge without practice, or practice without knowledge or reference to the spiritual state (*ḥāl*), or spiritual state without knowledge or practice; non-substantiation of his knowledge, practice, spiritual state, or religious conviction in the sources of the Muslim community, such as the books of Ibn ʿAṭāʾ Allāh concerning esoteric knowledge, especially the *Tanwīr*,[10] or the

10 Ibn ʿAṭāʾ Allāh al-Iskandarī (d. 1309), *Kitāb al-tanwīr fī isqāt al-tadbīr* has been described as the "basic training manual for Sufis in North Africa." It has been translated by Scott Kugle, *The Book of Illumination* (Fons Vitae, 2005).

Madkhal of Ibn al-Ḥājj[11] concerning exoteric knowledge, or the book of his Shaykh Ibn Abī Jamra,[12] and the works of the scholars who followed them. But if such an aspirant accepts the teachings of these authorities, he will be saved as a Muslim, if Allah wills. Virtuousness and success are from Allah.

"Allah's Messenger ﷺ was asked about the verse of the Qurʾān: *O you who believe! Guard your own souls!* (5:105). He replied, 'When you see greedy lust being obeyed, passionate desire being pursued, and every holder of an opinion taking conceited pride in his opinion; be on special guard for your own soul (*nafs*)'[13] He ﷺ also related a statement from the Scrolls of Abraham (*ṣuḥuf Ibrāhīm*):

> The intelligent person should be aware of his age (*zaman*), hold his tongue, and mind his business. The intelligent one should also hold on to four times: a time in which he calls himself to account; a time he confides in his Lord; a time he spends with his brothers, the ones who make him aware of his faults and guide him toward his Lord; and a time in which he allows himself to enjoy permissible desires.

May Allah provide us with this and help us in it. May He enable us and our companions to benefit thereby, for we are helpless without Him! He is sufficient for us, an excellent Custodian. May Allah bless our master, Prophet and patron, Muḥammad, and peace upon his family and companions."

Careful study of Shaykh Abū al-ʿAbbās al-Ḥaḍramī's above statement reveals its true meaning. This is why the gnostic of Allah, al-Sayyid al-ʿArabī b. al-Sāʾiḥ explained:

> The meaning of spiritual training (*tarbiya*) in this context (alluded to by Zarrūq) is spiritual training in the technical sense, which was developed after the first three centuries (following the Prophet ﷺ). This is the spiritual training which Shaykh al-Zarrūq believed, on the authority of some of his masters, had ceased to be practiced. He was

11 Muḥammad b. al-Ḥājj al-Abdārī al-Fāsī (d. 1336) taught at the Qarawiyyin University in Fes, Morocco, but traveled throughout North Africa and is buried in Egypt. His work, *Madkhal al-sharʿ al-sharīf ʿala al-madhāhib* is a four-volume work discussing various points of Islamic law.

12 Ibn Abī Jamra (d. 1300) was a renowned *ḥadīth* scholar and jurist of the Mālikī school, originally from Andalusia but who settled in Cairo. His major work was *Bahja al-nufūs*, which is a commentary on *Ṣaḥīḥ Bukhārī*.

13 Reported by Abū Dāwūd in his *Sunan*, by Tirmidhī in his *Sunan*, and by Ibn Māja in his *Sunan*.

followed in this regard by the scholarly researcher Yūsī,[14] may Allah have mercy on him, who said: "In the opinion of Ḥaḍramī and Zarrūq, the meaning was not that spiritual training has ceased in the sense of providing guidance based on the Qurʾān and the Sunna, and the teaching of remembrance (*dhikr*). Nor did it mean the end of removing falsehood from the soul, ridding it of attachments and obstacles, with the support and spiritual zeal of the shaykh. Indeed, this (role of the shaykh) is by the permission he receives in his innermost being from the Presence of Allah, or the Presence of His Messenger ﷺ, either in a state of wakefulness or sleep. Far be it from the people of Allah to think (such training has ceased)!" For more on this subject, consult *al-Dhahab al-ibrīz*.[15]

Here is the relevant text from *al-Dhahab al-ibrīz* recording the words of Shaykh ʿAbd al-ʿAzīz al-Dabbāgh ؓ in response to the issue at hand:

> Spiritual training (*tarbiya*) entails purifying the soul (*nafs*) and purging it of its deficiencies, so that it becomes capable of bearing the Secret. There is no way to achieve this other than removing the darkness from the soul and severing the ties of falsehood that bind it. The severance of falsehood is sometimes due to an innate purity, so Allah cleanses the soul without any intermediary. This was the state of affairs in the first three virtuous centuries. These were the best of the centuries; then, people were devoted to the Truth and constantly focused upon it. When they slept, they slept upon it. When they awoke, they woke with it. When they moved, they moved in it. If Allah were to permit someone to examine their inner beings, he would find their minds devoted exclusively to Allah and His Messenger, seeking His good pleasure. What goodness abounded in them because of this! The light of the Truth shone in their natures. Such knowledge and high degrees of independent scholarly reasoning (*ijtihād*) appeared in them as cannot be qualified or defined.

---

14 Abū ʿAlī al-Hassan b. Masʿud al-Yusi (d. 1691) was one of the more famous Moroccan Sufis of the seventeenth century. He was associated with the Nāṣiriyya branch of the Shādhiliyya Sufi order and authored numerous works covering a range of Islamic sciences. For more information, see Jacques Berque, *Al-Yousi: Problèmes de la Culture Marocaine au 17e Siècle* (Paris: Mouton, 1958).

15 *al-Dhahab al-ibrīz* was written in 1720 by the disciple of the Shādhilī Sufi, Shaykh ʿAbd al-ʿAzīz al-Dabbāgh (d. 1717, Fes), Aḥmad al-Lamaṭī. The work has remained extremely influential around the Muslim world ever since, and is one of the sources for emergence of the *Ṭarīqa Muḥammadiyya* phenomenon since the late eighteenth century. For a translation see John O'Kane and Bernd Radtke, *Pure Gold from the Words of Sayyidī ʿAbd al-ʿAzīz al-Dabbāgh: Al-Dhahab al-Ibrīz min Kalām Sayyidī ʿAbd al-ʿAzīz al-Dabbāgh* (Leiden: Brill, 2007).

There was no need for spiritual training in these centuries. The master (*shaykh*) would simply meet with his disciple, the companion (*ṣāḥib*) of his secret and inheritor of his light; then speak to him in his ear (*udhn*), and illumination (*fatḥ*) would come to the disciple without further ado. This was because of the pure natures and clear minds of these people, and their ardent yearning for the path of right guidance.

The severance of darkness from people's essential beings may sometimes be due to the instrumental influence of the shaykh. This came to be the case following the virtuous centuries, when people's intentions had become corrupted, when their innermost thoughts became empty of aspiration, their minds attached to this world, focused on satisfying lusts and giving the ego-self its full share. The shaykh possessing spiritual insight (*baṣīra*) began to meet his disciple and inheritor to get to know him first. He would look into him, and find that his mind was attached to falsehood and the gratification of lusts, and that his essential being (*dhāt*) followed his errant mind. He would find the disciple seeking distraction with the heedless, lost in the company of the negligent, and wavering to and fro with the purveyors of falsehood. Since the mind was yoked to falsehood, unattached to the Truth, the disciple's limbs and organs moved only for blameworthy purposes.

When the shaykh found the disciple in this condition, he would command him to practice secluded retreat (*khalwa*), remembrance (*dhikr*) and to eat less. In the retreat, the disciple could be separated from the prattling liars, who are counted among the dead. The remembrance of Allah would bring to an end the false words, the distraction of his mind, and the nonsense on his tongue. The frugal diet would diminish the steam in the blood, lessening his lustful appetites. The mind could then return to the dedication to Allah and His Messenger. When the disciple attained to this extent of purity and clarity, his essential being would be capable of bearing the Secret. So this was the aim of the masters (*shuyūkh*) in their use of spiritual training (*tarbiya*) and secluded retreat (*khalwa*).

The affair continued like this for a period of time. Then, the truth became mixed with falsehood, and the light overshadowed by darkness. The people of falsehood began to undertake the spiritual training of those who came to them, putting them in secluded retreat and teaching them the divine Names. But their intention was corrupt, and their purpose diverged from the Truth. They added spellbinding incantations and ambiguous figures of speech. The result was cunning deceit (*makr*) and false enticements away from Allah the Exalted. Such practices were widespread in the time of Shaykh al-Zarrūq ﵁ and his Shaykh (al-Ḥaḍramī). It became clear to them that the counsel of Allah and His Messenger in this case was to warn people to desist from this training since the people of falsehood had become engaged in it. Their advice was that people should stand in the open square of security: that of adherence to the Sunna and the Qur'ān, in which there was neither fear nor sorrow. Indeed, those who are guided by the Qur'ān and the Sunna do not go astray.

The statement of Zarrūq and al-Ḥaḍramī, may Allah be pleased with them, emerged from this context of giving advice and warning. Their intention was not to insist on the absolute cessation of genuine spiritual training. Far be it from them to say such a thing! Indeed, the light of the Prophet ﷺ remains with us. His message (*khabar*) is inclusive and comprehensive, and his blessings (*barakāt*) are universal, lasting to the Day of Resurrection.

There are several Qur'ānic verses and prophetic traditions which contain indications and glad tidings concerning this group (*ṭā'ifa*) manifestly committed to the Truth. And they are not limited to a particular time or place. For example, Allah the Exalted said: *And among those whom We have created there is a community who guide with the Truth and establish justice therewith* (Qur'ān, 7:181). In his commentary on the margins of the *Jalālayn*, the scholarly gnostic, Shaykh Sīdī al-Ṣāwī[16] said of this verse: "They are the community of Muḥammad ﷺ, since in a prophetic tradition he ﷺ said: 'A group from my community will not cease being committed to the Truth, until Allah's (final) command arrives.'"[17] Muʿāwiya once said while delivering a sermon: "I once heard Allah's Messenger ﷺ say, 'Among my community there will never cease being a group obedient to Allah's command. They will not be harmed by those who forsake or oppose them, until Allah's (final) command arrives while they are committed to this.'"[18]

This group is not limited to any particular time, or to any particular location. Indeed, they are present in every place and time, for Islam always will be raised high and never be surpassed. The wanton sinners and purveyors of evil, however many they are, bear no consequence (on the ascendency of Islam). This is glad tidings for the community of Muḥammad, making it known that Islam and the Muslims are endowed with sublimity and honor until the Day of Resurrection draws near. At this point, the bearers of the Qur'ān and the religious scholars will die. The Qur'ān will be erased from the books. The gentle wind will blow, and all in whom there is a tiny speck of faith will die. And this will not happen until after the (return

16 Aḥmad al-Ṣāwī (d. 1825) was an important Indian scholar of the Mālikī school of jurisprudence (*madhhab*) who wrote a commentary (*ḥāshiya*) on the *Tafsīr al-Jalālayn* of Jalāl al-Dīn al-Suyūṭī and Jalāl al-Dīn al-Maḥallī. Ṣāwī's *Ḥāshiya* became popular among West African scholars, for whom the *Tafsīr al-Jalālayn* has been one of the most important works of exegesis for centuries.

17 Reported by Bukhārī in his *Ṣaḥīḥ*, by Muslim in his *Ṣaḥīḥ*, by Abū Dāwūd in his *Sunan*, by Tirmidhī in his *Sunan*, and by Ibn Ḥanbal in his *Musnad*.

18 *Ḥadīth* reported in the collections of Muslim and Abū Dāwūd.

and) death of Jesus, peace be upon him. Jesus will not die until after he slays the Antichrist (al-Dajjāl) and lives for forty years, as the prophetic traditions have repeatedly confirmed. The Antichrist will not come until one hundred and seven years after the Mahdī.

One narration reports the Prophet's words: "There will always be a group in the West (al-Maghrib). . ."[19] Muḥyī al-Dīn Ibn al-ʿArabī al-Ḥātimī[20] explained, "Allah placed the station of the Seal (*al-khatmiyya*) and Concealment (*al-katmiyya*) in Morocco (*al-Maghrib*), for that is the place of secrets and concealment." For more on this, consult Ibn al-ʿArabī's *al-Futūḥāt* (*al-Makkiyya*) and his *ʿAnqāʾ mughrib fī khatm al-awliyāʾ wa shams al-maghrib*. See also the *Bughyat* (*al-mustafīd* of Muḥammad al-ʿArabī b. al-Sāʾiḥ).

Allah the Exalted has said: *A multitude from the earlier generations, and a multitude from the later generations* (Qurʾān, 56:39–40). Ibn ʿAbbās reported that Allah's Messenger ﷺ said: "The two multitudes are from my community."[21] This is found in *al-Jawāhir al-ḥisān*.[22] According to Shihāb al-Dīn al-Khafājī in *Nasīm al-riyāḍ*:[23]

> The Prophet's saying, "The best of you are my generation, then those who will follow them, then those who will follow them,"[24] is not inconsistent with his saying, "My community is like the rain, for it is not

19 The full version of this *ḥadīth*, found in *Ṣaḥīḥ Muslim* on the authority of Abū Hurayra: "The people of the West (*al-Maghrib*) will remain manifestly committed to the Truth, they will not be harmed by those who go against them or forsake them until the Final Hour." Imam Aḥmad b. Ḥanbal considered this to refer to the people of Shām (Syria), but other scholars considered this to refer to North Africa, as *al-Maghrib* is the Arabic name for Morocco. Certainly this latter opinion was held by Ibn al-ʿArabī.

20 Muḥyī al-Dīn Ibn al-ʿArabī al-Ḥātimī (d. 1240) was born in Andalusia and later settled in Syria. He was known as "the Greatest Shaykh," and his writings have influenced later Sufi scholars, including those of the Tijāniyya. His most comprehensive work is the multi-volume *Futūḥāt al-Makkiyya* [Meccan Illuminations]. Other writings include the *Fusus al-ḥikam* and the *ʿAnqāʾ mughrib*. This latter work speaks about the Seal of the Saints that will be found in Fes, Morocco. Numerous studies have appeared on the Shaykh and his writings. Noteworthy among these are the works of Henry Corbin, Michel Chodkiewicz, William Chittick, Titus Burckhardt, Claude Addas, Michael Sells, and Alexander Knysh.

21 Reported by Imam Ibn Jarīr al-Ṭabarī in his *Tafsīr*, and cited by Haythamī in *Majmaʿ al-zawāʾid wa manbaʿ al-fawāʾid*.

22 This is the multi-volume Qurʾān exegesis, *Jawāhir al-ḥisān fī tafsīr al-Qurʾān*, by ʿAbd al-Raḥmān al-Thaʿālibī (d. 1471).

23 This is the *Nasīm al-riyāḍ fī sharḥ Shifāʾ al-Qāḍī ʿIyāḍ*, a commentary on the *Shifāʾ* of Qāḍī ʿIyāḍ (work of *ḥadīth* and prophetic biography from the twelfth century) by the Egyptian Ḥanafī scholar Shihāb al-Dīn al-Khafājī (d. 1659).

24 Reported by Bukhārī in his *Ṣaḥīḥ*, by Muslim in his *Ṣaḥīḥ*, by Nasāʾī in his *Sunan*, by Ibn Ḥanbal in his *Musnad*, by al-Ṭaḥāwī in *Sharḥ Maʿānī al-āthār*, and by Ṭabarānī in *al-Muʿjam al-kabīr*.

> known whether the best is in its first part or in its last."[25] The first part comes in one valley, and the last comes in another; meaning that somebody may come in this community (of Muḥammad) who provides people with tremendous benefit, beyond the means of anyone who preceded him. The first rain refers to particular individuals (from the earlier generations), while the second rain refers to the complete span of time (comprising the later generations); and indeed, what a difference there is between the two (for individuals to equal the whole span of time)!

Shaykh al-Zarrūq ﷺ said in *Taʾsīs al-qawāʿid*:

> The preferential regard for certain times and people is a vestige of pagan ignorance and has no legal foundation. Thus the unbelievers said, *If only this Qurʾān had been revealed to some great man from the two towns* (Qurʾān, 43:31)![26] So Allah the Exalted responded to them with His saying, *Are they the ones who apportion the mercy of your Lord* (43:32)? And when they said, *We found our fathers following a religion, and we are guided by their footprints* (43:22), Allah responded to them by saying, *(The one sent to warn them) said: "What, even though I bring you better guidance than what you found your fathers following"* (43:24)?
>
> It is necessary to consider the universality of Allah's gracious favor (*faḍl*), without regard for a certain time or an individual, except in the case of someone specifically distinguished by the Word of the Most High. In this respect (of being distinguished by Allah), the saints followed the Prophets; for the saintly miracle (*karāma*) bears witness to the prophetic miracle (*muʿjiza*), and the scholars are the heirs of the Prophets in sanctity and mercy. Nonetheless, they are differentiated by the extent of their endowment with divine grace (*faḍl*), so understand this well.

Concerning Allah's saying, *And a multitude from the later generations (are among the companions of the Right)* (56:40), our Shaykh (al-Tijānī), our means of access, the nourishment of our spirits, our supporter, the saintly pole (*quṭb*), the succor (*ghawth*), the Seal of Muḥammadan sainthood (*al-khatim al-Muḥammadī*), said: "They are our companions!" Consider this fairly, and you will find that Shaykh al-Tijānī acquired the complete inheritance (of the Prophet), so that the two multitudes came to be in the Muslim community. One multitude belongs to his grandfather, they being the companions of the Allah's Messenger ﷺ. The other multitude belongs to him ﷺ, they being his own companions. My pen recoils from inscribing the rest of the implications here.

---

25 Reported by Tirmidhī in his *Sunan* and by Ibn Ḥanbal in his *Musnad*.

26 The "two towns" referred to here are the main cities of Arabia at the time: Mecca and Yathrib (later called Medina).

> In the secret of secrets are subtle details
> If we were to reveal them, our blood would be shed publicly.

Know that not even those with the lowest degree of faith can maintain the cessation of the Prophet's spiritual support (*madad*), or the waning of the light of his Prophecy. Our Shaykh (al-Tijānī) ؓ said, as recording in *al-Jāmiʿ* and *al-Jawāhir (al-maʿānī)*:[27]

> Know that the Prophet ﷺ used to impose general rules on the general populace (*al-ʿāma*) during his lifetime. Thus when he declared something unlawful, it became unlawful for everyone. When he prescribed something, he prescribed it for everyone. This was the case for all the manifest rulings of the sacred law.
>
> In addition to all of these general rulings, he ﷺ used to instruct the elite (*al-khāṣṣa*) with special knowledge (*khāṣṣa*), and he used to single out certain of his companions and not others for certain affairs. This is something well-known and thoroughly recorded in the traditional reports concerning him ﷺ.
>
> When he was transferred to the abode of the Hereafter, the situation was therefore the same as it had been during his life in this world. He had begun to entrust to his community the special command for the elite, but without modification of the general command given to everyone. So modification of the general command ceased with his death ﷺ, while the flood of his grace (*fayḍahu*) persisted in providing the special command to the elite.
>
> Whoever imagines that all of his support for his community came to an end with his death ﷺ, as in the case of other dead men, he is ignorant of the Prophet's rank ﷺ. He is guilty of treating him indecently, and he is therefore in danger of dying as an unbeliever if he does not repent of his deluded conviction.

This brings us to the end of the Introduction. Praise be to Allah, the Lord of all the worlds! Additional explanation of this issue will come later, in the description of the shaykh who provides spiritual training (*tarbiya*), if Allah the Exalted so wills. With Allah is success on the straight path, to Him, the Glorious, is the return and final destination.

---

27 The *Jawāhir al-maʿānī wa bulūgh al-amānī fī fayḍ Sīdī Abī al-ʿAbbās al-Tijānī* was written in 1799 by ʿAlī Harāzim al-Barāda, the closest companion of Shaykh Aḥmad al-Tijānī. The work is considered the most important primary source of the Tijāniyya.

Section I

Chapter 1

Concerning the Reality of Sufism

With Allah is the success for whatever I say, and He is the Guide to the straight path.

Sufism (*taṣawwuf*) is a science possessing a definition (*ḥadd*), a subject matter (*mawḍūʿ*), a founder (*wāḍiʿ*), a name (*ism*), a derivation (*istimdād*), a legal status (*ḥukm*), particular issues (*masāʾil*), an excellence (*faḍīla*), an attribution (*nisba*) and a fruit (*thamara*). Ṣāwī said: "It is incumbent on every person who would pass a judgment on a discipline (*fann*) to first know (these) ten basic principles." One of the scholars put this in verse:

> The definition and the subject matter, then the founder
> And the name, the derivation, and the ruling according to the sacred law
>
> The development of particular issues, the excellence
> And an attribution, (and) a sublime benefit (*fāʾida*)
>
> All are a right on the student, knowing that understanding
> Is comprised in these ten, the distinction in which he is entrusted
>
> He must know them before beginning to seek knowledge
> So that he may keep his sight on what he is seeking.

As for its definition, Zarrūq said, "Sufism has been defined, described and explained in approximately two thousand ways, all of them related to the importance of genuine dedication to Allah, and each explanation represents one aspect of the science, but Allah knows best." In the *Īqāẓ al-himam*, Junayd[1] has been quoted as saying, "It means that the Real makes you die to yourself and live for Him." He also said, "It means that you exist for the sake of Allah without any other attachment." It has similarly been said, "It is the entrance into every sublime character trait and the escape from every base characteristic." And it has been said that Sufism is when "noble characteristics appear among distinguished people in a distinguished age." It has also been said, "It means that you do not possess anything, and nothing possesses you." And in another saying, "It means devoting yourself to Allah with what He wants." One of the Sufis has said, "Sufism is not the wearing of wool and threadbare garments, rather it is excellent conduct and character." Another has said:

> Sufism is not wearing a robe that you patch
> And it is not the shedding of tears when the singers sing
> It is not crying out, nor dancing, nor musical entertainment
> And it is not swooning as if you had become possessed
> Sufism is rather your serenity (*taṣūfū*), without distress
> And following the truth of the Qurʾān and the religion.

In *Īqāẓ al-himam*, Ibn ʿAjība quoted Sīdī Zarrūq's commentary on the saying of our Imam Mālik:[2] "If someone practices Sufism (*taṣawwuf*) without acquiring knowledge of the law (*fiqh*), he has become an infidel (*zindiq*), while he who practices the law without acquiring knowledge of Sufism has become a debauched degenerate (*fāsiq*). He who combines the two is on the truth." Sīdī Zarrūq commented thus:

> The infidelity of the first is due to the fact that he professes the doctrine of fatalism (*jabr*), which entails the negation of wisdom and legal rulings. The moral depravity of the second is due to the fact that his conduct is devoid of genuine dedication that prevents disobedience to Allah, and of the sincere devotion that is required in all actions. The correctness of the third is due to his sincere, steadfast adherence to the Truth. So know this: there is no existence of Sufism except in the

---

1 Junayd b. Muḥammad Abū Qāsim al-Khazzaz (d. 910) of Baghdad was "perhaps the most famous of the early Sufis within Islam," articulating ideas of sobriety in mysticism and the annihilation (*fanāʾ*) of the ego-self in Allah. See Michael Sells, *Early Islamic Mysticism: Sufi, Qurʾān, Miʿraj, Poetic and Theological Writings* (New Jersey: Paulist Press, 1996), p. 21–22. Nearly all the Sufi orders, except the Tijāniyya (whose *silsila* goes directly from the Prophet ﷺ to Shaykh Aḥmad al-Tijānī), provide their followers with a chain of spiritual transmission (*silsila*) passing through Junayd.

2 Imam Mālik b. Anas (d. 795) is the eponym for the Mālikī school of jurisprudence. He lived in Medina, the city of the Prophet, and authored the *Muwaṭṭāʾ*, an early collection of traditions mostly with legal bearing. For more on Imam Mālik's role in the development of Islamic jurisprudence, see Yasin Dutton, *The Origins of Islamic Law: The Qurʾān, the Muwaṭṭāʾ and the Madinan ʿAmal* (London: Routledge, 2002).

Law, and there is no perfection of the Law without Sufism. This you must understand well.

As for the subject matter (*mawḍūᶜ*) of Sufism, it is nothing less than the exalted Essence of Allah. The science of Sufism searches a means of knowing Him, either by demonstrable evidence or witnessing with the eyes. The first is for the seekers, and the second for those who have arrived. It has also been said that the subject matter of Sufism is the souls, hearts, and spirits, since it deals with their purification and training. This definition is close to the first, for "he who knows himself knows his Lord."[3]

As for the founder (*wāḍiᶜ*) of Sufism, it is the Prophet ﷺ, to whom Allah taught it by means of both revelation (*waḥy*) and inspiration (*ilhām*). First, He sent down Gabriel with the sacred law (*sharīᶜa*), and once it had been firmly established, He next sent down the Reality (*al-ḥaqīqa*). Then, the Prophet favored some of his companions with this (latter) knowledge and not others. The first of those to speak of Sufism thereafter and to manifest its reality was our master ᶜAlī, may Allah ennoble his countenance. From him and through the well-known chains of knowledge transmission (*silsila*) found in their books, the Sufis have received this science. The exception is our master, our patron, our Shaykh and our means of access to our Lord, Abū al-ᶜAbbās Aḥmad b. Muḥammad al-Tijānī al-Ḥasanī, whom Allah blessed with receiving from the Prophet by word of mouth, without the mediation of any of the shaykhs. Our chain of authority derives from him.

As for its proper name (*ism*), it is the "Science of Sufism" (*ᶜilm al-taṣawwuf*). The experts have held different opinions regarding the origins of the name "Sufi," however. According to *Īqāẓ al-himam*, Sīdī Zarrūq stated that its origin may be attributed to five different sources. First from *ṣūfa*, the name for the caretaker in charge of the Kaᶜba in Mecca, because the Sufi is with Allah like the Kaᶜba's manager has himself been cast away (from the rest of the world's affairs), and there is no planning left with him. Secondly, it could be derived from the delicate *ṣūfa al-qafā*, the silky hair on the back of the neck, because the Sufi is likewise delicate and (considers himself) of little importance. Thirdly, it may be derived from the word *ṣifa*, quality or virtue, since the term is generally applied to the possession of praiseworthy qualities and the abandonment of blameworthy characteristics. Fourthly, it may be derived from the word *ṣafāʾ*, pure sincerity. This statement has been authenticated to the point that Abū al-Fatḥ al-Bastī said, concerning the Sufi:

> People have differed concerning the term "Sufi," but they have differed only due to ignorance, for they have supposed it to be derived from

3 Saying sometimes attributed to the Prophet Muḥammad, the meaning of which has been considered sound by numerous scholars even if its line of transmission from the Prophet has not been settled. More discussion of this saying can be found in Imam Sakhāwī's *Maqāṣid al-ḥasana.*

"wool" (*ṣūf*). I would never give this name to any but a chivalrous one, who behaved with pure sincerity (*ṣāfa*) and was requited with pure sincerity (*ṣūfiya*), so that he came to be called "Sufi."

This appears to me the most plausible explanation, and Allah knows best. The fifth possibility is that it could be derived from the *ṣuffa*, the porch or bench of the Prophet's mosque, which was a shelter for the (indigent devotees known as) the "people of the bench" (*ahl al-ṣuffa*). Indeed, the Sufi matches Allah's description of these people: *And restrain yourself along with those who cry unto their Lord in the morning and evening, seeking His countenance* (Qurʾān, 18:28). So this comprehensive explanation of the origin of the name "Sufi" provided by Shaykh al-Zarrūq is the foundation to which return all statements on the subject.

As for the source (*istimdād*) of Sufism, it is extracted from the Qurʾān, the prophetic Sunna, the inspirations (*ilhāmāt*) of the righteous, and the illuminations (*futūḥāt*) of the gnostics. The Sufis have incorporated elements of the science of jurisprudence in order to substantiate the incumbent need of the Law within the science of Sufism, and Ghazālī[4] has expounded this in four books of his *Iḥyāʾ ʿulūm al-dīn*: the "Book of the Rites of Worship," the "Book of Customary Practices," the "Book of the Causes of Perdition," and the "Book of the Causes of Salvation."

As for its legal status (*ḥukm*), Ghazālī said: "It is a duty incumbent on every individual Muslim (*farḍ ʿayn*), since no one is free from fault or sickness, except the Prophets." Shādhilī[5] said: "If someone does not become immersed in this science of ours, he will die as one who persists in the major sins, without being aware of his condition."

As for the issues (*masāʾil*) involved in Sufism, it is necessary to know its technical terms and the words its people use. These include: sincerity (*ikhlāṣ*), truthfulness (*ṣidq*), reliance (*tawakkul*), asceticism (*zuhd*), piety (*waraʿ*), contentment (*riḍā*), surrender (*taslīm*), love (*maḥabba*), annihilation (*fanāʾ*), and remaining (*baqāʾ*). It is likewise important to understand words such as Essence (*dhāt*), Attributes (*Ṣifāt*), capability (*qudra*), wisdom (*ḥikma*), spirituality (*rūḥāniyya*), and humanity (*bashariyya*). Also signifi-

---

4 Abū Ḥāmid al-Ghazālī (d. 1111, Baghdad), was known as the "Proof (*ḥujja*) of Islam," and is credited with the most comprehensive reconciliation of Sufism with the Islamic legal tradition. His primary work is the *Iḥyāʾ ʿulūm al-dīn* [The Revival of the Religious Sciences] comprising four volumes of ten chapters (or books) each. The most reliable translations are the "Ghazali series" published by the Islamic Texts Society, which has completed books 9, 11–13, 15, 32, 34, and 37. The website www.ghazali.org has collected translations and primary texts of most of the *Iḥyāʾ*'s forty chapters from various sources and has made them available online.

5 Abū Ḥasan al-Shādhilī (d. 1258), the renowned Sufi scholar of Moroccan origin who settled in Egypt and became the eponym for the Shādhiliyya Sufi order found primarily in North Africa.

cant is the knowledge of the reality of state (*ḥāl*), the coming (*wārid*) of mystical insights, the spiritual station (*maqām*), and other matters.

As for the excellence (*faḍīla*) of Sufism, it has already been mentioned that its subject matter is nothing less than the Exalted divine Essence (*dhāt*). There is no limit to the excellence of this subject, so the science that pertains to it also has no limit to its excellence. Its first stage deals with the fear (*khashya*) of Allah, its middle stage with proper conduct (*muʿāmala*) with Him and the last with the knowledge (*maʿrifa*) of Him and complete dedication to Him. That is why Junayd said, "If we knew that there was a more noble science under heaven to discuss with our companions, surely I would have speedily found it." In his book *Anwār al-qulūb fī al-ʿilm al-mawhūb*,[6] Shaykh al-Ṣiqillī said, "Anyone who testifies to this science is included among the elite. Anyone who understands it is included among the elite of the elite. Anyone who expounds it and speaks about it is the star that can never be reached, the ocean that can never be drained." Another person has said:

> If you see someone who has been opened to believing in this Path, congratulate him. If you see someone who has been illuminated with understanding it, rejoice on his account. If you see someone who has been enabled to speak about it, exalt him. But if you find someone finding fault with it, flee from him as you would flee from the lion, and emigrate from him completely. There is no science that cannot be dispensed with occasionally except the science of Sufism: one cannot do without it for a single moment.

As for its attribution or relationship (*nisba*) to the other sciences, it is comprehensive of them all as well as their prerequisite, since there is no knowledge and no good deed without genuine dedication to Allah. So too from the standpoint of legal validity, penalty and reward, sincerity is the precondition in every instance. From the standpoint of the external existence, the religious sciences may exist superficially without Sufism, but they become defective and disreputable. That is why al-Suyūṭī[7] said, "In relation to the sciences, Sufism is like the science of rhetoric (*balāgha*) in relation to grammar (*naḥw*): it perfects and beautifies them." According to Shaykh al-Zarrūq:

---

6 The title translates as "Lights of the hearts in divinely-bestowed knowledge." This work by Shaykh al-Ṣiqillī (sometimes pronounced Ṣaqlī; the 2001 Arabic printing "Maqlī" appears to be a misprint) is also known as *Nūr al-qulūb*, the title given by Shaykh Aḥmad al-ʿAlawī al-Mālikī's *al-Risala al-qawl al-maʿruf*, where the very same passage appears.

7 Jalal al-Dīn al-Suyūṭī (d. 1505), renowned Egyptian scholar was known as the renewer (*mujaddid*) of the faith in his century. He was also an accomplished Sufi. He authored numerous works, many of which quickly became widespread in West Africa. Most significant has been the work of Qurʾānic exegesis, *Tafsīr al-Jalālayn*.

The relationship of Sufism to the religion is the relationship of the spirit to the body, because it represents spiritual excellence (*iḥsān*), which Allah's Messenger explained to Gabriel by saying, "*Iḥsān* means that you must worship Allah as if you see Him."[8] Sufism is nothing other than this, since it hinges on the vigilant awareness of Allah (*marāqaba*) after witnessing Him (*mushāhada*),[9] or witnessing after vigilant awareness, where no other existence or existent beings appear to the seer (other than Allah).

And as for the benefit (*fāʾida*) of Sufism, it lies in the gilding of the hearts and (the granting of) of thorough knowledge of the Unseen. Or we might say: its fruit (*thamara*) is the generosity of the self, the serenity of the breast and good disposition with every created entity.

Know that this science we mention is not mere wagging of the tongue. Its contents are spiritual experiences (*adhwāq*) and ecstasy (*wijdān*). It cannot be acquired through talking or written texts, but can only be received directly from the people of experience (*ahl al-adhwāq*). It can only be gained through serving (*khidma*) the people of spiritual distinction (*rijāl*), and companionship with the perfected ones. By Allah, no one has ever succeeded (on this path) except by companionship with one who has succeeded, and the achievement is from Allah.

Our master, patron and teacher, Sīdī Abū al-ʿAbbās al-Tijānī, was once asked about the reality of Sufism. He responded by saying, "Know that Sufism is compliance with Allah's command and avoidance of His prohibition, externally and internally, with regard to what pleases Him, not what pleases you." There is no way to accomplish this without keeping company with a shaykh who is a perfect spiritual guide. Allah has said, *O you who truly believe, fulfill your duty to Allah, and seek the means of access (wasīla) to Him* (Qurʾān, 5:35).

The means of access to Allah are many. Among them is following the Prophet in his words and deeds, as Allah has said, "*Say (O Muḥammad), if you love Allah, follow me and Allah will love you*" (3:31); and in the *ḥadīth* (Allah says), "And when I love him, I become him."[10] This is the door to

8 *Ḥadīth* related in Bukhārī, reported by Abū Hurayra; and related in Muslim as reported by ʿUmar b. al-Khaṭṭāb.

9 This appears to be a reference to the nine steps of traveling the Sufi path (*sulūk*), where the last three comprising the station of spiritual excellence (*iḥsān*) entail witnessing (*mushāhada*), observation (*murāqaba*), and gnosis (*maʿrifa*). These steps are detailed in Shaykh Ibrāhīm Niasse's *Maqāmāt al-dīn al-thalāth* [The three stations of the religion].

10 A similar version of this *ḥadīth qudsī* (sacred tradition, in which the Prophet relays the words of Allah by inspiration, but without them being revelation), is related on the authority of Abū Hurayra and included in Bukhārī, in which Allah says, "When I love him, I am his hearing with which he hears, his seeing with which he sees, his hand with which he strikes, and his foot with which he walks. Were he to ask of Me, I would surely give it to him."

gnosis (*maʿrifa*). Among the means of access is also the companionship with the consummate gnostic (*al-ʿārif al-wāṣil*). Allah has said, *Follow the path of him who has turned to Me* (31:15). Among them as well is the perseverance in remembering Allah, as Allah has said, *Restrain yourself along with those who call on their Lord morning and evening seeking His countenance* (18:28). It is well known among the people of the spiritual path that the remembrance which benefits its practitioner is the one received from the perfected shaykhs.

As for the source for the phenomenon of instructing (*talqīn*) the remembrances (*adhkār*) and litanies (*awrād*), it derives from the Prophet ﷺ. It has been reported by Imam Aḥmad (b. Ḥanbal) in his *Musnad*, with an excellent train of transmission, and by Ṭabarānī and others, that Yaʿlā b. Shaddād said:

> My father Shaddād b. Aws told me, in the presence of ʿUbāda b. al-Ṣāmit, who said he was telling the truth: "We were together with the Prophet ﷺ, and he asked, 'Is there a stranger amongst you?' By this he meant one of the people of the (preceding) scriptures (*ahl al-kitāb*). We said, 'No, O Messenger of Allah."
>
> "So he ordered the door to be locked, then he said, 'Raise your hands and say: There is nothing worthy of worship but Allah (*lā ilāha ill-Allāh*).' So we held up our hands for a moment.
>
> "Then he said, 'Praise be to Allah! O Allah, You have sent me with this declaration, You have entrusted me with it, and You have promised me Paradise on account of it, and You do not fail to keep Your promise.'
>
> "Then he said, 'Rejoice, for Allah has granted you forgiveness.'"

Ibn Ḥajar al-ʿAsqalānī[11] confirmed this narration with an excellent chain of transmission reported by Imam Aḥmad and Ṭabarānī, and also reported in a slightly different version, ending with the words: "Allah's Mesenger ﷺ then raised (his hands), and we raised (ours). Then he said, 'Lower your hands and rejoice, for you have been granted forgiveness.'"

Shaykh Yūsuf al-Kūzānī, [12] known as al-ʿAjamī, reported in his *Risāla* that ʿAlī b. Abī Ṭālib once implored the Prophet, "O Messenger of Allah, point me to the shortest of paths to Allah, the easiest on His servants and the best in the sight of Allah." The Prophet ﷺ replied, "O ʿAlī, persist in the remembrance of Allah in spiritual retreat (*khalwa*)." ʿAlī then asked, "Does this excellent merit of remembrance depend on its being practiced by all human beings?" To this the Prophet ﷺ replied, "O ʿAlī, the Final

---

11 Ibn Ḥajar al-ʿAsqalānī (d. 1448) was a prominent Egypt *ḥadīth* scholar who authored numerous works, the most widely known being *Fatḥ al-Bārī*, a commentary on the *ḥadīth* collection of Bukhārī.

12 This is likely Shaykh Yūsuf al-ʿAjamī al-ʿAdawī, a thirteenth-century Egyptian scholar.

Hour will not arrive so long as someone on the face of the earth is saying '*lā ilāha ill-Allāh*.'"[13]

ʿAlī then asked, "How should I perform the remembrance, O Messenger?" He ﷺ replied, "You must close your eyes and hear it from me three times, then you must say it three times while I am listening." The Prophet then said, "*lā ilāha ill-Allāh*," three times, closing his eyes and raising his voice while ʿAlī listened. Then ʿAlī said the same three times, closing his eyes and raising his voice while the Prophet listened.

These prophetic traditions have been mentioned as well by the author of *Kitāb al-rimāḥ* (ʿUmar al-Fūtī),[14] in which it is mentioned that ʿAlī taught these (litanies) to Ḥasan al-Baṣrī,[15] who taught them to Ḥabīb al-ʿAjamī,[16] who taught them to Dāwūd al-Ṭāʾī,[17] who taught them to Maʿrūf al-Karkhī,[18] who taught them to al-Sarī,[19] who taught them to Junayd. They have been transmitted since then to the masters of spiritual training to the extent that Allah willed. So this is the source of the instruction of the litanies and the remembrances.

Much has been said about the necessity of seeking the spiritually-guiding shaykh, as the reader will discover in due course. One poet has said:

---

13 A similar narration of this section of the *ḥadīth* is reported on the authority of Anas in *Ṣaḥīḥ Muslim*, *Sunan al-Tirmidhī* and Ibn Ḥanbal's *Musnad*. The wording in the narration from Anas is: "The Final Hour will not arrive while 'Allah, Allah' is spoken on earth."

14 Al-Ḥājj ʿUmar al-Fūtī Tāl (d. 1864), originally of Senegal, died in Mali fighting *jihād* against the pagan Bambara kingdoms, and in opposition to the encroaching French influence. He briefly established an Islamic state in what is now part of Mali, Senegal, and Guinea. Al-Ḥājj Umar was a well-known nineteenth century Tijānī scholar, author, of the *Kitāb al-rimāḥ ḥizb al-raḥīm ʿala nuhūr ḥizb al-rajīm*, since printed with the Tijānī order's primary text, the *Jawāhir al-maʿānī*. For more on al-Ḥājj ʿUmar's social and political activities, see David Robinson, *The Holy War of Umar Tal* (New York: Oxford University Press, 1985).

15 Abū Saʿīd al-Ḥasan al-Baṣrī (d. 737) became a student of ʿAlī b. Abī Ṭālib at a young age. He moved from Medina to Iraq, where he formed a school and taught both juristic and ascetic sciences. Most lines of Sufi knowledge transmission pass through him to ʿAlī.

16 Ḥabīb b. Muḥammad al-ʿAjamī of Basra is mentioned in Abū Nuʿaym al-Iṣfahānī's *Tadhkira al-awliyāʾ* (vol. 6) as Ḥasan al-Baṣrī's closest student, renowned for his saintliness and ability to work miracles. He was nicknamed "ʿAjamī" because he spoke Persian and had difficulty learning the Qurʾān.

17 Abū Sulayman Dāwūd b. Nusayr al-Ṭāʾī (d. 790) of Kufa, Iraq, studied with Abū Ḥanīfa and later devoted his entire life to asceticism.

18 Abū Maḥfūẓ Maʿrūf b. Firūz al-Karkhī was born of Christian parents and converted to Islam at the hands of ʿAlī b. Mūsa al-Riḍā.

19 Abū Ḥasan Sarī b. Mughalis al-Saqatī (d. 870) was the disciple of al-Karkhī who elaborated on spiritual stations (*maqam*) and states (*ḥal*). He was the brother of al-Junayd's mother.

> Keep company with the shaykh knowledgeable of the ways of seeking (*masālik*)
> He will protect you from the dangers on the spiritual path.

You simply cannot do without a shaykh if you wish to acquire knowledge and correct practice. A shaykh is also necessary for acquiring the benefit of spiritual aspiration (*himma*) and state (*ḥāl*). According to *al-Shamāʾil*,[20] Anas said:

> The day Allah's Messenger ﷺ entered Medina, every part of it became radiant. On the day he died there, every part of it fell into darkness. No sooner had we dusted off our hands from burying him ﷺ than we had renounced our hearts.

He clearly meant that the presence of the Prophet's noble person ﷺ benefitted their hearts, and this is the meaning of benefitting from spiritual aspiration and state. It is well-known that the religious scholars are the heirs of the Prophets,[21] so seeking nearness to them is absolutely essential. It has been said concerning them: "Whoever is afflicted by a condition he cannot cure (himself), they will persuade him out of it." The author of *Risāla al-Qushayriyya*[22] said: "The aspirant must be refined (*yataʾaddab*) by the shaykh, for if he has no teacher, he will never succeed." This was put in a similar way by Abū Yazīd (al-Bistāmī): "Whoever has no teacher, his leader (*imām*) is Satan." Our master and our teacher, Abū al-ʿAbbās Aḥmad b. Muḥammad al-Tijānī al-Sharīf, may Allah be pleased with him, and allow us to benefit from him in this world and the next, was asked: "Is (seeking a shaykh) strictly incumbent on every individual, or on some but not others, and what is the reason in either case?" His complete answer will be presented in the relevant chapter (Section III, Chapter 2).

According to Sīdī Mukhtār al-Kuntī, the reality of the litanies is that they are contracts and covenants that Allah has imposed upon His servants by means of the shaykhs. If someone reveres the shaykhs, complies with the contracts and fulfills the covenants, he will have the good of this life and the next. On the other hand, if someone belittles the shaykhs and

---

20 *Al-Shamāʾil al-Muḥammadiyya* by the great *ḥadīth* scholar Muḥammad b. ʿĪsā al-Tirmidhī (d. 912) is a work of prophetic biography (*sīra*). A translation by Muhtar Holland entitled *A Portrait of the Prophet as Seen by His Contemporaries: Ash-Shamaʾil al-Muḥammadiyya* (Fons Vitae & Muslim Literary Society) is forthcoming.

21 This a prophetic tradition ("The scholars are the heirs of the Prophets"), reported by Abū al-Dardāʾ, and related by Abū Dāwūd.

22 This is Abū al-Qāsim al-Qushayrī (d. 1072), an important Persian scholar, famous for *ḥadīth* transmission, Qurʾān exegesis and his Sufi teachings. His most influential work is *Risāla ila al-Ṣūfiyya* [Epistle to the Sufis]. For a translation of al-Qushayrī's *Risāla*, see Barbara Von Schlegell (trans.), *Principals of Sufism by al-Qushayri* (Berkeley, CA: Mizan Press, 1990), or Alexander Knysh (trans.), *al-Qushayri's Epistle on Sufism: al-Risala al-Qushayriyya fī ʿilm al-Tasawwuf* (Reading, UK: Garnet Publishing, 2007).

neglects the contracts and the covenants, he will be led astray, sinking the ship of his religion. Allah has said, *O you who believe, fulfill your contracts!* (Qurʾān, 5:1). And He has said, *It is most hateful in the sight of Allah that you say what you do not do* (61:3), and, *Among the believers there are men who are true to what they covenanted with Allah. Some of them have paid their vow with death, and some of them are still waiting, and they have not altered in the least; so that Allah may reward the truthful ones for their truth* (33:23–24).

This explains why the Prophet ﷺ would not engage in any good work without tackling it with determination and persistent commitment, for this is among the signs of perfected resolve. These verses of the Qurʾān have been the source of the litanies, from the time of the Prophet to this time of ours. The Prophet (mentioned the use of litanies), saying, "If someone would normally perform a litany (*wird*) in connection with a ritual prayer, fast, or some other religious observance, but he is prevented by sickness, traveling, or old age, he is fully entitled to the reward." He also said, "Venerate the shaykhs, for revering them is part of exalting the Mightiness of Allah."[23]

23 A similar version of this *ḥadīth* has been reported by Ibn ʿAdī in *al-Kāmil fī ḍuʿafāʾ al-rijāl* and by Ibn al-Jawzī in *al-Mawḍuʿāt* on the authority of Anas b. Mālik: "Venerate the shaykhs, for surely reverence for the shaykhs is part of exalting Allah."

Chapter 2

The Excellence of Allah's Remembrance (*dhikr*)

Let us begin with reference to the work of the erudite scholar al-Nawawī,[1] may Allah bestow His mercy upon him, on the subject of the liturgical remembrances (*adhkār*). He cited the verse of Allah the Exalted, *Surely men who submit (to Allah), and women who submit,* to the words, *and men who remember Allah frequently and women who remember, for them has Allah promised forgiveness and a great reward* (Qur'ān, 44:35).[2] Then he related the *ḥadīth* in *Saḥīḥ Muslim* on the authority of Abū Hurayra ﷺ where the Messenger of Allah said: "Precedence is for those who are singled out (*munfarridūn*)." The companions asked, "O Messenger of Allah, who are those singled out?" He replied, "The men

1 Imam Yaḥya b. Sharaf al-Nawawī (d. 1278) was an eminent *ḥadīth* scholar and Shāfiʿī jurist in Damascus. He wrote numerous books, including *ḥadīth* compilations such as *Riyāḍ al-ṣāliḥīn*, works on jurisprudence such as *Minhaj al-ṭālibīn*, a book on prophetic supplications and remembrances called *Kitāb al-adhkār* (from which Shaykh Ibrāhīm cites here) and a work on inner sincerity, *Bustān al-ʿārifīn*.

2 The full verse reads: *Men who submit, and women who submit; and men who believe and women who believe; and men who obey and women who obey; and men who speak the truth and women who speak the truth; and men who are patient and women who are patient; and men who are humble and women who are humble; and men who give in charity and women who give in charity; and men who keep the fast and women who keep the fast; and men who are chaste and women who are chaste; and men who remember Allah frequently and women who remember: for them as Allah promised forgiveness and a great reward* (44:35). In one lesson, Shaykh Ḥasan Cisse explained that the mention of those who remember Him last in this verse indicates that Allah gives them precedence over the other groups mentioned.

who remember Allah frequently and women who remember."[3] It should be noted that both *munfarridūn* (those who are singled out) and *mufradūn* (the unique ones) have been reported in alternate narrations; but the majority opinion favors *munfarridūn*.

Pay careful attention to the true meaning of this noble verse of the Qur'ān, which has been the subject of scholarly discussion. According to Imam Abū al-Ḥasan al-Wāḥidī:[4] "The meaning is that they remember Allah in the wake of the ritual prayers, in the morning and in the evening, and in their beds. Whenever one of them wakes from sleeping, or whenever he leaves his home, he remembers Allah the Exalted." According to Mujāhid:[5] "A person is not included among the men and women who remember Allah frequently unless he remembers Allah while standing, while sitting and while lying down." He also said:

> The scholars are unanimously agreed on the permissibility of a person making remembrance with the heart and the tongue in whatever state, even in a state of ritual impurity resulting from excretion, seminal emission, menstruation, or childbirth. This applies to the glorification of Allah (*tasbīḥ*), the declaration of Allah's Oneness (*tahlīl*), the praise of Allah (*taḥmīd*), the exaltation of Allah (*takbīr*), the invocation of blessing on Allah's Messenger ﷺ, supplication (*duʿā'*), and other forms of remembrance.

According to the distinguished scholar and divine gnostic, Sīdī Aḥmad Zarrūq ﵁, as recorded in *Ta'sīs al-qawā'id*:

> The attachment to Him is found in the necessary commitment (*al-iltizām al-lāzim*)[6] to that for which one is liable. It is on this premise that the remembrance is more excellent than anything else, since your desire is for Him to be inseparable from you, so your duty is to make the commitment to Him (to remember Him regularly). Allah the Exalted said: *Remember Me, and I will remember you* (Qur'ān, 2:152). There is no greater miraculous bounty (*karāma*) than this promise from Allah that He will remember us if we remember Him.

---

3 Reported by Muslim in his *Ṣaḥīḥ*, by Tirmidhī in his *Sunan*, by Ibn Ḥanbal in his *Musnad*, and by Imam al-Baghawī in *Kitāb sharḥ al-Sunna*.

4 Abū al-Ḥasan al-Wāḥidī (d. 1076) was a famous interpreter of the Qur'ān from Persia who wrote *Kitāb asbāb nuzūl al-Qur'ān*, concerning the circumstances of revelation of various verses of the Qur'ān. This book is the likely source of the citation here.

5 Abū al-Ḥājjāj Mujāhid b. Jubayr (d. 723) was an early scholar of Persian descent who studied with ʿAlī b. Abī Ṭālib and Ibn ʿAbbās, and is said to have authored the first exegesis of the Qur'ān.

6 The adjective *lāzim* (necessary, indispensable) is often used in Sufi circles as another word for the daily liturgy (*wird*).

Allah has assigned a limit and a fixed period for everything except the remembrance of Him, as is evident in the following verses: *O you who believe, remember Allah frequently* (33:41); *Remember Allah, while standing and while sitting* (4:103); *Remember Allah as you remember your fathers, or with a more intense remembrance* (2:200).

A man once said: "O Messenger of Allah, the duties of Islam are too many for me to observe, so guide me to a deed by which I can make up for what I have missed." He told him: "Your tongue must not cease to be moist with the remembrance of Allah, to the point that they call you a crazy person."[7] The remembrance is the ordinance of sainthood, so who is entrusted with the remembrance is entrusted with the ordinance.

Our Shaykh Abū al-ʿAbbās al-Ḥaḍramī ﷺ said: "If the aspirant should not encounter the spiritually-guiding shaykh, he must practice constant remembrance and invocation of blessings upon Allah's Messenger ﷺ. This practice is a ladder, an ascending stairway to Allah the Exalted. I heard one of the righteous people narrate this from one of Allah's truthful folk, in the year 846 (1442 C.E.) in the Noble Sanctuary (in Mecca). Both men were known for their reliable reporting, and Allah knows best."

He also said: "The special distinction of each remembrance and divine Name derives from its meaning, and its power (*taṣrīf*) is according to what is needed. The secret of the remembrance is in its number of repetitions. Its fulfillment depends on the spiritual aspiration (*himma*) of the one practicing it (*ṣāḥibihi*). This explains why the scholar does not benefit (from a *dhikr*) unless the meaning is clear, and why the ignorant person (does not benefit) unless the meaning is hidden and unknown to him. In this way their (divergent) understandings persist. As for how many times a specific formula of remembrance is repeated, this is either taken from the legal sources, or derived by spiritual discovery. Success is thus dependent on Allah's established custom (*sunnat Allah*)."

As for writing, and indulging in patterned formulation (*shakl*) and the like, it is useful according to the knowledge of the one writing and the natural sciences, provided it is not obscured from the Truth or from verification. For this reason, Ibn al-Bināʾ ﷺ spoke on behalf of Ibn al-Būnī[8] and the like, disagreeing with al-Nassāj and his ilk.

---

7 Reported by Tirmidhī in his *Sunan*, by Ibn Māja in his *Sunan*, and by Ibn Ḥanbal in his *Musnad*.

8 Aḥmad b. al-Būnī (d. 1225) was an Arab author and Sufi who wrote the most comprehensive book on the Islamic esoteric sciences, called *Shams al-maʿārif al-kubrā*. His work has stirred controversy among Muslim scholars, even though he claimed that he cited lines of knowledge transmission from Ibn al-ʿArabī, Abū Madyan, and Ḥasan al-Baṣrī.

Shaykh (Ibn al-ʿArabī) al-Ḥātimī ﷺ said: "The science of letters (*ʿilm al-ḥurūf*)[9] is a noble science, but it has become blameworthy in this world and the next, so be aware of this, and with Allah the Glorious is all success." As for (its blameworthiness in) this world, the one who practices this science becomes preoccupied with illusionary secondary causes without verification. This diminishes his reliance on Allah, due to the effort expended for the instrumental cause. Such is analogous to undertaking cauterization in medical treatment, for he bleeds himself to death while seeking to hasten the recovery. As for (its blameworthiness in) the next world, this is because he has occupied himself with something of little importance.

The distinguished scholar and gnostic of Allah, Sīdī Muḥammad al-Yadālī[10] said in *Sharḥ khātima al-taṣawwuf*:

> It has been said that the quickest way to enter the divine Presence is through the remembrance, because the Name is inseparable from the One named. Since the one engaged in remembrance ceaselessly mentions the Name of Allah, the veils are torn to shreds bit by bit, until the heart comes to witness Allah directly. When this happens, the aspirant dispenses with the remembrance due to his witnessing of the One remembered. So this is what the Sufi people mean by entering the Presence of Allah: the removal of veils so that you enter the Presence while you remain sitting in your place.

He also said in *Sharḥ shahiyya al-samāʾ*:

> A servant does not draw near to His Exalted Presence unless he displays a deep sense of shame and bashfulness. He does not perfect this (disposition) unless he obtains spiritual disclosure (*kashf*) and the lifting of the veils; and he does not perfect this unless he perseveres in the remembrance. Constant engagement in the remembrance is only way to perfect the station of complete sincerity, where one sees all actions as the creation of Allah. There is no other means to extinguish the fire of the internal sicknesses. There is no other way to cut off the evil thoughts (*al-khawāṭir al-shayṭāniyya*), nor are the egocentric delusions weakened by any other means. The continued practice of the remembrance causes the anxiety and sadness with the world to disappear; for such emotions are only a result of the heedlessness of Allah. Indeed,

9 The technical term in English would be Arithmomancy or Numerology. Based on the Pythagorean idea that all things can be expressed in numerical terms, each letter is assigned a specific number that is thought to encapsulate the inherent power of the letter and the names formed from those letters.

10 Muḥammad al-Yadālī (d. 1753) was a famous Mauritanian jurist and Shādhilī Sufi of the Daymānī tribe. Besides the works on Sufism mentioned here, he also wrote an exegesis of the Qurʾān called *al-Dhahab*.

the servant has no one to blame but himself if anxieties and sorrows should afflict him in unrelenting succession, for these are only the consequence of turning away from his Lord. He who desires persistent happiness, he must devote himself to persistent remembrance.

Some of the misguided have become stagnant, contenting themselves with the gatherings of remembrance (*majlis al-dhikr*) in the morning and evening, while remaining heedless of Allah in between. But this practice is of no use for the spiritual wayfarer seeking the stations of the Sufi people. Perhaps he who contends with this will cite the prophetic saying: "If the servant remembers his Lord for a time (*sāʾa*) at beginning and end of the day, he will be forgiven whatever comes between." Forgiveness, however, does not include spiritual advancement. The result of forgiveness is to equate the sinner with someone who has not committed that sin, not to equate him with the one who has performed acts of worshipful obedience. Understand that the desire of the Sufi people is continuous spiritual elevation, with each breath, through all the stations. This is achieved by the constant remembrance of Allah, so that they do not regard themselves as having fulfilled one atom of Allah's right on them.

Ibn ʿAbbād commented on this aphorism in the *Ḥikam*:[11]

> Do not abandon the remembrance for your lack of mindful presence with Allah therein. Your heedlessness in the absence of remembering Him is worse than your heedlessness while remembering Him. It may be that He will raise you from the heedless remembrance to wakeful remembrance, from wakeful remembrance to a remembrance with presence of mind, from present remembrance to a remembrance absent from everything apart from the One remembered. And that is not difficult for Allah.

He said in his commentary:

> Remembrance is the shortest path to Allah the Exalted. It is the sign of sainthood, as has been said: "The remembrance is the edict of sainthood, so whoever achieves the remembrance, the edict is granted him." Likewise, whoever is deprived of the remembrance has his sainthood withdrawn. A poet has said: "And the remembrance is the greatest of doors you are entering; for the sake of Allah, devote to Him every guarded breath."

Imam Abū al-Qāsim al-Qushayrī ﷺ said:

11 The *Kitāb al-ḥikam*, or "Book of Aphorisms," is a Sufi text by the Egyptian Shādhili Sufi and scholar Ibn ʿAṭāʾ Allāh al-Iskandarī (d. 1309). It has been translated by Victor Danner as *The Book of Wisdoms* (New York: Paulist Press, 1979).

> The remembrance is the symbol of sainthood, the shining beacon of divine connection, the realization of the desire, and the sign of a sound beginning and a happy end. There is nothing besides the remembrance. All praiseworthy qualities return to the remembrance and originate from the remembrance.

The excellent merits of remembrance are too many to be counted. Sufficient is the saying of the Most High in His Mighty Book: *Remember Me and I will remember you* (Qurʾān, 2:152). There is also His statement, Exalted and Mighty is He, narrated from Allah's Messenger ﷺ (in a *ḥadīth qudsī*) that has been authenicated by a consensus of scholars.

I am alongside My servant's thinking of Me. I am with him when he remembers Me. If he remembers Me within himself, I remember him within Myself. If he remembers Me in a congregation, I remember him in a congregation better than that. If he draws near to Me by the span of a hand, I draw near to him by an arm's length. If he draws near to Me by an arm's length, I draw near to him by the span of outspread arms. If he comes to Me walking, I come to him at high speed.[12]

The scholars have said that the special merits of the remembrance include the fact that, unlike other forms of worship, it is not limited to a particular period of time. So there is no time when the servant is not invited to the remembrance, either as a matter of strict obligation or a strongly recommended practice. According to Ibn ʿAbbās ﷺ:

> Allah the Exalted has not imposed any religious duty upon His servant without fixing a known limit to it and granting an exception in the case of a valid excuse. The sole exception in the remembrance, for He has not fixed any limit at which it may end, nor has He permitted anyone to neglect it unless afflicted by mental absence. He has commanded His servants to remember Him in all situations, saying: *Remember Allah while standing, while sitting, and while reclining on your sides* (Qurʾān, 4:103). He, the Exalted, has also said: *O you who believe, remember Allah with frequent remembrance* (33:41). This is to say: remember Him by night and by day, on the land and sea, while traveling or while staying home, while rich or while poor, in health and in sickness, in private and in public; indeed, in every state.

Mujāhid ﷺ said: "Frequent remembrance means that one never forgets Him." As has been related from Allah's Messenger ﷺ, "Make frequent remembrance of Allah, to the point you are called crazy."[13] So the servant must practice frequent remembrance in all states, immersing himself in

---

12 This sacred tradition, in which the Prophet related Allah's words outside of the Qurʾān, is reported in the canonical collections of Bukhārī, Muslim, and Tirmidhī on the authority of Abū Hurayra.

13 *Ḥadīth* on the authority of Abū Saʿīd al-Khudrī reported in the *Musnad* of Ibn Ḥanbal.

it in all of his moments, removing himself from heedlessness. It is not permissible to abandon the remembrance due to the presence of heedlessness in it. Indeed, if he should leave it altogether, his heedlessness in the absence of Allah's remembrance is worse than his heedlessness in the course of remembering Him. So he must remember Allah the Exalted with his tongue, even if he is heedless in the remembrance. Perhaps the heedless remembrance will raise him to the remembrance absent from everything apart from the One remembered. And this is the degree of the spiritually-realized gnostics among the saints.

Allah the Exalted said, *And remember your Lord when you forget* (Qurʾān, 18:24). This is to say, "When you forget everything apart from Allah, then you will be remembering Allah." In this station (*maqām*), the remembrance of the tongue comes to a halt, and the servant becomes erased in the presence of the witnessing. In this context a poet has said:

> I do not remember You except that an anxiety disturbs me:
> My secret self, my heart, my spirit; in the presence of Your remembrance
> Until it is as if an observer is calling out to me
> Woe to you, what is this remembrance of yours?
> Do you not see the Truth? Its signs are shining everywhere
> The totality of existence emerging from His signification has fused with your meaning.

Wāsitī[14] was referring to this station when he said: "Those who remember His remembrance are more heedless than those who forget His remembrance; for the remembrance is other than He."

In the introduction of *al-Asrār al-ʿaqliyya fī al-kalimāt al-nabawiyya* by Abū al-ʿIzz Taqiyy al-Dīn b. Muẓaffar al-Shāfiʿī,[15] Abū al-ʿAbbās b. al-Bannāʾ included the following passage, which I saw in his own handwriting, may Allah have mercy on him:

> Among the greatest forms of the remembrance is that which arises from inspiration received from the One who is remembered, magnificent is His remembrance. According to the Sufis, this is the hidden remembrance, made continuously and in secret. As for their saying, "to the point the one making the remembrance masters a state of immersion beyond the remembrance," this mastery is neither a state of incarnation (*ḥulūl*) nor of theosophical union (*ittiḥād*), only a faculty obtained from Him who is Almighty, Wise.

---

14 Muḥammad b. Mūsa al-Wāsitī (d. 932) was a Sufi and jurist contemporary to Junayd in Baghdad. This citation of his is likely from al-Qushayrī's *Risāla* or Ibn ʿAbd al-Salām Sulamī's *Ṭabaqāt*.

15 The *al-Asrār al-ʿaqliyya* is a work of religious principles (*uṣūl*) by the Egyptian Shāfiʿī scholar and Imam Taqiyy al-Dīn al-Maqtaraḥ (d. 1215).

The explanation for this is that the heart becomes, in the presence of the remembrance, empty of the entirety of existence, so that nothing remains in it other than Allah, mighty is His remembrance. The heart thus becomes the house of the Manifest Truth. Allah becomes the tongue with which the servant speaks. If the one possessing such a heart were to strike a blow, He would be the hand with which he strikes. If he hears, He is the hearing with which he hears.[16] The Exalted One being remembered has taken possession of the heart, so He controls it. He has taken possession of the limbs of the body, so He uses them for what is pleasing to Him. He has taken possession of all the attributes of this servant, so he alternates them however He wills for His pleasure. For this reason, the remembrance emerges without any effort. Good deeds and obedience are undertaken with cheerful animation and delight rather than as a wearisome burden. *Such is Allah's bounty, He bestows it on whom He wills. And Allah is the Owner of infinite bounty* (Qurʾān, 57:21). *Surely Allah is with those who fear Him, the doers of good* (16:128).

Allah described the heart of the mother of Moses, peace be upon him, in this sense (of emptiness): *And the heart of the mother of Moses became empty* (Qurʾān, 28:10); meaning, "empty of everything but the memory of Moses." Unintentionally, she nearly betrayed him (when entrusting him to the care of Pharaoh's wife) due to her involuntary remembrance of her son. Her refraining was only the result of Allah fortifying her heart with patient endurance. She thus was included among the believers by what He inspired her concerning the condition of Moses as one of the Messengers.

This accounts for the incongruity mentioned by Abū al-ʿIzz, and to which he attached great importance. Namely, the simultaneous combination of two opposites: the remembrance and the inattention to the remembrance. No one knows the realities of these indications and paths of elevation except the spiritual seekers, by way of ecstatic experience, and the religious scholars, by way of faith and belief. So beware of denying the signs of Allah, for then you will become deaf and dumb, left in the darkness.

The One remembered cannot be described as missing or nonexisting. No veil obstructs Him, no place contains Him, and no time enfolds Him. Absence cannot be attributed to Him. He is not comprehended by speech, nor can He be attributed the qualities of created beings.

---

16 This is a reference to the well-known sacred tradition (*ḥadīth qudsī*) in which the Prophet relates Allah's words: "My believing servant continues to draw near Me, through supererogatory acts of worship, until I love him; and when I love him, I become his hearing, his sight, his tongue, his hand, his foot, and his heart; so through Me he hears, through Me he sees, through Me he speaks, through Me he understands, and through Me he strikes."

> Indeed, He is Present, both visibly and symbolically. He witnesses every secret and intimate thing, for He is Near every single atom. He is closer to the person remembering Him than the person is to himself, for He is creating him, knowing him, depositing will and capacity in him, managing his affairs and taking care of him. He has created the creations, so their characteristics cannot be applied to Him. He brought into being multiplicity, so its meaning does not encompass Him. Glory be to Him, the Exalted, the Magnificent.

This ends the words of Shaykh Abū al-ʿAbbās (al-Bannāʾ), may Allah have mercy on him, explaining the third station of the remembrance. This station of utmost excellence and spiritual realization points to the essential unity of the elite within this spiritual path (*ṭarīqa*). The servant should not consider the arrival to this station out of reach or far away, for it is no difficult matter for the Opener, the Omniscient, to make him attain it. So let the servant occupy himself with the necessary duties; the removal of the veil will come from Allah the Exalted. The distinguished scholar Yadālī said in the fifth section of *Sharḥ al-khātima*, entitled, "Concerning the jewels of the Qurʾān:"

> Know that the masters of spiritual insight have discovered that remembrance is the best of all good deeds. It has three husks, however, one nearer to the core than the other. And underneath the three husks is the core. The merit of the husks is only due to their being a path to the core. The outer husk is the remembrance of the tongue alone. The middle husk is the remembrance of the heart. The heart requires vigilant observation to be present in the remembrance, for if left to follow its natural inclination, it will wander about in the valleys of thought. The inner husk is the remembrance where the practitioner takes charge of the heart and brings it under control, so that it may be directed where required; (and this requires effort) just as effort was needed in the second husk to keep the heart focused and constantly devoted to the remembrance. Last is the sought-after core. This is where the servant is not concerned with directing the heart's attention to the remembrance, or with the heart itself: he is wholly absorbed by the One who is remembered. Whatever appears to him in the course of this that may divert his attention is a veil to be overcome.
>
> The gnostics refer to this (last) condition as "annihilation" (*fanāʾ*), because the servant has become extinct to himself. He is not conscious of the externals of his material form, nor of his internal disturbances. He has become absent from all of this, and all of this has become absent from him. So he proceeds to his Lord from the beginning to the end. Should his own annihilation appear to him in the course thereof, this represents a blemish and a vexation. Perfect annihilation entails the

extinction from the self, and then extinction from the extinction. So annihilation from annihilation is the ultimate form of annihilation.

The official jurist may find this an illogical phenomenon. But this is not the case. This condition of the Sufis pertains to their Beloved, just as your condition in most of your states is attributable to the object of your love; whether prestige, wealth, or lover. Similarly, when you are angry, you become absorbed in the intensity of your anger, thinking about your enemy. When you are filled with passionate desire, you become absorbed in the intensity of your desire, thinking about your lover. Your heart becomes incapable of anything else, so you speak about it involuntarily. Someone else may pass by in front of your eyes, but you will not see him though your eyes are wide open. Someone may speak to you, but you will not hear, though there is no deafness in your ears. You are totally absorbed, heedless of everything, including your own absorption. Indeed, the one who notices his own absorption has turned his attention away from the object of his absorption.

We have enabled you to understand annihilation (*fanāʾ*), so now you must refrain from slander and denying what you do not comprehend. Allah the Exalted said: *Nay they have belied the knowledge which they could not comprehend* (Qurʾān, 10:39). *And since they would not be guided by it, they said, "This is an ancient lie"* (46:11).

Then Yadālī went on to say:

Annihilation (*fanāʾ*) and total absorption (*istighrāq*) come first like a lightning-flash, seldom remaining or persisting. Once the experience does persist, becoming a deeply rooted habit and an established condition, the servant ascends by it to the highest realm. He is raised to the purest real existence. The breath of the Heavenly Kingdom (*al-Malakūt*) is instilled in him, and the Holiness of the divine Kingdom (*al-Lāhūt*) becomes manifest to him. Here, first to be presented to him in beautiful form will be the essential natures of the angels, and the spirits of the prophets and the saints. By this means, some of the realities will make themselves known to him. This is in the beginning. Then his degree transcends the symbolic (*al-mithāl*), and he encounters the unambiguous truth in every single thing.

When he returns to this world of metaphor, which is like shadows, he will regard the created beings with pity, pleading for mercy for them, because of their being deprived of ascending to the beauty of the Holy Presence. He will be amazed at their being deceived by the world of illusion, so he will be present with them in his person, but absent from them in his heart. While he is amazed at their preoccupation, they will be amazed at his absence.

And this is the fruit of the core of remembrance. The first stage of the remembrance is that of the tongue, then the remembrance of

> the heart under obligation, then the remembrance of the obedient heart, then the servant's occupation by the One remembered and the erasure of the remembrance. As long as the heart is conscious of the remembrance, it has turned away from Allah. The heart is not rid of hidden polytheism (*shirk*) until it comes to be totally absorbed in the One, the Real. So this is the true doctrine of Oneness (*tawḥīd*). The same might be said of gnosis (*maʿrifa*), for if someone is seeking gnosis, he has expressed duality. Whoever finds gnosis, it is as if he did not find it. Gnosis is found by none except by the One who is known. So He is the One who encompasses the reality of communion (*wiṣāl*) and the arrival of His loved one in the Presence of Holiness.

This concludes the excerpts from *Sharḥ khātima al-taṣawwuf* by the distinguished scholar Yadālī. May Allah be pleased with him, and make him pleased, and may He be pleased with us on account of him. Amen.

In his account of what is required of the aspirant by way of spiritual discipline (*riyaḍa*), our Shaykh and our means of access to our Lord, the hidden saintly pole (al-Quṭb al-Maktūm), the Seal of Muḥammadan sainthood (al-Khātim al-Muḥammadī), said:

> The truthful aspirant wishing to practice spiritual discipline in the secluded retreat (*khalwa*), or by other means, needs several things. First is an awareness of the proper balance. Next is the knowledge of the goal of the endeavor, then comes knowing how to hasten towards it. There is also the knowledge of the veil that cuts him off from the goal, and how this veil can be removed. Then there is the understanding of the sources of the veil, and the effort required to cut off these sources. Then there comes the knowledge of how to remove the veil, either totally or partially. Lastly there is the drawing of the sword of determination and mounting the stallion of struggle, in compliance with what he has become aware of in these matters and acting according to their requirements.
>
> The knowledge of striking the proper balance entails moderation in eating and drinking, neither indulging in excess or neglect. Also included is an awareness of the time and location (in which to undertake spiritual exercise), with regard to heat and cold, humidity and aridity. A person must also consider his age, and know what will strengthen him from falling ill.
>
> The goal of the endeavor is the removal of the veil from the individual's divine spirit (*rūḥ*) and its restoration to the state of purity with which it was endowed before its installation in the physical body. This is the means of realizing (*idrāk*) all knowledge (*ʿulūm*), gnosis (*maʿārif*), spiritual states (*aḥwāl*), virtues (*akhlāq*), stations (*maqāmāt*), illuminations (*futūḥāt*), divine gifts, and genuine nearness to Allah. So it is through the purity of the spirit that all happiness in this world

and the next is realized. Whoever loses this purity will not obtain the felicity of the Hereafter.

Proceeding at a rapid pace necessitates following the Messenger ﷺ in the entirety of his words and deeds, and imitating his state and his virtuous character. This is achieved by fulfilling the rights of Allah the Exalted, secretly and publicly, all the while sincerely devoted to Allah the Exalted, free from the entirety of faults found in this world and the next. This must be performed for the sake of glorifying and exalting Allah the Most High, offering Him reverence on the carpet of good pleasure, submission, commitment and reliance on Him in every single thing.

The removal of the veil is dependent on quickly detaching oneself from worldly goods and carnal lusts, desisting from exalting their worth and hasty procurement of their benefits. Their harmful effects can be prevented by gracious and gentle abstinence (*zuhd*), rather than complete renunciation.

The causes of the veil consist of excessive eating, drinking, social mixing, talking, sleeping, and continual heedlessness of the remembrance of Allah, Exalted is He. These causes are severed by hunger and thirst in gentle moderation, removing oneself from social mixing, persistent, absolute silence except in rare cases of necessity, keeping the night vigil in gentle moderation, and constant remembrance of Allah the Exalted with the heart and tongue, unceasingly, and with any form of remembrance.

The types of remembrance that remove the veils include those that tear away the veil from the spirit completely, and those that are partially effective, removing a veil of a particular kind. The remembrances that are totally effective are the following: "There is no god but Allah" (*la ilāha ill-Allāh*), the invocation of blessing upon Allah's Messenger ﷺ, "Glory be to Allah" (*subḥān-Allāh*), "Praise be to Allah" (*al-ḥamdu li-Llāh*), "Allah is Supreme" (*Allāhu akbar*), "In the Name of Allah, the Compassionate, the Merciful," (*bism-Llāh al-Raḥmān al-Raḥīm*) "Allah, Allah, Allah," and "Allah, there is no god but Him, the Ever-Living, Eternally Self-Subsisting" (*al-Ḥayy, al-Qayyūm*) The remembrances partially effective include the rest of Allah's beautiful Names (*al-asmāʾ al-ḥusna*). Each Name removes one type of veil, but does not apply to another. And the success is with Allah the Most High.

These words of his are worthy of being inscribed with golden ink! If someone wants more information on how to tear away the veils, in addition to what is provided here, let him keep company with the distinguished experts on this subject. Sayyid al-ʿArabī b. al-Sāʾiḥ ﵁ said: "The *Jawāhir al-maʿānī* contains numerous methods, all of them leading to Allah the Exalted." I would point out that more has been concealed that what has been made public.[17] The Director of fortune directs some people (to this discovery), while the divine Averter misguides others. As one poet has said:

The rain pours down and the earth becomes green
Whether the seeker of goodness settles there or migrates

This marks the end of the chapter. With Allah is the success on the straight path, and to Him, the Glorious, is the final destination.

17 Shaykh Ibrāhīm meant by this, said Shaykh Tijānī b. ʿAlī Cisse (interview, Medina-Baye, Kaolack, 21 May 2009), that *al-Fayḍa al-Tijāniyya* would bring forth more (of the secrets and remembrances of Shaykh Aḥmad al-Tijānī) than what al-ʿArabī b. al-Sāʾiḥ was pointing to in the *Jawāhir al-maʿānī*. Shaykh Muḥammad al-Māḥī Cisse added that this is a reference to the various types of spiritual retreat (*khalwa*) taught by Shaykh Aḥmad al-Tijānī to his close disciples; and these are not included in the texts (interview, Medina-Baye, Kaolack, 14 November 2008).

Chapter 3

Congregating for the Remembrance and Awakening the Desire for Reading the Qurʾān

With Allah is all success, and He is the Guide by His Grace to the balanced path.

The distinguished scholar, the gnostic of Allah, the missionary of the spiritual path, Shaykh ʿUmar b. Saʿīd al-Fūtī ﷺ said in *al-Rimāḥ*: "Know that congregating for the remembrance of Allah was something to which our Prophet, the Lawgiver ﷺ, prompted and invited people. So it has continued as the practice of the leaders of the spiritual path among the folk of Allah, from the East to the West."

The Prophet ﷺ said, as reported in the *ḥadīth* collections of Bukhārī, Muslim, Tirmidhī, Nasāʾī, Ibn Māja, and others: "Allah the Almighty and Glorious says, 'I am with my servant's thought of Me, and I am with him when he remembers Me. If he remembers Me within himself, I remember him within Myself. If he remembers Me in a congregation, I remember him in a better congregation.'"

He ﷺ is also reported as having said, in collection of Ṭabarānī, with an excellent chain of transmission: "Allah the Magnificent has said, 'Whenever My servant remembers Me within himself, I remember him in a congregation of the angels. Whenever he remembers Me in a congregation, I remember him among the Heavenly Host.'"

Imam Aḥmad (b. Ḥanbal) reported, on the authority of Abū Saʿīd al-Khudrī, ﷺ that Allah's Messenger ﷺ said: "Whenever a group of people gather to remember Allah, seeking nothing but His Countenance, a heavenly herald calls to them, 'Arise! You have been granted forgiveness, and your evil deeds have been converted into good deeds.'"[1]

In another narration, on the authority of Sahl b. Ḥanẓala as reported by Ṭabarānī, and on the authority of ʿAbd-Allāh b. Mughaffal as reported by Bayhaqī, Allah's Messenger said ﷺ: "A group of people does not sit together for the remembrance of Allah the Most High except that, when they stand up to depart, they are told, 'Rise with forgiveness granted, and your evil deed converted into good deeds.'"[2]

In a *ḥadīth* related by ʿAbd-Allāh b. ʿUmar ؓ, Allah's Messenger ﷺ came out to his companions and said: "O people, Allah has flying columns of angels who descend to attend the gatherings of remembrance on earth, so graze in the meadows of the Garden of Paradise!" He was asked, "And where are the meadows of Paradise's Garden?" He replied, "The gatherings of remembrance, so feast and relax in the remembrance of Allah, and have yourselves remembered by Him. If someone wants to know his position with Allah the Exalted, let him consider Allah's position with himself. He gives the servant the same status with Himself as the servant gives Him with himself." This narration was reported by Ibn Abī Dunya, Abū Yaʿlā, al-Bazār, Ṭabarānī, Ḥākim, and Bayhaqī. Ḥākim confirmed that it has an excellent chain of transmission.[3] As for the "meadow" referred to here, it means delicious victuals and refreshments in copious abundance.

According to Abū al-Dardāʾ ؓ, Allah's Messenger ﷺ said: "On the Day of Resurrection, Allah will bring forth a people with radiant light on their faces, installed on pearled pulpits. They will be the envy of all mankind, though they are neither prophets nor martyrs." An Arab of the desert fell on his knees and asked, "O Messenger of Allah, describe them for us so we may recognize them!" He responded by saying, "They are a people who love each other from diverse tribes and distant lands, who join in concurrence on the remembrance of Allah the Most High, so they remember Him."[4] This has been reported in Ṭabarānī with an excellent chain of transmission.

On the authority of Amr b. ʿAnbasa, ؓ Allah's Messenger ﷺ once said: "At the right-hand of the Merciful—and both of His hands are right hands—there will be men who are neither prophets nor martyrs. The brightness of their faces will dazzle the sight of the onlookers. They will be the envy of the prophets and the martyrs for where they sit in proximity to Allah, Mighty and Glorious is He." He was asked, "O Messenger of Allah, who are these people?" He said, "They are a collection of people from removed

1 Reported by Ibn Ḥanbal in his *Musnad*, Abū Nuʿaym in his *Ḥilya al-awliyāʾ* and Abū Yaʿlā in his *Musnad*

2 Cited by Haythamī in *Majmaʿ al-zawāʾid* and Bayhaqī in *Shuʿab al-īmān*.

3 See also Haythamī, *Majmaʿ al-zawāʾid*, and Bayhaqī, *Sunan al-kubrā*.

4 Reported by Ṭabarānī, cited by Haythamī in *Majmaʿ al-zawāʾid* and by Mundhirī in *al-Targhīb wa al-tarhīb*.

tribes who are joined in concurrence on the remembrance of Allah the Most High. So they select the best of words, just as one picks out the choicest of dates."⁵ This has been reported by Ṭabarānī, with a chain of transmission bearing no defect. The meaning of "collection" (*jummāʾ*) here is a mixture of distant tribes from various places. The meaning of "removed" (*nawāziʾ*) is that they are strangers. They do not gather because of nearness to each other, or because they share a relation, or because they know each other. They only gather for the remembrance of Allah the Most High.

Anas b. Mālik ⬥ reported that Allah's Messenger ⬥ said: "When you pass by the Garden of Paradise, revel therein." His companions asked, "And what is the Garden of the Paradise?" He said, "The circles of remembrance (*ḥilaq al-dhikr*)." This has been included in the collection of Tirmidhī.⁶ Ḥasan al-Baṣrī ⬥ related that he (the Prophet) said: "The remembrance of Allah is a very good thing, without any doubt. It takes away sin and contains no sin." And it is related from Abū al-Dardāʾ ⬥: "To attend a gathering of remembrance (*majlis dhikr*) is better than performing one thousand cycles (*rakʿa*) of ritual prayer, attending one thousand funeral prayers, and visiting one thousand sick people." According to Abū Hurayra, ⬥ Allah's Messenger ⬥ said:

> Allah has angels who roam the streets, searching for the people of remembrance. If they find a people remembering Allah the Exalted, they call out, "Come here to fulfill your need!" The angels then enfold them with their wings, one of top of the other, reaching up to the heavens. Their Lord will ask them, although He is well acquainted with them, "What are my servants saying?" Their reply will be: "They are glorifying You, proclaiming Your Supreme Greatness, praising You and exalting You." He will then ask, "Have they seen me?" Their reply will be, "No, by Allah, they have not seen You!" He will then ask, "How would it be if they had seen Me?" Their reply will be: "If they had seen You, they would be more intensely devoted to worshipping You, to praising You, and to glorifying You."
>
> He will then ask, "What are they asking from Me?" Their reply will be: "They are asking You for Paradise." He will ask: "And have they seen it?" Their reply will be: "No, by Allah, they have not seen it!" He will then ask, "How would it be if they had seen it?" Their reply will be: "If they had seen it, their desire for it would be more passionate, their longing for it would be more intense, and their yearning for it would even be greater."
>
> He will then ask: "From what do they seek refuge?" Their reply will be: "From the Fire of Hell." He will then ask, "And have they seen

---

5   Cited by Haythamī in *Majmaʿ al-zawāʾid*.

6   *Ḥadīth* reported by Tirmidhī in his *Sunan*, by Abū Nuʿaym in *Ḥilya al-awliyāʾ*, and by Ṭabarānī in *al-Muʿjam al-kabīr*.

> it?" Their reply will be: "No, by Allah, they have not seen it!" He will then ask, "How would it be if they had seen it?" Their reply will be: "If they had seen it, their effort to escape from it would be more intense, and their fear of it would be more severe."
>
> He will then say: "I call upon you to bear witness that I have granted them forgiveness!" One of the angels will say: "Among them is so-and-so, who is not one of them. He came only because of a certain need of his." The Lord will say: "They are a group whose sitting companions are never unfortunate."[7]

The distinguished scholar Imam al-Nawawī ﷺ said in *al-Adhkār*: "Know that just as the remembrance is deemed desirable, so too is sitting in the circle of its practitioners. The evidence of this is clearly apparent." He mentions some of the prophetic traditions cited above, then mentions this tradition in the *Ṣaḥīḥ* of Muslim related by Muʿāwiya ﷺ:

> Allah's Messenger ﷺ came out to a circle of his companions, and asked them, "What has caused you to gather together?" They replied: "We have met together to remember Allah the Exalted, and to praise Him for having guided us to Islam and for the gracious favor He has bestowed upon us!" Then he said: "By Allah, nothing else caused you to meet together? I would surely not extract an oath from you, implying suspicion of you, but Gabriel came to me and informed me that Allah the Exalted is taking pride in you before the angels."[8]

Nawawī also mentioned the tradition in *Ṣaḥīḥ Muslim*, in which Abū Saʿīd al-Khudrī and Abū Hurayra both testified that Allah's Messenger ﷺ said: "Whenever a group of people are seated together remembering Allah the Exalted, the angels surround them, mercy envelops them, tranquility descends upon them, and Allah the Exalted mentions them to those who are in His presence."[9] In *Taʾsīs al-qawāʾid*, Shaykh al-Zarrūq ﷺ said:

> The granting of general wisdom does not require specific substantiation for its application. This is the case for the public recital of the remembrance and supplications, for its proof is the sacred tradition in which Allah says: "If someone remembers Me in a congregation, I remember him in a better congregation." And its proofs also include the verse of the Qurʾān: "Remember Allah as you remember your fathers, or with an even more intense remembrance" (2:200). As reported by al-Bukhārī, Ibn ʿAbbās said: "I was not aware of the people's departure

---

7 *Ḥadīth* reported by Bukhārī in his *Ṣaḥīḥ*, and by Ibn Ḥanbal in his *Musnad*.

8 Reported by Abū Dāwūd in his *Sunan*, by Ibn Māja in his *Sunan*, and by Ibn Ḥanbal in his *Musnad*.

9 Reported by Muslim in his *Ṣaḥīḥ*, by Abū Dāwūd in his Sunan, by Ibn Māja in his *Sunan*, and by Ibn Ḥanbal in his *Musnad*.

from the ritual prayer in the time of Allah's Messenger ﷺ except by (hearing) the remembrance (following the prayer)."

Public recital of the remembrance was practiced during the *ʿĪd* festivals, in the wake of the ritual prayers, and on the frontiers and journeys, to the point that the Prophet ﷺ said: "Deal gently with yourselves! You are not calling One who is deaf, or One who is absent. Surely He is with you. He is the All-Hearing, the Ever-Near. Blessed is His Name and Exalted is His Majesty."[10] The Prophet ﷺ used to publicly recite the remembrance and supplication in numerous situations, and so did the righteous early believers (*salaf*). In one authentic report, he said in response to the companions in the trench during the battle of Khandaq: "O Allah! There is no goodness except the goodness of the Hereafter, so forgive the Helpers (*al-Anṣār*) and the Emigrants (*al-Muhājira*)!"

All of this provides evidence for the public and congregational remembrance. In special cases, however, there may be a motive for potentially abstaining from it depending on the circumstance. The remembrance after all is not the goal in itself. But such special cases require their reason.

The *Iḥyāʾ* of Imam Abū Ḥāmid al-Ghazālī narrates the statement from Allah's Messenger ﷺ: "If ever a group of people hold a gathering in which Allah the Most High is not remembered, and where blessings are not invoked on the Prophet ﷺ, an affliction will surely befall them on the Day of Resurrection."[11] Ghazālī then related the following narrations:

> Prophet David, peace be upon him, said: "O my God, if You see me passing by a gathering of people remembering You, and heading toward a congregation of heedless folk, break my leg before I get to them, for You have a gracious favor that You will bestow on me."
>
> The Prophet Muḥammad ﷺ said: "Attending one righteous gathering (*majlis*) grants the believer pardon for attending two million gatherings of wickedness."
>
> Abū Hurayra ؓ said: "The people of heaven see the houses on earth in which the Name of Allah the Exalted is remembered as you see the stars in the sky."
>
> Sufyān b. ʿUyayna, may Allah have mercy on him, said: "Whenever a group of people gather for the remembrance of Allah the Exalted, Satan and this lower world (*dunyā*) will step aside. Satan will say to the world, 'Do you not see what they are doing?' The world will reply,

---

10 Reported by Imam Bukhārī in his *Ṣaḥīḥ*, by Abū Dāwūd in his *Sunan*, and by Muslim in his *Ṣaḥīḥ*.

11 This *ḥadīth*, on the authority of Abū Hurayra, is also reported in the *Musnad* of Ibn Ḥanbal and the *Sunan* of Tirmidhī.

> 'Desist from them, for if they have come together in harmony, they will drive you out by their embrace."
>
> One day Abū Hurayra ﷺ entered the market and said: "I see you people here, while the inheritance (*mīrāth*) of the Allah's Messenger ﷺ is being distributed in the mosque." So the people left the market and went to the mosque, but they did not see any inheritance being distributed. They said, "O Abū Hurayra, we did not see any inheritance being distributed in the mosque." He said, "Well, what did you see?" They said, "We saw a group of people remembering Allah the Almighty and Glorious, and reciting the Qur'ān." He said: "That is the inheritance of Allah's Messenger ﷺ."

According to the author of *al-Rimāḥ* (ʿUmar al-Fūtī):

> As reported in the *Kashf al-qināʾ*,[12] Jalāl al-Dīn al-Suyūṭī ﷺ was once asked about the permissibility of the Sufi practice of convening circles of remembrance, performing it publicly in the mosque, and raising the voice in declaration of divine Oneness (*al-tahlīl*). He responded: "There is no reprehensibility in any of this. Some prophetic traditions emphasize the desirability of making public, audible remembrance; and some emphasize the desirability of making secret, silent remembrance. When these narrations are considered together, the conclusion is that the choice of performing the remembrance out loud or in secret depends on the circumstance and the person. This is similar to the conclusion of al-Nawawī when he considered the narrations emphasizing public, audible recitation of the Qur'ān in conjunction with those emphasizing silent recitation."

Al-Ḥājj ʿUmar al-Fūtī also related the statement of Sīdī ʿAlī al-Khawwāṣ on this subject:

> The disciple should perform the remembrance with his voice in full force, for this will have a stronger influence over all segments of his heart. He should also perform the remembrance with a congregation, for the remembrance in congregation is more effective in removing the veils. The Exalted Lord of Truth has likened the hearts to rocks, and it is well-known that the rock cannot be shattered except by the combined strength of a group. The hardness of the heart is likewise impenetrable, except by the congregational remembrance of people gathered as a single heart. This is because the power of the congregation is stronger than one individual. As for the individual's reward in the remembrance, he is entitled to his personal reward as well as the reward of the group's spiritual concert (*samāʾ*).

---

12 The *Kashf al-qināʾ ʿan wajh al-samāʾ* by ʿAlī b. Aḥmad al-Kāzuwānī (d. 1548), a work that describes the practice of the Sufi spiritual concert (*samāʿ*).

To this I would add that they are also entitled to the reward of the intention of the Sufi people, and their consideration of that which focuses their hearts on Allah the Exalted. Shaykh al-Zarrūq said: "The main consideration of the Sufi people is that which focuses their hearts on their Lord." Then he said:

> This explains why those who have not understood their purpose have criticized the Sufi people on the subject of proper conduct. They have been misconstrued by people who do not understand their spiritual state, so their critics have fallen into error and delusion with regard to the spiritual concert (*samāʾ*) and other matters. When asked about the spiritual concert, Junayd, may Allah have mercy on him, replied: "Anything that focuses the servant on his Lord is permissible." As he made its permissibility conditional on the focus (on Allah), his ruling applies to the issue at hand, and cannot be disputed. And Allah knows best.

This passage is from Shaykh al-Zarrūq's *Taʾsīs al-qawāʾid*. Later in the same work he goes on to say:

> The excellent merit (*faḍīla*) of a thing is not its ultimate excellence (*afḍaliyya*), and the rule of the moment is not the rule of the fundamental principle (*aṣl*). It is not imperative to insist on something's ultimate excellence, or to refrain from an action because of a temporary problem in applying the rule of the fundamental principle. As for congregational performance of the remembrance, supplications, and Qurʾān recitation, approval of these has been established by the prophetic traditions cited previously. The best practice in a circumstance may not necessarily be the most effective absolutely; neither does the rule of the moment indicate ultimate superiority over other things. The superiority of silent remembrance in the time of the Prophet's companions must be seen in light of other acts of beneficial worship—such as seeking knowledge, fighting *jihād* and working to earn a livelihood for their families—which occupied their attention so that the congregational remembrance was not performed regularly. But you should notice that whenever an opportunity presented itself during a journey, in the course of a campaign, during festivals, or following the ritual prayers, they readily performed the congregational remembrance. The preference to what is momentarily more beneficial can be observed in the tradition relating a situation in which the Prophet ﷺ passed by a congregational circle of remembrance to sit with another congregation exchanging knowledge. This was because those engaged in seeking knowledge at that particular time were more relevant for spreading the religion, while the congregational remembrance was more for personal benefit. However, he never criticized the first group,

even though his actions showed the second group to be superior in this instance. And Allah knows best.

As stated previously, the righteous folk are concerned with focusing themselves on Allah. Our Imam, the Imam of the Imams, Mālik b. Anas, once said, "If I had known that my heart would benefit by sitting next to heap of rubbish, I would have done so." Something to this effect has also been transmitted from the exemplary behavior of the Prophet's companions. According to *Sharḥ al-mawāqif*:[13] "When ʿUmar b. al-Khaṭṭāb ﷺ used to see Abū Mūsā al-Ashʿarī, he would say, 'He has reminded us of our Lord.' He used to recite the Qurʾān with a beautiful voice, and ʿUmar used to attribute the tenderness of his own heart to hearing his recitation of the Qurʾān." So there is no harm in performing the remembrance for the sake of benefitting the heart.

As for the Sufis and some of the righteous singling out certain nights over others for drawing near to Allah, Qāḍī ʿĪyāḍ had this to say: "In the fact that the Prophet ﷺ used to visit the mosque of Qubāʾ every Saturday, there is evidence to support the Imams and the righteous in their assignment of special properties in seeking nearness to Allah to certain days of the week, one of them being Saturday."

Let us conclude the subject of the congregational spiritual concert (*samāʾ*) with the words of our Shaykh (al-Tijānī) ﷺ from the *Jawāhir al-maʿānī*, sealing the issue at hand:

> How many a gnostic has poured on him floods (*fuyūḍ*) of spiritual states and gnosis from the Holy Presence during the spiritual concert! He ascends to stations to which he does not attain by ordinary worship; and he experiences the serenity of all the moments of one hundred thousand years (descending on him) from the spiritual stations.

The Recitation of the Qurʾān

As for the recitation of the Qurʾān, al-Nawawī had this to say in *al-Adhkār* in the section entitled, "The necessity of reciting the Qurʾān, day and night, whether traveling or staying at home:"

> The righteous early believers, may Allah be pleased with them, maintained various practices with regard to the complete recitation of the Qurʾān. Some of them used to conclude a complete recital (*khatma*) once every two months, while others would do so every month. Others would conclude a complete recital in eight nights, and others in every seven. This latter was the practice of most of the righteous early believers (*salaf*). Others would complete the Qurʾān every six nights, others

---

13 The *Sharḥ al-mawāqif* is an eight-volume work on Islamic theology according to the Ashʿarī school by ʿAlī b. Muḥammad al-Jurjānī (d. 1413).

every five, others every four, and many in every three. Many would conclude one complete recital in every day and night, and some would conclude two complete recitals in every day and night. Others would conclude three in every day and night. Some would conclude eight complete recitals in every day and night: four in the day and four in the night. Among this latter category of people was the venerable Sayyid Ibn al-Kātib al-Ṣūfi.

According to Sayyid Aḥmad al-Dawraqī,[14] Manṣūr b. Zādhān b. ʿAbbād al-Tābiʿī ﵁ used to recite the entire Qurʾān between the midday prayer and the afternoon prayer. He would also recite it completely in the interval between the sunset prayer and the night prayer. During Ramadan, he would perform two complete recitals and something extra in the interval between the sunset prayer and the night prayer. They used to postpone the night prayer during Ramadan, until one quarter of the night had elapsed. As reported by Ibn Abī Dāwūd, with an authentic chain of transmission, Mujāhid ﵁ used to recite the entire Qurʾān during Ramadan in the interval between the sunset prayer and the night prayer. As for those who recited the entire Qurʾān in a cycle of ritual prayer (*rakʿa*), they are too many to be counted. Among the companions of the Prophet they included ʿUthmān b. ʿAffan, Tamīm al-Dārī and Saʿīd b. Jubayr.

The reasons for this wide disparity are best explained in relation to the diversity of the individuals concerned. If someone is accustomed to discovering subtleties and mystical insights through the exercise of meticulous contemplation, he must limit himself to the amount of recitation from which he gains perfect understanding of what he is reciting. On the other hand, if someone is preoccupied with the dissemination of knowledge and the resolution of legal issues among the Muslims, or other matters of importance to the religion and the general interests of the Muslims, he must limit himself to an amount that neither conflicts with his purpose nor impedes its accomplishment. As for someone who is not included among those mentioned, he must do as much as he possibly can, short of reaching the point of exhaustion or slurring the recitation.

Some of the early authorities disapproved of the recital of the entire Qurʾān in a day and a night, as indicated by a report contained in the *Sunan* of Abū Dāwūd, Tirmidhī, Nasāʾī and others. According to this report, which is confirmed by authentic chains of transmission, ʿAbd-Allāh b. Amr b. al-ʿĀṣī ﵁ reported that Allah's Messenger ﷺ said:

---

14 ʿAbd-Allāh Aḥmad al-Dawraqī was an early scholar who lived in the eighth century C.E. He was a contemporary of Abū Ḥanīfa.

"Someone who recites the Qur'ān in less than three days and nights does not understand (what he is reciting)."[15]

As for the timing of when to begin and to conclude the Qur'ān, it is a matter of choice for the reader. If he is one of those who complete the recitation once a week, perhaps he will be like 'Uthmān ♦, who used to begin on Friday night and conclude on the evening of the following Thursday.[16] Imam Abū Ḥāmid al-Ghazālī has said in the *Iḥyā'*: "The most meritorious practice is to conclude one complete recitation in the nighttime and another in the daytime. The daytime recitation should be commenced on Monday, during or after the voluntary prayer before the dawn ritual prayer. The nighttime recitation should be commenced on the night of Friday, during or after the voluntary prayer following the sunset ritual prayer. This is to receive the blessings of the beginning of daytime and the beginning of nighttime."

As reported by Ibn Abī Dāwūd, the noble Amr b. Murra al-Tābi'ī ♦ said: "They used to love to recite the entire Qur'ān from the beginning of the night and from the beginning of the day." He also reported the saying of the noble Imam Ṭalḥa b. Muṣarrif al-Tābi'ī: "If someone recites the entire Qur'ān at any time of the day, the angels will invoke blessing upon him until the evening arrives, and if he does so at any time of the night, the angels will invoke blessing upon him until the dawn arrives." A similar saying is attributed to Mujāhid.

Sa'd b. Abī Waqqās ♦ said, as reported in the *Musnad* of Imam Abū Muḥammad al-Dārimī, may Allah have mercy on him: "If one's complete recital of the Qur'ān coincides with the beginning of the nighttime, the angels will invoke blessing upon him until the dawn arrives, and if one's complete recitation of the Qur'ān coincides with the beginning the daytime, the angels will invoke blessing upon him until the evening arrives."

As for how the Qur'ān should be completed, it has been previously mentioned that it is recommended to conclude the recitation during a ritual prayer. As for someone who is unable to conclude it in a ritual prayer because, for example, the Imam's recitation does not give him sufficient time, the recommended time for concluding the recitation is either at the beginning of the nighttime or the beginning of the daytime.

In the appendix of *al-Kawākib*, Shaykh Sīdī al-Mukhtār al-Kuntī cited the statement of Abū al-Layth: "One should try to recite the entire Qur'ān two times in the course of the year, unless he is capable of more than that." He then related the statement of Abū Ḥanīfa as reported by Ḥasan b. Ziyād: "If someone recites the entire Qur'ān two times in every year, he

---

15   Reported in the *Sunan* of Abū Dāwūd, Tirmidhī, and Ibn Māja.

16   In the Islamic calendar, each day begins at sunset, so the "night of Friday" is the night before Friday beginning after sunset on Thursday night.

has fulfilled his duty, because the Prophet ﷺ recited it to Gabriel two times during the year in which he died." He also included the tradition reported by Aḥmad b. Ḥanbal: "For someone who knows the Qurʾān by heart, it is reprehensible to postpone its complete recitation for more than forty days, without a valid excuse, because ʿAbd-Allāh b. ʿAmr asked the Prophet ﷺ: "In how many days should one recite the entire Qurʾān?" To this he replied, "In forty days." This has been reported in the *Sunan* of Abū Dāwūd.

On this subject, Mālik b. Anas said: "It is highly commendable to read and recite the Qurʾān regularly, for Allah the Exalted has applauded those whose habit is the regular recitation of the Qurʾān. He said: *Among the People of the Book there are upright people who recite the revelations of Allah in the watches of the night* (Qurʾān, 3:113)." According to a prophetic tradition on the authority of Ibn ʿUmar and reported in the collections of Bukhārī and Muslim: "Only two people are worthy of envy: one on whom Allah has bestowed the Qurʾān, so that he busies himself with it in the watches of the night and day; and a man to whom Allah has granted wealth, so he becomes charged with dispensing it for the sake of the Truth."[17]

In one sacred tradition (*ḥadīth qudsī*) reported on the authority of Abū Saʿīd, the Prophet ﷺ said: "The Lord, Glorious and Exalted is He, says: 'Whomever the Qurʾān and the remembrance of Me has occupied from asking Me, I give him better than what is given to those who ask.' And the superiority of Allah's speech over all other speech is like Allah's superiority over all His creation."[18]

According to a prophetic tradition reported in the *Ṣaḥīḥ* of Muslim, on the authority of Abū Umāma al-Bāhilī: "You must recite the Qurʾān, for it will serve on the Day of Resurrection as an intercessor for its companions."[19] And the Prophet ﷺ said, on the authority of ʿĀʾisha and reported by Bayhaqī: "The house in which the Qurʾān is recited will make itself apparent to the people of Heaven, just as the stars make themselves apparent to the people of the earth."[20] In another tradition on the authority of Anas: "You should illuminate your dwellings with the ritual prayer and the recitation of the Qurʾān."[21] And in a narration on the authority of al-Nuʿmān b. al-Bashīr, the Prophet ﷺ said: "The most excellent worship performed by my community is the recitation of the Qur an."[22] There is also the narration on the authority of Samra b. Jundub: "Every host loves his banquet to be attended, and Allah's banquet is the Qurʾān, so you must not stay away

17 Reported by Bukhārī in his *Ṣaḥīḥ*, by Muslim in his *Ṣaḥīḥ*, by Tirmidhī in his *Sunan*, and by Ibn Māja in his *Sunan*.

18 Reported by Tirmidhī in his *Sunan*.

19 Reported by Muslim in his *Ṣaḥīḥ*, and by Ṭabarānī in *al-Muʿjam al-kabīr*.

20 Cited by ʿAlāʾ al-Dīn al-Hindī in *Kanz al-ʿummāl fī sunan al-aqwāl wa al-afʿāl*.

21 Cited by Hindī in *Kanz al-ʿummāl*.

22 Cited by Hindī in *Kanz al-ʿummāl*.

from it."[23] And on the authority of ʿUbayda al-Mālikī is the narration: "O people of the Qurʾān, do not treat the Qurʾān with nonchalant familiarity (*la tatawassadū*), but recite it correctly in the watches of the night and at the ends of the day. Broadcast it widely and contemplate what it contains, for then you may achieve success!"[24]

In accordance with established custom, recitation of the Qurʾān should be performed in clean place, preferably in the mosque. Some scholars have disapproved of reciting the Qurʾān in the public bath-house (*ḥammām*) or on the road, while others have not found objection to it. Shaʿbī[25] disapproved of its performance in a mill-house while the wheel is turning. It is commendable for the one reciting to sit facing the direction of Mecca (*qibla*) in a state of humility, tranquility, and seriousness, while bowing his head. The established custom is to clean the teeth before the recitation, as an act of reverence and purification. This is due to the saying of the Prophet ﷺ: "You must clean your mouths by picking the teeth and brushing, for they are the pathways of the Qurʾān and the sitting rooms of the angels."[26]

It is reported that Allah the Exalted has assigned an angel to watch over the one reciting. When he recites, the angel places his mouth on his mouth, in honor of the Qurʾān. The angels, blessing and peace be upon them, are severely offended by unpleasant breath, but they enjoy pleasant odors and have a special affection for them. According to one report: "You must use the toothbrush (*siwāk*), for it pleases the Merciful and infuriates Satan. It freshens the breath, strengthens the gums, and increases the eloquence of the speaker."[27]

The established custom is to recite the Qurʾān with contemplation and understanding, for this is the most significant purpose and important objective of the recitation. ʿAlī said: "There is no benefit in a recitation in which there is no contemplation, because contemplation causes the heart to expand and the mind to become enlightened." Allah the Exalted has said: *A Book that We have sent down to you (O Muḥammad), full of blessing, that they may contemplate its verses* (Qurʾān, 38:29). *Will they not, then, try to understand this Qurʾān?* (4:82).

This means that during the recitation, one's heart must be devoted to reflecting on the meaning of what he is reading. He must strive to grasp the meaning of each verse, and pay careful attention to the command-

23 Cited by Hindī in *Kanz al-ʿummāl.*

24 Cited by Haythamī in *Majmaʿ al-zawāʾid*, reported by Abū Nuʿaym in *Dhikr al-akhbar*, and cited by Hindī in *Kanz al-ʿummāl.*

25 Qāḍī al-Shaʿbī (d. 721, Iraq) was an early interpretor of the Qurʾān and jurist in Kufa, Iraq.

26 Reported by Daylamī in *al-Firdaws*, and cited by al-ʿAjlūnī in *Kashf al-khafāʾ wa muzil al-ilbas* and by Hindī in *Kanz al-ʿummāl.*

27 Reported by Ibn Ḥanbal in his *Musnad*, and cited by Haythamī in *Majmaʿ al-zawāʾid.*

ments and prohibitions, with confidence in the acceptability of what he is doing. When he comes across a reference to something he has failed to observe in the time of his life that has passed, he should seek forgiveness, and beg Allah the Exalted to overlook his mistakes. When he comes upon a verse that offers mercy, he should welcome the good news and beg Allah for that mercy. When he comes upon a verse that threatens torment, he should be fearful and seek refuge in Allah. When he comes upon a verse that proclaims the transcendence (*al-tanzīh*) of Allah, he should affirm His transcendence and magnify Him. When he comes upon a verse that invites supplication, he should humble himself and make a request. According to a narration reported in the *Ṣaḥīḥ* of Muslim, Hudhayfa ☙ said:

> When I performed the ritual prayer together with the Prophet ☙ one night, he recited the Chapter of the Cow (*Sūra al-baqara*) and then the Chapter of the Family of ʿImrān (*Sūra Āl-ʿImrān*), reciting in a calm and distinct manner. When he came upon a verse containing a glorification of the Lord, he pronounced a glorification. When he came upon a request, he made a request. When he came upon a plea for refuge, he sought refuge.[28]

In another report found in the collections of Abū Dāwūd and Nasāʾī, ʿAwf b. Mālik said: "I stood in prayer with the Prophet ☙ one night, and he recited the Chapter of the Cow (*Sūra al-baqara*). Whenever he came upon a verse concerning mercy, he paused and made a request, and whenever he came upon a verse about torment, he sought refuge." As reported in the *Musnad* of Abū Dāwūd and the *Ṣaḥīḥ* of Tirmidhī, the Prophet ☙ said:

> When someone recites the chapter of the Qurʾān, "By the fig and the olive" (Chapter 95) and reaches the last verse, *Is not Allah the fairest of judges?* he should say: "Yes indeed, and I am one of those who bear witness to that!"
>
> Likewise, when someone recites the Chapter, "No! I swear by the Day of Resurrection" (Chapter 75), and gets to the last verse: "Is He not Capable of bringing the dead to life?" let him say: "Yes indeed!"
>
> And whenever someone recites the Chapter: "By the winds sent one after another" (Chapter 77), then gets to the end: "In what statement, after this, will they believe?" Let him say: "We believe in Allah and His Messenger and His angels, and in what He has revealed in His Book!"

As reported in the collections of Aḥmad (Ibn Ḥanbal) and Abū Dāwūd, on the authority of Ibn ʿAbbās: "When the Prophet used to recite the verse: *Glorify the Name of your Lord the Most High* (Qurʾān, 87:1), he used to say, 'Glory to my Lord the Most High!'"

---

28 Reported by Muslim in his *Ṣaḥīḥ*, by Nasāʾī in his *Sunan*, and by Ibn Ḥanbal in his *Musnad*.

When Ibn Masʿūd recited the Qurʾān to the Prophet ﷺ, as reported in the collections of Bukhārī and Muslim, the Prophet's eyes would overflow in tears. On the authority of Saʿd b. Mālik and reported in the *Shuʿab al-īmān*,[29] the Prophet ﷺ said: "This Qurʾān has come down with sorrow and grief, so weep when you recite it, and if your weeping does not come, force it to come." According to ʿAbd al-Mālik b. ʿUmayr: "One day Allah's Messenger ﷺ came out to his companions and said, 'I am reciting a chapter of the Qurʾān to you; if someone weeps, the Garden of Paradise is for him, and if you do not weep, then try to weep!" In the *Musnad* of Abū Yaʿlā[30] is the narration: "Read the Qurʾān with sadness, for it has come down in sadness."[31] Among the traditions included by Ṭabarānī is the following: "The best of those who read the Qurʾān are those who, when they read the Qurʾān, they discuss it among themselves."[32]

Weeping from reading the Qurʾān is caused by contemplating the meaning of what is being recited. This includes the threats and dire warnings, the covenants and the promises. The one reciting the Qurʾān should reflect on his own shortcomings in these respects. If this does not afflict him with sorrow and weeping, let him weep for himself on account of his distance from the Truth and the lack of his humility, for this is itself a calamitous misfortune.

The Qurʾān is properly recited in a distinct and measured manner, according to the Allah's saying, *And recite the Qurʾān in a distinct and measured manner* (Qurʾān, 73:4). Umm Salama described the recitation of Allah's Messenger ﷺ as a measured recitation, pronounced letter by letter. This has been reported by *Sunan* of Abū Dāwūd.[33]

Concerning the collective performance of the Qurʾān recitation by a whole congregation, either in unison or when members recite different sections at once, Shaykh Sīdī al-Mukhtār (al-Kuntī) said that there is no legal objection to this. On this subject, it has been said concerning the practice (of collective recitation) in Fes: "And the remembrance, together with the recitation of the Qurʾān in congregation, has become widespread since long ago." In one poem, Sīdī Muḥniḍ Bāb al-Daymānī al-Tijānī[34] رضي الله عنه said:

---

29 The *Shuʿab al-īmān* [The branches of belief] was the multi-volume work of Imam al-Bayhaqī discussing the *ḥadīth*, "Belief has seventy-odd branches."

30 This is the multi-volume collection of *ḥadīth* by Abū Yaʿlā (or Yaʿlī) al-Mawṣilī (d. 919).

31 *Ḥadīth* cited by Hindī in *Kanz al-ʿummāl.*

32 *Ḥadīth* cited by Ṭabarānī, *al-Muʿjam al-awsaṭ*, Haythamī in *Majmaʿ al-zawāʾid* and Hindī in *Kanz al-ʿummāl.*

33 It is also reported by Tirmidhī in his *Sunan*, by Ibn Ḥanbal in his *Musnad*, and by Ṭabarānī in *al-Muʿjam al-kabīr*.

34 Muḥniḍ Bāb al-Daymānī al-Tijānī was a nineteenth-century Tijānī scholar from the Daymānī tribe of Mauritania. He may have been the same Muḥammad Bābā al-Daymānī who was one of the teachers of Ousmane Sy, the father of al-Ḥājj Mālik Sy.

They denounced the public openness and congregation in the remembrance
Even though it is permissible by the consensus of the scholars
The consensus has been established after disagreement
So today it is permissible without any disagreement.

Concerning the merit of reciting the Qurʾān, our Shaykh al-Tijānī, the Seal of Saints, had this to say in *al-Kunnāsh*:[35]

> As for the external portion of the hidden, internal degree—that being the recitation (*tilāwa*) of the Qurʾān—it relates to the Supreme Assembly, in which there is no 'where,' no 'how,' and no demarcation. There is only the immersion in the divine and the Eternal Secret, which cannot be analyzed or known, which no expression captures and no signification realizes. The holder of this degree of the Qurʾān comprehends all remembrance of our Lord, on the tongues of all creatures, in the eternal past and eternal future. The means, goal, and end of this degree of recitation are not understood or realized except by its holder, who is the Prophet ﷺ alone.
>
> The reward for reciting the Qurʾān is allotted by degrees according to the ranks of the creation concerned. The degree of the one who is veiled is not the same as the one for whom the secrets of lesser sainthood has been opened. The degree of this lesser saint (*al-walī al-ṣaghīr*) is not like that of the gnostic (*ʿārif*), who has attained the rank of the most truthful (*ṣiddīqiyya*). And the degree of this gnostic is not like that of the unique and comprehensive saintly pole (*quṭb*). The reward for recitation at each of these degrees reaches a certain limit. At every degree there is an external reward and an internal reward. As for the external one, it is mentioned tradition. Namely, whoever recites the Qurʾān without ablution (*wuḍūʾ*), he is credited ten good deeds for every letter (he pronounces). Whoever recites with ablution, but outside of the ritual prayer, he is credited twenty-five good deeds for every letter. Whoever recites with ablution, while sitting in the ritual prayer, he is credited with fifty good deeds for every letter. Whoever recites with ablution while standing in the ritual prayer, he is credited with one hundred good deeds for every letter. Such is the degree of the external aspect.
>
> As for the degree of the inner aspect, it is beyond definition and likeness. It cannot be measured or quantified, and its essential nature is inaccessible for all eternity to the entirety of created beings. Even

35 The *Kunnāsh* is the term for a collection of secret prayers or papers belonging to a certain Shaykh. But in this case, the *Kunnāsh* seems to be another word for the *Jawāhir al-maʿānī* itself; although we have not located this exact passage in the *Jawāhir*. It is likely Shaykh Ibrāhīm refers here to a manuscript from the time of Shaykh al-Tijānī, perhaps the original manuscript of the *Jawāhir* known to have been in his possession.

> if all the liturgical remembrances were combined, with all the Names, with all the Attributes, with all the good deeds, with all the acts of devotion from the beginning of time till the end, it would fall short of one single letter of the Qurʾān. This is the internal degree.

This concludes what we wanted to gather in this chapter. With Allah is the success on the straight path, and to Him, the Glorious, is the return and final destination.

Section II

Chapter 1

Mention of the Flood (*fayḍa*) within the Tijāniyya

It has been a matter of general consensus among the companions of the Saintly Seal, Shaykh Aḥmad al-Tijānī ﷺ, and a topic of frequent discussion by the authors of the books of his spiritual path that the Shaykh said: "A flood (*fayḍa*) will come upon my companions, and people will enter our spiritual path group upon group. This *fayḍa* will come when people are in their utmost state of distress and hardship."[1] According to (al-Ṭayyib al-Ṣufyānī) the author of the *Ifāda*: "What he meant by *fayḍa* was that many of his companions would obtain spiritual illumination (*fatḥ*), but he used to consider its time remote."

Sīdī ʿAlī Harāzim al-Barāda, the closest disciple (*khalīfa*) of Shaykh Aḥmad al-Tijānī, reported in *Risāla al-faḍl wa al-imtinān*:[2]

> Our Shaykh said that among the assurances given him by Allah's Messenger was that the Prophet's support would remain with the Shaykh's disciples until the advent of the Final Hour. He ﷺ also said that among the children of Adam, the Shaykh's spiritual path (*ṭarīqa*) would exceed ten thousand paths (*ṭarīq*),[3] each one of them headed by

---

1 This statement of Shaykh Aḥmad al-Tijānī appears in the *Ifāda al-Aḥmadiyya li murīd al-saʿada wa al-ʿabadiyya*, a collection of the Shaykh's sayings written by his companion, Muḥammad al-Ṭayyib al-Ṣufyānī (d. 1843).

2 The *Risāla al-faḍl wa al-imtinān ilā kāffa al-aṣḥāb wa al-ikhwān* [The letter of grace and gratitude to the entirety of the companions and brothers] of ʿAlī Harāzim al-Barāda is a lengthy epistle written in 1803 discussing various details of the Tijānī Path. It has been translated in draft form by Muḥammad Bokreta al-Hassani (2007).

3 According to Shaykh Tijānī ʿAlī Cisse (interview 23 December 2008, Medina-Baye, Kaolack, Senegal), this statement does not mean that the Tijāniyya Order would fracture into several subsidiary orders as in the case of other Sufi orders such as the

one of the Shaykh's disciples. Each path would branch into many paths of gnosis (ma'rifa), and then each of these paths would also branch into more paths until the advent of the Hour. The spiritual path will consist of more than twenty thousand paths among the jinn, branching into many more branches until the advent of the Hour, and this will not end until Allah inherits the earth and everything on it. Indeed He is the best of inheritors. And the Tijānī litany (wird), so long as it is remembered and recited, will retain its special quality until the advent of the Hour.

This fayḍa mentioned by our Shaykh has also been discussed by his companions, deputies and those who inherited his secrets after him. Many of them claimed it for themselves, and they spoke about it, but their words became convoluted. I have happened upon some questions the scholar Aḥmad b. Maḥamm al-ʿAlawī once asked Shaykh ʿUmar al-Fūtī,[4] may Allah be pleased with them both. The third of these questions concerned the saying of Shaykh al-Tijānī: "A fayḍa will come upon my companions, so people will enter our spiritual path group upon group. This fayḍa will come when people are in their utmost state of distress and hardship." Shaykh ʿUmar was asked, "Has this fayḍa already arrived, or does it remain to come?" Shaykh ʿUmar responded: "As for the fayḍa, I hope from Allah for your sakes that I am its intended target, poor servant that I am; and the Fāṭimid Imam ☙."[5] I also discovered some commentary of Shaykh al-ʿArabī b. al-Sāʾiḥ on these responses by Shaykh ʿUmar. He ☙ said:

Shādhiliyya (Nāṣiriyya, Ḥamdiyya, Darqāwiyya, Maryamiyya, etc) or the Qādiriyya (Qādiriyya-Rifāʾiyya, Murīdiyya, ʿUthmāniyya, etc). Each ṭarīq, or branch, adds nothing to the litany of the Tijāniyya. The reference here is to coming of a multitude of charasmatic personalities within the Tijāniyya who attract disciples and continue to spread the Ṭarīqa.

4   Al-Ḥajj ʿUmar al-Fūtī Tāl (1797–1864) was a Tijānī scholar from Futa Toro (Senegal) influential in spreading Islam and the Tijāniyya Order in nineteenth-century West Africa through his writings and through armed jihād. He was the author of the Rimāḥ, one of the most important works of the Tijāniyya. Aḥmad b. Maḥamm b. al-ʿAbbās al-ʿAlawī al-Shinqīṭī was a prominent Mauritanian scholar who studied with many of the companions of Shaykh al-Tijānī and became a companion of al-Ḥajj ʿUmar. He was the author of Rawd shamāʾil ahl al-ḥaqīqa fī al-taʿrīf bi akābir al-ṭarīqa, an early biography of the prominent scholars of the Tijāniyya. For more on this work, see Muḥammad al-Muntaqī Aḥmad Tāl, al-Jawāhir wa al-durar fī sīra al-Shaykh al-Ḥājj ʿUmar (Beirut: Dār Albouraq, 2005), especially p. 553–561. Aḥmad b. Muhimm's son, Muḥammad al-Kabir, was among those who granted Shaykh Ibrāhīm Niasse unlimited authorization (ijāza muṭlaqa) in the Tijāniyya.

5   This is a reference to the Mahdi, the awaited "rightly-guided one" mentioned in Islamic eschatological accounts, whose coming will presage the arrival of the Antichrist and Jesus.

As for Shaykh ʿUmar's saying, "I hope from Allah..." in response to the question concerning our master's saying, "A *fayḍa* will come...," we have observed that those distinguished companions of Shaykh al-Tijānī whom we have encountered disagree as to whether or not the *fayḍa* has yet arrived. Those inclined to believe it has arrived say, "It is that which arrived in the regions of Shinjīt, at the hand of Shaykh Muḥammad al-Ḥāfiz ☙." But others say, "It has not yet arrived, because the Shaykh said, 'People will enter our spiritual path group upon group.' He did not limit this to any particular town or district." All are in agreement that its time is far. Our own understanding, based on what has come to us from the Shaykh, is that it has not arrived until now, and that its arrival will coincide with the appearance of the awaited Mahdi, when all the spiritual paths will become one. And Allah knows best.

Allow me to point out here that people have now entered the Order group upon group. And perhaps the other spiritual paths have even been abrogated, since not one of them is maintained by someone capable of providing spiritual training (*tarbiya*). Moreover, this present time has witnessed unprecedented distress and hardship, never before witnessed by the eminent elders of whom we are aware. As for the abundance of spiritual illumination (*fatḥ*) among the companions of Shaykh al-Tijānī—and the gnosis (*maʿrifa*) of Allah and absorption (*istighrāq*) in Him to the exclusion of everything apart from Him—nothing like it has ever occurred in our Order, to the best of my knowledge, from its beginning to our present time. *Such is the grace of Allah, He bestows it on whom He wills* (Qurʾān, 57:21).

The knowledgeable one of Allah, Sīdī Muḥammad al-Ḥāfiz b. Khayr al-ʿAlawī,[6] once claimed the *fayḍa* for himself, and alluded to the qualities of its possessor in verse:

Suppose that I am the one to appear
From among the foremost of those in command

The one who will bring forth the *fayḍa* near the end of time
He is the foremost among men in knowledge of the Qurʾān

His ordinance has singled me out, at the age of thirty[7]
And by me have hearts been awakened from slumber.

---

6   Muḥammad al-Ḥāfiz b. Khayr al-ʿAlawī was a Mauritanian scholar and elder contemporary of Shaykh Ibrāhīm who renounced his claim to the *fayḍa* in favor of the Shaykh.

7   The reference to the *Ṣāḥib al-fayḍa* being thirty years old at the time of his appearance was in fact fulfilled by Shaykh Ibrāhīm himself. In one letter the Shaykh wrote: "And you may know that the Shaykh (al-Tijānī) ☙ mentioned a *fayḍa* would appear in the latter days, and some of the people of spiritual unveiling (*kashf*) from the disciples of Shaykh Muḥammad al-Ḥāfiz have said that the *Imām al-fayḍa* will be thirty years old (when he appears). So understand my indication" (*Jawāhir al-Rasāʾil*, v. 2, p. 144). Thanks to Fakhruddin Owaisi for pointing this out to us.

My shaykh and master, the greatest shaykh, rare like the red sulfur, al-Ḥājj ʿAbd-Allāh b. al-Ḥajj ⬥,[8] likewise claimed the *fayḍa* for himself. He received spiritual unveilings concerning the *fayḍa*, and he perceived that it belonged to himself. He started seeking for it among all the (Tijānī) disciples he encountered. When he found his death near at hand and it had not yet descended, he knew that it was being held for his disciples.[9] So he began to appoint many deputies, hoping to serve as the means of access to the *fayḍa*; and that was the cause of his wandering. Concerning this he said things that cannot be written on pages or seen with the eyes.

Evidence for the *fayḍa* is found in the Qurʾān. The Most High said: *Such of Our Signs as We abrogate or cause to be forgotten, We replace with one better than it or as good (2:106). Allah will surely bring a people whom He loves, and who love Him (5:54). We will entrust it with a people who will not be disbelievers therein (6:89). As well as others among them who have not yet joined them (62:3). When the help of Allah comes, and victory, and you see the people entering the religion group upon group, then proclaim the praise of your Lord and seek His forgiveness; for He is Oft-Relenting (110:1–3). And He creates that which you do not know (16:8).* Here are indications confirming what has been presented (concerning the *fayḍa*) for those whom Allah has given light to see. But you may draw your own conclusions.

As for (evidence from) the Sunna, the Messenger of Allah ⬥ said, "There will come a time when the one doing good deeds will have the reward of fifty."[10] His companions asked, "(Fifty) of us, or of them, O Messenger of Allah?" He said, "Of you!" His saying, "There will remain a group in my community..." and his saying "My community is like the rain..." have already been discussed at length.[11] He also said, "The best of my community is the first of it and the last of it, in the middle there is trouble." And he said, "By Him in whose hand is my soul, Jesus the son of Mary will surely acquire in my community inheritors of his disciples." Were we to cite all the relevant prophetic traditions and discuss their implications, we would require a separate work.

---

8   Al-Ḥājj ʿAbd-Allāh b. al-Ḥajj al-ʿAlawī (d. 1927) was a renowned scholar and gnostic from Mauritania who traveled widely in the Senegambian region, frequently visiting al-Ḥājj ʿAbd-Allāh Niasse. His *silsila* passes through Shaykh Aḥmad b. Baddi (known as "Abba," d. 1905), to his father Shaykh Muḥamdi "Baddi" (d. 1855), the most prominent disciple of Shaykh Muḥammad al-Ḥāfiẓ b. al-Mukhtār (d. 1830). He was especially famous for his expertise in the science of gnosis (*maʿrifa*). Al-Ḥājj ʿAbd-Allāh wuld al-Ḥajj was the father of Muḥammad (known as "al-Mishrī"), the father of the current Shaykh of Matamawlana (Mauritania), al-Ḥajj ʿAbd-Allāh Mishrī.

9   Meaning that he believed he would not live to see its appearance.

10   *Ḥadīth* reported by Abū Dāwūd, Tirmidhī and Ibn Māja.

11   See Shaykh Ibrāhīm's Introduction to the present work.

My dear brother: if you have not grasped the essential realities of the Qur'ānic verses and prophetic traditions cited here, let that not stop you from accepting them. Shaykh Aḥmad al-Tijānī said in *Jawāhir al-maʿānī*:

> My dear brother: you must believe in and submit to this (Sufi) confession (*ṭāʾifa*). Do not imagine that its method of interpreting the Qurʾān and the Sunna is only changing one apparent meaning for another. Surely the apparent meaning of a Qurʾānic verse or prophetic tradition has an understanding suited to the people and their varying capacities to understand. In this case, the understanding is determined by the wording of the verse or tradition: thus what the words signify in ordinary linguistic usage.
>
> But there are other, hidden understandings of Qurʾānic verses and *ḥadīth*, understood by those to whom Allah has granted illumination (*fatḥ*). It is reported in one prophetic tradition, "Every Qurʾānic verse has an external meaning, and a hidden meaning; as well as an ending point and an insight into seven or seventy secrets."[12] The apparent meaning is that which is logical, which is transmitted by the practical sciences concerned with righteous conduct. The hidden meaning pertains to divine gnosis. Insight refers to when the apparent and hidden meanings become united in one meaning. The ending point is a way of witnessing that is both universal and personal.
>
> Understand this well, dear brother, and do not let the speech of the quarrelsome protestors deter you from accepting meanings from this noble (Sufi) group, even if they are foreign to the minds of common folk. They say this is distorting the words of Allah and His Messenger, but it is not so. It is as if they want to say, "There is no meaning to the noble Qurʾānic verse or prophetic tradition except what we give it." But of course, they will not admit this. In fact, they are only privileging the external meanings over the internal meanings for specific purposes. They understand in their egos what Allah permits them out of His grace. The opening of their hearts is (only) by His mercy and kindness.

There is divine wisdom for the appearance of the *fayḍa* in this age of corruption. Faith has become weak in the hearts of men. Erring sects, misguided and misguiding others, have proliferated. But know that Allah has mercy for this community of Islam, and He has poured out gnosis and essential realities (*ḥaqāʾiq*) so that the Muslims may return to the original, pure state of faith. On this subject, the Greatest Shaykh, Sīdī al-Mukhtār al-Kuntī reported in *al-Kawkab al-waqqād*:

12 *Ḥadīth* traceable to *al-Itqān* of Imam al-Suyūṭī.

> Imam al-Ḥaramayn[13] said: "When the errant sects multiply, arousing themselves in rage, he whom Allah has protected in this Muḥammadan community becomes a guardian for the minds of the Muslims, focusing them on the affirmation of divine oneness (*tawḥīd*) and delivering them from their contentment with convention (*taqlīd*). He will actualize the gnosis (*ʿirfān*) of their innermost beings with a most beautiful support. Protection in the full sense does not mean the servant protects himself from affliction. Rather, real protection is the guarding of his heart from passionate desires."

Once you have understood this, know that a man may obtain a spiritual station (*maqām*) through the affirmation of divine oneness in which those who have no experience of it may think he is possessed (*majnūn*). But he is not possessed. Those with no understanding may consider him an atheist (*zindiq*), though he is no less than a champion of Truth (*ṣiddīq*). According to Shaykh Sīdī al-Mukhtār Kuntī, Junayd was reported as saying:

> Whoever worships Allah, and truly affirms His Oneness, Allah will enthrall him, single him out and choose him for Himself. He will separate him from his kind, making him a unique individual seeking only Him who is Unique. No possessed madman among the gnostic sages goes mad except by drinking the wine of divine Majesty. His divine Majesty bewilders the lovers, and His divine Beauty confounds the gnostic sages. He presents His Perfection to those who have arrived in the divine Presence, and it is He who interprets His Names, He who is the Source of all benefit, the Aggregate of all the divine Names.
>
> The lovers, according to their spiritual states, disagree concerning His Majesty. Among them is one whose mind becomes overwhelmed by the intense lights of his state, so delirium becomes manifest in his actions. He appears, to one with no spiritual experience, to have gone mad, but he is not crazy. Those who lack understanding suspect him of being an atheist, but in actuality he is a champion of Truth (*ṣiddīq*). He has only drunk the wine of divine Majesty and thereby become intoxicated. Let there only be hostility to the evil doers, not to such a one as mentioned here. One of the enraptured described his spiritual state in verse:
>
> And say to him who condemns the people of ecstasy
> If you have not tasted the drink of passion, leave us alone
>
> For when we have become joyful and light-headed,
> Intoxicated by the wine of ardent yearning—you will put us to shame

---

13 ʿAbd al-Mālik Abū al-Juwaynī al-Shāfiʿī (d. 1085, Hijaz), known as Imam al-Ḥaramayn, was one of the most famous scholars of the Ashʿarī school of theology. He was also the teacher of Abū Ḥāmid al-Ghazālī.

So do not blame the drunkard in his state of drunkenness
For burdensome ceremonies are lifted from us in our intoxication

How could we insist on patience from a woman filled with desire?
How can one bear patience when he is witnessing the real meaning?

O driver of the ardent lovers, come to the aid of the conspicuous one
Sing for us in the Name of the Beloved, and cheer our spirits
Preserve our secret in our drunkenness from those who envy us
And if you see something unworthy, forgive us.

Their stories move us, but if not for their passion
Burning inside, such reports would not affect us

Young man: have you not seen the caged bird?
When native lands are mentioned, it longs for its home

So it condoles itself giving song to the contents of its heart
The abdomen shakes only with feeling and meaning

O young man! So too the spirits of the lovers:
They are moved by ardent yearning for the realm of radiance.

Yaḥyā b. Muʿādh al-Rāzī[14] said:

If the tongues of the gnostics were to wander around with the people the same way their hearts revolve with Allah, they would surely be called mad. They might describe their condition in verse as follows:

Wherever the wineglass goes around, around we go
The ignorant think we have been possessed

But we have not been possessed, nor do we suffer insanity
We simply drank wine and became drunk.

Those drawn near to Allah are distinguished by increased affirmation of divine oneness. In this regard, it is sufficient to cite the words of the poet:

I was asked, "Have you ever seen anything more beautiful?"
I said, "Is there anything else but this in existence?"

If you were to follow the indications of divine oneness from us and the Sufi people, we would have escaped from our present situation (requiring explanation).

---

14 Abū Zakariya Yahya b. Muʿādh al-Rāzī (d. 871) was an eminent early Sufi of Central Asia. He is credited with several treatises on Sufism, but his words are mostly related through such early Sufi compendiums as the *Risāla* of Qushayrī or the *Ṭabaqāt al-ṣūfiyya* of Sulāmī. See N. Hanif, *Biographical Encyclopedia of Sufis: Central Asia and Middle East* (Sarup & Sons, 2002), p. 371–372.

So let us now give free reign to the discussion of *fayḍa*, its occurrence, and what has been said by the venerable shaykhs of our time. The magnanimous Shaykh and gnostic sage, the imam and master, ʿAbd-Allāh b. al-Ḥājj al-ʿAlawī, told me: "The *fayḍa* is coming at your hand, in actuality, not figuratively. You will see such jealousy as never witnessed before you." And he told me: "You are the glory of the Tijānī spiritual path in your time," as well as other things that modesty prevents my pen from recording. His speech derives from the purity of his thoughts in regards to Allah and His servants, may it be displayed on yet another occasion. As it is, I am nothing but a delinquent servant, stained with sins and offenses.

Among those who were certain of the arrival of the *fayḍa* mentioned by the gnostic Shaykh (al-Tijānī) was the scholarly master Muḥammad b. al-Shaykh Aḥmad b. al-Shaykh Muḥamdi Baddi,[15] who was known as the Ḥassān of the Tijānī path. He was admired by the finest of his age, whose grace outshone pearls and exquisite coral. All indications are that he was endowed with the greatest sainthood. He annihilated himself in the love of his Master, the Merciful, the Compassionate, and plunged into the oceans and spiritual presences of the best of the children of ʿAdnān. So he became crowned with the secrets of the Seal of Saints, indeed, the finest of crowns.

Such names cannot comprehend the knowledge of him
We only mention them for the sake of pleasure.

The splendid master and venerable erudite scholar, Muḥammad ʿAbd al-Raḥmān b. al-Ḥājj ʿAlawī, was also among those certain of the arrival of the *fayḍa*. He is the holder of the most holy secret and most valuable of spiritual stations, the successor of the righteous early believers (*salaf*). I have mentioned him elsewhere.[16] There is also the famous signpost and brightest full moon, the greatest shaykh, more rare than red sulfur, Muḥammad b. Shaykh Aḥmad b. Shaykh Muḥammad al-Ḥāfiẓ.[17] No one doubts his sainthood on account of his abundant gnosis, his righteousness, the power of his narration and the depth of his understanding.

Less explicit in regards to the *fayḍa* were the two greatest shaykhs, the most famous supports, the inheritors of Shaykh al-Tijānī, Shaykh

---

15 Shaykh Muḥammad b. Aḥmad b. Muḥamdi (d. c. 1955) was the inheritor and descendent of Muḥamdi Baddi b. Sīdina (d. 1855), the closest disciple and *khalīfa* of Shaykh Muḥammad al-Ḥāfiẓ al-Shinqīṭī (d. 1830), who first brought the Tijāniyya to Mauritania. He was known as the "Ḥassān of the Ṭarīqa" after the poet Ḥassān, famous for his eloquence in the time of the Prophet.

16 This Shaykh was entrusted by Shaykh Ibrāhīm's father, al-Ḥājj ʿAbd-Allāh Niasse, to give his son Ibrāhīm unlimited authorization (*ijāza muṭlaqa*) in the Tijāniyya after al-Ḥājj ʿAbd-Allāh's death. Shaykh Ibrāhīm includes the text of the authorization later in the conclusion of the *Kāshif*.

17 Muḥammad b. Aḥmad b. Muḥammad al-Ḥāfiẓ (d. 1945), the direct descendant of Muḥammad al-Ḥāfiẓ (d. 1830) through Aḥmad (d. 1907), known as "Abba."

Muḥammad Saʿīd b. Shaykh Aḥmad b. Shaykh Muḥammad al-Ḥāfiẓ and Shaykh Muḥammad al-Amīn b. Aḥmad b. Muḥamdi, may Allah be pleased with them both. But they confirmed us in our endeavor, praising Allah for what had reached them, and supported us with their prayers and with every kind of assistance. May Allah allow us to benefit from them.
Here is what I said years before the appearance of the *fayḍa*:

> Soon will the *fayḍa* of the saintly Seal come, so make ready
> Detach yourself from others, to obtain the position.

And I said:

> That is the isthmus (*barzakh*), that is the secret link (*surūr*)
> So my two loves are found in this flood (*fayḍ*).

In a long poem of praise for Shaykh Aḥmad al-Tijānī, I wrote:

> My companion, let us stop at the dwelling places
> To hear the stories of the beautiful women.[18]

Let us conclude this chapter with the commendation of the scholars for this *fayḍa* and its people. The following verses were written by the erudite scholar of comprehensive understanding, the most distinguished and excellent judge (*qāḍī*), Sīdī Muḥammad ʿAbd-Allāh b. al-Muṣṭafa al-ʿAlawī:[19]

> Is not the mosque of Ibrāhīm founded on piety (*taqwā*)?
> This, your land (O Shaykh), where there is neither misdeeds nor vain talk
>
> For the companions of Abū al-ʿAbbās (al-Tijānī) are gathered around you
> Obtaining from the Most High the greatest of ranks
>
> Your finest city is the best of cities
> For therein every stranger finds a place of refuge (*maʾwan*)
>
> For here the religion continues to spread in secret
> For a thing has a share in that which its name is enfolded
>
> One is immediately taken upon entry (into the city)
> By the fact that the religion has occupied the center of concentration
>
> We came in troubled conditions

18 Like wine, "pretty girls" or "beautiful women" is often meant as an allegorical allusion in Sufi poetry. According to Anne-Marie Hilsdon, "Women may be depicted in intimate relation with the Beloved, where the Beloved comes to the poet as a woman does in an intimate relationship." See Hilsdon, "Rindu (Longing)," in Joseph and Najmabadi (eds.), *Encyclopedia of Women and Islamic Cultures* (Leiden: Brill, 2003), p. 241.

19 The poetry of this Mauritanian scholar is also cited by Sīdī ʿAlī Cisse in his biography of Shaykh Ibrāhīm in the beginning of the *Kāshif*.

And we obtained there what lifted our distress

From among the successors (*khulafāʾ*) of the Shaykh (al-Tijānī), there is one deputy (*khalīfa*)
Throughout all time, none can attain his rank

A cup of love makes the rounds among the drinkers
And with this (drink), there is no drunkenness and no sobriety

When they are vigilantly engaged in the remembrance of the Guardian Lord (*al-Muhaymin*)
It is as if they quake, transported with joy and pleasure

They crave a draught from the sea of gnostic understandings
A sip that cures whatever worries they have acquired

Their spiritual states emerge as a testimony of what they have claimed
And not every state is a testimony to the soundness of the claim

Accept the Shaykh of the (Sufi) people and travel his path
Do not follow any direction except that set by him

The inheritance (*khilāfa*) of Abū al-ʿAbbas (al-Tijānī) is distributed by him
His command in every affair is followed

He dictates to his companions all sorts of knowledge
Filling them with jurisprudence and grammar

Who among the human race possesses such qualities
He has no like among people, this day or the next

So hold fast to this beautiful inheritance, which came at such sacrifice
It is pronouncing to you its wishes and desires

How its ranks have been arranged! Free from every fault
No support or reinforcement is required

Its end result is nothing but benefit
And surely every affair is (judged) by the goodness of its ending

Blessing and peace on the master of creation
Muḥammad, the one sent, who has no comparison.

He also said:

Felicitous is your star of fortune, each time
And the zodiac sign is one of happiness and safety

O sun of the Hashimite religion, congratulations are due to you
You are the returning point of all doctrines

I am speaking of Abū Isḥāq (Ibrāhīm Niasse), the shining vanguard of his age

He who gives men to drink from cups brimming with gnosis

He is naught but the master of his time
The Tijānī flood (*fayḍa*) is at his hand

If compared with his peers, all fingers point to him alone
What a wonder! To him belongs an ocean that includes oceans
From the flux of the Lord of the Throne and all created beings

In him, the divine Reality is an ocean at high tide
And the sacred law is a second ocean in him

As for jurisprudence (*fiqh*) and religious principles (*uṣūl*); along with their understandings
And their branches: each of them is an ocean (in him)

The same is true for the sciences of rhetoric
Linguistics and logic

The proof of my words is clear
And true is the speech with clear proofs

Ever and ceaselessly are all his moments
Filled with remembrance and the Qurʾān

From all around, people descend on him
Like pigeons flocking on seeds

Every most pious individual, possessed of high morals and intelligence
Who is keen on purifying his heart

Surely destiny will pull him to this Shaykh
For the pulling of destiny is like the pulling of the horse's reins

And nothing can prevent him, not the mention of his loved ones
Not his family or his country

When he finds himself far from the locus of his longing
Burning in love will you find his heart

And when Allah is mentioned, you find him swaying
Like the swaying of the drunkard

Among all creation, the Shaykh's position is raised ceaselessly
Until he has become higher than Orion (*jawzāʾ*), and the mansions of the moon

May Allah protect you, our Abū Isḥāq
From the evil of the enemies

And from those harboring evil intent and evil words
From the evil of enviers and oppressors

And may He award you to follow Muḥammad
And may He give you the most honorable virtues and excellence

And give you the love of the masters of knowledge and their sciences
And the love of the brotherhood of the Shaykh (al-Tijānī)

The following verses were composed by Muḥammad ʿAbd al-Raḥmān b. al-Sālik b. Bāb al-ʿAlawī,[20] unique of his kind, whose condition cannot be matched by those after him, the singular intellect, the most fortunate star.

The secret in Medina (Baye) is the secret of the Shaykh (al-Tijānī)
So Allah has chosen it for us as a dwelling place

And He has chosen him (Shaykh Ibrāhīm) as its beautification
Indeed, it has obtained a grace that illumines the face of grace itself

So follow the path of Medina and you will arrive
And hold fast to her pillars; but trouble ensues if you leave us

In pious visitation, you will obtain your needs
Or if you are afraid, you will find security in your visit

The habitual practice of Ibrāhīm is to lead the creation
So too is (mastery of) of knowledge his habit

My soul submitted to him at a young age
My passion was pulled to him by force

With his wealth and spiritual state will the poet purchase
Whatever beautiful acclamations (he must) from the eloquent ones

Here I erect high buildings of love
But before him, still I find them but small hovels.

And he also said:

O Shaykh! Kaʿba[21] of moral virtues
Arafat[22] of aims and aspirations

Mine of knowledge, well of the Secret
The goal on which the eyes of seekers and pious visitors are fixated

Fruit of noble dignity and honor
Key to the door at every veil

You have not doubted your succession (*khilāfa*) to the Shaykh (al-Tijānī)

---

20 This was another scholar of the ʿAlawī people of Mauritania, who claim descent from ʿAlī b. Abī Ṭālib.

21 The Kaʿba is the name for the Sacred House in Mecca around which the pilgrims circumambulate and the direction to which Muslims pray.

22 Mount Arafat is where pilgrims spend the day in prayer during the Ḥājj.

Nor have you lent your ear to the doubter

You are the innermost heart among those giving spiritual training
And rare among men is the heart of hearts

He commands the good, and forbids the wrong
He calls to the Truth, with gentle disposition

What a guide! Your disciple does not fear
Having to run this way and that

(For you are) both singular and plural, present and absent
Concealed and manifest; what is appropriate for every course

I ask Allah to grant you a long life
As a refuge for the distressed and afflicted

I ask Allah for the favor of our meeting
After this, and a beautiful journey's end

Blessing from Allah
On the best of creation, and on his family and companions

And goodly pleasure on the reality of the Secret
Meaning the support of the saintly saviors (*aghwāth*) and poles (*aqṭāb*).

Thus the shaykhs of Islam have spoken, the distinguished men of our spiritual path. All of them have confirmed the arrival of the *fayḍa* on the hand of this delinquent servant, the author of this blessed Tijānī compilation. The tongue of my spiritual state says:

I was not worthy, but they considered me worthy
So because of that I came to be worthy.

Such are they among whom this *fayḍa* has descended; for their preoccupation has always been with Allah, His Messenger, and Shaykh al-Tijānī. The Shaykh has utterly absorbed them, so that they do not do anything except for him and by him. They are devoted to restoring his houses of remembrance (*zawāyā*) with the remembrance of Allah, in the watches of the night and at the beginning and end of the day. This (devotion of theirs) is by the remembrance (of Allah) and the invocation of blessing on Muḥammad, is their mighty exemplar, their means of achieving the divine Presence. They follow his Sunna, his noble character traits, the tracks he has left behind and his moral virtues. They have been insulted by the heedless and foolish people, who accuse them of not being part of the Tijāniyya. But it is the revilers who have failed to give the Imam (Shaykh al-Tijānī) his proper due, so they have nothing of the Tijāniyya except their having taken the litany (*wird*). I find them laughably absurd, and say as the poet Maʿarri[23] said:

> When al-Ṭāʾiyy[24] has been reproached for being stingy
> And Qusu[25] has been called foolish and stupid;
>
> When the dim star tells the sun, "you are small"
> And the darkness tells the full moon, "your light is setting;"
>
> Visit us, O death, for life has become objectionable
> O self, take me seriously, for your lifespan has become a comedy

Notwithstanding what preceded us in terms of the signs and indications being subtly interwoven, not one of these respected shaykhs of the *Ṭarīqa* claimed the *fayḍa* for himself. It is true that some such claims did occur in the early stages, and this was a wise lesson from Allah. Zarrūq said, "A reality has never become manifest without being greeted by a pretension that resembles it, the insertion into it of something that does not belong to it, and the emergence of denial." All of this demonstrates the merit of focusing undivided attention on the *fayḍa*, and clarifying its real meaning in refutation of its opponents. *But Allah will annul what Satan has suggested; then Allah will establish His revelations* (Qurʾān, 22:52).

He who inherits bears an affinity to what he inherits from. Those most severely tried are the prophets, then the saints, then the next most eminent, and so on. A man is put to the test only in proportion to his religious conviction, so the people of this *Ṭarīqa* have been sorely tried, first by being subjected to criticism and abuse by their fellows; then by being made an object of their reverential treatment; and finally with both at once! Those so tested should not miss an opportunity to thank Allah (alone) for commendation, and to patiently endure blame. So if someone wishes to be among those of religious conviction, he must make himself accustomed to affliction. *Allah is the defender of those who believe* (Qurʾān, 22:38). *And if someone puts all his trust in Allah, He will be sufficient for him* (65:3). The following passage is excerpted from the *Rimāḥ*, here quoting from *Baḥr al-mawrūd*:[26]

---

23 Aḥmad al-Tanūkhī al-Maʿarri (d. 1057) was a Syrian poet and ascetic of great renown.

24 Hatim al-Ṭāʾiyy was a Christian Arab who lived before the time of the Prophet (but whose son ʿAdī later became a companion of the Prophet) who became famous for his generosity. His name later became synonymous with paradigmatic generosity in Arabic literature.

25 Qusu was a preacher in Mecca during the time of the Prophet Muḥammad's youth. The Prophet would later speak admirably of his intelligence, wisdom, and eloquence. It is said that the "Amā baʿd" standard in the Friday sermon (*khuṭba*) comes from Qusu.

26 The *Baḥr al-mawrūd* by ʿAbd al-Wahhāb al-Shaʿrānī (d. 1565).

> He (our Shaykh) took from us a solemn pledge—should we seek to be included in the league (*ḥizb*) of Allah—that we accustom ourselves to endure trials and tribulations, and abundant criticism from those we know and those we do not know. Anyone whom Allah wishes to select, whether sinful or righteous, will experience some such tests. Let it not surprise you then, my dear brother, that people turn against those seeking to be among those in the presence of Allah. Entry into this presence is forbidden to anyone who attaches importance to prestige in the eyes created beings. When Allah causes the seeker to be assaulted by his fellow creatures with falsehood, slander, and rending scorn, he ceases to rely on his fellow created beings, and comes to rely only on Allah. Like this, his dependence on Allah becomes a necessity, and he seeks prestige (*maqām*) from Him alone. In that place, Allah bestows the station on him, then continues to elevate him in degrees of proximity until he reaches the position that Allah has allotted him. So long as the servant seeks prestige in the sight of the creation, he is veiled from Allah, the Most High. So long as such repugnant characteristics multiply, the veils multiply as well; until he may become veiled from Allah by seventy thousand veils or even more. I once heard ʿAlī al-Khawwāṣ,[27] may Allah have mercy on him, say: "The Lord of Truth will not select a servant until the devils among men and jinn have joined forces against him, assaulting him with falsehood and slander. Then if he manages to estrange his ego (*nafs*) from the creation, coming to rely on none of them, Allah the Exalted will choose him."

And he (al-Ḥājj ʿUmar) said:

> Sīdī Abū al-Ḥasan al-Shādhilī, may Allah have mercy on him, used to say, "When Allah the Exalted came to know of the falsehood and slander people were saying about His prophets and bosom-friends, He condemned a (whole) people to wretched misfortune. We take refuge with Allah the Exalted, for people attributed to Him a wife and a son, and they said, *Allah's hand is shackled* (5:64), and other things. The saint who is sadly at a loss for words before his accusers has consolation in the example of his Almighty and Glorious Lord. They ascribed to Him a wife and son, and linked Him to that which does not befit His Majesty."
>
> Shaykh Tāj al-Dīn Ibn ʿAṭāʾ Allāh, may Allah have mercy on him, used to say, "It was Allah's custom to test the prophets and His purified ones, subjecting them to vexation at the outset of their careers. If they endured with patience, success would finally be theirs." He (Shaʿrānī)

---

27 ʿAlī al-Khawwāṣ (d. 1532), a shaykh of the Shādhiliyya Sufi order under whom Shaʿrānī studied in Egypt.

discussed this at length in *Muqaddamāt al-ṭabaqāt*,[28] so understand the point well. And may Allah take charge of your right guidance.

In *Arāʾis al-bayān*,[29] the author comments on the verse, *So those who emigrated, and were driven from their homes, and suffered for My cause* (3:195). He states that if the Sufi people had not tasted the bitter abuse of their critics, they would not have discovered the real meaning of taking refuge with Allah. When the saints are disturbed by their adversaries to the point of rage and constriction of the breast—that being the site of Allah's testing whether the saint can control a rage that would choke the throats of the critics—the doors will be opened after that. Then the way will be clear for freedom of speech, blissful serenity, and the flow of gracious benefit.

Junayd said, "May Allah reward our brethren on our behalf. By treating us roughly, they have turned us back toward Allah the Exalted. This is the customary practice of Allah in dealing with the people who pursue the path of gnosis and unveiling. Allah, the Most High said, *And you will not find any means of changing Allah's custom* (33:62)."

Al-Ḥājj ʿUmar referred to *al-Qawāʾid al-Zarrūqiyya*, then mentioned the statements of Sīdī Zarrūq which already have been discussed. Then he went on to say:

> Studying this carefully you will understand that a man is put to the test in proportion to his religious conviction, as was mentioned earlier. Every prophet [had] and most truthful people have an enemy. Adam had Iblīs. David had Goliath. Abraham had Nimrod. Moses had Pharaoh. Jesus had Nebuchadnezzar, the Antichrist, and the Jews. Muḥammad had Abū Jahl and others. Abū ʿAlī al-Khawwāṣ said: "The perfection of summoning to Allah is dependent on peoples' genuine belief in the propagator. So the foremost in this regard was the Allah's Messenger, Muḥammad ﷺ, and the rest of the prophets before him. Some people believed them, so Allah guided them by His gracious favor. Others disbelieved, so Allah afflicted them with His justice. And the bosom-friends and saints have had enemies from the age of the Companions (of the Prophet) until this time of ours; enemies who abuse them and say evil things about them. Evidence for this is found in Allah's saying, *And We have appointed some of you as a trial for others* (Qurʾān, 25:20)."

Since being put to the test is an honor, Allah has collected for the elite of this Muḥammadan community—because of the loftiness of their rank—

---

28 Likely the introduction of *Ṭabaqāt al-kubrā* of Shaʿrānī.

29 The *Arāʾis al-bayān* is a famous Sufi commentary on the Qurʾān written by Ruzbihan al-Baqlī (d. 1209) of Shiraz, Persia.

a combination of trials and tribulations that were never so combined for previous communities.

ᶜAbd-Allāh b. al-Zubayr[30] was possessed of great humility in prayer. They slandered him, saying, "He is an adulterous hypocrite!" They poured hot water on his head while he was in ritual prostration, but he did not notice what they were doing. He suffered a painful headache for a long time thereafter.

Ibn al-ᶜAbbās[31] was slandered by Nāfiᶜ b. al-Azraq,[32] who said of him, "He explains the Qurʾān without knowledge."

Saᶜd b. Abī Waqqās[33] was insulted by some of the ignorant folk of Kufa, who said, "He does not know how to perform the ritual prayer properly."

Abū Yazīd al-Bisṭāmī[34] was banished from his homeland seven times by al-Ḥusayn b. ᶜĪsā. This was simply because Bisṭāmī taught his countrymen things unfamiliar to them, such as the spiritual stations of the Prophets and saints. He did not return to his hometown until after Ḥusayn's death. After his return, his people befriended him and held him in high esteem.

Dhū al-Nūn al-Miṣrī[35] was likewise exiled from Egypt. He was brought to Baghdad fettered and shackled, while the people of Egypt followed him, accusing him of atheism.

Muḥammad b. Faḍl al-Balkhī[36] was expelled from Balkh because of his adherence to the school (*madhhab*) of *ḥadīth* as it relates to the verses of the divine Attributes. He thus interpreted them based on their apparent meanings, without explanation (*taʾwīl*) or speculation (*tajassus*) concerning the knowledge of Allah the Exalted. As he left, he told the people, "Allah has

---

30 ᶜAbd-Allāh b. al-Zubayr (624–692) was the son of Zubayr b. al-ᶜAwwām and Asmāʾ bint Abū Bakr. He was the first Muslim child born in Medina and was raised in the Prophet's household since ᶜĀʾisha was his aunt. He fought in many of the early military campaigns of the Muslims. Sometimes known as the "Seventh Caliph," he was no fan of the Umayyad Caliphate. He was killed during a civil war between Muslims in the Hijaz, beheaded, and crucified.

31 ᶜAbd-Allāh b. al-ᶜAbbās (d. 688) was a companion and cousin of the Prophet famous for his knowledge of the religion and especially for his ability to explain the Qurʾān.

32 Nāfiᶜ al-Azraq (d. 60) was the leader of one of the more powerful factions of the Khawārij (those who early on departed from the Muslim community, accusing ordinary Muslims of disbelief or idolatry), called the Azariqa.

33 Saᶜd b. Abī Waqqas (d. 664) was the Prophet's maternal uncle and one of the first converts to Islam.

34 Abū Yazīd al-Bisṭāmī (d. 874), a prominent Sufi from Bisṭām, Persia.

35 Dhū al-Nūn al-Miṣrī (d. 859) was an early Sufi of Egypt. He was arrested in 829 on charges of heresy and sent to prison in Baghdad. He later returned to Cairo, where he is buried.

36 Muḥammad b. Faḍl al-Balkhī (d. 931), of the Balkh province of Khurasan (modern day Afghanistan) was the disciple of Aḥmad Khadruya (d. 854). After his expulsion, he traveled to Samarqand and served the people as a Shāfiᶜī jurist and Sufi guide.

removed His knowledge from your hearts." No Sufi ever emerged in Balkh again after that, even though the region was one of the greatest Sufi lands.

Junayd was similarly accused of unbelief. He used to teach the science of divine oneness in public, but after such accusations, he began teaching in the basement of his home.

Shaykh Ibn Abī Jamra was censured by scholars convened in a special meeting, in which they rejected his saying, "I have met with the Prophet ﷺ." So he stayed in his house until he died, leaving only to attend the congregational prayer. Nonetheless, he was accused of unbelief, of declaring the permissibility of alcohol, and sodomy. He was accused of dressing up at night in the religious attire of non-Muslims. He was taken bound and shackled from Syria to Egypt.

Abū Madyan[37] was accused of atheism, and he was expelled from Bougie to Tlemcen, where he died and was buried.

Ḥakīm al-Tirmidhī[38] was banished on account of his books, *ʿIllal al-sharīʿa* and *Khatm al-awliyāʾ*. It was said, "He has declared the saints superior to the prophets," and he was insulted with crude language. Both books were thrown into the ocean, but a fish swallowed them and spat them out elsewhere.

Saʿd b. ʿAbd-Allāh was accused of shameful acts. He was exiled from Egypt, and he died in a foreign land. Abū Saʿīd al-Kharrāz[39] was accused of terrible sins and unbelief because of statements found in his books.

Yūsuf b. al-Ḥusayn[40] was accused of terrible sins, until the point of his death. But he remained firm in his dignity, paying no attention. Abū al-Ḥasan al-Būsanjī[41] was exiled to Nīsābūr, where he remained until he died.

Saḥnūn al-Muḥibb[42] was accused of terrible sins. A prostitute was bribed and made to say that he and his friends were in the habit of visiting her.

---

37 Abū Madyan Shuʿayb (d. 1198) was born in Andalusia and died in Tlemcen (Algeria). He was the teacher of ʿAbd al-Salām b. Mashish and thus an important figure in the development of the Shādhiliyya order. He had begun teaching in Bougie (Algeria) after returning from pilgrimage, influencing the likes of Ibn al-ʿArabī, ʿAbd al-Salām Ibn Mashish, and Abū Ḥasan al-Shādhilī. For more on his life and thinking, see Vincent Cornell, *The Way of Abū Madyan: Doctrinal and Poetic Works of Abū Madyan Shuʿayb ibn al-Husayn al-Ansari* (Cambridge: Islamic Texts Society, 1996).

38 Al-Ḥākīm al-Tirmidhī (d. 905–910) lived in Tirmidh, near Balkh in modern-day Afghanistan. He is the first known Sufi to expound on the concept of the Seal of Saints.

39 Abū Saʿīd al-Kharrāz (d. 899) was from Baghdad. He was famous for expounding ideas such as *fanāʾ* (annihilation) and *baqāʾ* (remaining).

40 Likely Yūsuf b. al-Ḥusayn al-Rāzī (d. 916), an early Sufi.

41 Likely Abū al-Ḥasan al-Haytham al-Būsanjī (d. 1009), who wrote *Qisas al-Qurʾān*.

42 Saḥnūn al-Muḥibb was a famous *majdhūb* (enraptured) Sufi contemporary to Junayd (ninth century) in Iraq.

Shiblī[43] was accused of unbelief on several occasions. Even those who used to love him accused him of lunacy, and he was committed to an insane asylum to keep people away from him. One of the shaykhs of Baghdad said, "If Allah did not yet have a Hellfire, He would have created it for those who abused al-Shiblī, calling him an unbeliever!" He also said, "If al-Shiblī does not enter the Garden of Paradise, who will?"

Imam Abū Bakr al-Qābisī was banished from Morocco and brought to Egypt in chains. While reciting the Qurʾān with contemplation and deep humility, he was seized and flayed alive. He was said to have subjected the people to temptations, so that when the matter was presented to the sultan, he said, "Kill him and flay his corpse!"

Nasafī[44] was likewise flayed in Aleppo. He would look at the person flaying him and smile. He composed five hundred verses of poetry affirming the Oneness of Allah while he was being flayed. He was condemned when his enemies cunningly entrapped him. They sent the Shaykh a pair of shoes as a present, into the soles of which had been inserted a piece of paper on which was written the Qurʾānic chapter *Ikhlāṣ*. The Shaykh put the shoes on without realizing what he was doing. His enemies then told the governor of Aleppo, "Nasafī has written the Chapter *Ikhlaṣ* and put it in his shoe to be stepped on." So the governor sent an agent who found the piece of paper. The Shaykh surrendered to the will of Allah and did not defend himself, for he knew he would inevitably be put to death.

Abū al-Qāsim al-Bahrabādhī was banished from Basra, as well as Abū ʿAbd-Allāh, the companion of Abū Ḥafṣ al-Ḥaddād.

Abū al-Ḥasan al-Baṣrī was accused of unbelief.

Foul things were said of Ibn Shamʿūn till the point of his death, and no funeral prayer was given him.

Imam Abū al-Qāsim b. Jamīl was accused of terrible sins to the point of death. But he was never distracted from his preoccupation with knowledge, the prophetic tradition, the night vigil, and his abstinence from the world until he wore the funeral shroud.

According to Abū Bakr al-Simṭānī, Abū Dīnār used to disparage Junayd, Ruwaym, Saḥnūn, Ibn ʿAṭāʾ Allāh and the shaykhs of Iraq. Whenever someone mentioned them in his presence, he became enraged and fell into a fit.

Abū al-Ḥasan al-Shādhilī was exiled from Morocco to Egypt, and accused of atheism, apostasy, and declaring lawful the forbidden things.

Imam Abū al-Qāsim b. Qusayy, Ibn Hayyān, Jawnī, and al-Marjānī were all killed.

---

43 Abū Bakr al-Shiblī (d. 946), a famous Sufi and Mālikī jurist of Baghdad.

44 This is likely ʿAzīz al-Nasafī, a thirteenth-century Persian Sufi of the Kubrāwiyya order. For more on his life and works, see Lloyd Ridgeon, *ʿAzīz Nasafī* (Surrey, UK: Curzon, 1998).

Ibn al-ʿArabī al-Ḥātimī and Ibn al-Fāriḍ have not ceased to be censured till the present time.

ʿIzz al-Dīn[45] was subjected to formal interrogation on account of a statement found in his book, *al-ʿAqāʾid*.

Taqī al-Dīn b. al-Layth al-Aʿzz was envied and falsely accused of maligning the sultan. He was threatened with execution, but Allah came to his rescue.

Suyūṭī said:

> Among the blessings bestowed on me by Allah is that He provided me with an enemy who abused me and defames my honor, so that I may have something in common with the prophets and the saints. Know that there has never been a great man in any time who did not have an enemy among those of base character; thus the nobles (*ashrāf*) are forever tested by the fringe groups (*aṭrāf*).

Sīdī Abū al-Ḥasan (al-Shādhilī) used to say:

> Since Allah, Almighty and Glorious is He, knew from His pre-eternal knowledge what would be said about this righteous company (*ṭāʾifa*), He began with Himself. Thus He condemned a people to wretched misfortune because they attributed to Him a wife and a son and incapacity, declaring His Hands tied. If a saint or truthful person should feel depressed because of his accusers smearing him with allegations of unbelief, atheism, sorcery, insanity or other defamations, subtle voices from the Lord of Truth call out to him, saying, "What is said about you would be your apt description, if not for My gracious favor to you! Have you not seen how your brethren among the children of Adam have also dishonored Me, attributing to Me improper things?" Then, if he is still depressed, the voices call to him again, "In regards to this defamation, you have an example in Me, for things are said about Me which do not befit My Majesty. And things have been said about Muḥammad and his brethren among the prophets, peace and blessings on them, which do not befit their dignity. They were accused of sorcery and insanity, and wanting nothing other than leadership."

Shaykh al-Tijānī, the Seal of Saints ﷺ, was also tried and tested. Ibn Māyāba[46] composed a book to discredit him and his companions, loaded

45 Likely ʿIzz al-Dīn al-Sulamī (d. 1261), a famous Shāfiʿī jurist and Shādhilī Sufi who spent most of his life in Syria and wrote *ʿAqaʾid ahl al-Islām*.

46 The book of Muḥammad Khidr b. Māyāba, *Mushtaha al-kharif al-jani fi radd zalaqa al-Tijānī al-Jani*, was first published in 1925. The most detailed refutation of this work was by Muḥammad Khalīfa b. ʿAbd-Allāh Niasse (the older brother of Shaykh Ibrāhīm Niasse), called *al-Juyūsh al-Ṭullaʿ bi Murhafāt al-Quṭṭaʿ ila Ibn Māyāba akhi al-Tanaṭṭuʿ*, published in 1930. For more on this subject see Ousmane Kane, "Muḥammad Niasse (1881–1956) et sa réplique contre le pamphlet anti-tijânî de Ibn Mayaba," in Triaud and

with vilification, slander, curses, accusations of unbelief, and misguidance. Nothing but envy causes the stubborn petrification of the jurists, inciting them to censure Allah's bosom friends (*aṣfiyāʾ*). According to the erudite scholar Zarrūq, in *Taʾsīs al-qawāʾid*:

> The meaning of envy is connected to duplicity. The goal of the envier is to subject his target of envy to character assassination. Whenever souls are endowed with excellent virtues, enviers become preoccupied with their characters and the means of destroying them. So enviers pursue their ends in various ways. If a common person is envied, in the market place, for example, he is not accused of anything except cheating, swindling, and the like. If a soldier is envied, he is accused of disrespect, neglect of his duties, and like things. When a jurist or one who recites the Qurʾān is envied, he is accused of unbelief, mistakes, and whatever else will ruin his reputation and cause people to doubt his character. When the Sufis (*fuqarāʾ*) are envied, they are accused of deceit and cunning, of being masters of delusion, and so on. Other examples abound, but would take too long to mention.

This ends the chapter. Allah the Glorious is the enabling guide to the straight path, to Him is the return and destination.

Robinson (eds.), *La Tijâniyya: un confrérie musulmane à la conquête de l'Afrique* (Paris: Karthala, 2001).

CHAPTER 2

Spiritual Experiences (*adhwāq*) and their Foundation in the Qurʾān and Sunna

With Allah the Most High is all success, and He is the Guide by His Grace to the balanced path.

In the beginning of his *Ṭabaqāt*,[1] Shaʿrānī said:

The purpose of this introduction is to explain that the way of the (Sufi) people is based on the Qurʾān and the Sunna. It is founded on exemplifying the characteristics of the prophets and the purified ones. This way cannot be considered blameworthy for any reason except if it is at variance with the unambiguous ruling of the Qurʾān, the Sunna, and the consensus of the Muslim scholars. And since it does not depart from these foundations, the final word on the subject is simply that it is an understanding that a Muslim adult has been given. Let he who wishes put it into practice, and let he who wishes ignore it. This leaves no motive for criticizing the Sufi people, except that the critic thinks badly of them and wants to cast doubt on their sincerity. Certainly this is not permitted according to the sacred law.

Dear brother, may Allah have mercy on you! Know that the science of Sufism is a knowledge kindled in the hearts of the saints, until the practical application of the Qurʾān and the Sunna completely illuminated their hearts. For anyone who puts the religion into practice like this has such sciences kindled in him, along with moral virtues, secrets,

1 Sharʿānī's *al-Ṭabaqāt al-kubrā al-musamma bi lawāqiḥ al-anwār fī ṭabaqāt al-akhyār* is a collection of 430 biographies of righteous Sufis, from the time of the Prophet's companions to the Shaykh's own time.

and divine realities that tongues are incapable of enunciating. This is similar to the way in which the scholars have had knowledge kindled in their hearts from studying the legal rules, and they likewise have put into practice what they have learned. Consider how the sciences of rhetoric and eloquence are the cream of the knowledge of grammar. Similarly, Sufism, provided the servant is free from false pretexts and self-indulgence, is simply the sweet cream of practicing the rulings of the sacred law. In the same way that rhetoric and eloquence may be considered either independent sciences or part of the science of grammar, so too Sufism can either be considered its own science or the essence of the sacred law.

Sufism stems from the essence of the sacred law. This cannot be tasted, however, save by the one who delves into the depths of the sacred law. When the servant enters the Sufi path, plunging into its ocean, Allah gives him the capacity of discovery. This pertains to both the external rulings as well as the obligations of the spiritual path; its recommended procedures, its proper conduct and manners, and what is forbidden or reprehensible. He is able to distinguish what is appropriate and what is not, similar to the scholars of independent legal reasoning (*mujtahidūn*). But it is not proper for a jurist endowed with the authority of independent legal reasoning to declare something obligatory unless its obligation is explicitly stated in the sacred law. It is equally improper for a saint of Allah to say that a rule within the spiritual path is obligatory, unless its obligation is made explicit in the sacred law. This has been said in no uncertain terms by al-Yāfiʿī[2] and others, who explain that all saints are equal before the Law; Allah has simply chosen them for His religion. Those who pay attention realize that the sciences of the Allah's people contain nothing that departs from the sacred law. How could it be otherwise, when these sciences have linked them to Allah in every moment?

He who doubts that the science of Sufism stems from the essence of the sacred law is unfamiliar with people of the spiritual path and has not thoroughly mastered the knowledge of the sacred law. This is why Junayd, may Allah have mercy on him, said, "This knowledge of ours is built of the Qurʾān and the Sunna," in reply to those of his time or any other who imagine that it has departed from them. The Sufi people unanimously concur that it not permitted to put up obstacles (*taṣaddur*) in the path of Allah the Almighty unless one has plunged into the depths of the sacred law. He should know the law's explicit and implicit rulings, which are of general applicability and which are particular, which supersede others and which are superseded. He must

2 Likely ʿAbd-Allāh al-Yāfiʿī (d. 1367), a famous Shāfiʿī jurist and Sufi writer known for his defense of Ibn al-ʿArabī against his detractors.

also have thorough knowledge of the Arabic language, its figurative and metaphorical expressions, and so forth.

Every Sufi is an expert on jurisprudence, but not every jurist is a Sufi. Generally speaking, no one dares to criticize the spiritual states of the Sufis unless he is wholly ignorant of their condition. Qushayrī used to say: "No era of Islamic history has had a shaykh of this Sufi group to whom the leading scholars of the time did not pay homage, show humility towards and seek blessing from. If the people of the spiritual path had not been endowed with special excellence and distinction, the opposite would have been the case."

In his commentary on *al-Shifā*ʾ, Sīdī ʿAlī al-Qārī[3] explained the saying of the Prophet ﷺ, "Whoever innovates something in our decree...;"[4] or the alternative narration in *Ṣaḥīḥ Muslim*, "Whoever behaves in a way not in accordance with our decree;" or in another narration, "Whoever introduces something into our religion," or in another, "in this decree of ours ..."

> In other words, "(innovation in) this clear and perfect decree, which needs no innovated addition." The word "addition" here means anything for which the Qurʾān and the Sunna provide no support, whether obvious or concealed, explicit or implicit. In one narration, the wording of the *ḥadīth* is: "(If someone introduces) what is not found in it, it (*huwa*) is rejected."[5] Depending on whether the pronoun *huwa* here denotes the innovation or the innovator, either it or he is the object of rejection. This prophetic tradition (in its various versions) is the ruling on which adherence to the Qurʾān and the Sunna and the rejection of heresies and innovation is based.

ʿAlī, may Allah ennoble his countenance, said in an authentic report: "If I had wished, I could have loaded eighty camels with books explaining the sciences concerning the dot beneath the Arabic letter *bā*ʾ."[6] Imam al-Shaʿrāni mentions this statement in his book *al-Mizān*.[7] In another of his books, *al-Jawhar al-maṣūn fi ʿulūm kitāb Allah al-maknūn*, he said he had enumerated approximately thirty thousand sciences. Sharʿānī relates

---

3 Mulla ʿAlī al-Qārī (d. 1605) was born in Herat, Afghanistan, and migrated to Mecca, where he became a renowned scholar of his time. He composed numerous commentaries on classical Islamic texts, such as the *Muwaṭṭā*ʾ of Imam Mālik and *al-Shifā*ʾ of Qāḍī ʿĪyād b. Mūsā.

4 *Ḥadīth* found in *Ṣaḥīḥ Bukhārī*.

5 The version of the *ḥadīth* reported by ʿĀʾisha is: "Whoever does something outside of our decree, it (or he) is rejected."

6 The letter *bā*ʾ, which is marked by a subscript dot, is the first letter of the phrase, *bismillāh al-raḥmān al-raḥīm*, which begins the Qurʾān and nearly every subsequent chapter. It is thus the first letter of the Qurʾān.

7 The *Mīzān al-kubrā* is Shaʿrānī's work on comparative jurisprudence between the four schools of Sunni Islamic Law.

that Shaykh Shihāb al-Dīn b. ʿAbd al-Ḥaqq studied the book for a month, but was incapable of comprehending the relevance of a single science, so he said, "For what reason have you written this book at this time?" Sharʿānī said, "I have written it to aid the people of Allah, because many people accuse them of being ignorant of the Qurʾān and the Sunna." Shihāb al-Dīn said, "I describe myself as a scholar of Egypt, Syria, the Hijāz, Asia Minor, and Persia, but I have been incapable of understanding the relevance to the Qurʾān of even one science you mention, and I understand nothing of its contents. Nevertheless, I cannot reject your book in every respect, because the direction of its discourse is not futile or vulgar."

Consider the words of Allah, *And We have revealed the Book to you as an exposition of all things* (Qurʾān, 16:89). And He said, *We have neglected nothing in the Book* (6:38). And He said, *And He created that which you do not know* (16:8). Ponder the response of our master ʿAlī, may Allah ennoble his countenance, when Abū Juḥayfa asked him, "Do you people have a book that Allah's Messenger, may Allah bless him and grant him peace, has dedicated exclusively to you?" He replied, "No, not apart from the Book of Allah the Exalted."[8] (And evidence of its dedication is provided by the Qurʾānic verse) *Glory be to Him who carried His servant by night* (17:1).[9] Abū Hurayra ﷺ used to say: "I received two vessels from Allah's Messenger, peace and blessings on him. One I have poured out for all of you. As for the other, if I poured it out, this throat of mine would have been cut."[10] A similar version is found in the appendix of Shaykh Sīdī Mukhtār (al-Kuntī):[11] "Abū Hurayra used to say, 'I have taken from Allah's Messenger two cases of knowledge. One of them I have shared with others. As for the other, by Allah, if I mentioned one word of it, you would have cut my throat before I finished speaking.'" In like manner, ʿAlī b. Abī Ṭālib used to say in poetic verse:

> O Lord, were I to reveal a certain jewel of knowledge
> I would be told, "You are among those who worship idols"
> And Muslim men would find it lawful to shed my blood
> Believing the vile sin they were committing to be a good deed.

The reason for all of this is that the burden of the divine Realities can only be borne by one whom Allah has prepared. Allah will expand the breast of such a one to cope with what is involved. Indeed, no one is capable of bearing the Realities except a noble prophet or a wise saint. Jaʿfar

8 The full *ḥadīth* is found in the *Ṣaḥīḥ* of Bukhārī. ʿAlī's full response was, "By Him Who made the grain split and created the soul, we have nothing except what is in the Qurʾān and the gift of understanding Allah's Book with which He may endow a man …"

9 This is in reference to the Prophet's Night Journey and Ascension (*isrāʾ wa miʿraj*).

10 Narration found in the *Ṣaḥīḥ* of Bukhārī.

11 This is the appendix of Kuntī's *al-Kawkab al-waqqād fī faḍl dhikr al-mashāʾikh wa ḥaqāʾiq*.

al-Ṣādiq said, "When the lover comes to the utmost point of proximity to the Beloved, he experiences the utmost sense of awe (*hayba*). So the Real treats him with the greatest kindness, since He says, *And He inspired His servant with what He inspired* (53:10)." In other words, what happens happens, and the Beloved says to His beloved what He says; and the secret is concealed, so momentous is the matter. No one is aware of it because no one knows what was inspired except the one who was inspired. The one inspired obscures his secret because of its weighty importance, and becomes devout in his worship on account of his trust in it.

The Prophet ﷺ, however, did make this knowledge available to the elite of his community, however. They are his true inheritors. The substance of this knowledge imparted directly from the divine Presence (*al-ʿilm al-ladunī*) cannot be comprehended or borne except by those to whom it belongs among the saintly poles (*aqṭāb*) of this noble Muḥammadan community. Fakhr al-Dīn al-Rāzī[12] mentions that his father once told him that he heard Abū al-Qāsim Sulaymān al-Anṣārī say:

> When Muḥammad ﷺ attained to the exalted rank of the heavenly ascension, Allah the Exalted informed him, 'O Muḥammad, the honor on you has been perfected.' To which Muḥammad replied, 'O Lord, by my devotion to You in loving servanthood (*ʿubūdiyya*).'[13] Allah the Exalted said, *Glory to Him who carried His servant by night* (Qurʾān, 17:1). Thus Allah named him "servant" (*ʿabd*) with this ascension so he would come to embody (*taḥaqqaqa*) Allah's greatest Name. In truth, this name ("servant") is not fitting for anybody but he, may Allah's peace and blessing be upon him. The saintly poles (*aqṭāb*) from his community after him also can be called "servant," but only as a consequence of the Prophet, they do not bear this reality in themselves. Others, besides the poles, realize this name (servant) but only metaphorically, not actually.
>
> In one narration, the Prophet said: "When I was alone with my Lord, He revealed to me three types of knowledge. One type of knowledge—He took an oath from me to hide it, for no one would be able to bear it except myself. Another type of knowledge—He commanded me to share it with the elite (*khawāṣṣ*) of my community, for they are the saintly Substitutes (Abdāl) for the prophets. The last type of

12 Muḥammad b. ʿUmar Fakhr al-Dīn al-Rāzī (d. 1210, Herat, Persia) was a great theologian, philosopher and scientist. His multi-volume *Tafsīr al-kabīr*, also known as *Mafātiḥ al-ghayb*, is a comprehensive exegesis of the Qurʾān.

13 A slightly different translation of this narration of Anṣārī, is cited by Hisham Kabbani: "It is related that when the Prophet reached the highest levels and distinguished stations, Allah revealed to him, 'With what shall I honor you?' The Prophet said, 'By relating me to You through servanthood (*ʿubūdiyya*).'" See Kabbani, "The Importance and Meaning of Prayer in Islam," in Vincent Cornell and Safi (eds.), *Voices of Islam*, vol. 2, *Voices of the Spirit* (Westport, CT: Praeger Publishers, 2007), p. 45.

knowledge—He took an oath from me to inform everyone, common folk and the elite. He taught me the Qurʾān, and I anticipated Gabriel in (the revelation of) a verse from Him, so my Lord reproved me, and said, *Do not be quick to recite the Qurʾān before its revelation to you is completed; but rather say: "My Lord, increase me in knowledge"* (Qurʾān, 20:114).

In another narration, the Prophet said: "I approached my Lord until I was as He said, *Till he was (the proximity) of two bow-lengths or nearer* (53:9), and my Lord asked me, but I was unable to respond. So He put His Hand between my shoulder blades, without qualification (*takyīf*) or delimitation (*taḥdīd*), until I discovered the chill (*bard*) of the divine Presence upon my heart. Then I inherited the knowledge of everything that came before and everything that was to follow. He taught me all the sciences, what had been scattered and dispersed. One knowledge—He took an oath from me to hide, knowing that none could bear it other than myself. Another knowledge—He gave me the option (of sharing it or not). And He taught me the Qurʾān, and Gabriel, peace be upon him, reminded me in this. Another knowledge—He commanded me to give to both the common people and the elite of my community." This has been related on the authority of Abū Hurayra.[14]

At this point, allow me to recollect certain verses of the Qurʾān that are relevant to the subject of spiritual experience. Allah the Exalted said:

So whichever way you turn, there is the Face of Allah (2:115).

And say, "Truth has come and falsehood vanished. Falsehood is ever bound to vanish" (17:81).

But We hurl the truth against the falsehood, and it shatters its skull, and behold! It vanishes (21:18).

That is because when Allah only was invoked, you disbelieved. But if partners were ascribed to Him, you believed (40:12).

14 These narrations related by Fakhr al-Dīn al-Rāzī are not found in the canonical *ḥadīth* collections. Further explanation of the three types of knowledge obtained by the Prophet during the Miʿrāj was provided by Shaykh Tijānī Cisse (Interview, Medina-Baye, Senegal, 9 January 2009): "The general knowledge to share with everybody is the sacred law (*sharīʿa*), the Qurʾān, and the Sunna. The second type of knowledge, for the elite, consists of the knowledge of the essential Reality (*ʿilm al-ḥaqīqa*), that nothing exists except Allah. The Prophet was teaching this knowledge to the elite of his companions, such as Abū Bakr and ʿUmar. The third type of knowledge, only shared between Allah and himself, is referred to as 'the knowledge of the secret of predestination' (*ʿilm sirr al-qadr*). It concerns the secret purpose for the creation of every single thing—even the rug you are sitting on now—from the beginning of time till the end. No one can bear this knowledge except the Prophet, so Allah took an oath from him not to share it with anyone."

He is the First, the Last, the Manifest, the Hidden; and He is Aware of all things (57:3).

We shall show them Our signs on the horizons and within themselves, until it becomes clear to them that this (Qurʾān) is the truth (41:53).

The Compassionate has firmly established Himself on the Heavenly Throne (20:5).

Say: "The Compassionate has no son. And I am the first of His worshipers" (43:81).

Whoever obeys the Messenger has obeyed Allah (4:80).

Those who swear allegiance to you (O Muḥammad), swear allegiance to Allah. The Hand of Allah is over their hands (48:10).

And it was not you (O Muḥammad) who threw when you threw (pebbles cutting down the enemy); but it was Allah who threw (8:17).

Say: "If you love Allah, follow me; Allah will love you" (3:31).

For those who believe and do righteous deeds, and believe in what is sent down to Muḥammad—and it is the Truth from their Lord—He will cover over their evil deeds and right their condition (47:2).

And Allah suffices as witness … Muḥammad is the Messenger of Allah (48:27–28).

Whoever obeys Allah and the Messenger, they are in the company of those whom Allah has blessed: the Prophets, the most truthful ones, the martyrs and the righteous. And the best of company are they (4:69)!

He who came with the truth, and he who confirmed it; they indeed are the God-fearing (39:33).

How many a sign there is in the heavens and the earth which they pass by with aversion! (12:105).

As well as in your own selves (are signs). What, do you not see (51:21)?

The Messenger of Allah ﷺ reported that his Lord told him: "I was a treasure. I was unknown and I wished to known, so I created the creations and made Myself known to them. So through Me they came to know Me."[15] The Prophet said, "Allah existed when there was nothing with Him." ʿAlī

15 *Ḥadīth qudsī* (sacred prophetic tradition) cited by ʿAjlūni in *Kashf al-khafāʾ*. According to ʿAjlūni, al-Qārī said: "Its meaning is correct according to Allah's saying, 'I did not create the jinn and humankind except to worship Me' (Qurʾān, 51:56). As Ibn ʿAbbās explained, 'to worship Me,' implies, 'to know Me.'" This *ḥadīth*, often quoted by Sufis, is sometimes related with the following wording: "I was a hidden treasure and I wished to be known, so I created the creations, and through Me they came to know Me."

said, "And He is now in the state He was then." He also said, "How true is the saying of the poet Labīd, 'Everything apart from Allah is surely unreal.'"[16] The Prophet ﷺ also reported that his Lord told him, "Neither My earth nor my heaven can contain Me, but the heart of My believing servant contains Me."[17]

These verses from the Qurʾān and sayings of the Prophet contain matters that cannot be discussed, and secrets that cannot be disclosed.

A small indication of this divine Beauty is enough for you
Then leave it guarded behind the veil of divine Majesty.

To put it another way:

As for the one seeking information of Layla's secret
I have sent him away in ignorance of her, with no certain knowledge
They say, "Inform us, for you are her custodian!"
But if I were to inform them, I would not have been the custodian.

It could also be said:

If you have not seen the newborn crescent moon
Submit to those whose eyes have seen it.

This is the end of what we wanted to gather in this chapter. With Allah is the success on the straight path, and to Him, the Glorified, is the return and final destination.

---

16 The poet Labīd b. Rabīʿa al-ʿĀmirī was well admired by the Prophet. This *ḥadīth* is on the authority of Abū Hurayra and reported in *Ṣaḥīḥ al-Bukhārī*.

17 *Ḥadīth qudsī* cited by Abū Ḥāmid al-Ghazālī in *Iḥyāʾ ʿulūm al-dīn* and by ʿAjlūni in *Kashf al-khafāʾ*.

CHAPTER 3

The Sphere of Spiritual Training in the Tijāniyya Order

With Allah is the success for what I say, and He is the Guide by His grace to the balanced path.

The sphere of spiritual training (*tarbiya*) revolves around two poles. The first is the establishment of the five ritual prayers in accordance with their proper conditions. The second is the invocation of blessing on the Prophet throughout the night and at the beginning and end of the day, with the intention of obeying Allah's command to do so; and this with magnification, reverence, and love (for the Prophet). This follows the strict observance of the obligatory daily litany (*wird*), which confirms the authenticity of being a Tijānī aspirant.

In the *Bughyat* (*al-mustafīd*), one of the main books of the Tijānī path, the illustrious spiritual master and venerable guide, the father of endowments, al-Sayyid ʿArabī b. Sāʾiḥ, said on the subject of spiritual training:

> The sphere of spiritual training and purification in this noble Muḥammadan path of ours is centered on five practices. The first is the obligatory daily litany, without which entry into this path is invalid, whatever a person's scholarly credentials. The second practice, linked to the first, is the attendance of the congregational remembrance; both the daily office (*waẓīfa*) and the weekly remembrance of "there is no god but Allah" (*haylala*) following the afternoon prayer on Friday.[1]
>
> The next essential practice is the attendance of the five daily ritual prayers. Certainly all the practices mentioned here require careful

1 Detailed descriptions of the obligatory Tijānī remembrances can be found in Appendix I of this book.

> observance of the stipulated conditions and proper modes of conduct in order to attain excellence and perfection. But of all the practices, the most imperative is the careful observance of the five daily prayers with their traditional elements as prescribed by the sacred law. You must comply with these stipulations as much as possible, perfectly fulfilling the basic elements of the prayer as established by customary practice.
>
> The next step in spiritual training is the aspirant's dedication to the invocation of blessing on the Prophet ﷺ (*ṣalāt ʿala al-nabī*) to the maximum extent possible, in all available moments. The best method thereof is with the Invocation of Opening what was Locked (*ṣalāt al-fātiḥ lima ughliq*), which is one of the most exalted and precious treasures.
>
> Lastly, the aspirant undergoing spiritual training must persist in loving affection for the Prophet ﷺ and gratitude to Allah the Most High. He should rely only on divine grace, the sole means of realizing sainthood. In this way, sainthood is realized without the necessity of secluded retreat (*khalwa*), excessive strenuous exertion, or any of the other methods of training adopted after the earliest centuries of Islam.
>
> The type of spiritual path described here is what our master (Shaykh Aḥmad al-Tijānī) ؓ was commanded to follow by the master of existence, the fountain of spiritual assistance and generosity ﷺ.

According to the *Jawāhir al-maʿānī*, the Prophet ﷺ informed our master and Shaykh (al-Tijānī) ؓ that he ﷺ was the sole intermediary between him and Allah the Exalted. He also told him that he ﷺ was definitely his spiritual sustainer, and the sole guardian in charge of his spiritual training in place of all the masters of the Sufi path. He informed him that not one of the spiritual masters had any favor to grant him, for everything he would receive from Allah would come by the assistance and mediation of the Prophet ﷺ. Then he advised him, "Adhere to this spiritual path (*ṭarīqa*) without seclusion (*khalwa*) or separation from people, until you arrive to the spiritual station (*maqām*) promised you, while maintaining your (current) condition, without deprivation, constriction, or a great deal of strenuous exertion."

The gnostic sage al-Buṣayrī, may Allah have mercy on him and be well pleased with him, indicated such a condition in verse:

> Excellence is not achieved by means
> Of excessive abstinence nor asceticism
>
> If it is said, "That is the medicine," say
> "The kohl of the healthy (for beautification) is not like the kohl used for eye-maladies."
>
> The one granted the right of disposal walks where he wills
> Others walk like stones, shackled.

Sīdī al-ʿArabī b. Sāʾiḥ said in *al-Jawāb al-Shāfī*:

> Whomever good fortune drives into entering this Aḥmadī spiritual path—whomever divine providence attracts to this chain of Muḥammadan transmission, whomever Allah's gracious favor has prepared to taste this great distinction, whomever His generosity has admitted to this marvelous store of treasure—his only remaining option is to bind himself to this greatest teacher (Shaykh al-Tijānī). He must finish himself at his door and cling to his threshold; and this by the path of love, submission, and acceptance of his will and judgment. He must apply himself with diligence and perseverance to this noble Muḥammadan litany, observing its conditions and keeping within its precise limits. Then Allah the Exalted may grant him success. And this can be achieved while he remains in his normal condition, without secluded retreat, strenuous exertion or conventional spiritual exercises of other kinds. Success will either come upon him suddenly or take him by surprise. Allah the Exalted will favor him by removing the veil from his heart, and he will become united with the spirituality of the Shaykh ﵁ or the spirituality of the Prophet ﷺ. Like this, his spiritual training comes by the flooding abundance (*istifāḍa*) from one of them, or from both of them together. *That is the grace of Allah, which He gives to whom He wills; and Allah is the owner of infinite grace* (Qurʾān, 57:21). This is the meaning of what is found in the *Jawāhir al-maʿānī* in regards to visualizing the presence of the Shaykh ﵁ or the Prophet ﷺ while performing the litanies for him who is able. The *Mīzāb al-Raḥma al-Rabbāniyya*, one of central books of the Tijāniyya, provides a lengthy explanation of this. The author said that Allah appoints for the aspirant a brother in the spiritual path, one who will take on himself the burdens of his spiritual training. Allah the Exalted will show the aspirant the secret of his specialness, and remove from between them the veil of the guide's human nature. He will travel with his guide toward Allah the Exalted, secretly and openly.

Whoever attains spiritual illumination (*fataḥa*) in this manner, his light will be complete, for the illumination is commensurate with the one followed. This is why Shaykh al-Zarrūq said, "Each individual's illumination and light is commensurate with the illumination and light of the one he follows." If someone receives directly from the texts of the Qurʾān and the Sunna, his illumination and light will be complete, provided that he is one of those qualified to receive from them. In doing so, however, he is failing to take advantage of the light and illumination of exemplary guidance. So the Imams were wary of this approach, to the point that Ibn Madīnī,[2]

2 ʿAlī b. al-Madīnī (d. 848, Iraq) was a prominent *ḥadīth* scholar who wrote a work on the companions of the Prophet, *Kitāb al-maʿrifa al-ṣaḥāba*.

may Allah have mercy on him, said, "Ibn Mahdī[3] used to go by the word of Mālik, while Mālik used to go by the word of Sulaymān b. Yasār,[4] and Sulaymān used to go by the word of ʿUmar b. al-Khaṭṭāb. The doctrine of Mālik is therefore the doctrine of ʿUmar ﷺ." Junayd, may Allah have mercy on him, said:

> Whoever did not hear the traditions by sitting with scholars of understanding and by receiving proper manners from the morally refined, he will have a corrupting influence on those who follow him. Allah the Exalted said, *Say, "This is my way. On clear evidence, I call to Allah, I and all my followers. Glory be to Allah! And I am not among the idolaters"* (Qurʾān, 12:108). And the Glorious One said: *And this path of Mine is straight, so follow it. Follow not other ways, lest you be parted from His way. This has He ordained for you, that you may fear Him* (6:153). So understand this well.

There is no harm at this juncture in presenting some of our poems on this subject, for they contain useful advice for the truthful person. Some of the following poetic verses concern the spiritual traveler (*sālik*), while some concern the enraptured one (*majdhūb*).

> Here is advice to anyone who would listen
> The one searching hastily for the path of the guided ones
>
> Let him take the spiritual path of the Shaykh (al-Tijānī), with permission from its people
> Not all of them are alike, so keep companionship with the one who follows
>
> This litany is nothing except asking for forgiveness, then declaring the Oneness of Allah
> Along with invoking blessing on the chosen one; and avoiding combining (litanies)
>
> And this with the condition of the heart's attentiveness, and leaving aside looking
> This way and that among the creation: listen well and protect yourself with this advice
>
> Do not rely on anything except the grace (*faḍl*) of our Lord
> Since you are full of limitations, you are of no benefit to yourself

---

3 ʿAbd al-Raḥmān b. Mahdī was one of the students of the Imam Mālik and his school of jurisprudence.

4 Sulayman b. Yasār (d. 733) was known as one of the seven scholars of Medina for his role in transmitting Islamic knowledge in the first century after the passing of the Prophet, peace be upon him. He was a slave of Maymūna bint al-Ḥārith (the wife of the Prophet), who attained his freedom and became the overseer of the Medina market during the time of ʿUmar b. al-Khaṭṭāb.

This by way of witnessing the favors of our God
So do not be taken with yourself, be humble

Think well of Allah, whatever may happen
And entrust your affairs completely to Him, let yourself be crushed in trembling fear

Blessings and peace from the Real throughout all time
On the first of existence, the most comprehensive being.

There are also the verses:

Leave behind your dwellings and the beautiful women
Leave the laden tables and soft couches

And keep company with any master successful in combining
The sacred law (*sharīʿa*) and the divine Reality (*ḥaqīqa*)

A brother, pious and ascetic, uninterested
In anything beyond what is right and proper

Beware of vain desires, and beware
The brother wrapped up in the passing of time

(To the pious brother) grant him sovereign leadership, since you know
There is none above him in this affair

Certainly he has obliterated external appearance
And has been made to arrive in the Presence of Holiness

Brought close, sanctified, and summoned
By divine permission, with the speech of everything near (to Allah)

When you see such a person, congratulations to you on the occasion of arrival
For seeing him is a most glorious treasure to the eyes

So the blessing of Allah, together with peace
Upon the chosen one, from the first to the last

These verses are also from us:

I advise you all, fellow companions
To be patient and forgive your brethren

Do not concern yourself with hearsay
Occupy the heart with the Prayer of Opening (*ṣalāt al-fātiḥ*)

So you will come to know, what our God wills is
Not what you might wish.

Also belonging to us:

Beware of your egos, if you would be rightly guided

The one going astray cannot harm the spiritual guide

Whenever you are told, "You are in error,"
Content yourself with knowledge of the Majestic Guardian Lord.

If the brother of communion should sever the communion
We fret not, for our communion is with the Guardian Lord

If you should happen upon what they say (foolishly), be generous
The brother of perfection is not diminished by words

Also there are the verses:

Muḥammad b. Mālik,[5] take up the remembrance
Of our litanies, and keep your heart attentive

Flee from the entirety of the creation and their influence
Seek your Guardian Lord, and abandon other than Him

This advice suffices you, and suffices
Every aspirant, for this is for you from me.

Also belonging to us are the verses:

O enraptured one, I advise you not to travel (this path)
For your own sake, rather (let it be) for the sake of the Real, Most High
Do not travel from nonexistence for (the sake of) nonexistence
For that is the work of a foolish, blind man

Indeed this lower world
All of it, including the world on high

Contains nothing that can bring benefit or cause harm
So in order to meet with the One who causes, leave aside the cause
Betake yourself to Allah, and do not trouble yourself
With other than Him, for this is the devotion (*taqwā*) of the saint

The matter is not about the discovery of created things
Or about peeping into unseen affairs

Allah is nearer, more exalted and more majestic
So spend your time in (seeking) Allah, the Glorious

Invoke blessings on the Messenger, the selected one
To him belongs the means of access, even before his selection

So blessings on him from Allah, so long as purity
Manifests in the heart's stillness.

---

5 Muḥammad b. Mālik was one of Shaykh Ibrāhīm's early disciples whom Shaykh Ibrāhīm was giving *tarbiya* at the time of the composition of these verses (Interview with Shaykh Muḥammad al-Māḥī Cisse, Medina-Baye, Kaolack, 13 March 2009).

There are also the verses:

> O enraptured one! If you do not travel the difficulties of the path
> Alas for you, you are incomplete; so continue seeking
>
> O seeker! If you do not become enraptured
> You remain veiled, so move and bestir yourself!
>
> The perfected one is he who combines
> The two states of rapture and seeking, it is he who progresses with speed
>
> May Allah include us among such perfected ones
> Who have become truly enraptured, but continued traveling the path
>
> By the blessing of the son of al-Ḥājj ʿAbd-Allāh (Niasse)
> The spiritual guide for every heedless one
>
> Appointed as Imam of the people of the Tijānī *fayḍa*
> The proof of gnosis (*ʿirfān*) in his age
>
> By the blessing of the saintly seal of our Tijānī company (*silk*)
> And by the blessing of his grandfather, the ʿAdnānī Prophet
>
> May the prayer of Allah be on him forever, eternity without end
> From before the beginning of an eternity without beginning
> For Allah is the One, Unique.

To us belong these verses as well:

> The arrived ones should not assume leadership
> Before permission is granted, for the secret is concealed
>
> I am pleased with the long silence
> For it is an indication of gnosis, and of an informed state
>
> There is no good in (mystical) interpretation at every gathering
> For secrets are removed with public mention
>
> May Allah, Lord of the Throne, care for us, by the secret of His secret
> Upon him the blessing of Allah, for he is the disposer.

He who desires something more on this subject should keep company with the men of spiritual distinction, and serve the people of spiritual perfection.

This concludes what we wished to gather in this chapter. With Allah is the success on the straight path, and to Him is the return and final destination.

Section III

CHAPTER 1

Warning against Criticizing the Spiritual Elite and Those for whom Criticism is Permissible

With Allah is all success, and He is the Guide by His grace to the straight path.

It is incumbent on the one who is concerned for his own safety and that of his religion to flee from becoming involved in criticizing Allah's saints. By criticism I mean slanderous defamation, showing hostility, looking for their weaknesses or mistakes, and denying, out of envy and hatred, the special favors Allah has bestowed on them. There is no reward for becoming involved in any of this except a painful punishment. Indeed, it has been said that the reward is no less than being forbidden from the presence of Allah, the loss of one's religion and an evil end. This is the result of waging war against Allah, the Vanquisher, the One endowed with severe force.

Imam al-Shaʿrānī said, "No one ever criticizes something coming from Allah's saints, those blessed with spiritual unveiling, except that he is punished with deprivation from the divine Presence. This is true even if the critic is himself a saint, no matter his spiritual station." He also reported the statement of his shaykh, Sīdī Muḥammad al-Maghribī: "If Allah wishes his servant to be stripped of faith by the time he dies, He will set him like a dog on one of His saints, bent on harming him."

The enmity of Allah's saints is the definition of "coming to a bad end." Indeed, Imam al-Ghazālī said in the *Iḥyāʾ* (*ʿulūm al-dīn*):

> Suppose you were to ask, "What most people are afraid of is coming to an evil end, so what is the meaning of coming to an evil end?" The answer would be: Coming to an evil end has two levels, the first more terrible than the second. The first, most horrifying level, is for the heart to be dominated with doubt or rejection of faith at the time of death's agony, so in the end, one's life-spirit is removed while in this state. In this case, the knot of doubt and unbelief forms a veil between him and Allah forever, causing permanent banishment and everlasting torment.
>
> The second, less horrifying level, is for the heart to be engaged in passions and lust for worldly things at the time of death's agony. One's heart is so engrossed that no room remains in his heart for anything else. So the life-spirit is removed while his attention and body are totally directed towards the world. So long as one's attention is directed away from Allah, a veil exists. And where there is a veil, there descends the punishment, since the blazing Hellfire does not seize any but those who are veiled from Him.

These words of Ghazālī are confirmed by the statement of Allah the Most High: *No indeed, but on that day they will be veiled from their Lord, then they shall enter the blazing Fire* (Qurʾān, 83:15–16). It has been said in *al-Ṭarāʾif wa al-talāʾid*:[1] "No matter how hard we look, we have yet to find a scholar of jurisprudence who denied and criticized the Sufis that Allah did not destroy with a disastrous end." ʿAlī al-Khawwāṣ, as reported in *Laṭāʾif al-minan*, said:

> Just as it is imperative to have faith in all the prophets without exception, to believe in them and love them, the same applies to the saints of Allah. If someone should believe in all the saints except one, without a valid legal reason, this person thereby has denied all the saints and declared war on Allah. Whoever rejects the claim of a saint has rejected the claim of a prophet.

Imam al-Shaʿrānī related:

> Ibn Labbān slandered Sīdī Aḥmad al-Badawī, may Allah bestow His mercy on him, and consequently lost his memory of the Glorious Qurʾān and other knowledge. But he persisted in seeking intercession from the saints, until he was guided to Sīdī Yaqūt al-ʿArshī, who came to the tomb of Aḥmad al-Badawī (on his behalf). He addressed him, "O you father of spiritual heroes! Restore to this wretched one

---

1 *al-Ṭarāʾif wa al-talāʾid bi karamāt al-shaykhayn al-Wālida wa al-Wālid* is the work of Muḥammad al-Kuntī, the son of Shaykh al-Mukhtār al-Kuntī, who dedicated the book to his parents. Researchers have had difficulty locating a copy of this work in its complete form (see Abdel Wedoud Ould Cheikh, "Harun Wuld al-Shaikh Sīdīyya," in Triaud and Robinson, eds., *Le Temps des Marabouts* [Karthala, 1997], p. 209); Shaykh Ibrāhīm's reference to this work is an indication of his extensive manuscript collection.

> his wealth!" Sīdī Aḥmad replied, "Only if he repents." So he repented, and his wealth (of knowledge) was restored to him.

He went on to say:

> Our Shaykh al-Shinnāwī informed me that a certain person criticized the birthday celebration of Sīdī Aḥmad al-Badawī,[2] so he was stripped of his faith to the point that he felt not the slightest trace of longing for Islam. So he sought help from Sīdī Aḥmad, who told him, "On the condition that you do not repeat your offense." He agreed, and was restored the garment of his faith. Then Sīdī Aḥmad asked him, "What was it you were criticizing?" The man replied, "The intermingling of men and women (at your celebration)." Sīdī Aḥmad answered, "That happens during the circumambulation of the Sacred House during the pilgrimage, and no one is prevented from performing the pilgrimage (because of that)."

Yadālī relates Ibn Ḥajar's saying, "The affair of the three individuals—Sīdī ʿAbd al-Qādir al-Jīlānī as a youth, Ibn Saqā, and Abū Saʿīd b. Abī Aṣrūn—who went to visit the spiritual succor (*al-ghawth*) provides a most forceful warning against negative criticism of the saints." Their story is well known, and will not be delved into now.[3]

The one who maligns the honor of a saint and is not immediately afflicted by misfortune should not assume his immunity from Allah's vengeance. Indeed, his affliction could be more disastrous, since he may be afflicted in his religion. Ibn ʿAṭāʾ Allāh has said, "The consequence (of maligning a saint) could be the hardening of his heart, or the development of incorrect views on religious issues, or difficulty in performing obligatory worship, or perpetual engagement in sinful acts. The refuge is with Allah the Most High." In *Laṭāʾif al-minan*,[4] Ibn ʿAṭāʾ Allāh has given the following wise counsel and guidance:

> Beware, O brother, of listening to those who slander and ridicule the Sufis so that you do not fall out of Allah's good pleasure and make yourself worthy of His displeasure. These Sufi people are with Allah, established in the reality of truthfulness, sincerity and genuine fidelity. With each breath, they vigilantly monitor their relationship with Allah. They have surrendered themselves completely before Him. They

---

2 Shaykh Aḥmad al-Badawī (d. 1276) became one of the most popular saints of Egypt. His *mawlid* (birthday celebration) in Tanta is attended by thousands every year.

3 Shaykh Ibrāhīm includes the full story in Appendix III, "The Ecstatic Utterances of the Enraptured Ones."

4 Both Ibn ʿAṭāʾ Allāh and Shaʿrānī authored books called *Laṭāʾif al-minan*. This is the first reference to Ibn ʿAṭāʾ Allāh's version, *Kitāb al-laṭāʾif fī manāqib Abī al-ʿAbbās al-Mursī wa Shaykhihi Abī al-Ḥasan*, a book which concerns the founders of the Shādhiliyya Sufi path.

> have abandoned seeking assistance for themselves in shyness of His Lordship over them, becoming content with His infinite provision. Indeed, He provides them with the fullest of provisions.
>
> It is He who fights for them against those who wage war on them, and it is He who vanquishes those who would triumph over them. Allah the Glorious has tested the Sufis with criticism from their fellow creatures, especially from the scholars of exoteric knowledge. You will seldom find anyone among them whose heart Allah has expanded to believe in a particular saint. He is more likely to say to you, "Yes, we know that the saints do exist, but where are they?" Then, if you mention one to him, he will proceed to refute the special qualities with which Allah has endowed him. And he will do so with eloquent arguments, but arguments devoid of the light of belief. So be on guard against the one who matches this description, and flee from him as you would flee from the lion. May Allah, by His gracious favor and noble generosity, include us among those who believe in His saints, for surely He has power over all things.

The author of *al-Rimāḥ* (ʿUmar al-Fūtī), distinguished for his deep probing of the sciences of divine Reality and the sacred law, has said:

> Among the disgusting attributes of negative criticism of Allah's saints is that you find such critics following the path of the Jews, the idolaters and the hypocrites. So there is no doubt that Allah the Exalted will make them suffer a punishment similar to the punishment He inflicts on these people, for they are characterized by the same attributes.
>
> Another bad behavior is their preference for immoral folk, such as disobedient sinners and transgressors, as companions.
>
> Another bad attribute is their maintaining that the practice of the kings, the tyrants, and their helpers constitute the true religion and the straight path. So the false path, in their minds, is that of the scholars concerned with the Hereafter, and the honorable men who call upon their Lord morning and evening, seeking His countenance.
>
> Another bad attribute is their belief that the blameworthy habits and heretical innovations inherited from misguided ancient traditions are part of the Sunna of Allah's Messenger ﷺ and his close followers.
>
> They also have the chronic malady of envy, which prevented the Jews from following the Prophet ﷺ for fear of losing their positions of leadership. Allah the Most High has said, *Or are they jealous of people for that which Allah has blessed them out of His bountiful grace?* (Qurʾān, 4:54). In another verse He said, *Have you not seen those who have received a portion of the Scriptures, when called to accept the judgment of Allah's Book between them, some turn their backs and pay no heed?* (3:23).

If you pay close attention, you will find in this magnificent speech of the saintly pole, ʿUmar al-Fūtī, that which uncovers the dangerous conditions of the negative critics. According to the *Baḥr al-mawrūd*:

> The solemn oaths extracted from us require that we (of the Sufi path) not accuse the righteous of lying when they inform us of something our minds consider impossible. The exception is if it contradicts the sacred law. Their purpose in telling us these things may only be to inform us that Allah is able to do anything He wills, nothing else.

As quoted in Shaʿrānī's *al-Yawāqīt wa al-jawāhir*, Shaykh al-Islam al-Makhzūmī[5] said:

> It is not permissible for a scholar (*ʿālim*) to criticize a Sufi unless he treads their path (*ṭarīq*) and sees him contradicting the Sunna. The scholar may not criticize the Sufis until he is fully acquainted with seventy matters, including but not limited to the following: 1) The understanding of their technical vocabulary: the essential and superficial manifestations; and the meaning of "Essence" (*dhāt*), and the meaning of the Essence of the Essence. 2) The knowledge of the presence of the Names and Attributes, and the difference between the divine Presences, and the difference between (the Presences of) Unique Oneness (*aḥadiyya*) and Singularity (*wāḥidiyya*). 3) The awareness of the secret of the manifest and the hidden, and of pre-eternity (*azal*) and perpetuity (*abad*), the world of the unseen (*ghayb*), the universe (*kawn*), the secret of witnessing (*shahāda*) and longing (*shawq*). 4) The knowledge of the subtle nature of things (*māhiyya*) and divine Identity (*huwiyya*); and of spiritual intoxication (*sukr*) and love; and how to recognize the one who is truly spiritually intoxicated, deserving forbearance, and one who is lying, deserving censure.

Shaykh Sīdī Mukhtār al-Kuntī, the Imam and magnanimous spiritual guide, said in his *Tahdbīl* [Appendix]:

> Quṭb al-Dīn al-Shīrāzī[6] said, "As for the riff-raff's censure of the (spiritual) elite, this does not detract from their high-ranking offices, just as the prophetic mission is not impaired by people accusing the prophets of sorcery, possession and the like."

---

5 ʿUmar b. Mūsā "Sirāj al-Dīn" al-Makhzūmī (fifteenth century) was head judge in Damascus. He was the student of Sirāj al-Dīn al-Bulqinī (d. 1403, Cairo), a famous *ḥadīth* specialist. Both Bulqinī and Makhzūmī came to defend Ibn al-ʿArabī, Bulqinī after originally criticizing him. Jalāl al-Dīn al-Suyūṭī listed al-Makhzūmī as one of his teachers.

6 Quṭb al-Dīn al-Shirāzī (d. 1311) was a Persian Sufi, mathematician, astronomer, and physician. His most famous work on Sufism is *Durra al-tāj li ghurratt al-dubāj*; but he also wrote on planetary movement and the possibility of heliocentrism.

According to Sahl b. ʿAbd-Allāh al-Tustarī,[7] "When you see someone reviling the saints (*awliyā*ʾ) and disparaging the talents of the bosom friends (*asfiyā*ʾ), know that person is at war with Allah and His Messenger." Abū Yazīd (al-Bisṭāmī) said, "The flesh of the saints is poisonous, and Allah's custom in dealing with those who hate them is well known. If someone defames them, Allah will afflict him before his death with a death of the heart: *So let those who go against the His command beware, lest a trial or painful torment befall them* (Qurʾān, 24:63)." Shaykh Abū ʿAbd-Allāh al-Qurashī[8] said, "If someone belittles a saint of Allah, his heart will be struck by a poisoned arrow, and he will not die until his faith has become corrupted."

According to Ghazālī, "If someone possesses no portion of the knowledge of the (Sufi) people, he is in danger of coming to a bad end. The least portion of this knowledge is to believe (in its existence) and to accept its possessors." He also said,

> The saintly Substitutes (Abdāl)[9] have isolated themselves in the extreme regions of the earth, concealing themselves from the eyes of the general public. They do not pay attention to the scholars of the time, whom they regard as ignorant of Allah. They see themselves as scholars, and consider avoiding the ignorant to be among the virtues of true believers, as Allah has said, *And turn away from the ignorant* (7:199).

Imam al-Nawawī has thus declared it strictly unlawful for any intelligent person to hold a bad opinion of Allah's saints. Rather, he must interpret favorably their sayings and actions, even if he does not attach himself to them or participate in their spiritual experiences. Shaykh Badr al-Dīn al-Zarkashī[10] said in this regard:

> Any formal legal opinion (*fatwā*) against the Sufi people should be ignored, unless its author has first made a thorough study of their technical terminology and understood the real meanings of their

7 Sahl al-Tustarī (d. 896) was an influential figure in the early development of Sufism. Qushayrī said of him, "He had no peer in his time for correct transactions and fearing Allah, and he was a man of miraculous occurrences."

8 Abū ʿAbd-Allāh al-Qurashī was an early Sufi known for his visionary encounters with Khiḍr, the mystical guide of Moses in the Qurʾān.

9 The Abdāl are so called because when one of them dies, Allah is said to substitute another in his place. According to a *ḥadīth* related on the authority of ʿAlī and found in Ibn Ḥanbal's *Musnad*, "The saintly Substitutes (Abdāl) are in Syria and they are forty men, every time one of them dies, Allah substitutes another in his place. By means of them Allah brings down the rain, gives (Muslims) victory over their enemies, and averts punishment from the people of Syria." Anas related a similar *ḥadīth* (found in Ṭabarānī), but without the reference to Syria.

10 Imam Badr al-Dīn al-Zarkashī al-Shāfiʿī (d. 1392) was a renowned scholar of Qurʾān and *ḥadīth* sciences and an expert on Shāfiʿī jurisprudence.

expressions. This is similar to the way the jurist ignores the *fatwā* of someone who may be an expert in grammar and *uṣūl*[11] but has not ascertained the realities of the Qurʾān and the Sunna and understood the basic principles of jurisprudence. The sciences of grammar and *uṣūl* are simply tools for studying jurisprudence; they are not jurisprudence itself, so mastery of them does not give a person adequate proficiency for issuing a *fatwā*. He who does so has only gone astray and is leading others astray.

The same applies to someone with no understanding of the technical terminology of the Sufi people. He regards them with suspicion when he hears them speak because he does not understand their intentions or the meaning of their symbolism. For example, he will be critical when he hears the statement, "The reality of repentance is repentance of repentance." But he will refrain from criticism when he realizes that what is meant here is the suspicion of the self with regard to false pretenses and the sincerity of repentance. Even more shocking is the statement, "The Lord is a servant and servant is a lord." When he hears this, the one with no spiritual experience will demand the execution of the one who says it. His response will be different, however, when he understands what is actually meant: namely, that when a servant devotes himself utterly to his Master, becoming extinct in His good pleasure and disappearing from his own presence into His Presence, the Lord empowers him with enormous power, putting the command at his disposal. If the servant says "Be!" it will be; and this by the creative power of the Creator Himself. As our Shaykh al-Jīlī[12] said in poetic verse,

> My command is by Allah's command. If I say: "Be!" It comes into being.
> Everything is at Allah's command, so judge the extent of my power!

Imam al-Ḥaramayn used to say:

> Suppose we were asked to provide a standard by which the statements of the Sufi people could be charged with unbelief or misguidance. Our response would be that this can hardly be determined, being a matter far beyond ordinary comprehension, a disgraceful course since the matter flows from the ocean currents of divine Oneness (*tawḥīd*). If someone is not endowed with comprehensive knowledge of the ultimate extent of the divine realities, he is not qualified to issue certificates

---

11 . The science of *uṣūl* refers to the methodology, or basic principles involved in ascertaining knowledge, jurisprudence or otherwise.

12 ʿAbd al-Karīm al-Jīlī (d. 1403) was born in Baghdad and traveled extensively throughout the Muslim world, including Yemen and India. He was a staunch defender of Ibn al-ʿArabī. His most influential work was *al-Insān al-kāmil*.

> of unbelief. Such a person is therefore like one digging his own grave, or one who sets himself on fire. His intention is to find unbelief in another person, but his arrow will pierce his own throat.

Nawawī used to say:

> Since Allah bestowed charismatic miracles (*karamāt*) on His saints as a branch of prophetic miracles (*muʿjizāt*), it is not surprising that He also granted them modes of expression that incapacitate even the most outstanding scholars, let alone others. This is because the saints derive their support from Allah and His Messenger. *So no soul knows what comfort is kept secretly in store for them, as a reward for what they used to do* (Qurʾān, 32:17).
>
> The saints, for the sake of Allah, have broken through the confines of their egos and ordinary conditions, so for them ordinary conditions have been rent apart. They have become the ones who give expression to Allah's Majesty with His consent, and who are protected by Allah's watchful care.

Shaykh al-Islam al-Makhzūmī said:

> A servant must master six subjects of knowledge before he engages in negative criticism (*inkār*):
>
> 1) The first such science to master is that of holding a good opinion (*ḥusna al-ẓann*) of Allah's saints, in order to draw near to their presence and to honor their goals. Surely, whoever has a bad opinion of the saints will be banished from their presence, and whoever is banished from their presence is banished from the presence of Allah and His Messenger. All lights will desert him and all secrets will elude him, for how can the lights be seen by someone whose eyesight is obscured by clouds of darkness and vexation. Allah the Exalted has said, *No indeed, their own deeds have cast a veil over their hearts* (Qurʾān, 83:14). And He described this state by saying, *Layer upon layer of darkness. If he reaches out his hand, he can hardly see it. And he to whom Allah has not given light, for him there is no light* (24:40).
> 2) He must have studied the miracles of the prophets (*muʿjizāt*) and the saints (*karāmāt*).
> 3) He must have studied diligently the books of Qurʾānic exegesis (*tafsīr*) and interpretation (*taʾwīl*), thereby acquiring intimate knowledge of the Qurʾān and the Sunna.
> 4) He must frequently contemplate the Qurʾānic verses and relevant reports concerning the divine Attributes. He must have studied thoroughly everything said on the subject by the righteous early believers and their successors. He must

know those who take the Attributes literally, and those whose interpretation is based on the Attribute's connotation; and who has the stronger and more convincing proof.[13]

5) He must frequently delve into the methods of the independent legal scholars (*mujtahidīn*), examining the proofs on which they rely, as derived from the Qurʾān, the Sunna and analogy (*qiyās*).
6) Most importantly, he must be familiar with the technical terms of the Sufi people. Such terms are used to explain a long list of realities, such as essential and superficial manifestations (*al-tajallī al-dhātī wa al-sūrī*), the complex of spiritual stations (*maqāmāt*), the types of mystical experience (*dhawq*), spiritual intoxication (*sukr*), obliteration (*maḥw*), annihilation (*fanāʾ*), and extra-worldly encounters (*mukāfaḥāt*). He who has not been promoted to such spiritual stations (*maqāmāt*), who has not smelled the perfume of the divine manifestations, who has not tasted of the fruit hanging suspended in the divine Presence, who has not sipped from the oceans of sainthood; how can he be permitted to judge their words, their conduct, or their spiritual stations? He is criticizing something from which he has been cut off. The saints are suns, whose rays are obscured by the cataracts of the eye. Their voices are not heard, except by someone who speaks in a whisper.

In *Baḥr al-mawrūd*, Imam al-Shaʿrānī said:

> We have solemnly vowed not to allow any of our (Muslim) brethren to criticize others for contradicting the teaching of a religious scholar. Criticism is only possible if one has comprehensive knowledge of the *sharīʿa* and its procedures, and has not discovered any difference of opinion (concerning the relevant contradiction). This (lack of diverging opinion) is something that happens very rarely. All of this is just to deter criticism without knowledge.

It has been related in Ṭabarānī that Allah's Messenger ﷺ once said: "My sacred way (*sharīʿa*) has come by 313 paths (*ṭarīqa*). Whoever meets his Lord through one of these paths, he will surely enter Paradise."[14] The

---

13 This refers to a long-standing debate in Islamic theology, whether or not Allah's Attributes (such as hand, eye, or the act of sitting on the throne) are to be taken literally or not.

14 Al-Ḥājj ʿUmar also cites this *ḥadīth* in a polemical exchange with Muḥammad al-Amīn al-Kanamī (of Bornu) and explains, "If you were actually informed about all these ways, my friend, and then discovered a rule contrary to them, then you would be in a position to object to them. Otherwise, acceptance (of an unfamiliar way) is better for you, and is to be preferred, since it is impossible to encounter someone who is informed on all 313 ways." See John Willis, *In the Path of Allah: The Passion of al-Ḥājj ʿUmar: An Essay*

greatest shaykh and saintly pole ʿAbd al-ʿAzīz al-Dabbāgh was recorded in *al-Dhahab al-ibrīz* as saying:

> You should know, may Allah enable you to succeed, that the illuminated saint is fully aware of the Truth and the best course (*ṣawāb*). He does not attach himself to any particular doctrine among the schools of jurisprudence (*madhāhib*). Even if these schools were to be shut down, he would be able to revive the sacred law. How could it be otherwise? The Prophet is not absent from him for the twinkling of an eye, and there is not an instant in which he is not witnessing the Real, exalted is His Majesty. In his ruling on issues of obligation and other matters, he is endowed with intimate knowledge of the Prophet's intent (*murād*) and the Will (*murād*) of the Real. This being the case, he is the authoritative source (*ḥujja*) over all others, and no one has authority over him since he is closer to the Truth than those who have not been illuminated. How then is it permissible to criticize someone with this description, saying he has contradicted the doctrine (*madhhab*) of so-and-so in regards to such-and-such?
>
> The one who criticizes the illuminated saint must surely fall into one of the following categories:
>
> He is ignorant of the sacred law. This is the usual condition of the negative critics. Criticism is of course improper for such a person, for the blind man can never deny the sight of one who sees. This person should rather work diligently to rid himself of his ignorance.
>
> He is a scholar (*ʿālim*) of one of the schools of jurisprudence, but ignorant of the other schools. Such a scholar is unlikely to engage in negative criticism unless he has become convinced that the truth is confined to his school alone, and thus has become unable to accept its existence elsewhere. There are both rightly guided scholars and those in error who have escaped this conviction. The rightly guided ones realize that the truth is found in every school, and see them all on the right path. Their view is that Allah's ruling may be determined in a variety of ways according to the reasoning of a consummate legal scholar (*mujtahid*). If one such scholar finds something prohibited, that is Allah's ruling; but if another finds it permissible, that is also Allah's ruling. As for the scholars in error (who do not limit themselves to one school), they believe Allah only has one ruling, but they do not restrict it to the doctrine of a particular school. The truth for them is limited to whatever a particular Imam says it is, or in another case

---

into the Nature of Charisma in Islam (London: Frank Cass, 1989), pp. 90–91. The *ḥadīth* was also cited by Shehu Usmane dan Fodio (d. 1817, Nigeria) in *Najm al-ikhwān*. The reader of the Arabic text should be aware that the 2001 Arabic printing of the *Kāshif* accidently omits the pronominal suffix on the word *rabb* (Lord or master), altering the meaning a good deal.

whatever someone else says it to be (but both cannot be right at the same time). The negative critic who falls into this category should be devoting his attention to ridding himself of his unsound conviction (instead of engaging in criticism).

There is also the case of the scholar who may be well-versed in the all four schools of jurisprudence.[15] He is unlikely to engage in negative criticism, unless he has become convinced that the truth is wholly absent from any of doctrines of the scholars (outside the four schools). He thus rejects scholars such as al-Thawrī, al-Awzāʿī, Ibn Jurayh, ʿIkrima, Mujāhid, Maʿbar, ʿAbd al-Razzāq, al-Bukhārī, Muslim, Ibn Jarīr, Ibn Khuzayma, Ibn al-Mundhir, Tāwūs, al-Nakhaʿī, Qatāda, and others from among the early generations (*tābiʿīn*) as far back as the Companions of the Prophet, ﷺ. This conviction is unsound. He should devote his time to something besides preoccupying himself with negative criticism of Allah's illuminated saints.

At this point, you will have understood that negative criticism of (the people) of the Reality (*ḥaqīqa*) is not permissible, except by one who has comprehensive knowledge of the sacred law (*sharīʿa*). No one has such comprehensive knowledge except the Prophet and his perfect inheritors, like the saintly succors (*aghwāth*) in every age. As for others, their silence is best for them!

Our discussion so far has concerned the criticism of the people of Truth (*ahl al-Ḥaqq*) by enlightened folk (*ahl al-fatḥ*). But the statements of the people of darkness and misguidance also are not unfamiliar to those who have to deal with them. A certain person once sought permission from his shaykh, that enlightened folk be able to criticize the saints, the people of Truth. He said, "My master, I will criticize them only where they depart from the sacred law. If I find someone on the right path, I will submit to him. If I find someone deviating from it, I will criticize him." His shaykh said, "I am afraid you are not equipped with all the tools needed to weigh (the truth). Having only some of the tools, but not others, your scale will not be accurate, pointing only to what other ignorant people have done before."

I once met an intelligent and shrewd man. He (told me he once) heard someone asking an illuminated saint, "Suppose someone making the ritual prayer forgets to recite a (second) Qurʾān chapter (*sūra*) after the "Mother of the Qurʾān" (the Opening chapter, *al-Fatiḥa*). He then forgets the compensatory act of (extra) prostration until after he has pronounced the final salutation. Is his ritual prayer invalidated by the omission of the compensatory act of prostration—on the basis of the assertion of there being three traditional rules (*sunan*) concerning the (recitation of the second) *sūra*—or does it remain valid? Shaykh

15 Thus Ḥanafī, Māliki, Shāfiʿī, and Ḥanbalī.

al-Khaṭṭāb[16] and others considered it invalid,[17] but the commentators of the *Risāla*[18] considered the prayer still valid."

The illuminated saint responded to the petitioner by saying, "The truth from Allah is that the omission of the (second) *sūra* absolutely does not require compensatory prostration. If someone does make the compensatory prostration because of it, then his ritual prayer is rendered null and void."

The illuminated saint happened to be blind and illiterate. Nonetheless the inquirer knew him well and recognized his lofty spiritual station. When he heard the response, he knew it was the truth and had no doubt. But the shrewd man (who related the story to me) was filled with doubt and suspicion. He said to the inquirer after leaving the saint, "This man is an ignoramus. Do you see how he was ignorant of Allah's judgment on this simple problem? He said that no act of compensatory prostration is incumbent on someone who omits the (second) *sūra*, even though Ibn Rushd[19] included it among the established customary practices, similar to the audible and inaudible recitations." The inquirer replied that the illuminated saint does not attach himself to a particular school (*madhhab*), but that he revolves with the Truth wherever it revolves. The shrewd man, who was a student of the classical Islamic sciences, said, "We do not depart from the teachings of our Imam Mālik." The inquirer responded to this by saying, "The statement made by the illuminated saint has been reported by Ashhab[20] on the authority of Mālik, as related in *al-Tawḍīḥ*. It has also been reported on the Imam's authority that the (recitation of the second) *sūra* is indeed highly recommended, but it is not one

---

16 Possibly Abū al-Khaṭṭāb al-Kalwadhānī (d. 1116, Baghdad), a prominent independent scholar (*mujtahid*) of the Ḥanbalī school.

17 Others would include ʿAbd al-Raḥmān al-Akhḍarī (d. 1585, Algeria), in whose classic summary of Māliki *fiqh* it is said (translation by Aisha Bewley), "If someone forgets the (second) sura, or recites aloud or silently in the nafila (supererogatory prayer) and remembers after the ruku', he continues and does not owe any prostration, which is not the case with the fard (obligatory) prayer." See Bewley, trans., *Summary on 'Ibadat according to the School of Imam Malik by Sayyidi 'Abdu'r-Rahman al-Akhdari* (available at http://bewley.virtualave.net/akhdari.html, accessed 12/29/2009).

18 The *Risāla* of Qāḍī ʿAbd-Allāh b. Abī Zayd al-Qayrawānī (d. 996, Fes) is one of the primary treatises on jurisprudence from the Māliki school and has been commented on by many scholars of jurisprudence since.

19 Qāḍī Muḥammad Ibn Rushd (d. 1198, Andalusia), known in Europe as Averroes, was an important figure for Mālikī jurisprudence, though he became more famous as a philosopher and physician. His book, *Bidaya al-mujtahid* is still studied by advanced students of Islamic jurisprudence.

20 Ashhab b. ʿAbd al-ʿAzīz al-ʿĀmirī (d. 819) was one of the primary students of Imam Mālik and author of a book called *Mudawwana*, though this should not be confused with the more famous *Mudawwanna* of Ashhab's student Saḥnūn.

of the prescribed traditional practices (requiring compensation for being missed). This was also the doctrine (*madhhab*) of Shāfiʿī ﷺ. He considered it one of the virtuous customs, but not one of the prescribed traditional practices, and if someone performs prostration to compensate for its omission, his prayer is rendered null and void. Furthermore, our question to the saint was only about the identification of the truth without qualification, not about the well-known doctrine of Mālik's school in particular. He answered our question, and his answer happened to coincide with a report from Mālik as well as the school of Shāfiʿī, ﷺ. So what charge can be brought against the response of the saint?" To this, the shrewd person dried up, not knowing what to say.

This is the way of negative critics and their habitual style. You will not find anything with them except complete inadequacy. One of the great jurists among our shaykhs, ﷺ, once engaged me in a discussion in this connection. He said to me one day, "O *Fulān* (unnamed person), because of my affection and perfect love for you, I have decided to give you some wise counsel."

I responded, "My master, I regard you with love and respect, and I am wholly at your disposal."

He said, "Everyone has criticized a certain man whose spiritual illumination and sainthood you have confirmed. How is it possible that all the people deny him, but you alone believe in him? It is inconceivable that you alone should be on the side of truth." He spoke at some length on this matter, but this was the gist of what he had to say.

Then I said, "My master, in order for your wise counsel to be complete, first please answer the question I will put to you. If you can answer it, your wise counsel will be complete and the reward will be with Allah."

He ﷺ said, "Ask whatever you wish."

So I said, "My master, have you met this man, heard his speech, and conferred with him about a particular matter, and then become convinced of the peoples' judgment in this regard?"

He said to me, "I have never met him, and I have never even seen him."

Having discarded shyness on account of the intimacy and loving friendship between us, I said, "My master, in your case, it is clear to me you have reversed the proper course. You have tried to bring certainty out of speculation. Certainty can never be found in speculation. But in the pursuit of certainty, you have satisfied yourself with speculation, doubt, even lies and false slander."

He said to me, "Explain what you mean by this."

I told him, "When you teach jurisprudence (*fiqh*), the source material is available to you directly, from *al-Mudawwana*,[21] or the *Tabṣira* of al-Lakhmī,[22] or the *Bayān* of Ibn Rushd,[23] or the *Jawāhir* of Ibn Shās,[24] and other encyclopedic works of jurisprudence. You do not need to rely on the reports of intermediaries, even if they be (people like) Ibn Marzūq,[25] al-Ḥaṭṭāb,[26] or the author of *al-Tawḍīḥ*.[27] Consulting them (only) would be like using secondary sources to form your opinion when the established and authoritative sources are available to you. You will never find certainty by intermediary reports. Taking a later intermediary report is only exchanging a stronger opinion for a weaker one, for the closer the intermediary report in time to the author of the source text, the more reliable the opinion, for these transmitters are certainly closer than we are to the original sources. Moreover, the text available to the earlier intermediaries was transmitted by an unbroken chain from the original sources. We, however, have no direct chain of transmission to the original source, or the authentic text at our disposal. Just as your own text has been tampered with, how can you be certain that the report of al-Ḥaṭṭāb, for example, is attributable to the original sources?

"As for all of you being content with speculation in the place of certainty, know that this man you have been informed about is present, living with you in the town. There is hardly any distance between the two of you. If Allah enables you to love him and submit to his guidance, happy is your acquaintance with him, a happiness after which there is no misfortune! So Allah has made it possible for you to find him. Now you can believe in him and enjoy happiness and prosperity, or you

---

21 The primary work on Mālikī *fiqh* is by ʿAbd al-Salām b. Saʿid, known as Saḥnūn (d. 854, Fes). Saḥnūn was the student of both Ibn Qāsim and Ashhab, both renowned students of Imam Mālik.

22 ʿAlī b. Muḥammad al-Ribʿī, known as al-Lakhmī (d. 1092, Fes), was another towering figure in early Mālikī jurisprudence.

23 Ibn Rushd's (d. 1126) *Bayān al-taḥṣīl wa al-tawjīh wa taʾlīf fī masāʾil al-mustakhraja* is a massive commentary on the *Mustakhraja al-Qurṭubī*. Note this Ibn Rushd (Muḥammad b. Aḥmad) was the grandfather of the more famous Ibn Rushd al-Ḥafīd (the grandson).

24 The *Jawāhir al-thamina* of ʿAbd-Allāh b. Muḥammad, known as Ibn Shās (d. 1188, Egypt).

25 There were two famous Mālikī jurists named Ibn Marzūq, the one, Muḥammad b. Aḥmad Ibn Marzūq (d. 1379, Egypt), was the grandfather of the second, Muḥammad b. Aḥmad b. Muḥammad Ibn Marzūq al-Tilimsānī (d. 1439, Algeria).

26 Muḥammad b. Muḥammad ʿAbd al-Raḥmān al-Ḥaṭṭāb (d. 1547, North Africa) was the author of *Muwāhib al-Jalīl sharḥ Mukhtaṣar Khalīl.*

27 Probably the *Tawḍīḥ al-aḥkām min bulūgh al-marām*, a commentary by ʿAbd-Allāh b. ʿAbd al-Raḥman al-Bassām on Ibn Ḥajar al-ʿAsqalānī's *Bulūgh al-marām*. The work concerns *ḥadīth* relating to issues of jurisprudence.

can deny him and be turned away. In either case, certainty will come to you, and the darkness of doubt will leave your heart. Then, if you become satisfied to accept this prosperous condition and prodigious blessing (of submitting to the saint), the benefit of which is undeniable, you will be enabled to push away the corrupt and the liars. You are usually dissatisfied with speculation, forming your own opinion on matters with little recourse to intermediary reports. Why have you not followed the same course here? Certainty this domain is to your benefit and brings clear good fortune. So does this not constitute on your part a reversal of the right path?"

After listening to all of this, he said, "Your argument has affected me profoundly. By Allah, I will never be able to respond to this! Bear witness that I am repenting to Allah, Almighty and Glorious is He."

Then I said to this shaykh, "If you must follow someone else's authority in this, you should follow my lead for two reasons. First, you acknowledge my discernment (*baṣīra*) in things. Second, you are aware that I spent many years in the company of this remarkable man, until I learned from him things that no one else knows. As for the corrupt liars, most of them, like you, have never met him. They rely on baseless hearsay, and their only reason (for such slander) is their own exclusion and forsakenness. May Allah grant us success by virtue of His Grace, Favor, and Generosity."

He said, "There is nothing else left for you to say!"

Subsequently, another jurist, in fact one of the shaykhs of the jurist above, approached me. He said to me, "I have heard you are someone who can provide decisive proof against any disputant." He turned to the same jurist and asked, "Did you not inform me of a certain person who told you such-and-such?" He said, "Yes." And they both said, "You have transformed us both with this speech of yours." These two jurists are among the leading scholars of their age, and no one can match them.

As for the negative critics of lesser ranks, most of them rely on baseless hearsay, as previously mentioned. The shrewdest of them supports his criticism by saying, "We used to be associated with so-and-so, and he was not like that!" meaning the man being criticized. Such a critic has not understood that flowers come in various colors:

And date-palms, like and unlike, which are watered with the same water. And We have made some of them to excel others in fruit. Surely in that there are signs for those who understand (Qur'ān, 13:4).

Once the Shaykh ⬥ and I entered a garden in the spring time. He gazed for a while at the diversity of flowers and splendors, then turned his head to me and said, "If someone wants to understand the diversity (*ikhtilāf*) of the saints—their dissimilarity in regard to spiritual stations and states, while all being righteously guided and able to instill sweetness in the hearts of the people—let him contemplate the diversity of these flowers and splendors and the sweetness each one is able to instill in the heart." When the critic says, "Sīdī so-and-so, whom we knew well, was not like this," his implication is that Allah's mercy has been restricted to the saint he knew. He has narrowed something expansive. The Bedouin who urinated in the mosque (and was excused by the Prophet despite the protests of his companions) said, "O Allah, have mercy on me and have mercy on Muḥammad, but do not have mercy on anyone else." So the Prophet, Allah bless him and grant him peace, said, "You have narrowed something wide!" The critic's assumption in this case is that no one can be a recipient of Allah's mercy unless he is like the saint he knew. But there are different types of saints. And this principle is applicable to the saint he knew as well, for certainly this saint was not like the one that preceded him. If the critic disapproves of the third (most recent) saint because he was not like the second (whom he knew), he has also disapproved of the second, because he was not like the first.

I have gone to great length discussing this subject of negative criticism. I have delved into the arguments with the jurists, only trying to benefit them and all seekers of knowledge (*ʿilm*). I only want to give them sound advice, out of loving affection for them, for they have plagued themselves with negative criticism of the pure, virtuous, and righteous masters throughout all centuries and ages, in all the deserts, villages, and cities. This chapter has covered fully (the reasons) for their criticism. If anyone among them is fair-minded and considers carefully what we have said here, he will come to his senses. The truth will become clear to him, and the right direction apparent. I have been reluctant to dispute with the jurists concerning the saints. I assumed they were basing their criticism on sound foundations, but when I put them to the test, I found the matter as I have described it. Allah is the Guide to the right path. There is no lord other than He, and there is no blessing (*khayr*) other than His blessing. In Him have I placed my trust, and to Him do I turn in repentence.

The reference to the saintly succor (*ghawth*) earlier in the chapter calls for an account of some of the spiritual stations with which he is endowed. The greatest shaykh, rare like red sulfur, the most magnificent secret, Ibn al-ʿArabī al-Ḥātimī, said:

> Every spiritual station (*maqām*) is a cover (*ḥijāb*) for whoever is below it, because they obtain assistance through it. Every one among the men of spiritual distinction obtains assistance through someone whose sphere of influence (*dāʾira*) is more comprehensive in scope than his own. So the one granting assistance becomes the cover for the one receiving assistance. All of them receive assistance through the saintly

> savior-pole (*al-quṭb al-ghawth*), for he is the cover for all of them. He obtains assistance through one of four prophets: Idrīs, Ilyās, Jesus, or Khiḍr. They in turn receive assistance through the supreme cover, ﷺ, who receives it from the Absolute Presence. He supports all of his deputies (*nawāb*), in both the visible and invisible worlds, according to this capacity. In fact, he assists every individual according to that individual's readiness, not according to his own capacity to provide assistance. Indeed, the Prophet is a vast overflowing ocean, with no beginning and no end. If someone allows the eye of his heart to look at the ocean of his effulgence (*fayḍ*) and the wide diffusion of his sublime assistance—observing how all existent beings receive from him, with or without intermediaries—his heart will be astounded and his mind bewildered. The saintly pole (*quṭb*) is in charge of sixteen worlds comprehensively, this lower world (*dunyā*) and the afterlife (*akhīra*) each being one of them. He supports all of these worlds and their inhabitants. Our Prophet is the one who furnishes him with this complete assistance, and who gives him the strength to bear this station (*maqām*).

This venerable Imam al-Ḥātimī, despite the depth of his experience in the sciences of gnosis, was not aware of the Hidden Presence through which the saintly pole derives support. He mentioned that the pole's support comes from the spirituality (*rūḥāniyya*) of the prophets. In fact, the saintly savior-pole (*al-quṭb al-ghawth*) receives support (from the Prophet) through the ocean of the greatest assistance, that of the hidden pole and well-known Seal of Muḥammadan Sainthood: he being our master, the means of access to our Lord, Shaykh Sīdī Aḥmad b. Muḥammad al-Tijānī al-Ḥasanī. May Allah be pleased with him and may He benefit us by him, Amen.

This marks the end of the chapter. With Allah is the success on the balanced path, and to Him, Glorious is He, is the return and final destination.

Chapter 2

Seeking the Shaykh, his Character and the State of Discipleship

Anyone who recognizes what the divine Presence requires of every human being, while observing the states of human nature, will be aware of the necessity of seeking the shaykh of spiritual guidance (*murshid*). In the words of the scholar and distinguished spiritual guide, Nāẓim:

> The aspirant must accompany the shaykh well versed in the routes to Allah (*masālik*)
> Who will protect him from the dangers of the spiritual path.
>
> Seeing the shaykh will remind him of Allah
> And he will escort the servant to his Master.

In *al-Durr al-thamīn*, the scholar Badr al-Dīn al-Mayyāra[1] explained, "As for the words, 'keeping company with a shaykh well versed in *masālik*,' the Arabic term *masālik* is the plural of *maslak*, the noun of place corresponding to the verbal noun, *sulūk* (traveling, seeking, or conduct). It thus signifies the path (*ṭarīq*) that arrives to Allah the Exalted."

In his commentary on the saying of the gnostic, Sīdī Ibn ʿAṭāʾ Allāh, "But for the battlegrounds of souls, the journey of the travelers could not be realized," Shaykh Muḥammad Ibn ʿAbbād (al-Rundī) had this to say:

> On this path, the aspirant (*murīd*) cannot dispense with the companionship of a shaykh who is a genuine spiritual guide, one who

---

1 Badr al-Dīn al-Mayyāra, or Abū ʿAbd-Allāh Muḥammad b. Aḥmad (d. 1662) was a prominent teacher of *ḥadīth* and Mālikī jurisprudence in Fes, Morocco. The work mentioned here was primarily a theological tract, the full title being, *al-Durr al-thamīn wa al-mawrid al-maʿīn fī sharḥ al-murshid al-muʿīn ʿala al-darurī min ʿulūm al-dīn.*

has completed his own training and rid himself of vain desires. The seeker must submit himself to him, persist in obedience to him, and comply with everything he instructs him to do, without deliberation, interpretation, or hesitation. As has been said: "If someone does not have a shaykh, Satan will become his shaykh."[2]

Indeed, Abū Yaʿlā al-Thaqafī[3] states that even if a man acquired all the sciences and kept company with all classes of people, he could not match the attainment of the men of distinction, except by means of spiritual training received from a shaykh, imam, or instructor (*muʾaddib*) of sound advice. If a person does not receive his education from someone who gives him commands and prohibitions, showing him the faults of his actions and his personal stupidities, his training will not result in attainment to the stations of spiritual progress (*maqāmāt*). Thus Sīdī Abū Madyan said, "If someone does not receive his training from those who are well trained, he whom he follows is even more corrupt than the follower." The author of *Laṭāʾif al-minan*[4] has said:

> The only guidance to follow is that of a saint to whom Allah has directed you, and has revealed to you the special quality with which He has endowed him, so the presence of his human nature has disappeared from you in the discovery of this special quality. You will therefore give him free rein, for he will transport you on the path of right guidance. He will make you aware of the frivolities of your lower self, in its hidden depths and its secret caverns. He will guide you to the total concentration on Allah, and teach you to flee from everything apart from Him. He will travel beside you on your road until you arrive in the presence of Allah. He will acquaint you with your personal misconduct and make you aware of Allah's mercy toward you. The recognition of your personal misconduct will help you to escape from it, and cease to justify it in the reliance on your own means. The knowledge of Allah's mercy toward you will help you approach Him, offer thanks to Him, and remain in His presence at all times.
>
> Perhaps you will ask, "Where is there anyone who fits such a description? You have spoken of a person more astonishing than a marvelous mythological bird (*ʿanqāʾ*)!" But the knowledge of where such guides are to be found is not necessary for you to know. All that you need is the sincerity in seeking them. If you are utterly sincere, you

---

2 This last statement is traced to Abū Yazīd al-Bisṭāmī (d. 874, Persia). See Section I, Chapter I, where a slightly different version is quoted from al-Bisṭāmī: "Whoever does not have a teacher (*ustadh*), his imam is Satan."

3 Likely Abū ʿAlī al-Thaqafī (d. 940), a famous Sufi and jurist from Nishapur, Persia. Thaqafī was the leading shaykh of the "Malāmatiyya," and was the teacher of al-Sulūkī, who taught Sulāmī, who taught Qushayrī.

4 This is the work of Shaʿrānī, the full title of which is: *Laṭāʾif al-minan wa al-akhlāq*.

will surely discover a spiritual guide. As Allah has said in two verses of the Qurʾān, *Is it not He who answers the needy when they call unto Him?* (27:62), and, *For if they had been sincerely truthful with Allah, it would be better for them* (47:21). So if you are in dire need of someone who will lead you toward Allah, like a thirsty person in dire need of water or a frightened person in dire need of protection, you will find your goal closer even than your having to ask. If you are in dire need of Allah, like the mother in need of her lost child, you will find the Real near you and ready to answer you. You will find the arrival in the divine Presence easy for you, and the encounter with the Real will be facilitated for you.

The author, may Allah have mercy on him, also speaks of the shaykh as one of Allah's gracious favors and gifts to the aspirant. But this is provided that the aspirant is sincere in his quest, and exerts himself to the full extent of his ability in the effort to follow his master's advice rather than the illusory whims of those without knowledge. At this point (of sincerity), Allah will establish him with the proper conduct in dealing with his shaykh, who will then guide him toward the loftiest degrees and the highest levels of attainment. According to Sīdī Abū Madyan:

> The shaykh is someone whom your essence (*dhāt*) has acknowledged with preference, and whom your innermost being (*sirr*) has acknowledged with reverence. The shaykh refines you with his exemplary character, trains (*addaba*) you by bowing his head in silence, and illuminates your inner being with his radiance. The shaykh is he who gathers you in his presence and preserves you in his absence.

According to the *Laṭāʾif al-minan*:

> Your shaykh is not someone from whom you hear; your shaykh is someone from whom you receive. Your shaykh is not someone whose expressions confront you; your shaykh is the one whose signals become secreted within you. Your shaykh is not he who summons you to the door; but he who removes the veil between himself and you. Your shaykh is not the one whose words challenge you; he is the one whose spiritual state uplifts you.
>
> Your shaykh is the one who releases you from the prison of your vain desires, and brings you into the presence of the Lord. Your shaykh is one who never ceases to polish the mirror of your heart, until the lights of your Lord become manifest therein. He will encourage you toward Allah so that you will set off toward Him, and he will be with you until you arrive in His Presence. He will not cease to be by your side until he has cast you between His hands, and thrust you into the light of the divine Presence. Then he will say to you, "Here you are and here is your Lord."

As for the rules of proper conduct for the shaykh in relation to the disciple and for the disciple in relation to the shaykh, they are frequently discussed in the books of the Sufi masters. One of the most eloquent and succinct account is that provided by Imam Abū al-Qāsim al-Qushayrī:

> The stipulation incumbent on the disciple is that he must not breathe a breath without his shaykh's permission. If someone disagrees with his shaykh, even concerning the drawing of a breath, either in private or public, he must quickly recognize his error. Concealed disagreement with the shaykh is more serious than public disagreement, because the former amounts to treachery. If someone contradicts his shaykh, he will not smell the fragrant aroma of truthfulness. If someone is guilty of anything of the kind, he must make haste to apologize and seek pardon for the contradiction and treachery he has committed, and his shaykh will direct him toward the means of atonement for his offense.
>
> If the disciple returns to his shaykh with sincere remorse, it is incumbent on his shaykh to make up for his disciple's shortcomings with his own magnetic spiritual energy (*himma*). Since the aspirants are manifestly dependent on their shaykhs, it is obligatory (*farḍ*) on the shaykhs to spend of the power of their spiritual states to make up for the shortcomings of the disciples.

The definitive statement on this subject is the response of our Shaykh, the hidden pole and well-known isthmus, or *barzakh* (Shaykh Aḥmad al-Tijānī), as has been recorded in the *Jawāhir al-maʿānī*:

> As for the question about seeking the shaykh (Shaykh Aḥmad al-Tijānī was asked): Is it strictly incumbent on every single individual, or on some but not others, and what is the reason in either case? The Shaykh replied: The quest for the shaykh is not a duty prescribed by the sacred law (*sharīʿa*), with the inevitable consequence of reward for its performance and punishment for its abandonment. There is nothing of this kind in the sacred law.
>
> But it is obligatory from the standpoint of common sense, just as the search for water is imperative for the thirsty person, for common sense tells him he will perish if he does not find water to satisfy his thirst. Such a perspective relates to what has been mentioned: namely, human beings have only been created for the worship of Allah, and the dedication to the divine Presence by the rejection of everything apart from Him. The seeker has recognized his own inability to make his lower self comply with the need to enter the divine Presence, and has recognized the weakness of his own self in what is required to enter the divine Presence, in terms of fulfilling the necessary duties and proper modes of conduct. He has come to know he has no refuge or safety from Allah if he should remain attached to his lower self, following its vain passions and turning away from Allah.

From this perspective, it is clearly necessary for him to seek the consummate shaykh. This necessity is strictly a matter of natural logic, not a rule derived from legal texts, since what is mentioned in the legal texts is only the duty to fulfill the rights of Allah, both outwardly and inwardly. This duty is obligatory on every single individual among His servants, and no one has any legally valid excuse for neglecting it, nor has he any excuse for his subservience to vain passions and his inability to control his lower self. There is nothing in the sacred law except the incumbency thereof, and the penalty incurred by violating the prohibition of neglecting that duty.

This is what is contained in the sacred law, so the shaykh who must be sought is the shaykh who is qualified to provide instruction, he being the one who teaches the nature of the legal observances demanded of the servant, in terms of performance of the commandments and avoidance of the prohibitions. Every ignorant person must seek out the shaykh, for no one can do without him.

There is nothing other than this from a legal perspective that requires seeking out the shaykhs. But it is definitely obligatory from the perspective of common sense, since the ignorant person is comparable to an invalid. If such a person has resigned himself to sickness, on account of his inability to cure himself by his own means, one can only conclude that he wishes to stay sick. On the other hand, if the patient should demand how he may obtain perfect health, one would tell him to seek out the expert physician. Indeed, the expert physician is familiar with the sickness and its cause, he knows the medicine that will cure it and knows how this medicine should be applied—how much should be taken, in what manner, how often, and under what circumstances.

As for the distinctive characteristics of the consummate shaykh, Sharīshī[5] has said in his *Anwār al-sarāʾir*:

The shaykh certainly has signs, for without them, the aspirant is merely adrift in the nights of vain passions. If the shaykh bears no distinguishing mark, either outwardly or inwardly, the aspirant will be swallowed by the depths of the ocean, for the sick man is in the state closest to perdition if there is no doctor informed of his condition. The signs of the shaykh are that he is not inclined to follow vain passions. For him, the ephemeral world (*dunyā*) has been folded up, and the hereafter has been spread before him.

---

5 The Andalusian scholar Abū al-ʿAbbās Aḥmad al-Qaysī al-Sharīshī was the author of *Sharḥ al-maqāma al-ḥarīrī*, a commentary on a well-known work of Arabic literature.

Our Shaykh (Aḥmad al-Tijānī)—our means of access to our Lord, the hidden pole and the renowned Seal of Muḥammadan sainthood—has this to say in the *Jawāhir al-maᶜānī*:

> As for the true nature of the consummate shaykh, he is the one for whom all the veils have been removed from the perfect beholding of the divine Presence, with visual perception and certain realization. The process begins with attentive awareness (*muḥādara*), which entails observing the realities from behind a thick curtain (*sitr*). Next comes disclosure (*mukāshafa*), which entails observing the realities from behind a thin curtain. Then comes witnessing (*mushāhada*), which entails the manifestation of the realities without a veil (*ḥijāb*), but with particularity. Last comes the direct vision (*muᶜāyana*), which entails observing the realities without veil or particularity, with absolutely no surviving trace of variation or alteration. This is the station of eradication, absolute truth, destruction, and the annihilation of annihilation. There is nothing in this station except the direct vision of the Real, in the Real, for the Real, and by the Real.
>
> So nothing remains except Allah, and nothing besides Him
> There is nothing to be added and nothing to be separated.
>
> Then comes true existence, in which one is able to distinguish the degrees (*marātib*) on the basis of direct knowledge (*maᶜrifa*) of their particularities, requirements and exigencies, and everything to which they are entitled. One will know as well the source for each degree, the reason for its existence, its intended purpose, and the return of its affairs. This is the station of the servant's comprehension of his personal identity and his knowledge of all its secrets and particularities; as well as his knowledge of the divine Presence, its grandeur, majesty, exalted attributes and perfection. And this knowledge of his will be the product of direct experience and indubitable vision.
>
> Vast deserts must be traversed for the holder of such a degree. In spite of the hardships, the effort is perfectly worthwhile, since the Real has granted him specific authorization to provide right guidance to His servants, and has charged him with the task of directing them toward the divine Presence. This is the shaykh who deserves to be sought, for he matches the description of "great" given in the *ḥadīth* reported by Abū Juḥayfa: "You must consult the scholars, mingle with the wise, and keep company with the great."
>
> Whenever the aspirant comes across someone who matches this description, it is obligatory upon him to place himself at his disposal without any personal choice or volition, like a corpse in the hands of its ritual washer. He must rely on the shaykh to deliver him from the distress in which he has been immersed, and transfer him to complete and pure serenity; and this through the contemplation of the divine

Presence and nothing else. The disciple must purge himself from all other options or desires for anything besides this. Whenever the shaykh advises or commands him to do something, he must beware of asking questions like, "Why?" "How?" "In what manner?" "For what purpose?" This is the cause for the shaykh's disgust and rejection. He must be firmly convinced that the shaykh is more aware of his best interests than he is, and more familiar with the means by which they can be achieved. He must therefore go along with him in everything, for the shaykh will only act for the sake of Allah and with Allah's help, in order to extract him from the darkness and lust of his lower self.

As for the shaykh who matches this description, how can he be contacted and how can he be recognized? The answer is that such shaykhs are many, and most of them are in the major cities where they have taken up residence. But as for recognizing them and contacting them, this is a difficult problem, obscure like red sulfur (*kabrīt al-aḥmar*), since they have blended with the styles and customs of the common people. If someone should question them about this state of affairs, they will shun him and chase him away, swearing to him they are in no way connected to the subject.

They have a compelling reason for this, because the regular order of existence has been disrupted by the Will of the Real, something no one can deny. Now, the only concern for every individual is the pursuit of his selfish interests and carnal desires, in total disregard of the divine Presence, and of the duties and proprieties he ought to fulfill. For the common folk at the present time, the pursuit of the saints is motivated only by their desire to achieve wayward objectives, such as the enjoyment of the world's pleasures and lusts, protection from calamities, and comfort in this abode. They are content to leave alone their stubborn addiction to terribly dangerous causes of perdition, like committing abominable major sins whose punishment is damnation in the Hellfire. In this state, they have no exit from their prison, and no way to return to the divine Presence.

When the knowledgeable people of Allah became aware of the extent to which this applied to the common people, they concealed themselves from ordinary folk, and kept away from them with every means and in every situation. So they began to live in the deserts and wastelands, but then the Real required them to live again among the common people, due to matters with which the Real obliged them by His decree, and no one can dispute with Him concerning His decree. Since they could no longer find any justification for avoiding the common people by escaping to the deserted areas, nor could they determine how to correct them and bring them back into the divine Presence, they became like one who lives in a society of ignorant fools. They pelt him with stones, but he is compelled to endure with patience and reside in their midst. This being the trap in which they found themselves, the saints concealed themselves from the common people, and kept them at bay in every possible way.

The common folk sometimes happen to smell the fragrant perfumes of the saints wafting from behind the veils and apparently joining them in their vain pursuits. Because of this, the gnostics use various pretenses designed to confuse them. To keep their real identity hidden from the common folk, they pretended to be involved in abominations such as adultery, fornication, obscene lying, drinking alcohol, or suicide, which condemn their perpetrator to Allah's displeasure and wrath.[6] There was absolutely no substance to these antics of the gnostics: they appeared to be violating the sacred law, but in reality were only thereby concealing themselves from the common folk, in order to conceal their spiritual station and to permit their good conduct free rein.

If you have understood this well, you will realize that the truthful and the liars are mingled together in the public arena, so the former cannot be distinguished from latter, and it is quite impossible to recognize the consummate gnostic, except in extremely rare cases. However, the possibility does exist, because some of the gnostics have manifested themselves in visible forms that are perfectly consistent with the sacred law. Suppose that someone should manifest himself in such a form, laying claim to being a shaykh on the strength of his being known to guide people toward Allah, for his abstinence from, and lack of interest in this world and its people, together with evidence of the success achieved by other people with his help. If it is clear to the aspirant that the person in question matches such a description, he must commit himself to him at the very moment of their encounter. What is normally required of the aspirant, however, is that he should refrain from committing himself until he has studied the transmission of reports about him from reliable sources and people closely acquainted with him. Then, if he clearly matches the above description, the aspirant should commit himself to him, but otherwise not.

He who wants to connect himself with a shaykh in the present age, but finds it difficult to recognize him—afraid of being ensnared by the liars—he must devote his attention to Allah with absolute sincerity. He must turn to Him with a steadfast heart and humbly entreat Him to reveal the consummate shaykh capable of delivering the disciple

---

6 Shaykh Aḥmad al-Tijānī is here of course referring to the Malamatiyya, or those who call blame on themselves by pretending to commit reprehensible behavior or be otherwise ordinary men. The earliest recorded mention of the term is from ʿAbd al-Raḥman al-Sulamī al-Nishāpūrī (d. 1021), in his *Risāla al-Malāmatiyya*. For more on the subject, see Kenneth Honnerkamp (introduction and translation), "Stations of the Righteous and The Stumbling of those Aspiring: Two Texts from the Path of Blame," in *Three Early Sufi Texts* (Louisville, KY: Fons Vitae, 2003).

from his affliction. He must beg Allah to guide him toward his shaykh, to enable him to comply with his command, and to let him plunge into the depths of the shaykh's ocean. This should be done with the knowledge that there is no other means at his disposal (for delivering him from affliction).

More importantly, he who is unable to discover the perfect shaykh should devote every available moment to invoking blessings on the Prophet (*ṣalāt ͑ala al-nabī*), ﷺ. This is the most appropriate, beneficial, speedy, and elevated way to reach the desired goal. The prayer on the Prophet must be performed with perfect manners, presence of mind, and the heartfelt conviction that one is sitting in front of him ﷺ, and this must be done persistently. If a person persists in this, yearning for Allah like the thirsty man yearning for water, Allah will take him by the hand and draw him close. Allah will entrust him with a perfect shaykh to be guided by the hand. Or Allah may entrust him directly to His Prophet to be trained. Or Allah may simply remove his obstacles and open for him the door of arrival. And all this is the result of the servant's dedication to invoking blessings on Allah's beloved ﷺ. Offering blessings on the Prophet is the most effective of all means of access to Allah: no one who has practiced it with constancy has ever been disappointed in the quest for Allah.

As for the question about choosing the shaykh, and weighing his actions and spiritual states, it is not proper. No one who has engaged in that has ever achieved success, for this closes the doors to Allah. If a person is bent on this, he applies it to all his fellow creatures and Allah will show him deficiency in every creature, so he will not feel comfortable with anyone. Trusting the shaykh is a divine command which Allah has placed in the hearts, so the shaykh's companion cannot detach himself from him, even if he considers him guilty of a thousand sins. If the aspirant is sincere, however, the reward for his sincerity is that he will see nothing in his shaykh except that which puts his heart at ease, for he will encounter none but the truthful shaykh. As for the aspirant whose heart is not clean, he will see only that which he finds repugnant and inadequate, causing him to run away and take flight.

Shaykh Sīdī Mukhtār al-Kuntī said:

> There is no rational explanation for (the insight contained in) the shaykh's verbal expressions. The shaykh's statements and actions are based on divine faculties of wisdom. This is the meaning of the Sufi saying, "If someone does not understand our spiritual states, he cannot understand our verbal statements." Even if the shaykh should command you to do something in which you expect disaster, you must plunge headlong into it. Success will be found in it. Essential meanings are manifested to the shaykhs in forms peculiar to a particular individual.

Should your shaykh put you to the test, stand firm beneath the scourge of his trial. He will then deliver you from the prison of tribulation. Then the burden of such trials will become light with your knowledge that the tests (*miḥan*) of the shaykhs are actually acts of kindness (*minaḥ*). Remember the case of Abū Lubāba,[7] for his is a perfect example of proper behavior (*adab*).

You are the shaykh's brother, and he is the inheritor. Allah is the liberator, and the goal is one. Beware of impatient haste. This (submission to the shaykh's command) presents a difficult challenge, since it marks the end of the life you have known and deprives you of illusionary hopes. The shaykh only tests you to draw you near. He only draws you near is to make you humble. He only makes you humble to shake you up. He only shakes you up to plant you. He only plants you to make you blossom. He only makes you blossom to make you bear fruit. He only makes you bear fruit to make you thrive. He only makes you thrive so that you can repent. He only causes you to repent so that you become his deputy in withholding and giving, in hardship and comfort.

Beware of walking beside him with shoes on your feet, or while wearing any signs of luxury, unless he permits you to do so because of a valid excuse. You must not sleep in a house in which he is sleeping, nor spit in his presence, nor blow your nose, nor stretch your legs, nor show a great deal of curiosity, nor sit on his carpet. You may handle his clothes for the sake of blessing, for the masters used to avail themselves of their shaykh's garments for that purpose. This was likewise the habit of the Companions of the Messenger ﷺ in respect to his clothing, his hair, his cleansing agents, the remnants of his ablutions, his blessed saliva, his perspiration, his riding animal, his drinking vessel, the sites of his ritual prayer, and his private seclusion. They witnessed their effectiveness in the prevention of physical ailments and spiritual evils. Surely you are aware of the time Khālid b. Walīd returned to the fray of battle only to rescue a turban he had lost which contained some hair of the Prophet. When he was told that a large number of Muslims had died because of his rejoining the battle, he said, "I did not return for the sake of the turban itself, but only to keep the hair of Allah's Messenger from falling into the hands of the polytheists, and so dispossess them of its blessing (*baraka*)." The way the Sufis wear the

---

7 Abū Lubāba b. ʿAbd al-Mundhir was a companion of the Prophet who, after realizing he had betrayed the Prophet during the siege of the Banū Qurayza in Medina, tied himself in the mosque for six days until Allah sent revelation to forgive him, *And others have admitted their sins, those who have mixed a righteous deed with an evil one. Perhaps Allah will turn to them in mercy. He is Forgiving, Merciful* (Qurʾān, 9:102).

tattered gown (*khirqa*) is another example.[8] This is worn when they recognize a certain perfection in themselves, for it represents the flag of the army's commander.

Habits worth cultivating include respect for everything connected with the shaykh, even a dog, and affection for his disciples, his kinsfolk, his friends, and all his favorite things, even including types of food and clothing. Every form of reverence and respect for the shaykh is actually for Allah. The Messenger once said, "You must venerate the shaykhs, for the veneration paid to them is part of the reverence due to Allah."[9] He also said, "Commensurate with the reverence will be the blessing." The disciple must therefore emulate the righteous early believers (*salaf*) in their respect for the shaykhs, both outwardly and inwardly. He must also call to mind the intention (of his commitment), in a state (of reverence) received and learned from his shaykh. For his shaykh receives and learns from none but Allah and His Messenger, since he is the inheritor and deputy of the Messenger.

Allah says, *If an idolater seeks your protection, then protect him so he may hear the word of Allah* (Qurʾān, 9:6). And He says, *Nor does he (the Prophet) speak from his own desire* (53:3). All this is to dismiss the illusionary allegories (concerning the shaykh), and to set firm the decree of divine Reality (*ḥukm al-ḥaqīqa*). The Prophet ﷺ said: "You must say, 'Our Lord, to You belongs the praise!' Allah will respond on the tongue of His Prophet, 'Allah listens to those who praise Him!'"[10]

The shaykh is he who polishes you with his virtuous character traits, trains you by bowing his head in silence, and enlightens your inner being with his radiance. Zarrūq listed four things that must be included in the disciple's conduct: compliance with the prescriptions, abstinence from opposition, constant perseverance, and earnest pursuit of the goals. How beautifully put! You should also know that four things are bound to come to the disciple in the beginning: hurtfulness and honorable reception, and offenses and good deeds. So respond to the hurtfulness with patience, and to the honorable

8 The shaykh's bestowal of the *khirqa*, sometimes referred to as the "Sufi cloak," on his disciple indicates a symbolic recognition of his spiritual attainment, though in some cases it is bestowed simply to benefit the disciple in his spiritual progress. Hujwīrī claims the wearing of the *khirqa* is Sunna, quoting a *ḥadīth*, "See that you wear woolen clothing so that you might find the sweetness of faith." For more information see Jamal Elias, "The Sufi Robe (*Khirqa*) as a Vehicle of Spiritual Authority," in Gordon (ed.), *Robes and Honor: The Medieval World of Investiture* (New York: Palgrave, 2001).

9 Reported by Ibn ʿAdī in *al-Kāmil fī duʿafāʾ al-rijāl*; also cited by Daylamī in *al-Firdaws*.

10 These two formulaic statements are repeated in the ritual prayer when coming up from bowing. The citations in this paragraph are meant to remind the reader of Allah's proximity to the purified human being, most especially the Prophet and his inheritors, the shaykhs.

> reception with appreciation, without transgressing the limits of the sacred law in going to excess or falling short. Respond to the offenses with exoneration, without disputation or contempt; and to the good deeds with unhesitating approval. The spiritual health of the shaykh is damaged by the plague of conceit and pretentiousness, the roots of (the disciple's) aversion and protest. The remedy is repudiation (of the ego) and surrender.
>
> The conditions of being a shaykh are genuine knowledge (*ʿilm*), unambiguous spiritual experience (*dhawq*), lofty aspiration (*himma*), being in a state of divine satisfaction (*ḥāla marḍiyya*), and possessing penetrating spiritual insight (*baṣīra*).
>
> The secret of this all resides in the disciple's sincerity (*ṣidq*), for this is his real shaykh.

After some further discussion, Shaykh Mukhtār said:

> Know, dear brother, that the proof of Allah's wanting you to arrive (*wuṣūl*) to Him, and to commune (*ittiṣāl*) with Him, is your connection with the shaykh capable of spiritual training. He allows no one to reach the shaykhs, unless He wishes him to reach Himself. This means that no one can reach Him, except someone who connects himself with the shaykhs; and no one is veiled from the shaykhs except he who has become veiled by them. Allah the Exalted said, *Such was Allah's custom for those who passed away of old, and you will not find any change in Allah's custom* (33:62).

Tāj al-Dīn Ibn ʿAṭāʾ Allāh said in this regard, "Glory to Him who did not entrust His saints with guiding others, except for the purpose of guiding to Himself."

The one who understands what has been set forth above will surely comprehend the necessity of seeking the shaykh capable of spiritual training. As for the disciple's proper conduct in his company, this subject has been addressed by the words of the venerable shaykhs we have transmitted here. And know that the golden words of the perfected ones are not of trifling value!

As previously explained,[11] a true believer cannot profess the cessation of the Prophet's assistance, and the saints are the inheritors of the prophets. Thus, the spiritual training conveyed from Allah to His creatures will never be discontinued. In the first epoch, He used to send the prophets with training and guidance. Whenever an intermission (*fatra*) occurred,

---

11 See the end of the introduction to the *Kāshif*, where Shaykh Aḥmad al-Tijānī is quoted, "If anyone imagines that all of the Prophet's support for his community came to an end with his death, he is ignorant of the Prophet's degree, and guilty of treating him indecently. If he does not repent of this deluded conviction, he is guilty of dying as an unbeliever."

He would end it by sending a Prophet, until He sealed the mission of prophecy by sending the Seal of the Prophets and the Imam of Envoys, our master Muḥammad ﷺ. He then began to dispatch the gnostics, endowing them with special authorization to provide spiritual training. Whenever an intermission occurred, He would end it by dispatching a consummate saint as a spiritual guide. There are thus two kinds of intermission: that in the age of unbelief, which was abolished by sending a Prophet; and that in the age of Islam, which is abolished by dispatching a shaykh of spiritual training. Such is indicated by the *ḥadīth*s: "The religious scholars of my community are like the Prophets of the children of Israel," and "Allah will dispatch a reviver (*mujaddid*)."[12]

According to one traditional report, when the Prophet Muḥammad ﷺ died, the earth wept and said, "My God and Master! I am left here with no prophet to walk on my surface until the Day of Resurrection." Allah then informed the earth, "I shall set upon your surface members of this Muḥammadan community whose hearts are attached to the hearts of the prophets, and I shall not deprive you of them until the Day of Resurrection." May Allah include us among the greatest and most exalted of them, in the station facing the flower of His creation, ﷺ.

This ends the chapter. With Allah is the success on the straight path, and to Him the Glorious is the return and final destination.

12 The full *ḥadīth*, on the authority of Abū Hurayra and contained in the *Sunan* of Abū Dāwūd and Tirmidhī, is as follows: "Allah will send to this community at the advent of every century one who will renovate its religion for it."

CHAPTER 3

The Vision of Allah

With Allah is the success for what I say, and He guides by His Grace to the straight path.

Know that the Sufi people speak with their own technical vocabulary, not limited to the external meaning of words. No one understands them except those who have drunk from what they have drunk. They might be criticized by those blind of sight, deprived of the light of belief (*taṣdīq*) and thus unable to confirm what the Sufi people claim. The critic also may base his criticism on untenable arguments. He has not experienced the thing he is criticizing in order to know how to refute it.

If the critic hears someone claiming to have had the vision (*mushāhada*) of the Real, he will cite the verse, *The eyes do not perceive Him* (Qurʾān, 6:103). But the one seeing does not lay claim to ocular perception. He does not notice the eyes (*abṣār*), or anything else. The one who sees anything else besides Him who is seen (*mashhūd*), and is convinced of its existence, even a speck of dust, has associated a partner with Allah. Of all people, the one laying claim to the vision of Allah is completely convinced of Allah's statement, *The eyes do not perceive Him, but He perceives the eyes* (6:103).[1]

The one denying (the vision of Allah) also might try to prove his argument by citing the verse of the Qurʾān:

> *When Moses came to the place appointed by Us, and his Lord had spoken to him, he said, "My Lord, show (Yourself) to me, that I may look at You!" He said, "You will not see Me, but look at the mountain—if it stays still in its place, then you will see Me." When his Lord manifested Himself to the mountain, He made it crumble to dust. And Moses fell down in a*

1 This verse can be translated in a variety of ways. A popular alternative (Pickthal and others) reads, *Vision comprehends Him not, but He comprehends all vision* (6:103).

swoon. When he recovered consciousness, he said, Glory to You! To You I turn in repentance, and I am the first of the believers (7:143).

You should understand, however, that there is no incongruity between His saying, *You will not see Me*, and His saying, *Then you will see Me.*

Know that when a servant comes near to Allah through supererogatory good works, Allah enraptures (*yajdhabu*) him, loving him with a forceful attraction (*jadhban*). In this (rapture), the servant is not aware of himself, or anything else; not what came before, nor what will come after, not any part of himself, nor the whole of himself. He becomes absent from his personal witnessing (*shuhūd*), and is consumed in the intensity of His Master's summoning, Glorious and Exalted is He. In this state, he witnesses the divine Presence (*ḥaḍra*), as before the world and after the Hereafter, as before the before and after the after. This Presence has no beginning and no end, no above and no below, no right and no left, no explanation (*kayf*) and no definition, no name and no attribute, no going forward and no going back, no connection and no separation, no going in and no going out, no sensation and no realization (*idrāk*), no incarnation (*ḥulūl*) and no fusion (*ittiḥād*). The lover becomes extinct in his Beloved. And he becomes extinct to his own extinction (*fanāʾ*). Nothing remains except the divine Selfhood (*al-huwiyya*).

Words may emerge from the one entrusted with this (state), which those with no spiritual experience consider preposterous claims. Nonetheless, his conduct in this is perfect in the sight of Allah. In this regard, Abū Madyan al-Ghawth said:

> Do not blame the drunkard in his state of intoxication
> Our intoxication has relieved us of the burden of formality.

The one entrusted with this spiritual position (*maqām*) is not claiming something deceitful, he has only realized the desire of the Real, Glorious and Exalted is He. There are no words and no means of expression for the vision (*ruʾya*) claimed by those of spiritual distinction, for here all explanation comes to an end. Certain verses of the Qurʾān and sayings of the Prophet ﷺ provide evidence of this, and these will be presented in due course. If we assume for the sake of argument that they indeed are claiming the (ocular) vision of Allah, they are not claiming it in this world or the next. In this way, the vision of Allah is among the acceptable possibilities, according to the venerable scholars following the doctrine of the Sunna. Their opinions in this regard will be presented shortly. For now, let me say simply that Allah's statement, *The eyes do not perceive Him*, is a generalization that permits a particularization (*takhṣīṣ*). Since the miracle (*karāma*) of the saint particularizes the definitive sciences, how could it not be the same for a theoretical generalization? Once this has been established, we will present what the scholars have said, beginning with the jurists and moving on to the Sufi imams.

The erudite scholar Badr al-Dīn Mayyāra said in his commentary on Ibn ʿĀshir:[2]

> The creation's vision of our Lord, Glorious and Exalted is He, is among the legitimate possibilities according to the people of Truth (*ahl al-ḥaqq*). Since He exists—and it is permissible for every existent being to be seen with the faculty of vision—He can also be seen, but in a manner that befits Him, full of blessing and exalted is He; without spatiality, physicality or relativity.
>
> Some try to force the issue, as if issuing summons to see and encounter Him, forgetting that the authority belongs to Him. Unsatisfied with the middle course, they fluctuate between extreme proximity and extreme distance. They should know that He is the One who comes at speed, and there is no incumbency on Him to be seen, since He has already accepted non-appearance.
>
> It has been accepted as permissible to know (*yaʿlamu*) our Lord, Glorious and Exalted is He, in a manner befitting His Majesty, without delimitation. In a similar way, it is permissible to see Him, Glorious and Exalted is He, with the vision (*baṣar*), in a manner befitting his Exaltedness. It is impossible for this vision of Him to be tainted with confusion or distraction, because of the impossibility of any confusion being connected with Him. If the seer would associate the vision (*ruʾya*) of Him with any confusion whatsoever, the seer would not be permitted even a glance. For how could confusion be associated with Him, when in one glance He unveils Himself to the seer with the infinite manifestations of His Essence, without restriction or delimitation. If it were otherwise, He would not be distinguishable from the other things to which confusion is attached.

As recorded in Shanawānī's commentary on the *Mukhtaṣar* of Bukhārī,[3] Laqānī[4] said in one poem:

> He can indeed be seen with the eyes (*abṣār*)
> But without any explanation (*kayf*) or limitation

And in *al-Iḍāʾa*,[5] the author said:

---

2 This is the same text by Mayyāra (d. 1662, Fes) mentioned earlier, *Mukhtaṣar al-durr*, which is a commentary on *al-Murshid al-muʿīn* by Ibn ʿĀshir (d. 1631, Fes).

3 The *Ḥāshiya al-Shanawānī ʿala mukhtaṣar Ibn Abī Jamra li al-Bukhārī* is the commentary of Azhar University Rector Muḥammad b. ʿAlī al-Shanawānī (d. 1818) on Ibn Abī Jamra's abridgment of Bukhārī's *ḥadīth* collection.

4 Ibrāhīm al-Laqānī (d. 1631) was a famous theologian of the Ashʿarī school who authored the *Jawhara al-tawḥīd*.

5 The *Iḍāʾa al-dujanna fī ʿaqāʾid ahl al-sunna* is a versified theological tract by Shihāb al-Dīn Aḥmad al-Maqarrī (d. 1632, Tlemcen, Algeria). Maqarrī was a prominent scholar of *ḥadīth*, jurisprudence, theology, and history. He served as one time imam and mufti

The vision of Allah with the eyes (*abṣār*)
Is possible according to the people who can see (*ahl al-istabṣār*)

Sīdī Aḥmad al-Ṣāwī, the shaykh, the imam of exemplary aspiration, said in his *Ḥāshiyya ʿala al-Jalālayn* in reference to the verse, *The eyes do not perceive Him* (6:103):

> Jalāl said, "That is to say, 'You do not see Him.' This (denial) applies in particular (circumstances) since (it is accepted) that the believers will see Him in the Hereafter, as indicated by His words, *On that day faces will be radiant, gazing upon their Lord* (75:22–23). There is also the prophetic tradition of the two Shaykhs (Bukhārī and Muslim): 'Verily you shall see your Lord, as clearly as you see the full moon at night.'"
>
> It is said that the word "eyes" or "vision" (*abṣār*) in the verse, *The eyes (abṣār) do not perceive Him*, is the plural of *baṣar* and thus refers to the sense of sight, the ability to see; meaning, applying to the physical eye itself. Here the verse retains its general applicability in the sense that the physical eye cannot see Him, neither is this world nor the Hereafter. This does not contradict the ability of the believers to see Him in the Hereafter, for this vision is without any means (*kayf*) or delimitation. The possibility of seeing Allah is confirmed by both traditional proofs, based on the Qurʾān and the Sunna, and rational proofs. This latter includes the fact that Allah (when Moses asked to see Him on the mountain) made the vision of Him dependent on the stability of the mountain; and what is dependent on the possible is possible. Another rational proof is the fact that Moses would not have asked for the vision of Allah if it were impossible. It is unthinkable for a prophet to ask for the impossible, since doing so would be a form of pagan ignorance (*jahl*), and a prophet cannot conceivably be guilty of pagan ignorance. Another rational proof is the fact that Allah is said to be an existent entity (*mawjūd*), and it is permissible for an existent entity to be seen. So it is permissible to say Allah can be seen, contrary to the doctrines of the Muʿtazilī,[6] Murjiʾa,[7] or Khawārij,[8] who say that the vision of Allah is impossible.
>
> The argument of those who reject the vision of Allah is based on a superficial understanding of the verse of the Qurʾān quoted above.

---

of the Qarawiyyin mosque/university in Fes before traveling to lecture in Cairo and Damascus; he is buried in the latter.

6 The Muʿtaziliyya originated in eighth century and strove to reconcile Islamic doctrines with the Hellenistic framework of reason.

7 The Murjiʾa was an early theological school emerging soon after the passing of the Prophet; they believed, among other things, that no Muslim would enter Hellfire.

8 The Kharārij take their name from "going out" of the community by rejecting the authority of ʿAlī b. Abī Ṭālib, and any later imam who they believed went against the commandment of Allah. They were responsible for the assassination of ʿAlī.

> They assert that the vision (*ru'ya*) entails physical contact between the beams of the beholder's eye and the object seen. Thus, for them, the object must necessarily be a physical body, and of course Allah is exalted beyond physicality. This argument is refuted by what we have presented earlier. Moreover, the necessary connection (between eye and physical object) is only the usual method, and not entirely logical. So it is permissible to absent oneself from the usual.

After some more discussion of this subject, Imam al-Ṣāwī went on to say, "As for the vision (*ru'ya*) of Him, the hearts of the gnostic sages (*ʿārifīn*) experience it in this world—meaning the heart's witnessing of Him in everything—and it is permissible. Indeed, it is their quest, their goal, their purpose, their yearning." He also recited the poetic verses:

> Grant us the vision of You, (to include us) among Your beloved ones
> The vision to which are rushing the hearts of the saints.

And he went on to say: "This also applies to the vision of Him experienced in a dream." Shaykh Sīdī al-Mukhtār al-Kuntī said in *al-Kawākib*:

> The Prophets and the saints see Allah before everything, the righteous see Allah in everything, and the believers see Allah after everything. That is why Ibn ʿAṭā' Allāh said, "If someone looks at the existent phenomena, but does not see Allah before them or after them, the presence of the lights has eluded him. Those to whom He appears before every existent being, they are the ones who learn from Him about His creation. Those to whom He appears in every visible object, they are the ones who annihilate all existing things in the experience of witnessing Him. Those to whom He appears after the sight of His creation, they are the ones who learn about Him through the effects of His Power and the perfection of His attributes." Imam al-Rāzī said: "The manifest (*ẓāhir*) and the hidden (*bāṭin*) are two names that have been joined together, and it is not correct to separate them except when applied to Allah the Most High. He is the Manifest with regard to His Presence (*wujūd*) and Majesty (*majd*). He is the Hidden by virtue of the negation of definition and explanation. The Prophet ﷺ indicated this in the best possible way when he said: "You are the Manifest, and nothing can obscure You; and You are the Hidden, and nothing can unveil You."[9]

According to Imam al-Qushayrī's *Risāla*,

---

9 *Ḥadīth* reported in Muslim, Ibn Māja, Abū Dāwūd, Tirmidhī and the *Musnad* of Ibn Ḥanbal. A literal translation of this *ḥadīth* would read: "You are the Manifest, and nothing is above You; and You are the Hidden, and nothing is below You." This was among the favorite supplications of Shaykh Ibrāhīm Niasse, included after the daily congregational *waẓīfa*.

Suppose someone asks if it is possible to experience the vision (*ruʾya*) of Allah with the eyes (*abṣār*), today in this world, by virtue of the saintly miracle (*karāma*). The honest answer is that there is no general consensus on this matter. I once heard Imam Abū b. Fawrak[10] relating that Abū al-Ḥasan al-Ashʿarī stated two opinions on the subject in *Kitāb al-ruʾya al-kabīr*.

I might add here that the Prophet ﷺ certainly saw Him on the Night of Ascension (*al-isrāʾ*). What is possible to be a miracle (*muʿjiza*) for the Prophet is also possible to be a miracle (*karāma*) for a saint. There is hardly any difference between prophetic and saintly miracles, according to the opinion accepted as correct. The erudite Imam, Shaykh Muḥammad al-Yadālī, said in his *Sharḥ khātima al-taṣawwuf*:

> Anything that has been a miracle (*muʿjiza*) for a prophet can also be a miracle (*karāma*) for a saint, for there is hardly any difference between the two types (of miracles). This is the correct opinion, and the doctrine of the majority, preferred by Ghazālī, Fakhr (al-Dīn) al-Rāzī, Bayḍāwī, Nasafī, Ṭūsī, Imam al-Ḥaramayn (al-Juwaynī), Ibn al-Ṣalāḥ, Ibn Fawrak, Ṭabarī, Abū Naṣr al-Qushayrī, ʿIrāqī, Yāfiʿī, Zarkashī, and Ibn Jamāʿa.[11] One of their proofs is the prophetic tradition: "There is many a dusty and disheveled person who, if he entreats Allah, Allah will answer his prayer."[12] The answering of the prayer is universal for any such petitioner, even including the revival of the dead and similar things.

In *Ikmāl al-ikmāl*, the most competent scholar Ubayy[13] cites the words of Qarāfī[14] in response to the question, "If the saint's report of a miracle (*karāma*) is accepted as an extra-ordinary phenomenon in regard to the

---

10 Ibn Fawrak was among the teachers of Qushayrī. He was known as the "second Shāfiʿī" for his excellence in jurisprudence. He was also a famous early theologian of the Ashʿarī school.

11 The mention of these scholars together, all prominent theologians (among other things) is meant to indicate that this opinion was agreed upon by the greatest Muslim theologians.

12 This is a variation of a *ḥadīth* on the authority of Anas b. Mālik related by Tirmidhī: "It is possible that a disheveled, dusty person, with not many belongings, not noticed among people, if he asks of Allah, Allah will grant his prayer."

13 Ubayy al-Mālik (d. 1423) wrote his book *Ikmāl Ikmāl al-Muʿlim* as a commentary on Qāḍī ʿIyāḍ's *Ikmāl al-Muʿlim bi fawāʾid Muslim*, which was itself a commentary on Imam al-Mazari's *al-Muʿlim bi fawāʾid Muslim*, which was itself a commentary on the *ḥadīth* collection by Muslim.

14 Shihāb al-Dīn Aḥmad al-Qarāfī (d. 1285) was an Egyptian Mālikī jurist who is considered one of the greatest legal theoreticians of the thirteenth century. For more on this figure, see Sherman Jackson, *Islamic Law and the State: The Constitutional Jurisprudence of Shihab al-Din al-Qarafi* (Leiden: Brill, 1996).

categorical sciences, what about its appropriation by the general public who are acquainted with nothing but conjecture?"

> He said, "If it (the miracle) is claimed by someone unworthy, like a disobedient or negligent person, he certainly is a liar." In *al-Furūq*,[15] he said, "The vision of Allah the Most High while sleeping, in a manner befitting Him, is possible in this world as in the Hereafter. But if an unworthy person, disobedient or negligent, claims this experience, he is to be accused of lying. If one of the recognized saints claims it, we believe him and acknowledge his spiritual state. There are various interpretations of Allah's saying, *The eyes do not perceive Him*, for it is a generalization that permits particularization. The visionary experience of a saint trustworthy of religion and outstanding of integrity serves to reinforce some of the Qur'ānic interpretations (*ta'wīlāt*), and to particularize this generalization. The word of the honest person is accepted for such particularization, as is the word of the saints in regard to the saintly miracles falling outside of ordinary custom, which particularize the categorical sciences. But how can this particularization apply to the general populace, acquainted with nothing but conjecture?"

Shaykh Sīdī al-Mukhtār al-Kuntī said in *al-Kawākib*:

> Consider this allegory to understand the meaning of the Real's simultaneous visibility (*ẓuhūr*) and invisibility (*buṭūn*): sunlight makes things apparent to the senses, but the blind do not realize this, nor are the dim-sighted able to verify it. Sound faculties of vision can sometimes be dimmed in the presence of a desire (*irāda*). Ostensibly this desire is for the light of verification, but really the desire only wants (to see) its own light, and to have the knowledge of everything pass through its own light and presence.
>
> The same (visibility and invisibility) applies to the Creator's Essential Being (*dhāt*), Glorious and Exalted is He. The Essence, distinguished by perfection and majesty, is apparent to every individual. But they have been misguided by (secondary) causes extraneous to the divine Essence (*dhāt*) and the requirements of the divine Attributes. So they have wandered astray in the wastelands of misguidance.
>
> Things are known only by their opposites. If the sunlight was not followed by nighttime or was not covered sometimes by thick clouds, people would have belittled the light, thinking nothing of it at all. Būṣayrī, may Allah keep cool his tomb, meant something like this when he said:
>
> The close proximity of His mirror has hidden Him from them

---

15 *Kitāb al-furūq* was one of Qarāfī's most important works on Islamic law and legal theory.

So the concealment is due to the intensity of the divine manifestation.

This vision, concerning the possibility of which the scholars have argued, is not the same vision (*ruʾya*) claimed by those who have extinguished themselves (*ahl al-fanāʾ*) in the Essence of the Real, Glorious and Exalted is He. Their vision is not experienced with the human eye, nor with the heart, but rather with the Eye of the Real, Glorious and Exalted is He. And this Eye sees where there is no vision and no viewer. Imam al-Jīlī ﷺ referred to this when he wrote:

Allah has a manifestation behind the name and behind the description
From which the eyes of the worlds are shrouded by slumber

Beware of considering this matter far-fetched
Its reality is certainly close to those in whom is found the stamp of truth

The Compassionate does not see except with His own Eye
And that is the definitive ruling in regards to the divine Reality.

Imam al-ʿĀshiqīn[16] said:

Do not be one of those confused by sheets of paper
His understanding weighed down by trifling matters to the point of agitation

For beyond the intellect (*ʿaql*) is a knowledge so subtle—
Beyond the grasp of even the soundest minds

Its instruction is from me, and from me you have received it
My very soul has been an assistant in the giving.

One of the gnostic sages has said:

Say, "Allah!" and ignore the universe and what it contains,
As your goal is the attainment of perfection.

Once you truly recognize Him, everything else besides Allah
Will cease to exist, whether separately or as a whole.

Know that you and all the worlds, if not for Him,
Would be in a state of obliteration and evanescence

Before His divine Essence, nothing has existence in and of itself
Indeed, the (illusion of) existence other than Him is the essence of deceit

---

16 Many Sufis have been given this title, "Leader of the Lovers." The reference here may be to Manṣūr al-Hallāj (to whom the name seems to have been applied frequently) or to the less-renowned Urdu-speaking (Naqshbandī) Sufi who actually had the name, Imam al-ʿĀshiqīn Qadri Shakūrī.

So the gnostic sages have become extinct to themselves
Not seeing anything except Him, the Supreme, the Eminently Exalted

And they have perceived that everything apart from Him, in truth,
Is a vain deception, whether present, past or future.

Another gnostic sage has said:

Since coming to know Allah, I have not seen anything else
For (looking to) another is forbidden to us

Since being gathered (in the divine Presence), I have not feared being scattered
For today we have obtained the totality (of existence).

Another has said:

The secret of my secret is that, from the Paradise of Holiness, I have been annihilated
But with this annihilation from myself I have been brought to life

And I have been sent back to abide, in order to give expression
To the beauty of His Presence for all the thirsty ones, madly in love

I have brought forth in the heavenly kingdom (*malakūt*) astonishing things
I have not encountered another of the creation similarly endowed.

Another has said:

There are various passions in my heart
But when I see You, all my passions are gathered in one well of longing.

There are many other such expressions of the Sufi people, expressions drawing support from the flood (*tayyār*) of the ocean of exclusive divine Oneness (*baḥr al-tawḥīd al-khāṣ*). As has been said by one of the Sufis, "Our mode of expression is diverse, but the meaning of You is one; and we are all pointing to that perfection."

Whoever has any capacity for knowledge will understand from what we have compiled that the words of the enraptured saints (*majādhīb*) are based on a solid foundation. All of them are firmly established in the Presence of Him of the Heavenly Throne. Their expression comes from the light of a clean heart. The one who criticizes them has been misguided far away (from the truth), and is defective (of mind). He (the saint) does not utter a word except that a solemn warden is there watching him. We seek refuge from insolence before Allah, from misfortune, bad judgment, the malice of enemies, and from being distant after being close, and from withholding after giving. I include myself in this plea, together with the entirety of my brethren, believing men and women, by the blessing of greatest cover (*ḥijāb*), the source of the most precious gnosis, may Allah bless him, grant him peace; and may He honor, exalt, ennoble, and glorify him.

My way is clear to someone who is rightly guided
But passions obscure, so you have been rendered blind.

Our complaint is to Allah concerning a people among whom we find ourselves. They do not know, they do not learn, they do not ask, they will not accept the truth, they will not submit, they will not hold their tongues. Each one is the most ignorant of fools, but he considers himself the most learned of scholars. Each one dares to issue formal legal opinions, though he does not possess the requisite knowledge of what is involved. He is quick to accuse others of unbelief (*kufr*), though he does not know the definition of unbelief. Nor does he know the threat involved in making such an accusation, since an authentic report has the Prince of Messengers ﷺ saying: "If someone says to brother, 'O unbeliever!' one of the two is guilty of unbelief."[17] In other words, if the one who is accused is not an unbeliever, it is the accuser who is the unbeliever. We take refuge with Allah from ignorance. The Prophet ﷺ also said, "If someone says, 'The people have perished!' he is the one of them most surely doomed to perdition."[18] Our Shaykh al-Tijānī, may Allah be pleased with him and us for his sake, once said:

> We have a degree (*martaba*) in the Presence of Allah the Most High, the grandeur of which is not possible to divulge, and it is something other than which I told you about already. If I were to mention it, the people of Truth and gnosis would concur on my being put to death, let alone the enemies of the gnostics. The particularity of this degree includes the fact that if someone does not take care to amend his (bad) thoughts of our companions, he is doomed to perdition. The refuge from that is with Allah the Most High.

May Allah deliver us from affliction and include us among His chosen and beloved ones. May He enlist us among the elite of the elite companions of Shaykh al-Tijānī, the Seal of the Saints. May He quench our thirst from his ocean with the most splendid of goblets. May He unite us with him, and with his grandfather al-ʿAdnānī ﷺ in the abode of happiness. Surely Allah is the Guarantor of that, ultimately Capable.

---

17 This is a variation of a *ḥadīth* reported in the *ḥadīth* collections of Bukhārī, Abū Dāwūd, and Tirmidhī. Bukhārī's version (on the authority of Abū Darr) is: "No man accuses another man of being a sinner, or of being an unbeliever, but it reflects back on him if the other is not as he called him."

18 *Ḥadīth* reported in the collections of Bukhārī, Abū Dāwūd, the *Muwaṭṭāʾ* of Imam Mālik, and the *Musnad* of Ibn Ḥanbal.

This marks the end of the chapters. With Allah is the success on the straight path, and to Him, may He be glorified, is the return and final destination.

Conclusion

Our Confidant Reliance on the Tijānī Spiritual Path

Success is with Allah, and it is He who guides to the straight path by His grace.

It is no secret that the Tijānī spiritual path (*al-Ṭarīqa al-Tijāniyya*) is the most excellent of paths. The ones that hold to this path are the most exemplary of groups, since this is the Abrahamic, Muḥammadan, Aḥmadī path. Its exterior is the noble virtues of the sacred law (*sharīʿa*), and its interior is the product of the divine Reality (*ḥaqīqa*). There is nothing found in its practices or arrangements of litanies except something explicitly commanded by Allah in His Mighty Book. So you will not find anything of which Allah does not approve, either explicitly or implicitly. The Tijānī litany (*wird*) consists of seeking forgiveness, invoking blessings upon the Prophet ﷺ, saying "there is nothing worthy of worship but Allah," and reciting verses of the Qurʾān. Moreover, this litany was received from the Prophet ﷺ (by Shaykh Aḥmad al-Tijānī) in a waking state, not while sleeping. He it was who set firm its foundation with his noble hand, and arranged it for our Imam as a miraculous gift for this mercifully blessed Muslim community (*umma*).

Since the time Allah brought forth this Tijānī litany from the ocean of divine bounty, and people became aware of its benefit, it has profited humanity, in times gone by and times present, outwardly and inwardly, in all regions of the earth, in rural and urban areas. Even the negligent servant, far removed from his Lord—actually at war with Allah and those (saints) in charge of him—can meet this Imam or one of his disciples, and Allah will instill love for this Imam in his heart. He will receive the litany, his spiritual state will be transformed, and he will be included among the noble servants of Allah. He will purify himself, perform the ritual prayers and keep the fast (of Ramadan). He will love the people of Allah, and he will love the best of mankind ﷺ. In a very short time, it will be clear that he is among the chosen, select few. This is a matter witnessed by anyone who knows the spiritual path of this Imam, even if he is one of its enemies casting blame. So anyone aware of this magnanimous grace should strive to excel in performing this splendid (Tijānī) litany.

By the grace of Him who rules the unseen and the seen, good fortune drove me toward this Aḥmadī–Tijānī spiritual presence (*al-ḥaḍra al-Aḥmadiyya al-Tijāniyya*) to join the community of this Lordly Muḥammadan spiritual chain (*silsila*). I obtained this splendid litany and tremendous benefit from the Imam, my Shaykh and father, al-Ḥājj ʿAbd-Allāh b. al-Sayyid Muḥammad. He was surely the unique figure (*farīd*) of his age, the proof (*ḥujja*) for the people of his time, the sweet well (*zamzam*) of litanies and secrets, the confluence of remembrances and lights. He was the most erudite scholar, the most perceptive and understanding role model (*qudwa*), the deputy (*khalīfa*) of Shaykh al-Tijānī without doubt, and the bearer of his Path's banner in the lands of the West. He was surely one of the saints, among those who balance (knowledge of) the sacred law (*sharīʿa*) and the divine Reality (*ḥaqīqa*). May his Generous Lord never cease to promote him to the most praiseworthy station.

Time promised to produce the like of him (again)
Your promise was a lie, O time, so make amends.

He trained me (*rabbānī*) by means of this Aḥmadī litany, and took charge of my spiritual training (*tarbiya*) and learning (*taʿlīm*). Praise be to Allah, I received from him rare benefits (*fawāʾid*), blessed secrets, remembrances, and (spiritual) practices (*ʿawāʾid*). He was an accredited instructor (*muqaddam*) in the spiritual path, with absolute authorization from its leading folk. All of his shaykhs granted him unlimited sanction. Eleven chains of spiritual transmission (*silsila*) are linked to him, both unlimited and limited. These are well known and have been charted systematically by one of the brethren as a precious gift to all generations. He now has been taken from his life in this world. May Allah be pleased with him and us on his behalf. May Allah grant him the best reward, on my account and on account of all the Muslims.

He made an agreement with one of the shaykhs of the spiritual path who used to come to him, a true inheritor of its secrets. This was the distinguished Sharīf, the most competent scholar, Muḥammad Maḥmūd al-Shinjītī al-Tīshītī b. Muḥammad al-Ṣaghīr b. Aḥmad al-Ṣaghīr.[1] The

1 Muḥammad Maḥmūd b. Muḥammad al-Ṣaghīr al-Shinqītī, of the Idaw ʿAlī tribe in Mauritania, was the son of Muḥammad b. Muḥammad al-Ṣaghīr al-Shinqītī, author of *al-Jaysh al-kafīl*, and nephew of ʿUbayda b. Muḥammad al-Ṣaghīr, author of *Mīzāb al-raḥma*.

Shaykh, my father, gave him authorization for everything he had, and indicated to him that he did that in order for the Sharīf to grant me unlimited permission, saying explicitly that I was worthy of that. One of the spiritually unveiled people said to him concerning this, "There is no need to appoint one of the creation (to appoint your son), he already has been appointed by the Creator, Most High." This happened when I was still young. When my father passed, the Sharīf came to me and granted me unlimited authorization according to the instruction of my father. Just as my father's shaykhs gave him unlimited authorization, and he gave unlimited authorization to the Sharīf, so did he give me unlimited authorization. Praise be to Allah, in the beginning and end. Here is the text of his certificate of authorization (*ijāza*):

> In the Name of Allah, all praise is due to Allah.
> O Allah, bless our master Muḥammad and grant him peace.
>
> This poorest slave of Allah, Muḥammad Maḥmūd b. Muḥammad b. Aḥmad al-Ṣaghīr says: I have authorized my brother in Allah, in the Messenger and in the Shaykh (al-Tijānī), Ibrāhīm b. al-Ḥājj ʿAbd-Allāh, to assume the role of instructor and director. I have granted him unconditional authorization in everything coming to me from the Shaykh (al-Tijānī), just as Shaykh al-Ḥājj ʿAbd-Allāh granted me unlimited authorization. In his certificate of authorization to me (which now also applies to Shaykh Ibrāhīm), he said: "Allah blessed me to encounter some of the distinguished companions of the Shaykh (al-Tijānī), may Allah be pleased with them. I conversed with them concerning the secrets and gnostic sciences, and they appointed me with their true authorizations. I hereby grant permission and authorization to this beloved brother, according to what has been conferred on me, in regard to the secrets, the supplications, the Names, the secret of the Greatest Name, the Qurʾānic chapter of Power (*sūra al-qadr*), the incantation of the sea (*ḥizb al-baḥr*), the (prayer of the) Opener (*al-fātiḥ*) and its three degrees, the key of being the saintly pole (*miftāḥ al-quṭbaniyya*), and every secret established as having come from the Shaykh (al-Tijānī). I have taken from him the oath to fear Allah, that he seeks nothing by this except the Noble Countenance of Allah, and that he not give the secret to anyone except the deserving. Sufficient for me is Allah, the most excellent Custodian. There is no strength or power except by Allah, the Most High, the Almighty. May Allah's blessing and peace be upon our master Muḥammad."

This certificate of authorization was written in the year 1340 (1922), the year of my father's passing, the year of the sun.[2] Permission also came

---

2 If the numerological equivalent of the Arabic letters in *ʿām shams* (year of the sun) are added together, they equal 1340. Apparently the year was well-known by this name in

to me from the Shaykh (al-Tijānī) himself. I met him while asleep, but a sleep that was like wakefulness. He came to me many times. I also met my father (like this) many times, and he would say to me, "Everything I have left is for you, so take it from others." He told me other things as well, but they cannot be written here.

Unlimited authorization also came to me from the marvel of the age, my shaykh, my support (*sanad*), my master, al-Ḥājj ᶜAbd-Allāh b. al-Ḥājj al-ᶜAlawī.[3] All fingers point to him as the one endowed with the greatest sainthood. He was a lordly gnostic, inheritor of the Imam al-Tijānī's spiritual training due to his knowledge of the sciences of gnosis and divine realities, to the point that no concealment or hiding could cover up his widespread fame in these areas. He received his own authorization from his shaykh, Shaykh Aḥmad, and he from his shaykh, Shaykh Muḥamdi—known as "Baddi b. Sayyidayn"—who received it from Shaykh Muḥammad al-Ḥāfiẓ, and he from the Seal of Saints, Shaykh Aḥmad al-Tijānī. May Allah be pleased with them all and allow us to benefit from them. By the hand of this Shaykh, I benefited from the sciences and secrets that cannot be written on paper or seen by mere glances. With him is my dependence in the domain of spiritual experience (*adhwāq*), for he was the proof thereof in his time. May Allah be pleased with him and us for his sake. Here is the text of the certificate of authorization he gave me (written on his behalf by his disciple):

> In the Name of Allah, the Compassionate, the Merciful, He who is known, who commanded the invocation on the hidden master (*al-sayyid al-maktūm*). Praise be to Allah, praise which is due from His entire creation. And blessings and peace upon him who was made the original source.
>
> I have been commanded by my shaykh, father and guide, al-Ḥājj ᶜAbd-Allāh b. al-Ḥājj, to write for Ibrāhīm b. al-Ḥājj ᶜAbd-Allāh, that he has granted him permission to give the creation (*khalq*) spiritual guidance (*irshād*) and training (*tarbiya*) through word and deed. He is authorized to teach the litanies (*awrād*) and the remembrances (*adhkār*), both obligatory and supererogatory, the general ones and the special ones. This is a complete permission for everything for which exists an authentic report from the Shaykh (al-Tijānī) ﷺ. He has granted him an unlimited authorization, linking his rope in this

---

the Senegambian region: the Mouride scholar Shaykh Mbacke Boussou eulogized the deaths of al-Ḥājj ᶜAbd-Allāh Niasse and al-Ḥājj Mālik Sy in this year, "A sun and a sun disappeared in the year of the sun / And mankind cried for the overwhelming darkness" (See Shaykh Ḥasan Cisse, "al-Ṭarīqa al-Tijāniyya: Al-Khaṣāʾiṣ wa al-Mamayyazāt," speech at the Forum for the Followers of the Tijāniyya Order (Fes, 29 June 2007).

3 Al-Ḥājj ᶜAbd-Allāh b. al-Ḥājj al-ᶜAlawī (d. 1927) has been mentioned previously for his statements concerning the *fayḍa*.

> to his own until the Day of Judgment, or rather for all eternity. This is because he sees him as deserving of all of that. This document has been written by Muḥammad ʿAbd al-Raḥmān b. al-Ḥājj ʿAbd-Allāh b. al-Ḥājj, who gives witness to the above, in the year 1345 (1926–7).

Unlimited authorization also came to me by way of the consummate scholar, the knowledgeable one of Allah, Sīdī Muḥammad al-Kabīr b. al-Sayyid Aḥmad b. Miḥamm b. al-ʿAbbās al-ʿAlawī, who received it from Shaykh Aḥmad b. Baddi, and him from Shaykh Muḥamdi, and him from Shaykh Muḥammad al-Ḥāfiẓ, and him from the Seal of the Saints, Shaykh Aḥmad al-Tijānī[4] ﷺ. Sayyid Muḥammad al-Kabīr had other certificates of authorization from several paths. One linked him to Sīdī Mūsā b. Maʿzūz, to Sīdī Muḥammad b. Abī al-Naṣr,[5] and to Sīdī al-Ḥājj ʿAbd al-Wahhāb b. al-Aḥmar.[6] May Allah be pleased with them all, and may He allow us to benefit from them. Here is the text of his certificate of authorization to me:

> Praise be to Allah in His Oneness, and may the blessing of Allah be upon our master and patron Muḥammad, and may it include his family and companions.
>
> I have authorized our most excellent brother, the consummate scholar who has arrived (in the divine Presence), who has combined the knowledge of the sacred law and of the divine Reality. I authorize him in the spiritual path for all the remembrances originating from Shaykh al-Tijānī, the obligatory and supererogatory. This is a complete authorization, in general and particular, just as I received it from Sīdī al-Ghālī b. Mūsā b. Maʿzūz, who received it from his father, who received it from our Shaykh al-Tijānī. May Allah be pleased with them and pleased with us for their sake. Sīdī al-Ghālī b. Mūsā said that his father, who had given him his authorization, had received authorizations from Muḥammad b. Abī al-Naṣr and ʿAbd al-Wahhāb b. al-Aḥmar.[7] This authorization is also as I have received it from my Shaykh Aḥmad b. Baddi, who received it from his father, who received it from Shaykh Muḥammad al-Ḥāfiẓ, who received it from Shaykh

4 This is the same *silsila* of al-Ḥājj ʿAbd-Allāh b. al-Ḥājj. The significance of these certificates of authorization is that early on Shaykh Ibrāhīm was given license by some of renowned "Ḥāfiẓiyya"–Tijāniyya shaykhs in Mauritania.

5 Sīdī Muḥammad b. Abī al-Naṣr was a companion of Shaykh Aḥmad al-Tijānī in Fes, and one of fourteen which he granted unlimited authorization (*ijāza muṭlaqa*).

6 Sīdī ʿAbd al-Wahhāb al-Aḥmar was a close companion of Shaykh Aḥmad al-Tijānī, one of ten concerning whom the Prophet guaranteed the "grand illumination" (*fatḥ al-akbar*) in a vision to Shaykh Aḥmad al-Tijānī. He accompanied Sīdī ʿAlī Harāzim to the Hijaz and buried him there when he died, before returning back to Fes.

7 The implication here is that although Mūsā b. Maʿzūz took from Shaykh Aḥmad al-Tijānī directly, he received his unlimited authorization (*ijāza muṭlaqa*) from these other two fully-licensed companions of the Shaykh.

> al-Tijānī, who received it from Allah's Messenger ﷺ. The recipient of this authorization is the master previously mentioned, Ibrāhīm, son of the perfect gnostic and arrived shaykh, al-Ḥājj Sīdī ʿAbd-Allāh Niasse, may Allah never cease to raise him in the Holy Presence. I grant him permission to grant permission for what has been mentioned here to anybody else who is fully qualified. This has been written by Muḥammad al-Kabīr b. Aḥmad b. Miḥamm b. al-ʿAbbās al-ʿAlawī, may Allah reserve grace for them, on 22 Dhu al-Qaʿda 1345 (24 May 1927).

Absolute permission also came to this poor servant from the greatest deputy (*al-khalīfa al-akbar*), the most famous beacon, rare like red sulfur, the brightest full moon, the distinguished Shaykh Muḥammad Saʿīd b. al-Shaykh Aḥmad b. al-Shaykh Muḥammad al-Ḥāfiẓ. He received it from his father Sīdī Aḥmad, who received it from his Shaykh Baddi, who received from Shaykh Muḥammad al-Ḥāfiẓ, who received it from the Seal of Saints, Aḥmad al-Tijānī. May Allah be pleased with them and us on their account. Here is the text of the certificate of authorization:

> Praise be to Allah, Lord of all the worlds. Blessings and peace be upon the Master of Messengers. The writer is greeting his beloved and his bosom friend, the cultured and intelligent master, Shaykh Ibrāhīm the son of Shaykh ʿAbd-Allāh. May we continue to be blessed with assistance from the Generous Lord. I must inquire about your condition, the condition of your family, and the condition of those Tijānīs with you. May Allah include us and all of you among the elite of the elite among them.
>
> It is incumbent on me to grant you absolute authorization in the path of our Shaykh and means of access to our Lord, Sīdī Aḥmad al-Tijānī. This is an authorization to receive and to give, common knowledge to the common folk and special knowledge for the elite. Therein is the secret of the secret. This (authorization) is because I would deeply cherish being included in your spiritual chain (*silsila*), that I might enjoy the gracious favor of your supplication. I would dearly love for there to exist between us something special, and this for the Hereafter, since this world has little relevance to the subject at hand.
>
> I inform you of something I hope Allah will make you party to. I am the youngest of my father's children, and when he left me in charge of them, I became both a disciple (*talmīdh*) and father. When I did this, they became my children and disciples.[8] Pay no attention to what the people say, but ask Allah for help in everything that concerns you. May Allah reward you with the best, on our behalf and behalf of all Muslims.

---

8 The reference here is to the fact that Shaykh Ibrāhīm was one of the younger children of his own father, though his renown surpassed that of his brothers. Shaykh Muḥammad al-Saʿīd is advising Shaykh Ibrāhīm to treat his brothers with respect despite the talk of the naysayers.

This has been written by your brother and loving friend, Muḥammad Saʿīd b. Aḥmad b. Muḥammad al-Ḥāfiẓ in the year 1349 (1930–31).

Thus the staff shined, and by it was the destination attained,
As the traveler's eye is cooled by the homecoming.

Those are the forefathers, so bring me the like of them
Since you have joined us, O poet (Jarīr)[9] of the assemblies.

May Allah grant our masters the best reward on our behalf, and may He be well pleased with them, and they well pleased with Him.

In reality, our affiliation and link today are with Shaykh al-Tijānī, the Seal of Saints, without intermediary, since he is always present with us. Praise be to Allah, to Him belongs the favor. It is related that Abū al-Ḥasan al-Shādhilī once was asked about his shaykh. He said:

> I used to be affiliated with ʿAbd al-Salām b. al-Mashīsh, but today I am swimming in ten oceans. Five of them are Adamic beings: Muḥammad ﷺ, Abū Bakr, ʿUmar, ʿUthmān and ʿAlī, ؓ. The other five consist of spiritual beings: (the angels) Gabriel, Michael, Izrāʾīl, Isrāfīl and the Spirit (al-Rūḥ).

And we are in a single ocean, which has no shore, no limit, no termination, and no end. And this ocean derives from an ocean without shore, limit, termination, or end, which supplies its vastness. And this ocean derives from the Presence of the Absolute (*ḥaḍra al-iṭlāq*), which supplies its vastness and lordliness (*rubūbiyya*).[10] *And for this let those who strive aspire* (Qurʾān, 83:26).

Those are the forefathers, so bring me the like of them
Since you have joined us, O poet (Jarīr) of the assemblies.

This brings us to the end of the book. With Allah is the success on the straight path, and to Him the Glorified is the return and final destination. The book has been written with the permission and assistance of the Concealed Presence (*al-ḥaḍra al-katmiyya*)[11] by the poor servant in need of the Merciful's mercy, Ibrāhīm the son of Shaykh al-Ḥājj ʿAbd-Allāh. May he never cease to be enamored of the beauty of his Lord. I drafted

---

9   Jarīr b. ʿAṭiya al-Khaṭfī (d. 728) was a famous Arab poet in the court of ʿUmar b. ʿAbd al-ʿAzīz (ʿUmar II), the Umayyad sultan in Damascus. Among the three most famous poets of his age (Akhṭal, Farazdaq, and himself), he was the most apt to incorporate religious themes in his poetry, and was the only poet accepted into the court of the pious sultan ʿUmar II. See Louis Gardet, "Religion and Culture," in Holt, Lambton and Lewis (eds.), *Cambridge History of Islam*, vol. 2 (Cambridge: Cambridge University Press, 1977), p. 576.

10 The reference here is to the ocean of the Seal of Saints, deriving from the ocean of the Seal of Prophets, deriving from the Presence of Allah.

11 In other words, the hidden pole (*al-quṭb al-maktūm*), Shaykh Aḥmad al-Tijānī.

it in nine days, in an age of ignorance, encroaching darkness, increasing (worldly) preoccupation of human beings, stagnation of minds, languishing of thought, and extinction of sagacity. I am apologizing to those of understanding for any shortcomings found in this book. With Allah as my witness, I beseech the reader to consider it fairly and with the eye of approval.

The eye of approval blinks at every fault
While the eye of resentment makes appear the faults.

Whoever considers (this book) with eye of approval, he will see that it is from the Flood of the Tijānī Seal, owner of the divine secret; for it collects the cream of the books authored on this discipline. Seldom will you find a compilation (*majmūʿ*) containing what this contains. Whoever examines it closely and judges it fairly will know for certain that this compilation was authored by Shaykh al-Tijānī with his own hand.

I ask Allah the Most High—by means of Him, of the Seal of His Prophets and of the Seal of His Saints—to allow us and all Muslims to benefit by this book. May He accept it from us with beautiful approval. May He put tremendous blessing (*baraka*) in it, to the extent that it may bless any place it is found. May He make it a source of discernment for the spiritual path and its people, stringing them together (like pearls) in the company of the Noble Seal. *The day when neither wealth nor sons are of benefit, save him who comes to Allah with a sound heart* (Qurʾān, 26:88–9).

The rough draft was completed on Friday evening, the eighteenth of Muḥarram in the year 1350 (5 June 1931), in the town of Kaolack. Peace. With thanks to Allah and His most beautiful assistance, *The Removal of Confusion* has been completed. It is followed by an appendix by the author.

On Spiritual Training and Saintly Authority

In the Name of Allah, the Compassionate, the Merciful, and may Allah's blessing and peace be upon our master Muḥammad, as well as on his family and companions. We begin by offering Him the praise that befits His Majesty, and by invoking His blessing upon the best of His distinguished elite, and upon all his companions and family.

I have attached this Appendix of several sections to our work, *The Removal of Confusion*. Anyone interested in the sciences of the spiritual path will find it indispensably precious. I ask Allah for His acceptance and favor, from the beginning to the end. He is the Originator, the Restorer, the Forgiving, the Loving, the Lord of the Glorious Throne, who does what He wills. With Allah is all success, and He is the Guide by His Grace to the straight path.

More on the Continuance of Spiritual Training (*tarbiya*) and its Method

Here are the words of Shaykh Sīdī al-Mukhtār al-Kuntī in his book *Janna al-murīd*, as cited in *al-Jaysh*:[1]

> How astonishing is the negative criticism of the saintly miracles (*karāmāt*) by the Qurʾān readers (*qurrāʾ*) of the present time. And how amazing is their allegation that spiritual training (*tarbiya*) has ceased since the year 800 (1397 C.E.), basing their opinion on the statement of

1 *al-Jaysh al-kafīl bi akhdh al-thār mimman salla ʿala al-Tijānī sayf al-inkār* by Muḥammad b. Muḥammad al-Ṣaghīr Tashītī (d. 1869, Mauritania), a prominent Tijānī scholar tracing his initiation through Shaykh Muḥammad al-Ḥāfiẓ.

Zarrūq, may Allah have mercy on him: "Spiritual training has ceased to be practiced…" It does not occur to them that he was referring only to the Maghrib. The cessation of spiritual training is indeed possible for a particular time or particular place. No one maintains the existence of a spiritual trainer (*murabbī*) in every land, or such a trainer's fixed residence in one place indefinitely. Those endowed with powers of verification, from the righteous early forefathers to those that came later, have agreed on the (continued) existence of someone bearing the burdens of spiritual training, without reference to the number or place of such individuals. Thus the cessation of spiritual training in the Maghrib (in the time of Zarrūq) does not conflict with the unanimous agreement (*ijmāʾ*) of the scholars concerning its existence in general. There is sure to be a spiritual trainer (even if there is none in the Maghrib) in Black Africa (*sūdān*), for instance, or in Egypt, or in the two holy places (Mecca and Medina), or in Syria, or in Iraq. He may be assigned to a single place, or to a number of places. Whenever Allah the Exalted wishes the residents of a locality to benefit from his assistance, He reveals his special quality for the people living there. He may also reside in a place where Allah has decreed the inhabitants suffer deprivation and banishment from His Presence, so they fail to benefit by his help. Indeed, the special quality of the spiritual trainer is covered with the veil of human nature, so his contemporaries say, *This is only a human being like you, who eats what you eat and drinks what you drink* (Qurʾān, 23:33).

This denial is especially true of the Qurʾān readers associated with excellence in describing the sciences (*rasm al-ʿulūm*). It has been said of the likes of them:

They said so-and-so is an excellent scholar
So offer him the reverence he deserves

I replied, "since he has no fear (of Allah)
The divine Obstructer (al-Māniʿ) prevents compliance."

The denial by such scholars of the existence of spiritual masters and the continuance of spiritual training is nothing but conjecture. It is at general variance with the sacred law and in explicit contradiction with the textual sources. If they deny the very principle of sainthood, they have no basis for their disbelief. They are proven false by more than two hundred verses of Allah's book, either explicitly or by necessary implication, and by more than three hundred prophetic traditions. If the source for their denial is the alleged cessation of spiritual training, they are in fact claiming the cessation of the religion itself. For this they have no proof whatsoever, neither from the Qurʾān, the prophetic Sunna, nor the consensus of the scholars. They are disproved manifestly by several prophetic traditions, including the following:

> My community is like the rain: there is no telling whether the first of its members are the best, or the last of them.
>
> A party from my community will always be committed to the Truth. They will not be harmed by those who oppose and desert them, until Allah's command comes while they are in that state.
>
> Perhaps they allege the cessation of Sufism, while maintaining the continuation of the other formal sciences. Then the Qurʾān and the Sunna bear witness against them, censure them, refute them and utterly disprove them. The result of the knowledge of divine Reality (*ḥaqīqa*) is nothing less than the essential knowledge of the Real (*al-Ḥaqq*). Allah's Messenger ﷺ said, "Every truth (*ḥaqq*) has a reality (*ḥaqīqa*)."[2] Those who explain the prophetic traditions draw the analogy of a nut-shell and a kernel: the shell being the sacred law (*sharīʿa*) and the kernel being the Reality (*ḥaqīqa*). A kernel without a shell becomes rotten and putrid, and a shell with no kernel inside is worthless. This is also indicated by the verse, *They were only commanded to worship Allah, sincerely devoting the religion to Him* (Qurʾān, 98:5). So Allah the Almighty and Glorious has informed us that worship must include sincere devotion (*ikhlāṣ*), meaning pure intention free from hypocritical ostentation, from the beginning to end. Allah's Messenger ﷺ said: "Allah does not look at your bodies, or your forms, but he does look at your hearts."[3]
>
> It is indisputable that the rectification of hearts can only be achieved with the sciences of spiritual discipline and practice, which are a branch of the science of divine Reality (*ʿilm al-ḥaqīqa*). The person who alleges the cessation of this science is suggesting the bankruptcy of the sacred law and the disappearance of its harvest. For the harvest of the sacred law is steadfast righteousness (*istiqāma*). The sacred law establishes the formal structure of Islam, while the (science of) divine Reality determines the real meaning of Islam. The sacred law represents the body of Islam, the Reality represents its spirit.

In another instructive passage, Sīdī al-Mukhtār al-Kuntī said:

> Know that the shaykhs have two methods of spiritual training (*tarbiya*). The first one is centered on gratitude (*shukr*) and happiness on account of the Benefactor, without trouble or toil. The second one is centered on spiritual discipline (*riyāḍa*), labor, hardship, sleeplessness, and hunger.

When discussing the virtues of Sīdī ʿAbd al-ʿAzīz (al-Dabbāgh), the author of *al-Dhahab al-ibrīz* said:

---

2 *Ḥadīth* reported by Ṭabarānī in *al-Muʿjam al-kabīr* and by Ibn Shayba in *al-Musannaf*, and cited by Hindī in *Kanz al-ʿummāl*.

3 *Ḥadīth* reported in the collections of Muslim and Ibn Māja.

> The path of gratitude (*ṭarīqa al-shukr*) is the original way, practiced by the hearts of the Prophets and the bosom friends among their companions. It means to worship Him with sincere devotion and detachment from all worldly interests. The servant acknowledges his incapacity and shortcoming, and his failure to fulfill the right of Divinity. By necessity, this preoccupies his heart at all times. When Allah recognizes truthfulness (*ṣidq*) in such servants, He grants them favors commensurate with His generosity: spiritual illumination in knowing (*maʿrifa*) Him, and obtainment of the secrets of belief (*imān*) in Him, Mighty and Glorious is He.
>
> When the people of spiritual discipline (*riyāḍa*) heard of the illumination (*fatḥ*) achieved by these people, they made such illumination their goal. They pursued it by means of fasting, standing in supererogatory prayer, sleeplessness, and constant seclusion (*khalwa*), until they achieved what they achieved. The emigration (*hijra*) of the first way (gratitude) is only to Allah and His Messenger, not for the sake of spiritual illumination (*fatḥ*) and the attainment of mystical discoveries (*kashūfāt*). The emigration of the second way (discipline and deprivation) is for the sake of illumination and the attainment of degrees (*marātib*). The journey in the first is the journey of hearts. The journey in the second is the journey of bodies. Illumination in the first comes as a sudden surprise, for the servant has no expectation of it, contrary to the illumination of the second.
>
> The two paths are both correct, but the path of gratitude is more correct and more sincere. Both practice spiritual exercise, but the exercise of the first is of the hearts. The exertion is in their attachment to Allah the Glorious, their persistent attendance at His door, their turning back to Him in all moments of movement and stillness. The people of the first path remain constantly devoted to this, even if their appearance is not clothed in a great deal of worshipful activities (*ʿibāda*). For this reason, the master of this path may fast, or break his fast, stay awake (at night) or sleep. He may spend time with women, and perform any other of the duties within the sacred law that conflict with the discipline (*riyāḍa*) of physical bodies.

Our Shaykh Abū al-ʿAbbās Sīdī Aḥmad b. Muḥammad al-Tijānī ﵁ used to say:

> Gratitude (*shukr*) is the door of Allah, and the closest of doors to Him. That is why Satan sits next to it, for Allah the Most High relates his statement, *I shall lurk in ambush for them on Your straight path* (Qurʾān, 7:16). In this time, whoever does not enter through the door of gratitude does not enter (the divine Presence). This is because the egos have become thick and rebellious, so they are not restrained by being called to account or argumentation, and they are impervious to

discipline (*riyāḍa*). But if they are drowned in rejoicing (*faraḥ*) with the Benefactor, they will absent themselves from this (rebellion), and end their distance (from their Lord).

The Continued Existence of Saints in the Present Time

In *Rūḥ al-bayān fī tafsīr al-Qurʾān*, Ismāʿīl al-Ḥaqqī al-Burūsī[4]—the erudite Shaykh who combines (knowledge) of the sacred law with (knowledge) of the divine Reality, the seal of Qurʾān interpreters, may Allah sanctify his innermost being—gave the following commentary on the verse, *And among those whom We created there is a community who guide with the Truth and by it establish justice* (Qurʾān, 7:181).

> The Prophet ﷺ is reported as having said, "Among my community there will be people devoted to the Truth, until Jesus, peace upon him, comes down (from Heaven)."[5] The meaning is that no period of time will be without them. The great Shaykh Ṣadr al-Dīn al-Qunawī,[6] may Allah sanctify his inner being, quoted the prophetic tradition, "The Final Hour will not arrive until 'Allah, Allah' ceases to be uttered on the earth." The Shaykh explained in *Kitāb al-fukūk*, "The Prophet confirmed it repeatedly. There is no doubt that no one genuinely remembers Allah—and especially with this Comprehensive Supreme Name, which carries with it the attributes of all the divine Names—except that he knows the Real with complete gnosis (*maʿrifa*). In every era, the one of creation with the most complete knowledge of Allah is His deputy (*khalīfa*), for he is the perfect one of that time. The Prophet ﷺ said, 'The Final Hour will not arrive as long as there is a perfect human being (*insān kāmil*) upon the earth.'[7] He is the delegated spiritual pillar. If you want you could call him the one for whose sake the universe is kept intact. If (this position) were taken away, the sky would be shattered, the sun would be divested of light, the stars would fall, the pages (*ṣuḥuf*) would be scattered, the earth would split asunder, and the Resurrection would be at hand."

He (Ismāʿīl al-Ḥaqqī) also related the report transmitted by Ibn Masʿūd ﷺ in which the Prophet ﷺ said:

---

4 The ten-volume Qurʾānic exegesis of Ismāʿīl al-Ḥaqqī Burūsī (or Burusawi or Bursawi, d. 1724, Anatolia), *Rūḥ al-bayān*, is one of the most comprehensive Sufi exegeses of the Qurʾān.

5 A *ḥadīth* cited by Suyūṭī in *al-Durr al-manthūr*, and by Ibn Abī Ḥātim in his commentary of the Qurʾān.

6 Shaykh al-Islām Ṣadr al-Dīn al-Qunāwī (d. 1274, Konya) was the closest disciple of Ibn al-ʿArabī al-Ḥatimī, through whom most of his works are related. The work cited from here, *Kitāb al-fukuk*, is a commentary on Ibn al-ʿArabī's *Fuṣūṣ al-ḥikam*.

7 A *ḥadīth* related in the *Ṣaḥīḥ* of Muslim and the *Musnad* of Ibn Ḥanbal.

> Allah has on the earth three hundred (servants) whose hearts are upon the heart of Adam. He has forty whose hearts are on the heart of Moses. He has seven whose hearts are on the heart of Abraham. He has five whose hearts are on the heart of (the angel) Gabriel. He has three whose hearts are on the heart of (the angel) Michael, and He has one whose heart is on the heart of (the angel) Isrāfīl.[8] If the one (on the heart of Isrāfīl) dies, Allah replaces him with one of the three (on the heart of Michael). If one of the three dies, Allah replaces him with one of the five (on the heart of Gabriel). If one of the five dies, Allah replaces him with one of the seven (on the heart of Abraham). If one of the seven dies, Allah replaces him with one of the forty (on the heart of Moses). If one of the forty dies, Allah replaces him with one of the three hundred (on the heart of Adam). If one of the three hundred dies, Allah replaces him with one of the ordinary people (*al-ʿāmma*). By them, Allah drives away affliction from the community.[9]

He commented:

> The unique one mentioned in this prophetic tradition is the saintly pole (*al-quṭb*), the Succor (*al-ghawth*). His position and rank among the saints is like the point at the center of a circle: the focal point of the universe's well-being.

He then cited a narration from Abū al-Dardāʾ:

> Allah has servants called the Substitutes (Abdāl). They have not achieved what they have achieved through a great deal of fasting, ritual prayer, outward displays of humility, or beautiful embellishment. They have achieved it through genuine piety, good intention, peaceful hearts, and compassion for the entirety of the Muslim community. Allah favored them with His knowledge and has chosen them for Himself. They are forty men whose character is like the heart of Abraham. No man among them will die until Allah has created someone to replace him. They do not revile or curse anything. They do not abuse those who are beneath them. They do not treat anything with contempt. They do not envy those above them. They are the best of people in goodness, gentleness of temperament, and generosity of disposition. In what is between them and their Lord, spurred horses and tempestuous winds cannot overtake. Their hearts find contentment in the highest firmaments, ascending to Allah. They compete with one another in good deeds: *They are Allah's party. Surely Allah's party are the ones who prosper* (Qurʾān, 58:22).

---

8 The angel Isrāfīl, or Raphael, is the angel responsible for blowing the horn on the Day of Judgment.

9 A *ḥadīth* reported by Ibn al-Jawzī in *al-Mawdūʿāt*, and Imam al-Dhahabī in *Mīzān al-iʿtidāl*. A similar narration is found in Hindī, *Kanz al-ʿummāl*.

> Imam Abū al-Mawāhib al-Tūnisī[10] said in one of his wise counsels: Beware of saying, "The great saints and truthful dervishes (*fuqarāʾ*) have disappeared." They have not really disappeared: they are like a treasure belonging to the owner of the vault. Allah may grant someone who comes near the End of Time what He withheld from the people of earlier times. In this way, Allah the Most High gave to Muḥammad ﷺ what He did not give to the Prophets before him, thus glorifying him over them.

In *Qawāwīn al-ishrāq ilā kulli al-ṣūfiyya fī jamīʿi al-āfāq*, he (al-Tūnisī) also said:

> Do not say, "The approaching End of Time necessitates the departure of the people of spiritual distinction," but say, "By Allah, they are in these times like treasure in the owner's vault."
>
> There is no harm for me if I do not come before,
> The One who owns the arena is aware (of my place).
>
> Even if the garden of eloquence should become a wasteland
> The Lord still has treasure in the depths of the vault.
>
> Someone who comes at the end of the cycles of existence will not suffer deprivation, so long as his knowledge distinguishes him among the most excellent of his peers. Allah deferred the coming of the Prophet (Muḥammad) ﷺ but put him first in degree of praise and mention.

Majd al-Dīn said in the preface of *al-Qāmūs*:[11]

> I say, as the speaker of truth, Abū al-ʿAbbās al-Mubarrad,[12] said in his book, *al-Kāmil*, "The interlocutor should not be given preference because he comes from an ancient time, nor should the righteous person be treated unfairly because he is a contemporary. Each should be awarded his rightful due."

---

10 Abū al-Mawāhib al-Tūnisī (d. 1477) was a renowned scholar of Tunisia and saint of the Shādhiliyya Sufi path. His major work was *Qawanīn ḥikam al-ishrāq*, which has been translated into English by Edward Jurji as *Illumination in Islamic Mysticism* (Princeton, NJ: Princeton Oriental Texts, 1938).

11 *Al-Qāmūs al-muḥīt* [The comprehensive dictionary], by Abū al-Ṭāhir b. Ibrāhīm Majd al-Dīn al-Fayrūzābādī, an expert of Arabic lexicon and Mālikī jurisprudence. Born in Shiraz (Persia), he served as a judge in Yemen and eventually settled in Mecca, where he died in 1414.

12 Abū al-ʿAbbās Muḥammad b. Yazīd (known as Mubarrad) was an early Arabic grammarian. Originally from Azerbaijan, he settled in Baghdad during the ʿAbbāsid caliphate and died in 898. *Al-Kāmil* was his major work on Arabic grammar.

According to the agreeable gnostic sage (*al-ʿārif al-murtaḍā*), Shaykh Murtaḍā,[13] in his commentary entitled *Tāj al-ʿarūs*: "The point is that neither the remoteness of time nor its recentness has superior merit in itself. All times are on equal footing. Of sole importance are the distinguished folk who exist in those times." Imam Ibn Mālik said in the preface of *al-Tashīl*:[14]

> Since the Islamic sciences are divine bounties and precious gifts, it is possible that what was difficult for past men to obtain is kept in store for people of the present. The point is that neither the remoteness of time nor its recentness has superior merit in itself. All times are on equal footing. Of sole importance are the distinguished folk who exist in those times. One who is correct in his opinion or critique is not impaired by the recentness of the time in which Allah brought him into being. The erroneous person, wrong in his opinion and wrong in his understanding, gains no advantage by the ancientness of his time. Being a present contemporary, as has been said before, is only a veil. Pure following of convention (*taqlīd*) is a curse and torment for its adherent. Our refined Shaykh, the muezzin, ʿAbd-Allāh b. ʿAbd-Allāh b. Salāma, recited to us these poetic verses:
>
> > Tell the one who thinks nothing of the present age,
> > And sees all preeminence owned by the ancients:
> >
> > "That person of the past was once a contemporary,
> > And this contemporary person one day will be considered one of the ancients."
>
> He also recited to me these verses by Ibn Rashīq:[15]
>
> > Those most bent on extolling the ancients
> > And belittling the blameless newcomer
> >
> > Are motivated only by envy for the modest
> > So they have climbed high on rotten bones.

The intention in all of this is to encourage people to look fairly at their contemporaries, and all people. Sincerity and fairness are the goal of knowledge.

---

13 Shaykh Muḥammad al-Ḥusaynī, known as Murtaḍā al-Zabīdi (originally from India, d. 1790, Egypt) was one of the most famous *ḥadīth* scholars of his time, a Ḥanafī jurist, and lexicographer. *Tāj al-ʿarūs min jawāhir al-qāmūs* is one of the largest Arabic dictionaries, originally meant as a commentary on *al-Qāmūs al-muḥīt*.

14 The *Tashīl al-fawāʾid wa takmīl al-maqāṣid*, a work on Arabic syntax, was written by the Andalusian Jamal al-Dīn Muḥammad al-Jayānī, known as Ibn Mālik (d. 1274, Damascus). Ibn Mālik is more famous for another of his works on grammar, the *Alfiyya*. Ibn ʿAqīl (d. 1374) later produced an important commentary on this work, *al-Musāʾid*.

15 Ibn Rashīq was an Andalusian scholar (d. 1064) who wrote a major study of Arabic poetry, *al-ʿUmda fī mahāsin al-shiʿr wa adabihi wa naqdihi*.

The following passage is from the book, *Nawādir al-uṣūl*, section 122, by the wise Imam al-Tirmidhī:[16]

> Concerning the assertion that the best of this (Muslim) community is its first and its last, and in the middle there is confusion; consider the prophetic tradition related by Ibn ʿUmar: ﷺ "My community is like the rain. There is no knowing whether the first of its members are the best, or the last of them."[17] ʿAbd al-Raḥmān b. Samura ﷺ relates:[18] "Khālid b. al-Walīd sent me to bring news to Allah's Messenger ﷺ during (the battle of) Muʾta. When I entered his presence, I said, "O Messenger of Allah!" and he said,
>
> > Take it easy, O ʿAbd al-Raḥmān. Zayd b. Ḥāritha took the battle standard, and fought until he was killed. May Allah have mercy on Zayd. Then Jaʿfar took the standard, and Jaʿfar fought until he was killed. May Allah have mercy on him. Then ʿAbd-Allāh b. Rawāḥa took the standard and fought until he was killed. May Allah have mercy on ʿAbd-Allāh. Then Khālid took the standard, and victory was granted to Khālid, for Khālid is a sword among the swords of Allah the Most High.
>
> The companions of Allah's Messenger ﷺ wept as they were gathered around him, so he said, "What is causing you to weep?" They replied, "How can we not weep, since the best, noblest, and most meritorious of us have been killed?" He said:
>
> > Do not weep, for the likeness of my community is the likeness of a garden cultivated by its owner. He dug its wells, set up its dwellings and pruned its date palms. One year the garden nourished one group of people, and another year it nourished another group. Perhaps its last fruits will be the finest bunches of dates. By Him who sent me as a Prophet with the Truth, (Jesus) the son of Mary surely will find in my community a substitute for his apostles.
>
> In another narration, the Prophet ﷺ said:
>
> > Among this community (Jesus) the Messiah will surely notice certain groups of people who are either just like you, or three times better than you. Surely Allah will not disgrace a community in which I am the first of its members and Jesus is the last.

---

16 *Nawādir al-uṣūl fī maʿrifat aḥādīth al-rasūl*, a work examining prophetic traditions, was written by Muḥammad b. ʿAlī al-Ḥakīm al-Tirmidhī (d. 910, Khurasan, Persia), a jurist, *ḥadīth* scholar (though he is not the same Tirmidhī who collected one of the six canonical *Sunan*), and influential early Sufi.

17 A *ḥadīth* reported in the *Sunan* of Tirmidhī, in the *Musnad* of Ibn Ḥanbal; and cited by Suyūṭī in *al-Ḥāwī ʿala al-Fatāwī*.

18 The narration is found Bayhaqī's *Sunan al-kubrā*.

Abū ʿAbd-Allāh al-Ḥakīm[19] once said:

> Allah has blessed this community, for He has said, *You are the best community that has ever been brought forth for the sake of mankind* (Qurʾān, 3:110). He also said, *And thus We have made you a moderate community* (2:143). This is to say (we are) a balanced community, not leaning toward excess or deficiency, for the scale's balance point is in the middle, steadying the two extremes, and two scale pans remain even. So the measurement begins. You put the ends of this community in each of the two weighing pans, and they balance. This is because they both guide to the Truth and by it establish justice. What is between them is a group idle in the balance, standing upright for the steadying of the scale pans. If the middle should incline to either side, it will return to the reliable sources. The steadiness of the two scale pans prevails over any deviation in the middle. According to one narration: "Knowledge will become manifest at the End of Time, and people will dedicate themselves to Allah's commandment, Exalted is He, so that Allah's proof for His servants may be perfected."

Concerning Disagreement among Sufis

Know that the disagreement between the Sufis does not detract from them. According to the author of *Rūḥ al-bayān*:

> There is a discordant party in this community that loathes the scholars and regards the jurists with hostility. This was far from the case among the religious communities that preceded us, for they were obedient and friendly to their religious authorities. Allah the Exalted says (of the Jews and Christians): *They took their rabbis and monks as lords apart from Allah* (Qurʾān, 9:31). If the jurist (*fāqih*) is detested by the people, what do you think is the case for the scholar knowledgeable of Allah (*al-ʿālim bi-Llāh*)? When they find a man with perfect knowledge of the external and esoteric sciences, who is unique in knowledge, who is distinguished of his kind and superior to his peers, some of them surely will say, "He is an atheist (*zindīq*)!" Others will say, "He is a heretical innovator (*mubtadiʾ*)! Seldom will you hear them saying, "He is a most truthful one." So consider the jealous concern (*ghayra*) of Allah. Allah has shielded such a scholar from others, and concealed his secret from the evildoers.

19 This is likely Abū ʿAbd-Allāh Muḥammad al-Ḥakīm al-Nishāpūrī (d. 1012, Nishapur), the famous *ḥadīth* scholar of Khurasan who was the teacher of Imam al-Bayhaqī. His most famous works were *al-Mustadrak ʿala al-Ṣaḥīḥayn* and *Mustadrak al-Ḥakīm*.

> According to the noble Shaykh Ruwaym,[20] "The Sufis will always benefit from their disagreement, for if they agree, they will perish. If they accepted each other, they would become attached to each another, and come to rely (*sakana*) on each other. Among the spiritual elite, reliance on anything other than Allah is comparable to the worship of idols among the common folk. This disagreement between the spiritually realized Sufis is not like the disagreement among the Jews and the Christians. The disagreement of the Sufis concerns the Truth and is for the sake of Truth. The disagreement of others concerns falsehood and is for the sake of falsehood."
>
> The gist of the matter is that disagreement can be both blameworthy and praiseworthy. The blameworthy disagreement relates to the beliefs and principles of the religion. That which is praiseworthy relates to various courses of action (*ʿamāl*) or the branches of the religion. The Prophet ﷺ meant this latter disagreement when he said, "Scholarly disagreement (*ikhtilāf*) in my community is a mercy."[21]
>
> A Jewish man once said to ʿAlī, may Allah ennoble his countenance, "No sooner had you buried your Prophet than you differed!" ʿAlī replied, "We differed about him (*ʿanhu*), not with him (*fīhi*). As for your people, no sooner had your feet become dry outside the womb than you said to your Prophet, 'Appoint for us a god, just as they have gods.'" This is the kind of response that seizes a person by the throat! *But Allah speaks the truth, and He shows the way* (Qurʾān, 33:4).

This (notion of permissible disagreement) is confirmed by what Ubayy mentioned in *Ikmāl al-ikmāl.*

> According to Āmidī, the Muslims at the time of the Prophet's death ﷺ were in a state of accordance. There was no disagreement among them, except with regard to matters open to independent judgment (*al-masāʾil al-ijtihādiyya*), which do not carry a charge of unbelief. For instance, the Prophet ﷺ said, "Bring me some ink and a tablet, so that I may write something whereby you will never be misguided."[22] The companions disagreed about whether they should bring him what he asked for, until ʿUmar said, "Allah's Messenger ﷺ has been overcome by pain. The Book of Allah is sufficient for us."[23]

---

20 Ruwaym b. Aḥmad (d. 915–6, Baghdad) was a master of jurisprudence (of the Ẓāhirī school), Qurʾān recitation, and Sufism.

21 A *ḥadīth* cited by Imam al-ʿAjlūnī in *Kashf al-khafāʾ wa muzīl al-ilbās.* Al-Ḥāfiẓ al-Sakhāwī also cites the *ḥadīth* in *Maqāṣid al-ḥasana;* he finds it written earlier in Ibn al-Ḥājib's *Mukhtaṣar,* who in turn cites Khaṭṭāb's *Gharīb al-ḥadīth.*

22 A *ḥadīth* reported in the *Ṣaḥīḥ* of Muslim. Similar variations are found in the *Ṣaḥīḥ* of Bukhārī and the *Musnad* of Ibn Ḥanbal.

23 Narration related in the *Ṣaḥīḥ* of Muslim.

Another example of their disagreement occurred when he ﷺ said, "Equip the army of Usāma!" One group said, "Let us do it," and another group said, "Let us wait and see what becomes of his sickness." Another example occurred when he ﷺ died, for the companions disagreed as to whether he died. And ʿUmar said, "If someone says he has died, I will smite him with my sword. He simply has been raised up like Jesus!" Another example was their disagreement about the succession (*khilāfa*), to the point that the Anṣār ("Helpers", those native to Medina) said, "Let one of us be a commander (*amīr*) and let one of you be a commander." Another example was their disagreement about the (legislative) council (*shūra*), until the matter was entrusted to ʿUthmān. Yet another example was their disagreement about fighting those who withheld the alms tax (*zakāt*). They also disagreed about the inheritance of distant relatives or of a grandfather.

Disagreement over matters of independent judgment continued progressively until the appearance of Muʿabbad, Ghaylān al-Dimashqī, and Yūnus al-Aswārī. They maintained that there is no predestination (*qadar*). This was the first difference of opinion to emerge in relation to the principles of faith (*iʿtiqādāt*). Difference of opinion then continued to diverge, until the people of Islam became divided into seventy-three sects, just as the Prophet ﷺ had predicted in his saying, "The Jews became separated into seventy-one sects, the Christians became separated into seventy-two sects, and my community will become separated into seventy-three sects. All of them will be doomed to the Fire except one." His companions asked him, "Which one is that?" He replied, "The one to which I and my companions belong."[24] So this (prediction) was one of his prophetic miracles.

In *al-Jāmiʿ*, Shaykh Aḥmad al-Tijānī is recorded as saying (in reference to the Prophet's request for pen and paper on his deathbed): "What he ﷺ intended to set down in writing was the unity of gnostic sages (*ʿārifīn*), for that is a clear distinguishing factor. And Allah is the best of knowers."

The *Sharḥ al-arbaʿīn al-Nawawiyya* of the jurist ʿAlī b. al-Sultān Muḥammad al-Ḥanafī[25] lists seven sources of heretical innovation.

(1) The Muʿtazila ("Separatists") maintain that Allah's servants are the creators of their own deeds. They deny the vision of the Creator, Glorious and Exalted is He. They consist of twenty sects.

(2) The Shīʿa ("Partisans" of ʿAlī) are extravagant in their love for ʿAlī ؓ. They consist of twenty-two sects.

---

24 A *ḥadīth* related in the *Sunan* of Abū Dāwūd and the *Sunan* of Ibn Māja.

25 This is likely ʿAlī b. Sultan Muḥammad al-Qārī (d. 1605, Mecca), a great Ḥanafī jurist and *ḥadīth* scholar originally from Herat (Persia). He was a student of Aḥmad b. Ḥajar al-Haythamī. The work in question is a commentary on the "Forty *ḥadīth*" collection of Imam Nawawī (d. 1277).

(3) The Murji'a ("Procrastinators") maintain that sinful disobedience is harmless if combined with faith, just as obedience is useless when combined with disbelief.

(4) The Khawārij ("Rebels") have detached themselves through their hatred of ʿAlī ☙, charging him with unbelief as they charge anybody they consider to have committed a major sin. They consist of twenty sects.

(5) The Najjāriyya (followers of Muḥammd al-Najjār) agree with the people of the Sunna regarding the creation of deeds, but with the Muʿtazila regarding the denial of divine Attributes and the denial of divine Speech. They consist of three sects.

(6) The Jabariyya ("Compulsionists") maintain that the servant of Allah is deprived of free will. They form a single sect.

(7) The Mushabbiha ("Assimilators") maintain that the Real is similar to the creatures in physical shape and incarnation (*ḥulūl*). They also form a single sect.

These are the seventy-two sects doomed to the Fire of Hell. The sect that is saved from damnation is comprised of those who follow the pure Sunna.

The Authority of the Sufi Shaykhs

Rūḥ al-bayān contains the following commentary on the verse, *O you who believe, obey Allah and obey the Messenger, and those in authority (amr) among you* (Qurʾān, 4:59):

> Know that the words "those in authority" actually refers to the consummate religious leaders (*al-mashāyikh al-wāṣilūn*) and those in whose hand is the authority for spiritual training (*amr al-tarbiya*). The one in charge of the disciple is the shaykh. Whenever a mystical experience (*wārid*) knocks at the door of the disciple's heart, or he receives a directive (from the Unseen), or an inspiration, or something happens that conveys information about actions or spiritual states that concern him, he should submit the matter to the shaykh for scrutiny. The shaykh will consider what benefits it may contain, and either will encourage him or restrain him. Because he is the one in authority, the disciple must obey his commands and his prohibitions. As for the shaykh, his authorities are the Qurʾān and the Sunna. Whenever he receives truthful insights (*wārid al-ḥaqq*) from the Unseen, in the form of unveilings, visions, (revelations of) secrets and realities, he should put them to the test of the Qurʾān and Sunna. If they confirm his experiences, he accepts them; but if not, he leaves them. This is because the spiritual path (*ṭarīqa*) is determined by the Qurʾān and

Sunna, as was mentioned by the perfect Shaykh Najm al-Dīn al-Kubrā in *Taʾwīlāt*.[26]

The wicked scholars (*ʿulamāʾ al-sūʾ*), slaves of lustful desires, are not what is meant by this (reference to those in authority), for they are an evil scourge beneath Heaven. Concerning the verse, *Say, "O People of the Book, why do you bar those who believe from Allah's way?"* (Qurʾān, 3:99), the author of *Rūḥ al-bayān* said:

> While this is addressed explicitly to the People of the Book, you should know that it refers implicitly to the wicked scholars. They sell the religion for the price of this world and do not put their knowledge into practice. They disbelieve in what comes in the Qurʾān in regard to abstinence (*zuhd*) from the world, piety (*warʿ*), fear (*taqwā*), restraining the self from lustful desires, preferring what is lasting to what is passing, shunning the creation while turning to the Real, and making efforts to attain the objective.
>
> Allah witnesses what they do, observing their intentions in good deeds and bad. He surely will requite them for what they do. By their greed for this world and their pursuit of lustful desires, they mislead the believers who follow them with good intent, believing their actions are based on the sacred law (*sharīʿa*) and the spiritual path (*ṭarīqa*). Such scholars divert people from the way of Allah and the path of truth, the path to which He has commanded His Prophets to summon their fellow beings. They try to circumvent the path of truth with the path of falsehood. Allah has advised the believers, saying, *O you who believe, obey Allah and obey the Messenger, and those in authority among you.* This is so the believers will not desert the path of right guidance after having believed by following bad conduct and lustful desires. He also said, *And do not follow the vain desires of a people who erred of old, who led many astray and were (themselves) led astray from the plain road* (Qurʾān, 5:77).
>
> One of the shaykhs has said that the best knowledge is that accompanied by fear (*khashya*), for fear comes only from knowledge of the attributes of the Real. Fear is the evidence of real knowledge, the type one wishes Allah to bestow. The evidence of fear is compliance with the commandment. Consider the knowledge that is accompanied by desire for this world, adulation of its rulers, ambitious pursuit of wealth, accumulation and hoarding, boastful pride, greed, far-reaching expectations and forgetfulness of the Hereafter. The one with this type of knowledge is very far indeed from being included among the

---

26 Najm al-Dīn al-Kubrā (d. 1221, eastern Persia) was a famous Sufi shaykh, known as "the sculptor of saints." The Kubrāwiyya Sufi order traces its lineage through him. The work mentioned here is not one of his more well-known works, but it likely contains his interpretation (*taʾwīl*) of the Qurʾān.

inheritors of the Prophets.[27] How can something be passed to an inheritor if doing so would compromise the quality it had with its original possessor? The scholar with the above description is like a candle that, as it casts light for others, immolates itself. Allah's Messenger ﷺ said:

> There will come upon the people a time when nothing is left of Islam except its name, and nothing of the Qurʾān except its transcription. Their hearts will be ruins of right guidance, and their mosques will be filled with their bodies. Wicked will be those of their scholars beneath heaven that day. Trouble will issue from them, and to them will it return.[28]

It is reported that Fudayl b. ʿĪyāḍ[29] once said: "We have heard that the Day of Resurrection will begin with (recompensing) the profligates among the scholars and the bearers of the Qurʾān, before the idol worshipers." An intelligent person should not be deceived by their outward appearance, but should observe the weakness of their conviction and the depravity of their condition and all its implications. The intelligent man should avoid those who conduct themselves in this manner. He must follow the way of the best of examples, take refuge with Allah through detaching himself from everything other than Him, and persist in the genuine affirmation of divine Oneness. Like this, he will be guided to the straight path. If someone dedicates himself to Him through annihiliation (*fanāʾ*) in divine Oneness, his path is the path of Allah. No one can bar him from it. Nothing can harm him, and the cunning and wickedness of his enemy cannot lead him astray. Whoever is with Allah, Allah is with him. He becomes his Guardian and Helper.

Such dedication is not within the means of the spiritual seekers, but Allah the Exalted may take His servant by the hand and lead him to his goal. If the servant's quest is genuine, he certainly will not be deprived of the answer (to his prayers). If someone seeks and strives with earnest endeavor, he will find. If someone knocks on a door, and keeps knocking, he will enter. May Allah protect us and you from the cunning of Satan and the trickery of a lower self inciting to evil (*al-nafs al-ammāra bi al-sūʾ*)

In reference to the verse, *And let there arise from you a community that summons to goodness, enjoining what is right, and forbidding what is*

---

27 This is a reference to the famous *ḥadīth*, "The scholars are the heirs of the prophets; and the prophets did not leave behind dinars or dirhams, only knowledge. So whoever acquires knowledge has acquired an abundant portion" (in the *Sunan* of Abū Dāwūd).

28 Cited by Hindī, *Kanz al-ʿummāl.*.

29 Imam Fudayl b. ʿĪyāḍ (d. 803) was a scholar and Sufi in the Hijaz known for his sincerity. He was one of the teachers of the ʿAbbāsid sultan Harūn al-Rashīd.

wrong; such are they who are successful (Qurʾān 3:104), the author of *Rūḥ al-bayān* also said:

> The verse implies that the members of this community summon to goodness by their deeds, not their words. This is the way they command what is right and forbid what is wrong, and they are the successful ones. So this is a warning to those who command what is right but do not do it themselves. Such is indicated in the report of Usāma, who once heard Allah's Messenger ﷺ say:
>
> > A man will be brought forth on the Day of Resurrection. He will be thrown into the Fire, so his intestines will spill into the Fire and he will circle around in it, just as the donkey circles around in its mill. The inhabitants of the Fire will gather around him and say, "O so-and-so, what is the matter with you? Were you not the one who used to command us to do the right, and forbid us to do the wrong?" To this he will reply, "I used to command you, but I did not do it myself."
>
> Those who summon to goodness in reality are the shaykhs of the spiritual path, for if someone does not know Allah, he does not know what is good. Absolute goodness is the absolute perfection realized by the human being in accordance with the degree of his knowledge (*maʿrifa*) of the Real and arrival (*wuṣūl*) to Him. And this was the perfect goodness that belonged to the Prophet ﷺ. Perfection cannot be attained by something ephemeral, so the people should be summoned to the Real Himself, or to the means to arriving to Him. This is the goodness to summon people. The right (to be commanded) is everything that draws one near to the Real. The wrong is everything that keeps one far from Him.
>
> Whoever is not endowed with (the reality of) divine Oneness (*tawḥīd*) and resolute dedication (*istiqāma*) does not have the authority to summon (*maqām al-daʿwa*). He who is not resolutely dedicated, even if he affirms divine Oneness, will sometimes command the right, but it may be wrong in actuality, and sometimes forbid the wrong, but it may be right in actuality. (In his lack of authority to summon to Allah) he is like one who reaches the station of communion (*jamʿ*) and is barred from the creation by the Real. How often these people make permissible what is forbidden and forbid what is permissible, for they are a veiled folk. But no veil remains for the people of absolute success, for they are the deputies (*khulafāʾ*) of Allah on His earth. May Allah bring us to knowledge of the reality of this state (*ḥāl*), and may He honor us with the arrival to His Exalted Majesty.

According to the *Jawāhir al-maᶜānī*:

> Our Shaykh Muḥammad al-Maghribī al-Shādhilī ﷺ[30] used to say: "You must seek the path of the Sufi masters, even if they are little known, and beware of those who are ignorant of the spiritual path, even if they are highly renowned. The knowledge of the Sufi people has been sufficiently honored by what Moses said to Khiḍr:[31] *Moses said to him, "May I follow you, in order for you to teach me some of the right guidance you have been taught?"* (Qurʾān, 18:66). This is the most compelling proof of the need to seek knowledge of the divine Reality (*al-Ḥaqīqa*), just as it is necessary to seek knowledge of the sacred law (*al-sharīᶜa*)."

Elsewhere in the *Jawāhir al-maᶜānī*, ᶜAlī Harāzim writes: "I have seen a letter sent by Shaykh Muḥyī al-Dīn b. al-ᶜArabī ﷺ to Shaykh Fakhr al-Dīn al-Rāzī, author of *al-Tafsīr* (*al-kabīr*), in which he explains to him the deficiency of his degree of knowledge. This in spite of the fact that Fakhr al-Dīn was one of the preeminent scholars in every science." The letter reads:

> Know my brother, may Allah assist us and you with His enabling grace, that a man does not attain perfection in the station of knowledge until he receives his knowledge directly from Allah the Exalted without any intermediary, such as the transmitted report of a shaykh. If one's knowledge comes only from transmitted reports, one becomes obsessed with the study of temporal phenomenon (*muḥadīthāt*). This is well known by the people of Allah. If someone devotes his life to the study of temporal phenomenon and their detailed classification, this becomes his allotment with his Lord, Almighty and Glorious is He. Such a person becomes completely engrossed in temporal phenomenon and fails to realize their reality.
>
> O my brother, if you traveled (the path) with the help of a shaykh from among the people of Allah, you would be led to the presence of witnessing the Real. You would learn from Him knowledge of affairs through genuine inspiration, without difficulty, fatigue or sleeplessness, just as Khiḍr learned it. There is no true knowledge except that which comes from unveiling (*kashf*) and witnessing (*shuhūd*), rather than speculation, thinking, supposition, and conjecture. The perfect Shaykh Abū Yazīd al-Bisṭāmī ﷺ used to say to the scholars of his era: "You have taken your knowledge from the scholars of the written texts, like a dead man from a dead man. But we have received our knowledge from the Ever-Living who never dies."
>
> O my brother, it is incumbent on you to refrain from seeking any of the sciences except those by which your essential nature will

30 Muḥammad al-Maghribī was a fifteenth-century shaykh of the Shādhiliyya order who conferred the Shādhiliyya on Jalāl al-Dīn al-Suyūṭī, among others.

31 Khiḍr is the name given for the mystical guide of Moses mentioned in the Qurʾān.

be perfected, and which will travel with you wherever you go. This is only the knowledge of Allah (*al-ʿilm bi-Llāh*) the Exalted, whenever it is bestowed or witnessed. As for your knowledge of medicine, for example, you need it only for the world of sickness and disease. If you moved to a world in which there is no sickness and no disease, whom would you treat with that knowledge?

So you have come to know, my brother, that it is unnecessary for the intelligent person to acquire anything of the sciences except that which will travel with him between worlds (*barzakh*). Otherwise (leave the sciences that) will part with you at the time of your move to the world of the Hereafter. Only two forms of knowledge travel with a man to the Hereafter. The first is the knowledge of Allah, Glorious and Exalted is He. The second is the knowledge of the regions (*mawāṭin*) of the Hereafter, so he will not fail to recognize the manifestations that occur to him there. This is so he will not say to the Real when He manifests Himself to him, "We take refuge with Allah from you!" Therefore, my brother, you must discover these two forms of knowledge in this abode so you may reap the benefits of them in the next abode. You should refrain from carrying around anything from the sciences of this abode, except that for which there is a pressing need in your journey to Allah the Almighty and Glorious. And this is according to the consensus of the people of Allah the Exalted.

The two desired forms of knowledge can be discovered only by means of secluded retreat (*khalwa*), spiritual discipline (*riyāḍa*) and effort (*mujāhada*), and rapture (*jadhb*) in the divine. I was intending to describe for you the secluded retreat and its prerequisites, and what will appear to you during it—one thing and the next in its proper sequence—but shortage of time has prevented me from that.

The habitual practice of one with no interest in the secrets of the sacred law is disputation. So they have refuted everything of which they were ignorant. They have become addicted to fanaticism and the love of appearance and leadership. They use the religion to eat of the world, instead of yielding to the people of Allah and submitting to them.

Appendix I

Concerning the Sufi Path

In *Laṭāʾif al-minan*, Shaʿrānī said: "The path of the Sufi people (*ṭarīq al-qawm*) has always been a rarity, in every age. Few have had the stamina to endure their shaykh's training (*tarbiya*) and his examination of their actions." That is why the Shaykh began to see the Muḥammadan virtues, such as piety, abstinence, fear of Allah the Most High, and so on, as being in the hands of the people of Allah. It is impossible to obtain such characteristics by random means. The path of the Sufi people thus consists entirely of battling against the lower self (*mujāhadat li-l-nafs*). But where is the one who is capable of virtuous conduct and dedicated opposition to the lower self, preferring the desire of the Real to the self's desire? This can only be attained by sacrificing the soul (*badhl al-rūḥ*). We know that the true Sufis were the imams of independent scholarly judgment (*mujtahidī*) and the scholars who put their knowledge into practice.

Suppose someone said: "If the way of Sufism had been a matter prescribed by the sacred law, the imams of independent scholarly judgment would have produced books about it. But we do not see any book of theirs on that subject, none whatsoever." Our response would be: The fact that these imams did not produce a single book on this subject was simply due to the paucity of maladies among the people of their era, and their general immunity from ostentation and hypocrisy. Even if such immunity did not extend to all the people of their time, the exceptions were very few, and any shortcoming of theirs was hardly apparent. That being the case, the main concern of the scholars of independent judgment was the dispersal of all the legal proofs to the cities and frontier regions. This was similarly the case with the leaders among the generation succeeding (the Companions of the Prophet), as well as their successors. Those proofs (which they furnished) are the subject matter of every science, and the principles of all rules of law are known by them. That was more important, therefore, than criticizing some people with regard to the movement of their hearts, which does not comprise the ritual practice of the religion. No intelligent person would ever say about Imam Ḥanīfa, for instance, or Imam Mālik, or Imam al-Shāfiʿī or Imam Aḥmad (b. Ḥanbal), ﷺ that any one of them knew himself to be guilty of ostentation, vanity, arrogance, envy, or hypocrisy, but did not do battle with his lower self and subject it to criticism. If they had been aware of their susceptibility to these afflictions, they would have given precedence to curing them over every other science. So understand this well.

Qushayrī, may Allah have mercy on him, said: "The Sufis originally came to be called Sufis when lustful desires and innovations began to appear, during the time of Imam Aḥmad b. Ḥanbal ﷺ. The term 'Sufi' was then applied exclusively to anyone who faithfully adhered to the Qurʾān and the Sunna, and acted according to them." He also said, "We have been informed that Imam Abū al-Qāsim al-Junayd ﷺ used to say: 'This spiritual path (*ṭarīqa*) of ours is based on the Qurʾān and the Sunna. If someone does not read the Qurʾān and write the prophetic traditions, he is not to be emulated in this (path).'" In the seventy-third chapter of *al-Futūḥāt*, Shaykh Muḥyī al-Dīn (Ibn al-ʿArabī) said: "Know that we have no evidence that disproves the method of the Sufis, and no reproach that refutes it, either from the sacred law or from transmitted report. Those who attack Sufism do so out of sheer ignorance." In *al-Ibrīz*, Ibn al-Mubārak quoted the words of his Shaykh (al-Dabbāgh):

> Hidden knowledge (*ʿilm al-bāṭin*) is like ninety-nine lines of golden writing, while exoteric knowledge is like the final one-hundredth line in ordinary ink. Nevertheless, if this line in black ink were not together with the golden lines, they would not be of any benefit, and their owner would not be safe.

Ibn al-Mubārak also reported his Shaykh's words to him on another occasion:

> Exoteric knowledge is like the torch that shines at night, providing splendid benefit in the darkness. Hidden knowledge is like the rising sun and brilliance of the light at high noon. Perhaps its owner will say about the torch in his hand, "Allah has enabled me to dispense with it by the light of the day." So he will put it out. At that very moment, however, the light of the day will depart from him, and he will return to the darkness of the night. The persistence of his daylight is therefore conditional on his refraining from extinguishing the torch in his hand.

In *al-Jawāhir wa al-durar*,[1] Shaʿrānī said:

1 Shaʿrānī's *Kitāb al-jawāhir wa al-durar min-mā istafadu Sayyid ʿAbd al-Wahhāb al-Shaʿrānī min Shaykhihi Sayyidi ʿAlī al-Khawwāṣ* is a collection of teachings of Shaʿrānī's Shaykh ʿAlī al-Khawwāṣ.

> I once asked our Shaykh (ʿAlī al-Khawwāṣ) ﷺ about the statement of some of them, "The combination of two opposites is inconceivable." I said, "Is this statement valid in reference to the gnostic sages of Allah the Almighty and Glorious?" He replied, "I have heard one of the enraptured ones say, 'The combination of two opposites in not inconceivable, except for one whose mind is stuck. As for one whom Allah reinforces with divine strength, the judgment of his mind is included (in this strength), so he does not find this inconceivable.' It is known that the Real, Exalted is He, and the world are two opposites, yet they are joined together without incarnation, without unification or delimitation. If someone does not combine the two opposites (in this case), his (knowledge of) divine Oneness (*tawḥīd*) is imperfect. Moreover, he doubts many prophetic traditions, for the combination of two opposites is one of the strongest proofs of divine Singularity (*al-Waḥdāniyya*). This is because if a person sees himself as a necessary existent being, he has committed polytheism. On the other hand, the one who is not (seeing himself as) indispensable to existence, he (realizes himself as) nonexistent and present at the same time.
>
> Know that the combination of opposites is only something inconceivable to the mind, for (the person affirming divine Oneness) sees multiplicity as one, and one as many, at one and the same time, in one single realization, without interpretation or alteration. And this occurs while the conditions for contrariety are fulfilled. The degree of sainthood is other than what is familiar to the scholars whose judgment is determined solely by their minds. It should be clear to you, my brother that, in actuality, the combination of two opposites is impossible: there is nothing existing except Allah, and He has no opposite. This subject has once again become similar to the doctrine of the scholastic theologians, but with a perspective that is contrary to their point of view. So contemplate this with careful attention.

Consider this passage from *Rūḥ al-bayān*:

> Know that the spiritual seekers (*sālikīn*) are of various types. It takes some of them seventy years to cut through the obstacles and pierce the veils. It takes others ten years, or one year, or one month, or even one week, or even one hour. Some of them even reach their destination in a single instant, by special good fortune from Allah and His foreordained assistance. Remember the sorcerers of Pharaoh when they witnessed the miracle of Moses. They only took one instant to say, *We believe in the Lord of all the worlds* (Qurʾān, 7:121). They saw the way and traversed it without hesitation, so they came, moment to moment—or in even less time than that—to be endowed with the gnosis of Allah.

It is related that Ibrāhīm b. Adham[2] used to be involved in his worldly business, but then turned away from that to embark on the path to the Truth. His journey had taken him no farther than the distance from Balkh to Marw al-Rudh, when he saw a man fall off the bridge over a flooded river. He signaled to him, "Stop!" The man came to a halt in midair and was saved.

Rābiʿa al-ʿAdawiyya al-Baṣriyya was an elderly enslaved woman who was put up for sale in the market of Baṣra, but nobody wanted her because of her advanced age. One of the merchants took pity on her, so he bought her for one hundred dirhams (small silver coins), then promptly emancipated her. Then she chose to embark on the path of Truth, devoting herself to worship. Before one year had passed, she was being visited by the (Qurʾān) readers and scholars of Baṣra due to the grandeur of her status.

The one for whom divine assistance has not been foreordained, who has not practiced virtuous conduct, will put all his trust in his lower self. He may well get stuck in a ravine on the mountain path for seventy years, unable to make his way across it. How often will he yell and cry, "How dark and rough is this path! How difficult and problematic is this business!"

If you were to ask, "Why is one singled out for divine success, while the other is deprived, although both of them are partners in the rope of servitude?" The answer to that question comes from on the Majestic Heights: *You must adhere to virtuous conduct (adab), and you must know the secret of Lordship and the reality of servitude, for "He will not be questioned as to what He does, but they will be questioned"* (Qurʾān, 21:23). *Such is the judgment and ordering of (Him), the Mighty, the Wise* (6:96). *All bounty is in Allah's hand. He bestows it on whom He wills* (3:73). *Allah is the Lord of infinite bounty* (3:74).

May Allah include us among those for whom assistance is foreordained, who are destined to receive success and guidance from Him. Amen, O Lord of all the worlds.

In *Taʾsīs al-qawāʾid*, Shaykh Zarrūq has said:

> Receiving knowledge and practice from the spiritual masters (*mashāyikh*) is more perfect than receiving it from others. Allah the Exalted said, *Nay, here are Signs self-evident in the hearts of those endowed with knowledge* (Qurʾān, 29:49). And He said, *And follow the path of the one who has turned to Me* (31:15). This applies in particular to the spiritual masters. The companions received it from the Prophet ﷺ, who received it from (the angel) Gabriel. The Prophet followed his

2 Sultan Ibrāhīm b. Adham (d. 777) was the king of the Balkh (Khurasan, Persia) who abandoned his throne to take up the life of a Sufi ascetic upon the promptings of several visions, including one of Khiḍr, the mystical guide of Moses.

direction to be a prophet-servant, rather than a prophet-king. The generation succeeding that of the Prophet received from the Companions. So it came to be known by the likes of Ibn Sīrīn and Ibn al-Musayyab, or Aʿraj who received from Abū Hurayra; or Ṭāwūs, Wahb, and Mujāhid, who all received from Ibn ʿAbbās. What has been mentioned here clearly pertains to receiving both knowledge and practice.

As for acquiring the benefit of devotional zeal (*himma*) and spiritual state (*ḥāl*), this is something Anas referred to when he said, "No sooner had we dusted off our hands from burying him ﷺ than we had already abandoned our hearts." He clearly meant that the sight of his noble person was a benefit to their hearts. The religious scholars are the heirs of the prophets, in the present and in the future, even if they have not measured up to the status (of the prophets). This is the reason for seeking nearness to the people of Allah in general. That is why He commanded keeping fellowship with the righteous, and forbade companionship with the profligates. So understand this well.

Shaykh al-Ṣāwī[3] said, in his commentary of Allah's saying, *And do not hurry with the Qurʾān, before its revelation has been completed for you* (Qurʾān, 20:114):

> In other words, (Allah is telling the Prophet) "You must not be hasty in reciting what Gabriel has implanted in your heart, until he recites it to you." The reason for this instruction is that Gabriel used to come to the Prophet with the Qurʾān, then draw close to his body and place the revelation in his heart. Then the Prophet would wish to make haste and pronounce it. Allah therefore commanded him not to pronounce it until Gabriel recited it to him with clear verbal expression. This is the meaning of the saying of the Exalted, *Do not move your tongue with it to hasten it. It is for Us to gather it together, and to recite it. So, when We recite it, follow its recitation. Then it is for Us to explain it* (Qurʾān, 75:16–19). The wisdom in Allah's Messenger ﷺ receiving directly from Gabriel is that this becomes an exemplary custom practiced by his community. His community therefore is commanded to receive it from the mouths of the spiritual masters, for a person does not succeed by receiving knowledge of the Qurʾān from lines of writing. The means of his actual instruction is another secret entirely.

Shaykh al-Zarrūq also said in *Taʾsīs al-qawāʾid*:

> The spiritual elite are steadfast in their words, their deeds, and their essential beings. Preeminent among them are the masters of remem-

3 The work referred to is the *Tafsīr al-Ṣāwī ʿala al-Jalālayn*, thus Aḥmad al-Ṣāwī's commentary on the Qurʾān exegesis of Jalāl al-Dīn al-Maḥallī and Jalāl al-Dīn al-Suyūṭī.

brance, since no deed performed by a human being is more certain to deliver him from Allah's torment than the remembrance of Allah.

But Allah has created things that are beneficial only for certain ends, similar to liquor and drugs, so the general rule of the law must be observed. In the special case (of remembrances), however, the state and conduct of the individual evade assessment from the legal standpoint. This applies both to the intention and the action. On the subject of such unknown matters, Mālik, may Allah have mercy on him, asked, "How can you tell whether they constitute unbelief?"

Speaking for myself, I have seen someone making (protective) invocations (*raqiya*) by pronouncing blasphemous expressions. Allah knows best. Shaykh Zarrūq said later in the same work:

> The sacred law is decisively settled on the permissibility of adopting those remembrances and supplication of which the meaning is perfectly clear, even if it is not authenticated by a traditional report. This has been established by Ibn al-ʿArabī in *al-Sirāj*, as well as by others. Several prophetic traditions relate the effectiveness of the devoted servant's supplication proceeding from his spiritual zeal. In the chapter on prophetic supplications in the *Muwaṭṭāʾ*, Mālik, may Allah have mercy on him, included the saying reported by Abū al-Dardāʾ: "The eyes have gone to sleep and eyelids have calmly relaxed, and nothing remains but You, O Ever-Living, O Eternally Self-Sustaining." To someone who invoked Allah by saying, "I ask You, for You are Allah, the Unique," the Prophet ﷺ said, "You have appealed to Allah by invoking His Greatest Name."[4] He said the same to someone who supplicated, "O Ever-Loving, O Lord of the Splendid Throne," and to others (who made other supplications).
>
> This proves the correctness of accepting every supplication of clear meaning and which is commendable in its nature. This is especially the case when it is based on a valid source, like the dream of a righteous person, and when the merit of the inspiration has been established; as in the case of the prayers (*aḥzab*) of Shādhilī, Nawawī, and others like them. As for the prayers of Ibn Sabʿīn,[5] there are many obscure and dubious elements of them. It is necessary to shun them altogether due to the risk involved, except if the scholar considers the meaning and does not take them at face value. The liturgical offices (*waẓāʾif*) compiled from the prophetic traditions are more perfect, however, especially when they are received from the spiritual masters, since

4 *Ḥadīth* reported in the *Sunan* of Abū Dāwūd, the *Sunan* of Nasāʾī, and the *Musnad* of Ibn Ḥanbal.

5 Muḥammad b. ʿAbd al-Ḥaqq b. Sabʿīn (d. 1268, Mecca) was a renowned Sufi who taught of the unity of creation.

nothing is added to them apart from the compilation. The orisons of Shādhilī have passed the test of detailed analysis and complete examination by scholars well-versed in the prophetic traditions. This includes what these orisons contain by way of reminding and exerting influence over particular desired affairs. And Allah knows best.

APPENDIX II

Concerning the Tijānī Litanies

The litany (*wird*) of the Tijānī spiritual path consists of the following elements: 1) the plea for forgiveness, 2) the invocation of blessing upon the chosen Prophet, 3) the remembrance that there is no god but Allah, and 4) the recitation of certain verses of the Qurʾān. Its excellence exceeds other litanies, for our master (Shaykh al-Tijānī), according to his own account, received it by word of mouth from the Prophet. Shaykh al-Tijānī is an honest man, and the account of the honest man must be accepted. In this case especially, evidence proving his truthfulness is apparent to anyone whose perception has been enlightened by Allah.

Taking refuge in Allah

Our litany begins with the plea for refuge, made by saying, "I take refuge with Allah from Satan the accursed." As we are told in *Rūḥ al-bayān*:

> Know that the meaning of seeking refuge is asking permission to enter (the divine Presence), knocking at the door. When a person comes to the door of one of the kings, he cannot enter without the king's permission. In the same way, when someone intends to recite the Qurʾān, he is actually seeking to enter into intimate conversation with the Beloved. So he needs to purify his tongue by seeking refuge, because it has been soiled by gossip and slander. Some of the masters of gnosis have said: "This statement is the means of access for those who draw near (to the Lord), the safeguard of the fearful, the reformation of the criminals, the rescue of those doomed to perdition, and the good cheer of the lovers." It entails compliance with the saying of the Lord of all the worlds in the (Qurʾānic) Chapter of the Bee: *If you recited the Qurʾān, you must seek refuge with Allah from Satan the accursed* (16:98). This means that the plea for refuge must precede the recitation, according

to the vast majority of Muslims. There are others who say, "The main clause of the conditional sentence (involved in this verse) comes after the condition, so the plea for refuge must be postponed (until after the recitation)." In our opinion, however, the meaning is, "If you intend to perform the recitation (seek refuge)," and this is a widely accepted interpretation, compatible with conventional linguistic usage.

As for the wording of the plea for refuge, the preferred formulation is that of the majority, namely: "I take refuge with Allah from Satan the accursed." Such has been authenticated by the prophetic tradition (which goes on to say), "This is how Gabriel taught me to recite it, on the authority of the inscription on the Well-Preserved Tablet (*al-lawḥ al-maḥfūẓ*)."

After further discussion, the author said:

> Know that the words of the plea for refuge are of three kinds: 1) relating to the attributes of Allah, 2) relating to the actions of Allah, and 3) relating to the Essence of Allah. All of these types are referred to when the Prophet ﷺ supplicated, "I take refuge with Your good pleasure from Your disapproval, and with Your exemption from Your punishment, and with You from You."[1] Allah's comprehensive, majestic Name is preferred (in the supplication), so that the form in which the plea for refuge is expressed will incorporate these three types.

In *al-Tafsīr al-kabīr* (Fakhr al-Dīn al-Rāzī) said:

> Evils stem either from the false doctrines, including those of the seventy-two misguided sects, or from physical acts. Some (of these actions)—those that nullify religious duties and their correct performance—harm the religion, like the excuse of (religious duties) being impractical (*muta'adhdhir*). Some of them are not harmful to the religion, like diseases, aches and pains, burning, drowning, poverty, blindness, chronic illness, and other such tribulations and afflictions. The declaration, "I take refuge with Allah," comprises the plea for refuge from all of these evils of doctrine and action. So the intelligent person, when he makes the plea for refuge, should envision these different types of evil and their various forms. When he realizes that they are without limit, he will acknowledge his inability to repel them, so his mind will prompt him to say, "I take refuge with Allah, He who is Capable of dealing with all problems, all dangers, and all disasters."
>
> It is said that all knowledge is contained in the four (previous) books (of revelation), and that all of this knowledge is contained in the Qur'ān. All knowledge in the Qur'ān is contained in its opening

1 Prophetic supplication reported by Tirmidhī, by Nasā'i in his *Sunan*, and by Ibn Ḥanbal in his *Musnad*.

> chapter (*al-Fātiḥa*). All of *al-Fātiḥa* is contained in (its first line), "In the Name of Allah, the Compassionate, the Merciful" (*basmala*). All of the *basmala* is contained in its first letter, *bāʾ*, as Allah the Exalted wills.[2]

Later in *al-Tafsīr al-kabīr*, the author said:

> The reason for this is that the purpose of all knowledge is to allow the servant to attain to the Lord. The *bāʾ* that is linked to Allah[3] links the servant to Him. So he will discover the secrets of the *bāʾ* in the *basmala*, if Allah the Exalted wills.

After a lengthy discussion, the author then said:

> The real meaning of the plea for refuge is said to be beyond verbal utterance. Its discovery is impossible without presence of heart and harmony between speech, spiritual state, and action. It is useless for your tongue to say, "I take refuge with Allah," while your spiritual state and actions are saying, "I take refuge with Satan." This latter would be due to the lower self's partnership with Satan while committing sinful acts of disobedience and rebellion. The gnostic's plea is for refuge from the recognition of anything other than Allah, and from the veil of multiplicity, for surely Satan flees from the light of spiritual understandings (*maʿārif*).
>
> It is related that Abū Saʿīd al-Kharrāz, may Allah sanctify his innermost being, once saw Iblīs in a dream, so he threatened to strike him with his staff. But Iblīs said, "O Abū Saʿīd, I am not afraid of the staff. I am only afraid of the rays of the sun of gnosis when it rises in the firmament of the gnostic's heart."
>
> To those who say, "Pleading for refuge from Satan implies the fear of something other than Allah, and falls short of true worship," our response will be: "Treating the enemy as an enemy is a confirmation of love. It is fleeing to Allah from everything other than Allah, as a means of perfecting true worship and complying with Allah's commandment. The fear of someone who does not fear Allah is a display of wretchedness, as if he is saying, "I am afraid of Allah, but only from His punishment and anger. I am afraid of him of who fears Allah, but only from the injurious effect of his supplication. I am afraid of him who does not fear Allah, but only from the evil effect of his actions."

After further discussion, the author continues:

> When the Prophet ﷺ was asked about the whispering of Satan, he replied, "The thief does not enter a house that has nothing in it!" Thus

---

2 In the context at hand, this is meant to refer to the letter *bāʾ* in the plea for refuge, *aʿūdhu bi-Llāh*

3 The *bāʾ* in "*aʿūdhu bi-Llāh*" or "*bismi-Llāh*" has the meaning of "with" (Allah) or "in" (the Name of Allah).

> Satan's whispering is motivated by the presence of true belief. ʿAlī b. Abī Ṭālib ﷺ said, "The difference between our prayer and the prayer of the People of the Book (Jews and Christians) is the whispering of Satan. He has finished dealing with the unbelievers, since they have concurred with him, whereas the believers oppose and fight him; so with combat comes opposition."
>
> It is related that a man set out from his native Khurasan in the direction of Iraq. When he arrived in Iraq, he frequented one of the scholars, until he was taught four thousand counsels (*ḥadīth*) of wisdom. Then, when he wished to leave for his homeland, he sought permission from his teacher. The teacher said to him, "Shall I give you a word of advice that is worth more than all of your counsels?" He said, "What is it?" The teacher asked, "Will Iblīs be in Khurasan?" He said, "Yes." So the teacher asked, "Will he tempt you?" He said, "Yes." So the teacher asked, "How will you deal with his temptation?" He said, "We shall reject him." The teacher asked, "What if he tempts you again?" He said, "We shall reject him again." The teacher then said, "When the enemy of Allah annoys you, and distracts you from worshipful obedience, you must not become preoccupied with rejecting his temptation. Be with him like a stranger with the shepherd's dog. You must seek refuge with Allah, for Satan is a dog from among the dogs." May Allah keep us all safe from Satan's cunning and wickedness.

The real reason for beginning our litany with the plea for refuge is that Allah has taught us that Satan is an enemy to us, and He has commanded us to treat him as an enemy. The Exalted said, *Surely Satan is an enemy to you, so treat him as an enemy* (Qurʾān, 35:6). Treating the enemy as an enemy means remaining constantly on guard against him by taking protective measures. Once we have appealed for refuge, we have entered an impregnable fortress, and we are left free to experience the pleasure and comfort that become available in the remainder of the litany. Thus the prevention of bad things clears the way for the obtainment of benefits.

Beginning in the name of Allah

Next in our litany comes the *Basmala*, *In the Name of Allah, the Compassionate, the Merciful*, which is linked to the opening chapter of the Qurʾān (*al-Fātiḥa*). According to *Rūḥ al-bayān*:

> Allah the Exalted has three thousand Names. He made one thousand of them known to none but the angels, and He made one thousand of them known to none but the Prophets. Three hundred are in the Torah, three hundred are in the Gospel, three hundred are in the Psalms, and ninety-nine are in the Qurʾān. Allah has kept one Name to Himself. The meaning of all these three thousand Names is contained within these three Names (Allah, the Compassionate [al-Raḥmān], the Merciful

[al-Raḥīm]. If someone knows them and practices them, it is as if he has remembered Allah the Exalted by all His Names.[4]

The Prophet ﷺ is reported to have said: "On the night when I was transported to heaven, all the Gardens were displayed to me, and in them I saw four rivers: a river of water, a river of milk, a river of wine, and a river of honey. So I said, 'O Gabriel, from where do these rivers come from, and whither are they going?' He said, 'They are going to the Lake of Abundance (*ḥawḍ al-kawthar*), but I do not know where they come from, so ask Allah the Exalted to inform you.'" When he asked his Lord, an angel came and greeted the Prophet ﷺ and said, "O Muḥammad, close your eyes." He said, "So I closed my eyes. Then the angel said, 'Open your eyes,' so I opened my eyes, and there I found myself beside a tree. I saw a dome of white pearl, and it had a door of bright gold, with a lock. If all the jinn and human beings in this world were placed on that dome, they would be like a bird perched on a mountain. Then I saw these four rivers emerging from underneath this dome. When I wished to return, the angel said to me, 'Why did you not enter the dome?' I said, 'How can I enter, when there is a lock on its door for which I have no key?' The angel said, 'Its key is, *Bismi-Llāh al-Raḥmān al-Raḥīm* (In the Name of Allah, the Compassionate, the Merciful).'

"Then, when I approached the lock and said, 'In the Name of Allah, the Compassionate, the Merciful,' the lock opened and I entered the dome. There I saw these four rivers, flowing from the four pillars of the dome. Inscribed on the four pillars I saw, 'In the Name of Allah, the Compassionate, the Merciful.' I saw the river of water flowing from the letter *mīm* in *Bismi-Llāh* (In the Name of Allah). I saw the river of milk flowing from the letter *hāʾ* in Allah, the river of wine flowing from the letter *mīm* in *al-Raḥmān* (the Compassionate) and the river of honey flowing from the letter *mīm* in *al-Raḥīm* (the Merciful). I knew then that the source of these four rivers was the *basmala*.

"Then Allah the Almighty and Glorious said, 'O Muḥammad, if someone from your community remembers Me by these Names, with a heart free from hypocritical ostentation, and he says, *Bismi-Llāh al-Raḥmān al-Raḥīm*, I shall let him drink from these rivers.'"

According to a prophetic tradition, "A supplication that begins with *Bismi-Llāh al-Raḥmān al-Raḥīm*, will not be rejected." In another tradition, the Prophet ﷺ said: "If someone picks up from the ground a sheet of paper bearing the inscription, 'In the Name of Allah, the Compassionate, the Merciful,' respectfully preserving Allah's Name from being soiled, he will be included among the most truthful

4 This saying has also been reported by Suyūṭī in *al-Durr al-manthūr*.

(*ṣiddīqīn*) in Allah's sight. Even if his parents were polytheists, their burden will be lightened because of him."[5]

In *Laṭā'if al-ishārāt*, Shaykh Aḥmad al-Būnī[6] said, "The tree of existence has branched out from 'In the Name of Allah, the Compassionate, the Merciful,' and the entire universe is based on it, as a whole and in its individual details. So someone who remembers it frequently is endowed with dignity in both the higher and lower worlds. The Roman emperor wrote to ʿUmar ﷺ saying, 'I have a headache that will not go away, so send me a remedy if you have one at your disposal, for the physicians are incapable of treating it.' ʿUmar ﷺ responded by sending him a turban. When the Emperor put it on his head, his headache went away, and when he took it off, his headache came back. So he marveled at this. He examined the turban and found it contained a piece of paper on which was written, 'In the Name of Allah, the Compassionate, the Merciful.'"

The Greatest Shaykh (Ibn al-ʿArabī) said in *al-Futūḥāt*, "When you recited the opening chapter of the Qur'ān (*Fātiḥa al-Kitāb*), you must connect 'In the Name of Allah, the Compassionate, the Merciful,' with a single breath, without interruption. It is reported on the authority of Muḥammad the Chosen One ﷺ, who said he heard it from Gabriel, who said he heard it from (the angel) Michael, who said he heard it from (the angel) Isrāfīl, that Allah the Exalted said: 'O Isrāfīl, by My Might, My Majesty, and My Abundance, if someone recites *Bismi-Llāh al-Raḥmān al-Raḥīm* together with the opening chapter of the Qur'ān (*Fātiḥa al-Kitāb*), bear witness that I have forgiven him and accepted his good deeds. I shall not burn his tongue with the Fire, and I shall protect him from the torment of the grave, the torment of the Fire, the torment of the Day of Resurrection, and the most terrifying plight. He will meet with me before (he meets) all the prophets and saints.'"

The Opening Chapter of the Qur'ān, *al-Fātiḥa*

Sufficient proof of the excellence of *al-Fātiḥa* is the fact that it is called "Mother of the Book." It consists of the seven oft-repeated (verses).[7] As

---

5 This *ḥadīth* is also reported by Abū Nuʿaym, and cited by Suyūṭī. It is also reported by Khatīb al-Baghdadi.

6 There seems to be little record of a book by Shaykh al-Būnī (d. 1225, Maghrib) by this name. The early Sufi Qushayrī wrote an exegesis of the Qur'ān by the name, *Laṭā'if al-ishārāt*. There is also the *Laṭā'if al-ishārāt li funūn al-qirā'at* by Aḥmad b. Muḥammad al-Qastallanī (d. 1517). It is possible this later work cites Būnī, or it is possible that Būnī's work by this name has simply escaped our attention.

7 After the *Basmala*, these verses are: *Praise be to Allah, the Lord of all the worlds / The Compassionate, the Merciful / Master of the Day of Judgment / You alone do we worship, and You alone do we ask for help / Guide us to the straight path / The path of those whom*

mentioned in *Rūḥ al-bayān*, its special merits include those referred to by the Prophet ﷺ when he said:

> If it had been in the Torah, the people of Moses would not have adopted Judaism. If it had been in the Gospel, the people of Jesus would not have adopted Christianity. If it had been in the Psalms, the people of David would not have been transformed into monkeys. For any Muslim who recites it, Allah will grant him the same reward as if he had recited the whole Qurʾān, and as if he had made charitable donations to every believing man and believing woman.

Its special merits also include the fact that it contains twenty-two letters of the Arabic alphabet, and twenty-two was the number of those who helped the Prophet ﷺ after he received the revelation. Seven letters (of the Arabic alphabet) do not occur in *al-Fātiḥa*. They are the *thāʾ* of *al-thubūr* (destruction), the *jīm* of *al-jaḥīm* (Hellfire), the *khāʾ* of *al-khawf* (fear), the *zāy* of *al-zaqqūm* (the tree of bitter fruit in Hell), the *shīn* of *al-shaqāwa* (misfortune), the *ẓāʾ* of *al-ẓulma* (darkness), and the *fāʾ* of *al-firāq* (separation). If someone firmly believes in (the merit of) this Qurʾān chapter, and recites it in a state of reverence and veneration, he will be safe from these seven things.

According to Ḥudhayfa, the Prophet ﷺ said: "Allah will surely inflict the people with a prescribed and inevitable punishment, but when He hears one of the children in school (*maktab*) saying, 'Praise be to Allah, Lord of all the worlds,' He will relieve the people's punishment for forty years."[8]

As previously mentioned, the knowledge of all the revelations are contained not only in the Qurʾān, but also in the *Fātiḥa*. So if someone learns its interpretation, he is like someone who has learned the interpretation of the whole Qurʾān, and if someone recites it, it is as if he has recited the whole Qurʾān. According to *al-Tafsīr al-kabīr*, "The reason is that the purpose of all the revelations is to provide knowledge of the roots, branches, and discoveries, and the *Fātiḥa* is known to contain all of this." Nawawī said,

> That is because its first part, up to Allah's saying, *Master of the Day of Judgment* (1:4), indicates the basic articles of faith relating to divinity, in terms of divine Essence, Attributes, and Action. Understanding the notion of praise (*ḥamd*) requires comprehension of the essential, attributive, and acting perfections (of the One praised). It also alludes to the prophecy and sainthood, since the prophets and the saints are endowed with the finest and most special blessings. It also alludes to

You have favored / Not of those who have incurred Your wrath, nor of those who have gone astray (Qurʾān, 1:1–7).

8 A *ḥadīth* cited by Zamakhsharī in his Qurʾān exegesis entitled *al-Kashshāf ʿan ḥaqāʾiq ghawāmiḍ al-tanzīl*.

the belief in the Hereafter, because Allah is the Master of everything on the Day of Resurrection.

As for its middle part, namely, *You alone do we worship, of You alone do we seek help* (1:5), this refers to the rules governing the acts of true worship, which form a bond between the Real and the servant. This also concerns the business dealings and restraints imposed upon the servants, because seeking help is lawful only when its purpose is either the obtainment of benefits or the prevention of harmful things.

As for the conclusion, *Guide us to the straight path, the path of those whom You have blessed, not of those who earn Your wrath, nor of those who go astray* (1:6–7), this relates to the believers' quest for the kinds of guidance that are the consequence of true faith.

The submission (*islām*) mentioned in the second part (*You alone do we worship, of You alone do we seek help*) relates to the various aspects of spiritual excellence (*iḥsān*). By this I mean the three degrees of praiseworthy spiritual virtues (*akhlāq*). It also includes the covenanted witnessing (of Allah) in the saying of the Prophet ﷺ, "You must worship Allah as if you see Him." It also relates to the perfections witnessed at the point of total immersion in the manifestation of divine Majesty, as indicated by the expression, "as if" in the (above) prophetic tradition.

These (insights) are included among the sciences of revelations. And Allah is the One who knows the secrets of all mysteries.

As for the *Amīn* ("Amen," pronounced at the end of the recitation of the *Fātiḥa*), the Prophet ﷺ once said, "Gabriel taught me to say *Amīn* when I had finished reciting the *Fātiḥa*, and he said, 'It is like the seal on the Book.'"[9] ʿAlī ﷺ added a clarification to this when he said, "*Amīn* is the seal of the Lord of all the worlds, with which He seals His servant's supplication. The secret of this is that, just as a seal protects what is sealed from intrusion and mishandling, so does the *Amīn* protect the servant's supplication from disappointment." Wahb said, "With each of its letters, an angel has been created who says, "O Allah, forgive anyone who says, '*Amīn*.'" According to prophetic tradition, "The supplicant and the person who says *Amīn* are partners." This is in reference to Allah's saying, *He said, "The supplication of the two has been answered"* (Qurʾān, 10:89). The Prophet ﷺ said:

> When the prayer leader says (at the end of the *Fātiḥa*), "Nor of those who go astray," you must say, "*Amīn*," for the angels will say it, and if a person's saying *Amīn* coincides with the angels saying *Amīn*, he will be forgiven all his previous sins.[10]

9 A *ḥadīth* cited by Zamakhsharī in *al-Kashshāf*.

10 A *ḥadīth* reported in the *Ṣaḥīḥ* of Bukhārī, the *Ṣaḥīḥ* of Muslim, the *Sunan* of Nasāʾī and the *Musnad* of Ibn Ḥanbal.

Some say the coinciding (mentioned in this tradition) refers to the timing of the utterance. Others say it refers to sincerity and singular devotion. There is also difference of opinion with regard to (the identity of) these angels: some say they are the Guardian Angels, while some say they are others. The latter view is supported by the saying attributed to the Prophet: ﷺ "If a person's utterance coincides with the utterance of the Inhabitants of Heaven ..."[11] It is also possible for the two views to be reconciled by maintaining that the angels concerned are both the Guardian Angels and the Inhabitants of Heaven. This is a lengthy topic, so we have restrained the pen from writing more about it here.

The Plea for Forgiveness

Next in our litany comes the plea for Allah's forgiveness (*al-istighfār*), repeated one hundred times. Allah the Exalted has said, *And (you are instructed) that you must beg forgiveness of your Lord* (11:3). The Prophet ﷺ said, "My heart is surely distracted, so I plead for Allah's forgiveness seventy times each day."[12] I would add here that this distraction was the distraction of lights, not the distraction of others apart from Allah. Since he ﷺ was constantly elevated with each breath, he saw every spiritual station as deficient in comparison to the one above it. His plea for forgiveness should be understood in this sense. Allah knows best. In *al-Kawkab al-wahhāj*, (Shaykh Aḥmad Sukayrij) said:

> Know that it is incumbent on every intelligent and truthful person to preoccupy himself with pleading for forgiveness in the watches of the night and at the two ends of the day. The human being is not faultless, and if someone is overconfident of his obedience, he is debarred (from the divine Presence).
>
> If you should say, "I have not sinned," a voice will reply,
> "Your existence is a sin, with which no sin can be compared!"[13]
>
> Shaykh Abū al-Ḥasan al-Shādhilī ؓ said, "You must make the plea for forgiveness, even if no sin has been committed. Consider how the Prophet ﷺ begged forgiveness, even after receiving the glad tiding of Allah's forgiving all his previous and future sins. If this applies to the perfect being ﷺ, who never committed a sin and was sanctified from that, what do you think of someone who is not free from shortcoming and sin at any moment of time?"

---

11 A *ḥadīth* reported in the *Sunan* of Tirmidhī.

12 A *ḥadīth* reported in the *Ṣaḥīḥ* of Muslim, the *Sunan* of Abū Dāwūd, the *Ṣaḥīḥ* of Bukhārī and the *Sunan* of Tirmidhī.

13 These poetic verses are also cited in the *Jawāhir al-maʿānī*. The meaning draws on an understanding of *fanāʾ* (annihilation in the divine Presence), and the knowledge that nothing exists except Allah.

The excellence of the plea for forgiveness is the subject of many Qurʾānic verses and prophetic traditions. Allah's Messenger ﷺ once said:

> Allah the Exalted has sent down to me two assurances of immunity for my community: *Allah will not punish them while you (the Prophet) are among them* (Qurʾān, 8:33); and *Allah will not punish them while they are pleading for forgiveness* (8:33). So when I pass away, I will leave the plea for forgiveness among them.[14]

And Allah's Messenger ﷺ once said, as reported by Abū Dāwūd, Ṭabarānī, Abū Yaʿlā and Ibn Mardawayh:

> An angel came to me from my Lord, and he said, *Yet if someone commits an evil deed, or wrongs his own soul, but then seeks forgiveness of Allah, he will find Allah the Forgiving, the Merciful* (4:110). They (the companions) had been troubled by the Qurʾān verse revealed before, *If someone commits an evil deed, he will be requited for it* (4:123), so I was keen to give the good news to my companions.[15]

ʿUwaymir Abū al-Dardāʾ ؓ said:

> I asked, "O Messenger of Allah, will a person be forgiven even if he commits adultery or theft, but then seeks forgiveness?" He said, "Yes!" I asked again, "O Messenger of Allah, even if he commits adultery or theft, but then seeks forgiveness, will he be forgiven?" He said, "Yes!" Then I asked a third time, and he said, "Yes, just to put ʿUwaymir's nose out of joint!" Kaʿb b. Dhahl said, "I saw Abū al-Dardāʾ punch himself in the nose!"[16]

As reported by Ibn Jarīr and Ibn al-Mundhir, Ibn ʿAbbās, in reference to Allah's saying, *Yet if someone commits an evil deed, or wrongs his own soul, but then seeks forgiveness of Allah...* (4:110), said:

> Allah the Exalted has informed His servants of His clemency, His pardon, His noble generosity, and the vast extent of His mercy and His forgiveness. For if someone commits a sin, be it small or large, but then seeks forgiveness of Allah, he will find Allah the Forgiving, the Merciful, even if his sins were larger than the mountains, the earth and the heavens.[17]

Allah's Messenger ﷺ also said, on the authority of Abū Hurayra and reported in Muslim:

---

14 A *ḥadīth* on the authority of Abū Mūsā al-Ashʿarī, reported in the *Sunan* of Tirmidhī.

15 *Ḥadīth* on the authority of Abū al-Dardāʾ reported by Abū Dāwūd, Ṭabarānī, Abū Yaʿlā, and Ibn Mardawayh.

16 Narration cited by Suyūṭī in *al-Durr al-manthūr* and by Haythamī in *Majmaʿ al-zawāʾid*.

17 Narration reported by Ibn Jarīr in his Qurʾān commentary, *Jāmiʿ al-bayān*.

> By the One in whose Hand is my soul, if you do not sin and seek forgiveness, Allah will remove you and replace you with a people who will sin and beg forgiveness, and whom He will forgive.[18]

> According to the report of Imam Ibn Ḥanbal ﵁, the Prophet ﷺ said: Iblīs said (to Allah), "By Your Might, I will not desist from misleading Your servants, so long as their spirits remain in their bodies." Allah said in response, "By My Might and My Majesty, I will not cease to forgive them, so long as they seek My forgiveness."[19]

As reported by Ṭabarānī, Anas b. Mālik ﵁ said:

> A man once came to Allah's Messenger ﷺ and said, "O Messenger of Allah, I have sinned." So the Prophet ﷺ said to him, "Whenever you have committed a sin, appeal to your Lord for forgiveness."
>
> The man said, "I do appeal to my Lord for forgiveness, but then I backslide and sin again." The response was again, "Whenever you have committed a sin, appeal to your Lord for forgiveness."
>
> Then, when it came to his response to being asked the question a fourth time, the Prophet ﷺ said, "Appeal to your Lord, Almighty and Glorious is He, for forgiveness, so that Satan will be the one who is spurned."[20]

When relating what he had received from his Lord, Almighty and Glorious is He, Allah's Messenger ﷺ said, as reported by Bukhārī and Muslim:

> When a servant sins, and then says, "O Allah, forgive me my sins," He, Blessed and Exalted is He, will say, "My servant committed a sin, but he knows that he has a Lord who forgives sins and inflicts punishment for sin."
>
> Then, when he relapses and sins again, he says, "O Allah, forgive me my sins." He, Blessed and Exalted is He, will say, "My servant committed a sin, but he knows that he has a Lord who forgives sins and inflicts punishment for sin."
>
> Then, when he relapses and sins again, he says, "O Allah, forgive me my sins." He, Blessed and Exalted is He, will say, "My servant committed a sin, but he knows that he has a Lord who forgives sins and inflicts punishment for sin. I have granted (him) forgiveness, so let him do whatever he wishes."[21]

---

18 *Ḥadīth* on the authority of Abū Hurayra reported in the *Ṣaḥīḥ* of Muslim and the *Kitāb al-daʿawāt* of Tirmidhī.

19 A *ḥadīth* on the authority of Abū Saʿīd al-Khuḍrī, reported in the *Musnad* of Ibn Ḥanbal and *al-Tarhīb wa al-targhīb* of Mundhirī.

20 A *ḥadīth* in Ṭabarānī, also cited in Haythamī's *Majmaʿ al-zawāʾid.*

21 A *ḥadīth* on the authority of Abū Hurayra reported by Bukhārī and Muslim.

In another version of the prophetic tradition, the wording is, "Do whatever you wish, for I have forgiven you."[22]

As reported in *Kashf al-ghumma*, the Prophet ﷺ used to say: "Whenever a Muslim commits a sin, the angel will wait for three hours. Then, if he seeks forgiveness for his sins, the angel will not record his offense, and Allah will not punish him on the Day of Resurrection."[23] He ﷺ also used to say, "Hearts have a rust like the rust of iron, and the polish for hearts is the plea for forgiveness."[24] As reported in *Targhīb al-ṭālib*, the Prophet ﷺ also said:

> You must make a frequent practice of pleading for forgiveness, for the plea of forgiveness consumes sins, just as the fire consumes wood, and just as the sheep consume grass. If a man's record contains no plea for forgiveness, it will have no light when it is raised to heaven. If it does contain the plea for forgiveness, it will have a light that sparkles when it ascends, even if it contains no more than a slight trace of the plea for forgiveness. Whenever a group of people participate in a session of idle sport, and then conclude it with the plea for forgiveness, the whole of that session of theirs will be recorded in their favor as a plea for forgiveness.

As reported by Nasafi,[25] the Prophet ﷺ said:

> There is not one Muslim for whom a record sheet is not inscribed each day. If it contains no plea for forgiveness by the time it is folded up, it will be pitch-black when folded. But if it does contain a plea for forgiveness by the time it is folded up, it will have a light that sparkles when folded.

As reported by Bayhaqī, on the authority of Anas b. Mālik, Allah's Messenger ﷺ said, "Let me direct your attention to your sickness and your remedy: your sins are your sickness, and your remedy is the plea for forgiveness."[26] On the authority of ʿAbd-Allāh, as reported by Ibn Māja, Bashshār ؓ said, "I once heard Allah's Messenger ﷺ say, 'Congratulations to someone who finds many a plea for forgiveness in his record!'"[27] Anas b. Mālik ؓ, as reported by Tirmidhī, said:

---

22 Aside from Bukhārī and Muslim as above, this version is found in Ḥakim's *al-Mustadrak* and Hindī, *Kanz al-ʿummāl*.

23 A *ḥadīth* cited by ʿAbd al-Wahhāb al-Shaʿrānī in his book, *Kashf al-ghumma ʿan jamiʿ al-umma*, and also in Hakim's *al-Mustadrak*.

24 This is also found in *Kashf al-ghumma*.

25 This is likely ʿAbd-Allāh b. Aḥmad al-Nasafī (d. 1310), the great interpreter of the Qurʾān and Ḥanafī legal scholar.

26 A *ḥadīth* related in Bayhaqī's *Shuʿab al-īmān*.

27 A *ḥadīth* reported in the *Sunan* of Ibn Māja and in the *Sunan* of Abū Nuʿaym.

> I once heard Allah's Messenger ﷺ say, "Allah the Exalted has said, 'O son of Adam, whenever you appeal to Me and implore Me, I forgive you, whatever you have done, and I do not care. O son of Adam, if you came to Me with a load of sins equivalent to the volume of the earth, provided that you came to Me without attributing any partner to Me, I would grant you its equivalent volume in forgiveness.'"[28]

These are only a small sample of the well-known prophetic traditions on this subject. *And Allah speaks the truth, and He shows the way* (Qur'ān, 33:4).

The Invocation of Blessing on the Prophet ﷺ

Next in our litany comes the invocation, recited one hundred times:

> O Allah, bless our master Muḥammad, the opener of what was closed, the seal of what came before, the helper of Truth by the Truth, the guide to Your straight path. And on his family (blessing), may this prayer be commensurate with his worth, and the greatness of his extent in space and time.

Allah the Exalted has said, *Allah and His angels shower blessings on the Prophet. O you who believe, invoke blessings upon him and salute him with a worthy salutation* (Qur'ān, 33:56). In reference to this verse, it is reported in *Rūḥ al-bayān* that Sahl b. ʿAbd-Allāh al-Tustarī, may Allah sanctify his innermost being, said: "The invocation of blessing upon Muḥammad is the most meritorious of the acts of worship, because Allah has undertaken it, He and His angels, and then He has commanded the believers to perform it, and the other acts of worship are not like that." The point here is that Allah the Exalted has commanded the performance of the other acts of worship, but He has not performed them Himself. The most truthful (*al-Ṣaddīq al-Akbar*, Shaykh Aḥmad al-Tijānī) once said:

> The invocation of blessing upon him ﷺ is more effective in eradicating sins than cold water in extinguishing fire. It is more meritorious than the emancipation of slaves. The emancipation of slaves is analogous to emancipation from the Fire of Hell and entry into the Garden of Paradise. But the peace invoked upon the Prophet ﷺ is the Peace of Allah, and the Peace of Allah is more excellent than one thousand benefactions.

Wāsiṭī[29] said, "Invoke blessing upon him in abundance, and do not assign a fixed amount to them in your heart." According to prophetic tradition:

---

28 A *ḥadīth* reported by Ibn Māja in his *Sunan*, and by Abū Nuʿaym in *Ḥilya al-awliyā'*.

29 This is likely Aḥmad Imād al-Dīn al-Wāsiṭī (d. 1311), a Shādhilī Sufi and student of Ibn Taymiyya, who was one of the first to use the term, Ṭarīqa Muḥammadiyya.

> Allah has an angel whom He has empowered to listen to all creatures, and he will stand by my grave from the time of my death until the Day of Resurrection. Whenever any member of my community invokes a blessing on me, the angel will name him by his personal name and the name of his father. He will say, "O Muḥammad, so-and-so, the son of so-and-so has invoked so-and-so many blessings upon you." And for every single one of those blessings the Lord will bestow ten upon that man.[30]

In another tradition, the Prophet ﷺ said, "When you invoke blessing upon me, you must perform the invocation in an excellent manner, for you will be presented to me by your personal names and the names of your fathers, your kinsfolk and your paternal uncles."[31] The invocation of blessing is best performed with presence of the heart and concentration of the mind. One of the authorities has said:

> Invocations of blessing upon the Prophet are a form of obedience, a means of drawing near, a means of connection and a dutiful compliance; but only when they are performed with the intention of spiritual salutation, seeking access, and drawing near to the presence of the Aḥmadī prophecy. As you must surely be aware, drawing near the moon is like drawing near to the sun, for the moon is its mirror and the target of its rays of light.

According to tradition, the Prophet ﷺ said, "If someone invokes blessing upon me one time, Allah will command his guardian angel to refrain from recording anything to his discredit for three days."[32]

A woman saw her son after his death. He was suffering torment, so she was very sad. Some time later, however, she saw him bathed in light and mercy, so she asked him about it and he said, "When passing by the graveyard, a man invoked blessing on the Prophet ﷺ and presented its reward to the dead. Allah made forgiveness my share of that (reward), so I have been forgiven." It is related that Sufyān al-Thawrī,[33] may Allah bestow His mercy on him, said:

> While I was circumambulating the Sacred House (in Mecca), I was surprised to see a man who did not lift a foot without invoking blessing upon the Prophet ﷺ. I said, "You there, you have omitted glorifying Allah (*tasbīḥ*) and declaring Allah's Oneness (*tahlīl*), and gone straight to the invocation of blessing on the Prophet ﷺ. Have you any explanation for this?"

---

30 A *ḥadīth* cited by Albānī in *Silsila al-aḥadīth al-ṣaḥīḥa.*

31 A *ḥadīth* cited by Hindī in *Kanz al-ʿummāl.*

32 A *ḥadīth* found in Suyūṭī, *al-Ḥabāʾik fī akhbār al-malāʾik.*

33 Sufyan al-Thawri b. Saʿīd (d. 778) was an early scholar of the Qurʾān, jurisprudence, and *ḥadīth*. He is known as one of the "Eight Ascetics," along with Ḥasan al-Baṣrī, among others.

He said, "Who are you? May Allah protect you."
I said, "I am Sufyān al-Thawrī."

So he said, "Had you not been a stranger among the people of your time, I would not have informed you of my spiritual state, and I would not have revealed to you my secret." Then he went on to say: "My father and I set out as pilgrims toward Allah's Sacred House. When we were in one of the camping sites along the way, my father fell ill and died. His face turned dark, his eyes turned blue, and his stomach became inflated. So I wept and said, *To Allah we belong, to Him we return* (Qurʾān, 2:156). My father died like this, in a foreign land, so I drew the death shroud over his face.

"Then sleep got the better of my eyes. In my dream, I found myself with a man who was far more handsome, more finely dressed, and more fragrantly perfumed than anyone I had ever seen. He approached my father and removed the shroud from his face, and wiped it (with his hands). My father's face became whiter than milk. Then he rubbed his stomach, and it returned to its normal condition. He was then about to depart, so I went to him, caught hold of his cloak, and said, 'O my master, by the One who sent you to my father, as a mercy in a foreign land, who are you?' He said, 'I am Muḥammad, the Messenger of Allah. This father of yours was guilty of many acts of sinful disobedience, but he would often invoke blessing on me. Then when what happened to him happened, he appealed to me for help. So I came to his aid, for I am a source of help for anyone who often invokes blessing on me in the abode of this world.'

"I woke up from sleep at that point, and behold, my father's face had indeed turned white, and the bloating of his stomach had disappeared."

Kaʿb b. ʿUjra ﷺ said:

When the saying of Allah the Exalted—"O you who believe, invoke blessings upon him and salute him with a worthy salutation"—was revealed, we approach him ﷺ and said, "As for greeting you with the salutation with peace, we are familiar with that already; but what about the invocation of blessing upon you, O Messenger of Allah?"

He replied, "Say: 'O Allah, bestow blessing upon Muḥammad and upon the family of Muḥammad, as You have bestowed blessing upon Abraham and upon the family of Abraham. You are indeed the Praiseworthy, the Glorious. And sanctify Muḥammad and the family of Muḥammad, as You have sanctified Abraham and the family of Abraham. You are indeed the Praiseworthy, the Glorious.'"[34]

34 A *ḥadīth* reported in the *Ṣaḥīḥ* of Bukhārī, the *Ṣaḥīḥ* of Muslim, and the *Sunan* of Tirmidhī.

The above is found in *Tafsīr al-taysīr*.[35]

Concerning *ṣalāt al-fātiḥ*, the Invocation of the Opener

Our Shaykh, our master, and our means of access to our Lord, Aḥmad b. Muḥammad al-Tijānī, had this to say about *ṣalāt al-fātiḥ*, as recorded in the *Jawāhir al-maʿānī*:

> When I returned to Tlemcen (Algeria) from the pilgrimage, I became preoccupied with offering the "Invocation of the Opener of what was locked" (*ṣalāt al-fātih li-mā ʿughliq*), because I had discovered its excellence: offering it one time is worth six hundred thousand ritual prayers, as stated in *Warda al-juyūb*. According to the author of this work, the author of the invocation, Sīdī Muḥammad al-Bakrī al-Ṣiddīqī ﷺ[36]—a saintly pole (*quṭb*) and frequent visitor to Egypt—had said: "If someone offers it one time, and does not enter the Garden, let him arrest its author in the presence of Allah."
>
> I persisted in offering this invocation until I returned from Tlemcen to Abū Samghūn. Then, when I saw a prayer, one of which is worth seventy-thousand complete recitals of *Dalāʾil al-khayrāt*, I became preoccupied with that. This prayer is, "O Allah, bless our master Muḥammad and his family, with a blessing that is equal to all the blessings of those who enjoy Your loving affection, and grant our master Muḥammad and his family a peace that is equal to their peace."
>
> I saw great merit in that, but then the Prophet ﷺ commanded me to return to *ṣalāt al-fātiḥ li-mā ʿughliq*. When I asked him ﷺ about its merit, he first informed me that offering it once is equal to reciting the entire Qurʾān six times. He later told me that offering it one time is equal to all the glorification (*tasbīḥ*) that has ever been offered in the universe, to all the remembrance (*dhikr*), to all supplication (*duʿāʾ*), great or small, and to reciting the Qurʾān six thousand times.[37]

---

35 It is possible the work referred to here is the *Taysīr al-Karīm al-Raḥmān fī tafsīr al-Qurʾān* of ʿAbd al-Raḥmān b. Nāṣir al-Saʿdī al-Tamīmī (d. 1956, Saudi Arabia). If so, this would be one of the few contemporary works the Shaykh cites in the *Kāshif*.

36 According to Tijānī tradition, Muḥammad al-Bakrī (d. 1545) discovered this prayer on a sheet of light after spiritual retreat inside the Sacred House (Kaʿba) in Mecca.

37 This has been contextualized by numerous Tijānī authors, including by Shaykh Aḥmad al-Tijānī himself, by reference to different ranks of Qurʾān readers. According to the explanation of Shaykh Ḥasan Cisse based on the *Jāmiʿ*, those who fail to implement what the Qurʾān commands them are actually being cursed by the Qurʾān as they read it; so this statement applies to them. Otherwise, for the knowledgable person of Allah, nothing is better than reading the Qurʾān. Elsewhere in the *Jawāhir*, Shaykh al-Tijānī emphasized that the invocation of blessing on the Prophet is a supererogatory worship, while recitation of the Qurʾān is obligatory on the believer; so that the recitation can never be left aside. The Shaykh said: "Rather the recitation of the Qurʾān is more vital (than prayer on the Prophet), because it is required by the sacred law due to its merits

In *al-Kawkab al-wahhāj*, (Shaykh Sukayrij) said: "If you wish to acquire some knowledge of this reality so the matter will become clear to you and so that you will not slip into dangerous pitfalls, you should understand what our master ﷺ said in a written response to the *khalīfa*, our master ʿAlī Harāzim Barāda, sanctified be his innermost being." Here is the text of the letter, as recorded in *Jawāhir al-maʿānī*:

> The special quality of *ṣalāt al-fātiḥ li-mā ʿughliq* is a divine affair, to which the minds have no access. Imagine one hundred thousand nations, each nation consisting of one hundred thousand tribes, with one hundred thousand men in each tribe, each one of them living for one hundred thousand years, and each one of them offering invocation of blessing on the Prophet ﷺ, but with other than *ṣalāt al-fātiḥ li-mā ughliq*. If the reward of all these nations, for all these remembrances throughout all these years, were to be combined, they would not equal the reward of one single offering of *ṣalāt al-fātiḥ li-mā ughliq*.
>
> So pay no attention to the falsehoods of the liars, or to the accusations of the slanderers, for bountiful grace is at the disposal of Allah, who bestows it upon whomever He will. Allah the Glorious and Exalted has bountiful grace beyond the realm of comprehension. Enough for you is His saying, *And He creates that which you do not know* (Qurʾān, 16:8).
>
> For the one who would turn himself toward Allah the Exalted, there is no act of dedication to match it, none whatsoever. The one exception is the degree attained by someone who dedicates himself to Allah the Exalted by invoking His greatest Name. That is the ultimate act of dedication, and the highest degree of all acts of worship. There is no limit to its excellent merit, and no terminal point above it. This invocation (*ṣalāt al-fātiḥ*) ranks close to it in degree, dedication, reward, and the attainment of Allah's love for its practitioner, with the best of results. If someone dedicates himself to Allah sincerely in this manner, he will succeed in gaining Allah's good pleasure and His reward, in his worldly life and in his life in the next world, to an extent that all (other) good deeds would not allow him to reach. Thereby he will experience the divine bounty to an extent beyond his most hopeful expectations.
>
> This gracious favor cannot be achieved except by humble submission. If someone wishes to argue about this subject, he must desist, for he will derive no benefit from the examination of proofs. You must refrain from debating with someone who asks you for proofs, because that kind of discussion, involving refutation and response, is like the endless heaving of the ocean waves. Hearts are in Allah's hand. He

---

narrated to us, and because it is the foundation of the sacred law and the way of the Lord's dealing with creation. There is also the great punishment reserved for the one who leaves the Qurʾān" (*Jawāhir al-maʿānī*).

controls them and moves them to and fro. If someone wishes for good fortune and success in obtaining the reward of this matchless sapphire, he must enrapture his heart in belief of what he hears about it, and he must practice humble submission before the bountiful grace of Allah the Glorious by refraining from delimitation and analogical deduction. He must focus his attention on using it as a means of dedication to Allah the Exalted, and as a means of approaching Him. *So no soul knows what comfort is kept secretly in store for them, as a reward for what they used to do* (Qurʾān, 32:17). If Allah wishes to preclude someone from its benefit, He will distract his heart with whispers, and make him wonder, "Where does the news of it come from?" You must devote your attention to what we have told you. If someone follows you in that, and refrains from debating with you about the investigation of evidence, we shall accept him on the strength of what you say about him.

A full discussion of the matchless sapphire (*al-yāqūta al-farīda*)[38] could not be contained within many large volumes, but this small discussion provides sufficient provision.

The Glorification of Allah

Also in our litany are the words of Allah the Exalted:

> *Glory be to your Lord, the Lord of Majesty,*
> *Far from what they attribute!*
> *And peace be upon those sent as Messengers,*
> *And praise be to Allah, Lord of all the worlds!* (Qurʾān, 37:180–182).

Allah said, *And glorify Him at the dawn and in the evening* (33:42). According to an authentic prophetic tradition, cited in Suyūṭī's *al-Jāmiʿ al-ṣaghīr*, "The best of speech is, 'Glorify be to Allah, and praise be to Allah, and there is no god but Allah, and Allah is the Greatest.'"[39] As recorded in *Rūḥ al-bayān*, on the authority of ʿAlī ﷺ, the Prophet ﷺ said, "If someone would love to be measured by the fullest measure of reward on the Day of Resurrection, let him conclude his meeting with the words, *Glory be to the Lord, the Lord of Majesty, far from what they attribute…*" (33:42). The *Rūḥ al-bayān* goes on to say:

> The spiritual pauper, may Allah the All-Powerful improve him, urges the believer to correct his spiritual state by doing two things before he gets up from a meeting (with his fellows). The first is to obtain abundant reward by reciting the above mentioned verses of the Qurʾān. The second is to make atonement, as indicated by the Prophet ﷺ in

---

38 This is another name for *ṣalāt al-fātiḥ*, and should not be confused with a famous poem by the same name, written by Shaykh Muḥammad al-Naẓīfī (d. 1942, Morocco).

39 A *ḥadīth* reported by Bukhārī in his *Ṣaḥīḥ*.

his saying: "If someone sits in a meeting, during which he does a lot of talking, then he says before he gets up—'Glory be to You, O Allah, and with praise to You; I bear witness that there is no god but You; I seek Your forgiveness and I repent to You'—he surely will be granted forgiveness."

This is to say, (he will be granted forgiveness) for minor sins, which do not violate the rights of human beings, like slander. Instead of being heedless during his sitting with people, therefore, the intelligent person must remember his Lord and His intimate Presence, and conclude his meeting with the appropriate words: "And the conclusion of their supplication will be, *Praise be to Allah, Lord of all the worlds!*" (Qurʾān, 10:10).

Since our purpose is to discuss the glorification of Allah (*tasbīḥ*), and this conversation (by its nature) drifts from one topic to another, permit us to devote attention to the "Prayer of Glorification" (*ṣalāt al-tasbīḥ*). As reported by Imam al-Ṭabarānī and Abū Nuʿaym, Ibn ʿAbbās ﷺ said:

> ʿAbbās once came to the Prophet ﷺ at an unusual hour, so someone said, "O Messenger of Allah ﷺ, this is your paternal uncle at the door." He said, "Let him come in, for he must have come with some important business!" Then, when ʿAbbās entered his presence, the Prophet ﷺ asked him, "What has brought you at this hour, O my paternal uncle?" He replied, "O son of my brother, I recalled the age of ignorance (al-Jāhiliyya) and its stupidity, then this world oppressed me, regardless of its spaciousness. I cried, 'Who will comfort me?', but I realized that there is no one who can comfort me, except Allah the Exalted, and then you."
>
> The Prophet ﷺ responded by saying, "Praise be to Allah, who has instilled this in your heart! Shall I offer you a present?" His uncle said, "Yes!" He replied, "Shall I give you a gift?" His uncle said "Yes!"
>
> The Prophet ﷺ then told him: "During any time in which the ritual prayer can be performed—not following the afternoon prayer (*ʿasr*) and not after the rising of the sun (after the dawn prayer until the daylight), but anytime in between—you must perform your ritual ablution correctly, then stand in honor of Allah the Almighty and Glorious. Recite the Opening of the Qurʾān (*fātiḥa al-kitāb*) and another chapter (*sūra*), which you may select from the beginning of the final section of the Qurʾān. Then, when you have completed the chapter, you must say fifteen times: 'Glory be to Allah, and praise be to Allah, and there is no god but Allah, and Allah is Supremely Great!' Then, when you perform your act of bowing (*rukūʿ*), you must say that ten times. Then, when you raise your head from bowing, you must say that ten times. Then, when you perform the prostration (*sajda*), you must say that ten times. Then, when you raise your head and adopt the sitting posture

(*jalsa*), you must recite that ten times. Then, when you perform the act of prostration again, you must say it ten times. Then, when you raise your head and adopt the sitting posture again, you must say that ten times. This adds up to a total of seventy-five (glorifications).

"You must then stand up and perform another cycle (*rakʿa*), in which you must do what you did in the first. Then you must say it ten times before the profession of faith (*al-tashahhud*). This brings the total to one hundred and fifty. You must then perform two other cycles like that, so this brings the total to three hundred.

"If you have completed (this prayer), even if your sins are equal in number to the stars in the sky, Allah will erase them. (He will erase them) even if they are like a huge pile of sand, and even if they are like the foam of an ocean.

"If you can, perform this prayer once daily. If you cannot do so, then one time every Friday. If you cannot do that, then perform it once a month. If you cannot even do that, then every year as long as you are still alive."[40]

A similar narration is recorded in al-Ḥāfiẓ al-Mundhirī's *al-Targhīb wa al-tarhīb*.[41] On the authority of ʿIkrima, Ibn ʿAbbās ﷺ said:

> The Messenger of Allah ﷺ said to ʿAbbās b. ʿAbd al-Muṭṭalib: "O ʿAbbās, O my paternal uncle! Shall I not give you a gift? Shall I not grant you a favor? Shall I not offer you a present? Shall I not do something for you? (Let me tell you about) ten virtuous deeds (*khiṣāl*) that, when performed, Allah will grant you forgiveness for your sins, the first of them and the last, that which was committed long ago and that which was committed recently, that which was done mistakenly and that which was done deliberately, that which is major and that which is minor, and that which is committed in private and that which is committed in public.
>
> "There are ten virtuous deeds: Perform four cycles (*rakaʿāt*) of ritual prayer, reciting in each one the Opening of the Qurʾān (*fātiḥa al-kitāb*) and a chapter. When you have completed the recitation at the beginning of a cycle, say fifteen times, while you are standing erect, 'Glory be to Allah, and praise be to Allah, and there is no god but Allah, and Allah is Supremely Great!' Then perform the act of bowing, and then say it ten times while in this position. Then raise your head from the bowing posture, and repeat it another ten times. Then move into the prostrating position, and recite it ten times. Then raise your head

---

40 Reported by Abū Dāwūd is his *Sunan*, and by Ibn Māja in his *Sunan*.

41 Al-Ḥāfiẓ al-Mundhirī (d. 1258), whose proper name was ʿAbd al-ʿAẓīm b. ʿAbd al-Qawī, was originally from Damascus, but later moved to Egypt. He was a famous *ḥadīth* scholar, and his work, *al-Targhīb wa al-tarhīb* is an abridgment of *Ṣaḥīḥ Muslim*.

from the posture of prostration, and say it again ten times. Then move into the prostrating position again, reciting it ten times. Then raise yourself from prostrating and recite it ten times more. This adds up to a total of seventy-five times in each movement. Repeat all of this in three more cycles (*rakaʿāt*). If you are able to perform this prayer once a day, then do so. If you are unable to do so, then one time every Friday. If you cannot do that, then one time every month. If you cannot do that, then do it once a year. If you cannot even do that, then (do it at least) once in your lifetime."

In the version reported by Ṭabarānī, the prophetic tradition ends with the words: "Even if your sins are like the foam of the ocean or like a great pile of sand, Allah will grant you forgiveness." According to al-Ḥāfiẓ (al-Mundhirī):

> This prophetic tradition has been reported through many lines of transmission, and on the authority of a number of Companions. This version attributed to ʿIkrima is the best example, for it has been authenticated by a group of experts, including al-Ḥāfiẓ Abū Bakr al-Ajurrī, our Shaykh Abū Muḥammad b. ʿAbd al-Raḥīm al-Miṣrī, and our Shaykh al-Ḥāfiẓ Abū al-Ḥasan al-Maqdisī, may Allah the Exalted bestow His mercy upon them. Abū Bakr b. Abī Dāwūd said, "I heard my father say, 'On the subject of the prayer of glorification (*ṣalāt al-tasbīḥ*), there is no authentic prophetic tradition other than this.'" Muslim b. al-Ḥajjāj, may Allah have mercy on him, said, "Where this prophetic tradition is concerned, there is no finer chain of transmission (*isnād*) than this," referring to the chain of transmission that validates ʿIkrima's report on the authority of Ibn ʿAbbās ﷺ. He (Ibn ʿAbbās) also said about concluding the prayer, "When I come to the end (of the prayer of glorification), I say this after the profession of faith (*al-tashahhud*) and before the salutation of peace (*al-salām*):
>
> "'O Allah, I beseech You to grant me the success of the people of right guidance, the actions of the people of certitude, the sincere advice of the people of repentance, the firm resolve of the people of patience, the wariness of the people of apprehension, the quest of the people of yearning, the devotion of the people of piety, and the insight of the people of knowledge, so that I may be afraid of offending You.
>
> "'O Allah, I beseech You to grant me a sense of fear, by which you will prevent me from committing acts of sinful disobedience against You, so that I may practice obedience to You with conduct that makes me worthy of Your good pleasure; and so that I may be honest with You in repentance, for fear of offending You, and so that I may be completely sincere with You, for love of You, and so that I may place my trust in You regarding all affairs, because of my excellent opinion of You. Glory be to the Creator of Light...'"

I advise you to hold tightly to this mighty and exalted treasure!

The Declaration that there is no god but Allah

Let us now consider the declaration, "There is no god but Allah (*lā ilāha ill-Allāh*)," which is recited one hundred times in our litany. Allah the Exalted has said: *And remember Allah often, so that you may be successful* (Qurʾān, 8:45). The excellent qualities of this declaration are too many to be enumerated, and it is impossible to provide a complete account of the many authentic reports from Allah's Messenger ﷺ on the subject. But since this is an essential point, some examples in proof of the declaration's merit and meaning will be discussed here. According to the erudite scholar and gnostic, the eminent Sayyid Aḥmad b. al-Ḥājj al-ʿAyyāshī Sukayrij, in *al-Kawkab al-wahhāj*:

> With regard to this blessed declaration, you should know that the imams of exoteric and esoteric knowledge are unanimously agreed that nothing else will suffice the servants at the time of their death and that none of the other remembrances will serve as evidence of their profession of faith. Allah has commanded His servants to believe it with firm conviction, for He the Exalted has said, *So know that there is no god but Allah* (Qurʾān, 47:19)

According to a report from Abū Hurayra ﷺ, Allah's Messenger ﷺ said, "I have been commanded to fight the people until they bear witness that there is no god but Allah."[42] Our master ʿUthmān ﷺ is reported as having said, "I once heard Allah's Messenger ﷺ say: 'I surely know a declaration, which no servant can say without making him immune from the Fire, so long as it is said truthfully from his heart.'"[43] Our master ʿUmar ﷺ is recorded as saying, "I shall tell you what it is. It is the declaration of sincere devotion, which Muḥammad ﷺ and his companions imposed as a duty: 'There is no god but Allah!'" Abū Hurayra ﷺ is reported as having said,

> I said, "O Messenger of Allah ﷺ, who will be the most fortunate of all people as a result of your intercession on the Day of Ressurection?" He replied, "I had assumed, O Abū Hurayra, that no one would be more likely than you to ask me this question, because I had noticed your keen interest in what I have to say. The most fortunate of all people, as a result of my intercession on the Day of Resurrection, will be someone who says, 'There is no god but Allah,' sincerely from his heart and soul."[44]

The Prophet ﷺ also said:

42 Reported by Bukhārī in his *Ṣaḥīḥ*.

43 Reported by Ibn Ḥanbal in his *Musnad*.

44 Reported by Bukhārī in his *Ṣaḥīḥ*.

> Whenever a servant says, "There is no god but Allah," sincerely from his heart, his declaration will ascend with no barrier to obstruct it. Then when it reaches Allah the Exalted, He will look at the person who uttered it, and He never looks at someone who affirms His Oneness without bestowing His mercy upon him.

According to another prophetic tradition from Abū Hurayra ﵁, Allah's Messenger ﷺ said:

> Allah the Exalted has a pillar of light in front of the Heavenly Throne. When the servant says "There is no god but Allah," that pillar will shake. So Allah the Exalted will say "Be still!" It will reply, "How can I be still, when You have not granted forgiveness to the person who uttered this?" Allah the Exalted will then say, "I have already granted him forgiveness." And so the pillar will promptly come to rest.[45]

According to a report from Abū Saʿīd al-Khudrī ﵁, the Prophet ﷺ said:

> Moses, peace be upon him, said, "O my Lord, teach me something by which I may remember You and make supplication to You." His Lord replied, "O Moses, say, 'There is no god but Allah.'" Moses then said, "O my Lord, (but) all Your servants say this!" His Lord told him again, "Say, 'There is no god but Allah!'" Moses then replied, "I only wish for something by which You will show me special favor." His Lord replied, "O Moses, if the inhabitants of the seven heavens and the seven earths were on one side of a scale, and (the declaration) 'There is no god but Allah' was on the other side of the scale, 'There is no god but Allah' would outweigh them all!"[46]

Another tradition that is attributed to the Prophet ﷺ records him as saying:

> No loneliness will afflict the people of "There is no god but Allah," neither in their graves, nor at their resurrection. It is as if I am seeing the people of "There is no god but Allah" shaking off the dust from their heads and saying: "Praise be to Allah, for He has relieved us of sorrow!"[47]

> According to another tradition from Ibn ʿAbbās ﵁, the Prophet ﷺ said: Gabriel, peace be upon him, informed me: "'There is no god but Allah,' will be the solace of the Muslim at the time of his death, in his grave, and when he emerges from the grave. O Muḥammad, if only you could see how it will be when they are emerging from their graves, shaking the dust off of their heads! This one will say: 'There is no god but Allah,'

---

45 Reported by Abū Nuʿaym in *Ḥilya al-awliyāʾ*.

46 Reported by Ḥākim in *al-Mustadrak*.

47 Cited by Haythamī in *Majmaʿ al-zawāʾid*.

and his face will be bright. Another will say: 'Woe is me, because of my falling short in my duty to Allah,' and his face will be grim."[48]

There is a report (*khabar*) in which the Prophet ﷺ is recorded as saying, "Allah the Exalted says: 'There is no god but Allah' is My fortress; so if someone enters My fortress, he will be safe from My punishment."[49] As reported by Imam al-Qurṭubī, with a chain of transmission, the Prophet ﷺ said:

> The Angel of Death, peace be upon him, approached a man and penetrated every limb of his body, but found no goodness in it. Then he split his heart open, but found nothing in it. Then he tugged at his beard (and the man's mouth opened), and he found the tip of his tongue sticking to his palate, saying, "There is no god but Allah." (The Angel of Death) then told him, "You have earned the Garden of Paradise by uttering the declaration of sincere devotion!"

As reported by Anas b. Mālik ﷺ from Muʿādh b. Jabal, the Prophet ﷺ seated Muʿādh behind him on his donkey named ʿUfayr. He said, "O Muʿādh!" Muʿādh replied, "Doubly at your service, O Messenger of Allah ﷺ, time after time!" He called out to him a second time, and Muʿādh said again, "Doubly at your service, O Messenger of Allah, time after time!" Then he called out to him a third time, saying "O Muʿādh!" And again, Muʿādh replied, "Doubly at your service, O Messenger of Allah, time after time!" He ﷺ said, "No servant bears witness that there is no god but Allah, and that Muḥammad is Allah's Messenger, truthfully from his heart, without Allah the Exalted making him immune from the Hellfire." Muʿādh then related: "I said, 'O Messenger of Allah, should I not inform the people of this, so they may rejoice at the good news?' He replied, 'In that case, they will surely put their trust (in the Lord)!'" Muʿādh related this at the time of his death, while repenting of his sins.[50] According to a *ḥadīth* related by Ibn ʿAbbās, may Allah be well pleased with him and his father, the Prophet ﷺ said:

> Allah the Exalted will open the gates of the Garden of Paradise, and a herald will cry from beneath the Heavenly Throne, "O Garden of Paradise and all the bounties you contain, to whom do you belong?"
>
> The Garden of Paradise and everything within it will proclaim, "We belong to the people of 'There is no god but Allah.' We seek none but the people of 'There is no god but Allah,' and none but the people of

---

48 Shaykh Tijānī Cisse could not verify the relation of this *ḥadīth* through Ibn ʿAbbās, but found it related instead through Ibn ʿUmar.

49 Cited by Murtaḍā al-Zabīdī in a commentary on *Iḥyāʾ ʿulūm al-dīn*.

50 Reported by Bukhārī in his *Ṣaḥīḥ* and by Muslim in his *Ṣaḥīḥ*.

'There is no god but Allah' will enter our presence! We are forbidden to anyone who does not say 'There is no god but Allah.'"

At this point, the Hellfire and all of the torments it contains will say, "None will enter me except those who deny that there is no god but Allah. I seek only those who do not believe that there is no god but Allah. I am prohibited to those who declare 'There is no god but Allah.' I shall only be filled with those who refuse to accept that there is no god but Allah. My wrath and my blazing fury are for none but those who deny that there is no god but Allah."

Allah's Mercy will then arrive, with His Forgiveness, and it will say, "I belong to the people of 'There is no god but Allah.' I am the assistant of those who say 'There is no god but Allah,' and I am the lover of those who declare 'There is no god but Allah.'"

The Garden of Paradise is lawful to those who proclaim 'There is no god but Allah,' and the Hellfire is forbidden to those who say 'There is no god but Allah.' Forgiveness for every sin belongs to those who say 'There is no god but Allah.' Mercy and forgiveness are unveiled for the people of 'There is no god but Allah.'"

According to a report from Abū Hurayra ؓ, Allah's Messenger ﷺ said to Abū Darr al-Ghifārī ؓ, "Tell the people that if someone bears witness that there is no god but Allah, he is entitled to the Garden of Paradise." Abū Darr replied, "Even if he is guilty of sexual indecency and theft?" The Prophet ﷺ said, "Even if he is guilty of sexual indecency and theft." He repeated this three times, and on the third occasion, he said, "Even if he is guilty of sexual indecency and theft—in spite of Abū Darr's disapproval!"[51] As reported by Anas b. Mālik ؓ, Allah's Messenger ﷺ said:

> I have never ceased to intercede with my Lord, for He will always accept my intercession, unless I say, "O my Lord, accept my intercession on behalf of someone who says 'There is no god but Allah.'" In that case, Allah the Exalted will say, "This is not for you, O Muḥammad. It is only for Me! By My Might, My Majesty, My Clemency, and My Mercy, I shall not put someone who says, 'There is no god but Allah,' into the Hellfire!"[52]

There is a *ḥadīth* reported from Ibn ʿUmar ؓ, wherein Allah's Messenger ﷺ is recorded as having said:

> On the Day of Resurrection, a man from my community (*umma*) will be brought out in front of all his fellow creatures, and ninety-nine scrolls will list the charges against him, with each scroll stretching

---

51 Reported by Bukhārī in his *Ṣaḥīḥ* and by Ibn Ḥanbal in his *Musnad*.

52 Reported by Ibn Abī ʿĀṣim in *Kitāb al-sunna*, by Abū Nuʿaym, by Tirmidhī in his *Sunan*, by Ibn Māja in his *Sunan*, and by Ibn Ḥanbal in his *Musnad*.

> out as far as the eye can see. He will be asked, "Do you deny any part of this?" The man will reply, "No, O my Lord." Then he will be asked, "Do you have any valid excuse?" He will say again, "No, O my Lord." Allah the Exalted then will say to him, "You have a deposit with Me, and you will suffer no injustice today!" The man will receive a slip of paper inscribed with the words, 'I bear witness that there is no god but Allah, I bear witness that Muḥammad is Allah's Messenger.' Allah the Exalted will continue: "Prepare to be weighed in the balance." The man will respond, "O my Lord, what is this slip of paper in relation to the scrolls?"Allah the Exalted will say to him, "You will suffer no injustice today!" Then, when the scrolls are placed on the scale along with the slip of paper, the scrolls will be lighter in weight compared to the slip of paper, for nothing matches the weight of Allah's Name."

We will continue by exploring a fraction of the heavy weight of this declaration, and with Allah is all success.

The Names of *la ilāha ill-Allāh* and Associated Subtleties

The gnostic endowed with intimate knowledge of Allah, Sayyid al-Ḥasan b. Masʿūd al-Yūsī,[53] may his innermost being be sanctified, stated in his book entitled *Minhāj al-khalāṣ min kalima al-ikhlāṣ*:

> You should know that the honored declaration ("There is no god but Allah"), from the standpoint of the linguists, should be called "the declaration of negation and affirmation" (*kalima al-nafī wa al-ithbāt*) because of its contents. In the usage of the jurists and the legists, it is called the "the declaration of the testimony of faith" (*kalima al-shahāda*) because it consists of testimony to Allah's Singularity in divinity, and because the declaration of that testimony represents the beginning of surrender to the Will of Allah (*islām*) for the human being. These two points of view are mutually compatible.
>
> As for the grammatically dual expressions *kalimatā al-shahāda* ("the two declarations of the testimony of faith") and *kalima al-shahādatayn* ("the declaration of the two testimonies"), they refer to the words "I bear witness that there is no god but Allah; I bear witness that Muḥammad is Allah's Messenger." This is because true faith is not established unless the two are linked together.
>
> According to the jurists, it may also be called "the declaration of the affirmation of Oneness" (*kalima al-tawḥīd*), for either of two reasons: (1) It consists of the affirmation of Oneness of Allah the Exalted in respect of divinity, this being its explicit meaning. (2) It comprises all

53 Imam al-Ḥasan b. Masʿūd al-Yūsī (d. 1691) was considered a "renewer" (*mujaddid*) of the twelfth century A.H. He lived in the Maghrib and was one of the eminent students of Muḥammad b. Nāṣir, the eponym for the Naṣiriyya-Shādhiliyya order.

the subjects to which the affirmation of Oneness is relevant, includ-ing three matters: theological matters (*ilāhiyyāt*), prophetic matters (*nubuwiyyāt*), and traditionally-heard matters (*samᶜiyyāt*).

As for the Qurʾān commentators and the Sufis, they regard it as having many names, which have been elicited from the texts. The Proof of Islam (Imam al-Ghazālī) mentioned a number of them, and later scholars have added to the list. These names will be enumerated here, accompanied by the evidence on which the interpretations are based. And with Allah is all success.

The first Name, "the declaration of divine Oneness" (*kalima al-tawḥīd*), has already been mentioned. It is derived from the Qurʾān, where Allah the Exalted says, *And your God is One God. There is no god but He* (2:163).

The next three names are often grouped together. They are "the dec-laration of surrender" (*kalima al-islām*), "the declaration of faith" (*kalima al-īmān*), and "the declaration of spiritual excellence" (*kalima al-iḥsān*). They come from the words of Allah the Exalted, where He says:

There is no blame on those who believe and do righteous deeds as to what they may have eaten, so long as they are pious and believe and do righ-teous deeds! And again, are pious and believe! And again, are pious and excel in doing good, for Allah loves those who excel in doing good (5:93).

As for His saying, Exalted is He, *So long as they are pious and believe*—this has been said to refer to (the declaration), "There is no god but Allah," for this is the declaration of surrender and pious submission to the Will of Allah (*islām*). As for His saying, *And again, are pious and believe*, this is said to refer to, "There is no god but Allah," for this is the declaration of belief or faith (*īmān*). As for His saying, "And again, are pious and excel in doing good," this is said to refer to "There is no god but Allah," for this is the declaration of spiritual excellence (*iḥsān*). Indeed, in reference to His saying, *If you do good, it is for your own souls* (17:7), and His saying, *for those who do good* (3:172, 16:30, 39:10), it is said that the spiritual excellence (*iḥsān*) mentioned here means proclaiming, "There is no god but Allah."

The fifth name is "the declaration of mutuality" (*kalima al-sawāʾ*). This name is derived from the Qurʾān, in which Allah the Exalted says: *Say: "O People of the Book! Let us come to a mutual declaration between us and you"* (3:64). This is said to refer to the statement, "There is no god but Allah."

The sixth name is "the declaration of the covenant" (*kalima al-ᶜahd*). The name is derived from the Qurʾān, in which Allah the Exalted says: ... *except those who have made a covenant with the All-Merciful* (19:87). It has been said that this covenant is the declaration, "There is no god but Allah."

The seventh name is "the declaration of justice" (*kalima al-ᶜadl*). This is taken from Allah's saying: *Surely Allah commands justice* (16:90). As reported on the authority of Ibn ᶜAbbās 🙵, justice is the declaration: "There is no god but Allah."

The eighth name is "the declaration of truth" (*kalima al-ḥaqq*). It is derived from Allah's saying: *And those to whom they cry instead of Him possess no power of intercession, except someone who bears witness to the truth* (43:86). In this context, the one "who bears witness to the truth" is the one who declares, "There is no god but Allah."

The ninth name is "the declaration of sincere devotion" (*kalima al-ikhlāṣ*). This title is drawn from Allah's saying: *And they were commanded only to serve Allah, devoting the religion to Him sincerely* (98:5). This is to say that the People of the Book were commanded to affirm His Oneness by proclaiming, "There is no god but Allah."

The tenth name is "the declaration of truthfulness" (*kalima al-ṣidq*). This stems from the Qurʾān, where Allah the Exalted says: *And whoever brings truthfulness and believes therein, such are the truly devout* (39:33). The truthfulness alluded to in this verse is referring to the declaration, "There is no god but Allah."

The eleventh name is "the declaration of steadfastness" (*kalima al-istiqāma*). This is derived from the Qurʾān, where Allah the Exalted says: *Those who say, 'Our Lord is Allah,' and then are steadfast* (46:13). The steadfastness defined here is the declaration, "There is no god but Allah."

The twelfth name is "the declaration of the fear (of God)" (*kalima al-taqwā*). This name comes from the words of Allah the Exalted: *And He obligated them with the declaration of fear (of God)* (48:26). It has been said that this refers to the declaration, "There is no god but Allah," because the one who lives by it fears disbelief and the Hellfire.

The thirteenth name is "the good declaration" (*kalima al-ṭayyiba*). This name is defined in the Qurʾān, when Allah the Exalted says: *Do you see how Allah has coined a similitude? A good declaration, like a good tree, its root is set firmly and its branch is in the sky* (14:24). It has been said that this refers to the declaration, "There is no god but Allah," because it stems from the heart and its root is set firm, thus signifying gnosis (*maʿrifa*).

The fourteenth name is "the enduring declaration" (*kalima al-bāqiya*). This title is a derivative of the verse of the Qurʾān, where Allah the Exalted says, regarding the story of Ibrāhīm, blessings and peace be upon our Prophet and upon him: *And he made it an enduring declaration among his offspring* (43:28). This is the declaration, "There is no god but Allah," because this verse alludes to his disavowal of what people worship other than Allah. The declaration is also implicit when Ibrāhīm says: *except for the One who created me, for He will surely guide me* (43:27), for this (guidance) includes the declaration, "There is no god but Allah."

The fifteenth name is "the most exalted declaration" (*kalima al-ʿulyā*). It is derived from Allah's saying: *And the declaration of Allah is most Exalted* (9:40). This is to say that this affirmation, "There is no god but Allah," is the loftiest of declarations.

The sixteenth name is "the word that stands firm" (*al-qawl al-thābit*). It is mentioned in the Qurʾān, where Allah the Exalted says: *Allah firmly establishes those who believe, with the word that stands firm, in the life of this world and the Hereafter* (14:27). This "word that stands firm" is, "There is no god but Allah."

The seventeenth name is "the good statement" (*al-qawl al-ṭayyib*). It is derived from Allah's saying: *And they are guided to the good form of speech* (22:24). The "good form of speech" that is alluded to is, "There is no god but Allah."

The eighteenth name is "that which is right and proper" (*al-ṣawāb*). It is derived from Allah's saying: *They shall not speak, except someone to whom the All-Merciful has given permission, and who says that which is right and proper* (78:38). He is indicating the one who says, "There is no god but Allah."

The nineteenth name is "the sincere religion" (*al-dīn al-khāliṣ*). This comes from the words of Allah the Exalted: *Surely it is to Allah that sincere religion is due* (39:3). The "sincere religion" is to say, "There is no god but Allah."

The twentieth name is "the sublime similitude" (*al-mathal al-aʿlā*). In the Qurʾān, Allah the Exalted says: *And to Allah belongs the sublime similitude* (16:60). This is said to be, "There is no god but Allah." It is linguistically synonymous with "the sublime description" (*al-waṣf al-aʿlā*).

The twenty-first name is "the most secure handle" (*al-ʿurwa al-wuthqā*). It is derived from Allah's saying: "he has grasped the most secure handle" (2:256). The "secure handle" is said to be, "There is no god but Allah."

The twenty-second name is "the call to the truth" (*daʿwa al-ḥaqq*). This name is derived from Allah's saying: *to Him is the call of truth* (13:14). The "call to truth" is said to be, "There is no god but Allah."

The twenty-third name is "the keys of the heavens and the earth" (*maqālīd al-samāwāt wa al-arḍ*). Allah the Exalted says in His Qurʾān: *His are the keys of the heavens and the earth* (39:63). According to Ibn ʿAbbās ، the keys are: "There is no god but Allah." Those keys include the key to the Garden of Paradise, the key to the treasuries of the Unseen, and the keys to the heavens and the earth. The most noble of them all is the key to the souls, the bodies, the spirits, the hearts, the innermost feelings, and the minds. *Say: "To Allah belongs the East and West. He guides whom He wills to a straight path"* (2:142).

As the authorities have mentioned, the declaration, "There is no god but Allah," is called by many other names, including "the greatest verse" (*al-āya al-kubrā*), and "the success" (*al-falāḥ*) to which the believer is summoned.[54] It has also been called "Allah's safeguard," "Allah's fortress,"

---

54 The call to prayer (*adhān*) summons the believers by saying, "Come to success!" (*ḥayya ʿala al-falāḥ*).

and "the cream of the Qurʾān." It is said to be the best part of the Qurʾān (*al-dhikr*) and its tithe (*ʿushr*) or alms-due (*zakāt*). According to Imam (Ibn) al-ʿArabī, in his treatise *al-Futūḥāt al-Makkiyya:*

> Because it is repeated thirty-six times in the Qurʾān, it is said to be its alms-due (*zakāt*). These thirty-six repetitions in the Qurʾān are the tithe of the orbits of the celestial sphere, by the movements whereof Allah has brought into being the various types of entities existing in the universe, such as spirits and bodies, light and darkness. These thirty-six occurrences (of "There is no god but Allah") are Allah's rightful due from all things existing in the universe. They are within the very essence of the human utterance of the Qurʾān, so they are like the tithe from the produce of heavenly irrigation. "There is no god but Allah" is the most exalted appellation, proven where Allah says, *Glorify the Name of your Lord, the Most High* (87:1).
>
> The *tahlīl* (the declaration that there is no god but Allah) is therefore the tithe of the *dhikr*, meaning its *zakāt*, because it is Allah's rightful due. It is one-tenth of the three-hundred and sixty (degrees of a full circle).

Imam Ibn al-ʿArabī continues:

> Know that this noble declaration consists of four words: the negative particle (*lā*, "no"); the negated object (*ilāha*, "god"); an affirmative particle (*illa*, "but, except"); and an affirmed Existent ("Allāh"). Similarly, there are four divine essences which are the source of the existence of the universe. There are also four natural essences comprising the existence of material substances. Four elements are the source for the existence of the vegetation. Four humors are the source of the existence of the animals. Four realities are the source of existence of the human being.
>
> The divine four are Life, Knowledge, Will, and Speech, for these are the source of intellectual and legal faculty. The natural four (comprising material substance) are heat, cold, aridity, and moisture. The four elements (making up vegetable life) are fire, water, air, and earth. The four humors (comprising animal life) are yellow and black bile, blood, and phlegm. The four realities (comprising the human being) are the body, nourishment, sensory perception, and enunciation.
>
> If the servant says, "There is no god but Allah," in accordance with this fourfold arrangement, he will be the tongue of the world and the deputy of the Real in speech. Thus the world and the Real will remember him when he makes his remembrance.

According to Sayyid al-Ḥasan b. Masʿūd al-Yūsī, may his innermost being be sanctified, in his book *Minhāj al-khalāṣ*:

> It has been reported that Allah says: "The declaration, 'There is no god but Allah,' is My Fortress, so if someone enters My Fortress, he will be safe from My torment." The statement, "There is no god" is not a fortress by itself, but only part of the fortress, since the fortress is not completed unless "but Allah" is added."

He also said:

> Every fortress has four basic elements, and "There is no god but Allah" consists of four words (in Arabic), so each word is a basic element. When its parts are interconnected, the fortress becomes complete.
>
> Just as the declaration has four basic elements in its outer form, it has four basic elements in its inner meaning: namely, the ritual prayer (*ṣalāt*), the alms-due (*zakāt*), the fast (*ṣawm*), and the pilgrimage (*ḥajj*). It is itself the fifth, since "Islam is built upon five (pillars)."
>
> This declaration consists of four words, and the letters (in the Arabic spelling) add up to twelve.[55] Particularly significant are the four letters that spell the Name of Majesty (Allah) which occur in the declaration, because its affirmation is the purpose and the intention (of the declaration).
>
> The significance of this number "four" is truly remarkable. The elements are four, there are four natural humors, there are four Scriptures,[56] the Caliphs are four in number,[57] and the schools of Islamic law and jurisprudence (*madhāhib*) are four.[58]
>
> Most things that exist in the universe have been formed in a quadrilateral shape. The human being is a rectangular quadrilateral, and so are most of the animals. Houses have four sides, and so do doors. Books are bound in quadrilateral volumes. Mosques are quadrilateral, and it is actually considered reprehensible to perform the ritual prayer in any place of worship that is not quadrilateral (in dimension). The directions are four, and so are the winds. The degrees of nearness (to Allah) are four, they being the degree of the prophets, the champions of truth, the martyrs, and the righteous. Human subtleties are four in number, they being the mind, the soul, the heart, and the spirit. If four is multiplied by itself, the result is sixteen; this number is the sum of the seven heavens, the seven earths, the Throne and the Pedestal.
>
> Most of the things in existence are grouped in multiples of this number four. Twelve letters are the basis of the ennobled declaration

---

55 In the Arabic script, *lā ilāha ill-Allāh* is spelled "lām-alif, alif-lām-hāʾ, alif-lām-alif, alif-lām-lām-hāʾ."

56 The Torah of Moses, the Psalms (Zabūr) of David, the Gospels (Injīl) of Jesus, and the Qurʾān of Muḥammad.

57 Abū Bakr al-Ṣiddīq, ʿUmar b. al-Khaṭṭāb, ʿUthmān b. ʿAffān, ʿAlī b. Abī Ṭālib.

58 The schools of Abū Ḥanīfa (Ḥanafī), Imam Mālik (Mālikī), Imam Shāfiʿī (Shāfiʿī) and Aḥmad b. Ḥanbal (Ḥanbalī).

> (*lā ilāha ill-Allāh*, "There is no god but Allah"). Twelve is the number of the signs of the Zodiac, and there are twelve constellations that form the sphere of vicissitudes and transformations, by Allah's permission. The scholars have devoted considerable research to the peculiarities of numbers and the secrets of the letters of the alphabet.

The twelve letters (in the Arabic spelling) of, "There is no god but Allah," are full of light. If someone remembers this declaration, his heart will be filled with light, wisdom, and right guidance, and its blissful grace will envelop him. As for the declaration: "There is no god but Allah; Muḥammad is Allah's Messenger," it consists of twenty-four letters.[59] This is the number of hours in the full cycle of the night and day. If someone pronounces this declaration, any sins he has committed during those hours will be erased from his record. As for the number of different letters used in the declaration, they are nine in number.[60] That is the number of the nine spheres encompassing the upper and the lower world;[61] so if someone pronounces it one time, he obtains rewards amounting to the contents of the whole world.

The declaration ("There is no god but Allah; Muḥammad is the Messenger of Allah") consists of seven words (in the Arabic). There are seven doors to Hell, and the son of Adam has seven (main) body parts. If someone pronounces it one time, each word will therefore lock one of the seven doors and prevent him from entering the Fire.

Imam al-Fakhr al-Rāzī reported:

> A man was standing at (Mount) Arafat, holding seven stones in his hand. He said, "O stones, bear witness that I bear witness that there is no god but Allah, and that I bear witness that Muḥammad is Allah's Messenger!" Then he fell asleep and dreamed that the Day of Resurrection had arrived. The man was called to account and then condemned to the Hellfire; so when they escorted him to one of the doors of Hell, one of those seven stones came and threw itself into that door. The angels of torment made a concerted effort to remove it, but they were unable to do so. He was then escorted to the second door, and the same thing happened there. It happened at each of the seven doors, so he was then escorted to the Heavenly Throne, and

---

59 In the Arabic script, *Muḥammadan Rasūl-Allāh* is spelled "mīm-ḥā'-mīm-dāl, rā'-sīn-wāw-lām, alif-lām-lām-hā'."

60 Alif, lām, hā', mīm, ḥā', dal, rā', sīn, wāw.

61 Islamic cosmology defines nine spheres of the universe, seven planetary, one of the stars (comprising the divine Footstool), and the last beyond the stars (comprising the divine Throne). This ninth sphere was added by Muslim cosmologists to the eight Ptolemaic spheres of existence, and "symbolizes the transition between becoming and Being." See Seyyid Hossein Nasr, *An Introduction to Islamic Cosmological Doctrines* (Albany: State University of New York Press, 1993), p. 236.

Allah, Glorious and Exalted is He, said to the man, "My servant, you caused the stones to bear witness, so their rightful due will not be forfeited. I am a witness to you bearing witness to My Oneness. Enter the Garden of Paradise!" He promptly approached the doors of the Garden, only to find that its doors were locked. Then the testimony that there is no god but Allah came and opened the doors, and the man entered into the Garden.

The Perfection of "There is no god but Allah"

According to Imam Ibn ʿAṭiyya:[62]

> The religious scholars have disagreed as to which expression is better: "Praise belongs to Allah, the Lord of all the worlds (*al-ḥamdu li-Llāhi Rabb al-ʿālamīn*)," or, "There is no god but Allah (*lā ilāha ill-Allāh*)." One group has maintained the superiority of the former because the affirmation of divine Oneness (*al-tawḥīd*) is implicit therein, since the expression, "Praise belongs to Allah, the Lord of all the worlds," comprises both an affirmation of Oneness and praise, whereas the expression, "There is no god but Allah," contains only the affirmation of Oneness. In support of their opinion, they cite the prophetic tradition reported on the authority of Abū Hurayra ﵁ and Abū Saʿīd al-Khudrī ﵁, in which Allah's Messenger ﷺ said: "If someone says 'There is no god but Allah,' twenty good deeds will be recorded in his favor and twenty bad deeds will be removed (from his record). If someone says, 'Praise belongs to Allah, the Lord of all the worlds,' thirty good deeds will be recorded in his favor and thirty bad deeds will be erased."
>
> Another group maintained the superiority of the latter expression, because it repudiates unbelief, and people (are inspired to) fight for it. In support of their opinion, they cite the saying of the Prophet ﷺ: "The keys to the Garden of Paradise consist of, 'There is no god but Allah.'"[63]

After making this explanation his choice (in favor of the declaration, "There is no god but Allah"), Imam Ibn ʿAṭiyya said, "The decisive factor is the saying of the Prophet ﷺ: 'The best thing I have said, myself and the prophets preceding me, is 'There is no god but Allah Alone, He has no partner.'"[64]

Abū al-Walīd b. Rushd was once asked: "What is better, saying 'Praise be to Allah' (*al-ḥamdu li-Llāhi*) or saying 'There is no god but Allah' (*la*

62 This likely refers to Imam Ibn ʿAṭiyya (d. 1147, Andalusia), a famous interpreter of the Qurʾān who is cited frequently in the twenty-volume *Tafsīr* of Imam al-Qurṭubī (d. 1273).

63 Cited by Mundhirī in *al-Targhīb wa al-tarhīb*, and reported by Ibn Ḥanbal in his *Musnad*.

64 Reported by Tirmidhī in his *Sunan* and by Imam al-Bayhaqī in his *Sunan*.

ilāha ill-Allāh)? He responded that saying 'There is no god but Allah' is better. His response was conveyed to the eminent jurist Maymūn b. Mahdī, who wrote to Ibn Rushd in verse:

> I have just seen what you wrote, and you are not without arrows
> In this controversy, though you have plunged into it with undue haste
>
> Your error lies in your lack of submission to the people of knowledge
> And the fact that people will follow you will be part of your final reckoning.

So Imam Ibn Rushd responded to him by saying:

> Gently! You have not caught me sleeping
> So be careful, and listen if you can hear
>
> You have transgressed my rights as if I were like those with whom you are acquainted
> And in my absence you have met with a raging lion
>
> If you had only handed over the religious sciences intact to their owners
> You would not be now in the throes of death because of what you pretend
>
> Contention is guaranteed you within any scholarly sitting
> Without doubt, we have given you a drink infused with poison.

This should suffice for this matter. Allah is the Enabling Guide to the straight path, and to Him the Exalted and Glorified is the return and final destination.

The Supplication Concluding the Litany

The litany is concluded with the words:

> *Verily Allah and His angels shower blessings on the Prophet. O you who truly believe! Invoke blessings upon him and salute him with a worthy salutation* (33:56). May Allah the Exalted shower blessings upon him and upon his family, and may He salute them with a worthy salutation! *Glory be to your Lord, the Lord of Majesty, far from what they attribute! And peace be upon those sent as Messengers! And praise be to Allah, Lord of all the worlds!* (37:180–182).

The invocation of blessing upon the Prophet ﷺ and the glorification (*tasbīḥ*) of Allah the Almighty and Glorious have been discussed previously.

Concerning the Tijānī Daily Office *(waẓīfa)*

As for the remembrances included the Tijānī daily office (*waẓīfa*), the plea for refuge (*al-istiʿādha*), the invocation of Allah's Name (*al-basmala*) and the Opening chapter (*al-fātiḥa*), have already been discussed in length.

Following the Opening chapter (*al-fātiḥa*), the next part of the daily office (*waẓīfa*) is the plea for forgiveness (*istighfār*), recited thirty times: "I beg forgiveness of Allah the Almighty, for there is no god but He, the Ever-Living, Self-Subsisting." On the subject of this remembrance, it is reported in the *Sunan* of Abū Dāwūd and Tirmidhī, on the authority of Ibn Masʿūd ﷺ, that Allah's Messenger ﷺ said, "If someone says 'I beg forgiveness of Allah the Almighty, for there is no god but He, the Ever-Living, the Self-Subsisting, and I repent to Him,' his sins will be forgiven, even if he deserted an army!" According to Ḥākim, this is an authentic prophetic tradition.

Sayyid al-ʿArabī b. al-Sāʾiḥ, the master gnostic, explained in *Bughyat (al-mustafīd)* the reason for leaving out the statement "and I repent to Him" from the *waẓīfa*. It came this way by way of the Prophet ﷺ to Shaykh Aḥmad al-Tijānī, without the Shaykh having a choice in the matter. The reason is that if the plea for forgiveness should be accompanied with repentance, the servant will make himself a liar if he violates his repentance. If he says, "I repent to Him," but he is not repentant for his deeds, he has become a liar. The (reality of) repentance is returning (to Allah) with remorse. It is more fitting for the servant to ask for forgiveness, so that he will come to recognize his sins and have remorse for them. He will become determined to never return to them, and so will arrive at (true) repentance. The manner of the heedless in coming to repentance is devoid of remembering (the meaning of) repentance, unlike the coming to repentance of a person who has joined himself to the act. The former method risks the manifestation of deception and derision, unlike the latter which contains sincere seeking for forgiveness. This has been mentioned by al-Fakhr (al-Dīn) al-Rāzī in his exegesis of the Qurʾān, for it contains a sublime subtlety that should not be hidden. And Allah the Exalted knows best.

Let us mention here the sacred tradition (*ḥadīth qudsī*) related by Abū Dharr, on the authority of Allah's Messenger ﷺ, to whom Gabriel, peace be upon him, conveyed it from Allah the Exalted:

> Allah the Exalted has said: "O My servants, I have declared wrongdoing unlawful to Myself, and I have made it unlawful among you, so do not treat one another wrongfully! O My servants, you are the ones who err by night and by day, and I am the One who forgives sins. I do not mind, so seek My forgiveness and I will forgive you! O My servants, all of you are hungry except those whom I have fed; so ask Me for food and I shall feed you! O My servants, all of you are naked, except those whom I have clothed; so ask Me for clothing and I shall clothe you! O My servants, even if the first of you and the last of you, the human beings among you and the jinn among you, were in the (same) state as the most righteous-hearted man among you, that would not add anything to My Kingdom! O My servants, even if the first of you

and the last of you, the human beings among you and the jinn among you, were on equal footing, you should ask of Me, for I will give every one among you what he asks. That will not detract anything from My Kingdom, except to the extent that the ocean is diminished by a single prick of a needle! O My servants, it is only for your deeds that I hold you accountable, so if someone gains a benefit, let him praise Allah the Almighty and Exalted; and if someone gains anything other than that, let him blame no one but himself!"[65]

Additional Commentary on *ṣalāt al-fātiḥ*

Next comes the invocation, "O Allah, bestow blessings upon our master Muḥammad, the Opener of what was locked." The next invocation must be recited fifty times as part of the *waẓīfa* (following the plea for forgiveness). No other invocation (on the Prophet) can suffice in this part of the *waẓīfa*. It has already been explained at length, but it would be appropriate to include some of what has been related to us of its commentary here.

"O Allah" (*Allāhumma*): In the Arabic script, it is spelled *alif-lām-lām-hāʾ-mīm*. The initial letter *alif* is a sign of the presence (*ḥaḍra*) of Oneness and its manifestation, for which there is no connection, no separation, no entering, and no exiting. Its utterance melts from full realization, because it indicates the pure divine Essence (*al-dhāt al-sādhij*), and the source (*ʿayn*) of blindness and effacement. The two letters (*lām-lām*) are two hidden presences. The letter *hāʾ* is the presence of worshipful servitude, immersed in divine Uniqueness (*huwiyya*). The letter *mīm* is indicative of total immersion (*istighrāq*) of pure worship in the divine Uniqueness.

"Bestow blessings" (*ṣalli*): This verb in the imperative tense is an invocation of blessing that emerges from the totality of the four presences, one by one. With the invocation's emergence from the first presence, it is happily received by the next two presences, and so on through its successive emergence through each of the two hidden presences. The presence of *hāʾ* is a secret that cannot be divulged. With its emergence from the hidden presence of the last it becomes a (complete) invocation, for there is nothing beyond this in terms of capacity for expression; and it is the secret that cannot be divulged. With the invocation's emergence from the presence of *hāʾ*, there are thus three manifest degrees. So this is the rank of the true servant's invocation on his master.[66]

"Upon our master" (*ʿalā sayyidi-nā*): The inner meaning of "master" (*sayyid*) is a secret that cannot be divulged here. The pronominal suffix, "our" (*nā*) applies to "us" in the sense of all beings. The name of this rank

65 Reported in the *Ṣaḥīḥ* of Muslim.

66 The reference to and discussion of the "four presences" is perhaps meant to be hopelessly obscure for the uninitiated. Such concepts are meant to be understood during the process of spiritual training (*tarbiya*).

("master") implies the one most thoroughly immersed in the four presences, the link to the presence of the un-manifested *alif*, the support for the divine Attributes. The invocation of the *lām* after the *alif* is the absolute existence of the Attribute (*ṣifa*) upon what is described (*mawṣūf*). The invocation of the *hāʾ* represents the absolute unseen and total immersion. So *Glory be to your Lord, the Lord of Might, free is He from what they attribute to Him* (Qurʾān, 37:180).

"The opener of what was locked" (*al-fātiḥi li-mā ughliq*): meaning the (one who opened the) manifestations of prophecy and sainthood.

"And the seal of what had gone before" (*wa al-khātimi li-mā sabaq*): meaning (he who sealed) the manifestations of prophecy and the secret. In other words, he is the one who removed the veils, for he is the greatest veil (*ḥijāb*), meaning his being sealed the essence (*ʿayn*) of the veil. Thus the Prophet ﷺ is the confluence of all affairs and praises (*maḥāmid*), so he gave victory to the manifestations of Divinity.

"The helper of the Truth" (*nāṣir al-ḥaqq*): He is the one who helped or made possible the manifestations of divinity.

"With the Truth" (*bi al-ḥaqq*): In order to confirm the reality of divine Oneness (*Aḥadiyya*); so he is the helper and the one helped.

"And the guide" (*wa al-hādī*): He is the guide by means of divine manifestation or revelation.

"To Your straight path" (*ilā ṣirāṭi-ka al-mustaqīm*): This is the path that becomes apparent through divine manifestation or revelation.

"And upon his family" (*wa ʿalā āli-hi*): They are the site of sainthood's appearance (*maẓhar*).

"In keeping with his value and the greatness of his extent in space and time" (*ḥaqqa qadri-hi wa al-miqdāri-hi al-ʿaẓīm*): That is to say, in keeping with the value of his prophecy and his sainthood. His extent in space and time is a reality that is unfathomable, and thus a secret that cannot be mentioned or divulged.

O Allah! Bestow blessings on our master, the opener of what was closed, the seal of what came before, the helper of truth with the truth, and the guide to Your straight path; and upon his family; in keeping with his value and his tremendous worth. O Allah, care for me for his sake, for the sake of his secret of *alif*, of truthfulness (*ṣidq*), of mastery (*siyāda*), of praiseworthiness (*maḥāmid*), opening (*fatḥ*), graciousness (*luṭf*), deputyship (*khilāfa*), precedence (*sabq*), victory (*naṣr*), realization of Truth (*al-ḥaqq*), guidance (*hidāya*), steadfastness (*istiqāma*), proximity, value, worth, and greatness. Amen, O Lord of all the worlds.

The next portion of the daily office (*waẓīfa*) is the Qurʾānic verse: *Glory be to your Lord, the Lord of Majesty, far from what they attribute. And peace be upon those sent as messengers, and praise be to Allah, Lord of All the Worlds* (37:180–182). This has already been discussed.

This is followed by one hundred recitations of the blessed declaration 'There is no god but Allah." The virtue of this has also been expounded upon previously. However, let us remind ourselves here of the following *ḥadīth*, in the version reported by the author of *al-Bughyat* (*al-mustafīd*) on the authority of Ibn ʿAbbās ♦, in which the Prophet ﷺ said:

> Allah (Exalted is He) will open the gates of the Garden of Paradise, and a herald will cry from beneath the Heavenly Throne, "O Garden of Paradise and all the benefits you contain, to whom do you belong?"
>
> The Garden of Paradise and everything within it will then proclaim, "We belong to the people of 'There is no god but Allah,' and we are forbidden to anyone who does not say 'There is no god but Allah.'"
>
> At this point, the Hellfire and all of the torments it contains will be asked "To whom do you belong?" It will say, "None will enter me except those who deny that there is no god but Allah. I seek none but those who do not believe that there is no god but Allah. I am unlawful to those who declare 'There is no god but Allah.' I shall be filled with none but those who refuse to accept that there is no god but Allah. My wrath is for none but those who deny that there is no god but Allah."
>
> Allah's mercy will then arrive with His forgiveness, and they will say, "We belong to the people of 'There is no god but Allah.' We are the assistance of those who say 'There is no god but Allah,' and we love those who declare 'There is no god but Allah,' and we are graciously disposed to those who proclaim 'There is no god but Allah.'"
>
> Allah the Blessed and Exalted will say, "I have declared the Garden of Paradise lawful to those who say 'There is no god but Allah,' and the Garden of Paradise has not been created except for the people of 'There is no god but Allah.'"[67]

This portion of the daily office (*waẓīfa*) is concluded with an invocation upon the Prophet ﷺ, the benefits of which have already been enumerated. It reads, "Our master Muḥammad is Allah's Messenger. May Allah's peace be upon him."

Commentary on the Jewel of Perfection (*jawhara al-kamāl*)

The invocation of blessings upon the Prophet ﷺ described here is called the "Jewel of Perfection" (*jawhara al-kamāl*). It reads as follows:

> O Allah, bestow blessings and peace upon the source of divine mercy and Lordliness, and the veritable ruby that encircles the center of comprehensions and meanings. The light of all created entities, the Adamic being, the owner of the Lordly truth, the brightest flash of

---

67   A slightly different version of this *ḥadīth* has been provided in a previous sub-section, in which the declaration 'There is no god but Allāh (*lā ilāha ill-Allāh*)' is explained thoroughly.

lightning in the rain clouds filling all the seas and receptacles. Your radiant light with which You have filled Your universe, encompassing all places of abode.

O Allah, bestow blessings and peace upon the source of the truth, from which the thrones of the realities have become manifested, the source of the most precious gnosis. Your complete and straightest path.

O Allah, bestow blessings and peace upon the outward appearance of the Truth, with the Truth, the most splendid treasure, Your showering of blessing from You to You, the encompassment of the mystifying light.

May Allah bless him and his family, with a blessing by which You will make us well acquainted with him!

This invocation is recited twelve times in the daily office (*wazīfa*). There is good reason for its inclusion among the other invocations of blessings upon Allah's Messenger ﷺ, since it is distinguished by qualities that no other invocation can possess. Shaykh Aḥmad Sukayrij, the author of *al-Kawkab al-wahhāj*, said about the *jawhara al-kamāl*:

Know that this noble invocation of blessing is equal in content to all the wells of gnosis and secrets. Our master Shaykh Aḥmad al-Tijānī ⚭ received it by word of mouth from the venerable Master of Existence (Sayyid al-Wujūd) ﷺ. He told Shaykh al-Tijānī about some of its excellent merits, including the fact that if someone recites the Jewel (*al-jawhara*) twelve times, while fulfilling its preconditions, with the intention of visiting the Messenger, he will be granted the special favor of obtaining the benefit of visiting all the saints.

Its fundamental importance is explained by our master's ⚭ saying, "Allah's Messenger ﷺ gave me an invocation of blessing called the Jewel of Perfection (*jawhara al-kamāl*). If someone recites it twelve times, and says, 'This is a gift from me to you, O Messenger of Allah,' it is as if he has visited him in his noble garden (*rawḍa*), as well as visiting the saints (*awliyā'*) of Allah the Exalted and the righteous ones, from the beginning of existence until his own time." In another version, the narration is recorded as, "until eternity."

One of its special qualities is that a single recitation of it is equal to the glorification (*tasbīḥ*) recited three times by the entire universe. Another is that, if someone makes a regular practice of reciting it more than seven times daily, the Prophet ﷺ will love him with a special affection, and he will not die until he becomes a saint (*walī*). Another is that, if someone recites it seven times or more, the Prophet ﷺ and the four caliphs, may Allah be well pleased with them, will be in his presence as long as he is remembering it.

When one of the scholars, who was one of our master's companions, may Allah be pleased with them, came to hear about this, he wished to confirm its reality. So he approached our master 🌼 and mentioned what he had heard. Shaykh al-Tijānī 🌼 told him: "By Allah, if you were to remember it constantly throughout your life, without any intermission, the Prophet 🌺 would never separate himself from you in the entire course of your life."

The presence mentioned here will be that of their spirits and persons in reality. If the veil is removed from those who practice remembrance, or from some of them, they will surely witness the Prophet 🌺 in the state he was in when Allah took him away (from his life in this world), and the same is true for the four caliphs, may Allah be well pleased with them. The Prophet 🌺 and the caliphs may thus be witnessed time after time.

Another of its special qualities is that, if someone diligently persists in reciting it seven times before going to sleep, in a state of perfect ritual purity and on a clean bed, he will see the Prophet 🌺.

This should be sufficient for you in regard to its excellent benefit, worthy of any expenditure on the part of noble souls. The Prophet 🌺 is recorded as having said, "One of you would dearly love to see me, even at the cost of everything in his possession!" In the words of a poet, "If only He would favor me with the sight of a face—a face that relieves everyone who sees it of distress!"

You must view the arrangement of this litany (wird) and the daily office (wazīfa) with clarity of vision. Then you will realize that it contains amazing secrets, dazzling to the mind and beyond the grasp of intellectual comprehension. One day, I said to one of my dear friends, "In the daily office (wazīfa), the human being is first denuded and stripped bare of clothing, clad only in the intentions and the plea for forgiveness. The divine Essence then manifests itself to him, in all its perfection, in the invocation of blessings upon our master Muḥammad 🌺. Then he affirms the divine Oneness with: 'There is no god but Allah. Then he recites the Jewel of Perfection (jawhara al-kamāl)." The daily office (wazīfa) is then concluded with:

> Surely Allah and His angels shower blessings on the Prophet. O you who truly believe! Invoke blessings upon him and salute him with a worthy salutation (33:56). May Allah send His benediction upon him, his household and companions, and send many salutations. Glory be to your Lord, the Lord of Majesty, far from what they attribute. And peace be upon those sent as Messengers. And praise be to Allah, Lord of All the Worlds (37:180–182).

The Excellence of the Litanies and the *Shaykh al-Tarbiya*

Careful study of the Tijānī litanies (*awrād*) demonstrates that they are the finest and most excellent of all litanies.

According to the erudite scholar al-Ḥāfiẓ Ibn Ḥajar,[68] in his *Fatāwāt*:

As for the litanies of the Sufis, which they recite after the ritual prayer in accordance with the customary practices of their method of spiritual development, they have an authentic source; for Bayhaqī has reported, on the authority of Anas b. Mālik ◉, that the Prophet ﷺ said: "That I should remember Allah the Exalted in the company of a group of people, after the dawn prayer until the rising of the sun, is dearer to me than this world and what it contains. That I should remember Allah the Exalted in the company of a group of people, in the wake of the afternoon prayer until the sun sets, is dearer to me than this world and what is contains."[69]

As reported by Abū Dāwūd, he ﷺ also said: "That I should sit in the company of a group of people who are remembering Allah, from the early morning prayer until the sun rises, is dearer to me than emancipating four of the sons of Ismāʿīl, ◉. That I should sit in the company of a group of people who are remembering Allah, from the early morning prayer until the sun rises, is dearer to me than emancipating four (slaves)."[70]

As reported by Abū Naʿaym, he ﷺ also is reported as having said, "Tranquility descends upon the sessions of remembrance; the angels surround their participants, mercy envelops them, and Allah remembers them."[71]

Imam Aḥmad and Imam Muslim both reported that the Prophet ﷺ said: "Whenever a group of people sit and remember Allah, the angels surround them, and mercy envelops them. Tranquility descends upon them, and Allah mentions them to those in His presence."[72]

Since it has thus been established that the customary practice of the Sufis—meaning their general observance of the remembrances and litanies—has an authentic basis in the Sunna, no objection can be leveled against them in this regard. In a situation in which their

---

68 Ibn Ḥajar al-Haytami al-Makkī (d. 1556) was a prominent scholar of Mālikī jurisprudence and Sufism who wrote, among other works, *al-Fatāwā al-ḥadīthiyya*.

69 Reported by Imam al-Bayhaqī in *al-Sunan al-kubrā*, and cited on the authority of Anas b. Mālik ◉ by Imam al-Haythamī in *Majmaʿ al-zawāʾid*.

70 Reported by Abū Dāwūd is *al-Sunan al-kubrā* and by Imam Abū Nuʿaym in *Dhikr akhbār Iṣbahān*, and cited on the authority of Anas b. Mālik by Imam al-Haythamī in *Majmaʿ al-zawāʾid*.

71 Reported by Imam Abū Nuʿaym in *Ḥilya al-awliyāʾ*, and by al-Khaṭīb al-Baghdādī in *Tārīkh Baghdād*.

72 Reported in the *Ṣaḥīḥ* of Muslim, and by Ibn Ḥanbal in his *Musnad*.

audible recitation may disturb someone, especially someone who is performing the ritual prayer or someone who is sleeping, inaudible recitation is strongly recommended. Otherwise, they should follow the instruction of their teacher, who combines the sacred law (*sharīʿa*) and Reality (*ḥaqīqa*), for he is like the physician, as mentioned previously. He will not prescribe something unless he believes that it contains a remedy for the sickness.

This explains why you will find that some of them prefer audible recitation (*jahr*), in order to drive away devilish whisperings and carnal inclinations, to awaken heedless hearts, and to demonstrate perfect actions; while some of them prefer inaudible recitation (*isrār*) in order to discipline the self, and to teach it the ways of sincere devotion, and to make it accustomed to unobtrusive behavior. It is related that ʿUmar ﷺ used to recite his remembrance audibly, whereas Abū Bakr ﷺ would recite inaudibly. When the Prophet ﷺ asked them about this, each of them responded with the kind of explanation we have just mentioned, so he confirmed them both.

Taking from multiple spiritual masters (*mashāyikh*) differs in condition depending on whether the person desires blessing (*tabarruk*), or spiritual education (*tarbiya*) and traveling along the path (*sulūk*). The first takes from whom he wills unless there is something to prevent him from doing so. For the second, this (exclusive) affiliation is appointed for him, according to the school of the sound Sufi people, in order to avoid the prohibited and blameworthy things. May Allah gather us together in the company of such masters! May He not start the disciple except with the shaykh whose state (*ḥāl*) he has been attracted to. Like this, the shaykh will have full dominion over the disciple, so that his ego-self will vanish in the splendid state of this spiritually realized shaykh. So the shaykh will intervene between the disciple and the passions and desires of the disciple's ego-self. At this point, the disciple must hold tightly to the shaykh's guidance, submitting himself to the entirety of his commands, prohibitions, and prescriptions. He will then become like a corpse in the hands of the funeral washer, turning this way and that as the washer wills.

If the spiritual state of the shaykh does not enrapture him in this manner, the (first type of) disciple may free himself for one more pious among the shaykhs, and one more knowledgable of the rules of the sacred law and the divine Reality. So he will enter under his direction and prescriptions. This will lead to success in the case of the shaykh of the first description (the *shaykh al-tabarruk*).

As for the shaykh of the second description (the *shaykh al-tarbiya*), it is forbidden for the disciple, according to the Sufi people, to leave him and go to another, even if his lower self (*nafs*) should entice him to think that another shaykh is more complete. In such a case, it is simply the right of his shaykh that exasperates him, for the lower self wants to remove itself from its owner into further error.

The best solution is to choose, from the beginning, the best shaykh: endowed with the most gnosis, knowledge, piety, and righteousness. So after entering under the providential care of such a gnostic (*ʿārif*), he has no permissible excuse to leave him. Indeed, according to the Sufi people, the shaykh of spiritual training has no license to let an aspirant take from him if he knows that a perfected teacher is already causing him to tread the spiritual path. In this case, the shaykh should command him to return to his teacher, and let him know the right of his teacher, to not let his lower self turn away from him even if it wants to part with him for somebody else. Indeed, this (desire of the *nafs* for separation) is the first evidence of his teacher's perfection and the truth of his path. Many of the souls (*nufūs*) for whom failure has been decreed, if they should see a teacher of strong spiritual training, they will have an aversion to him, and heap on him all sorts of calumnies and criticisms of which he is innocent.

The fortunate one will be warned against this course, knowing that the ego-self actually desires nothing but the destruction of its owner (the disciple himself). So he must not obey it in refusing his shaykh, since he recognizes its most insidious condition, trying to rob his good deeds of their righteousness and his lofty goals of their acceptibility by the sacred law. Whoever has the door of correctly interpreting the spiritual masters opened for him, and out of modesty lowers his gaze from their spiritual states, and assigns their affairs to Allah, and devotes his attention to the condition of his self (*nafs*), waging holy war against it to the best of his ability; surely it is hoped that such a person will arrive to his goals and find success in his desires in the shortest amount of time.

As for the one for whom has been opened the door of disaproval of the spiritual masters, of searching into their spiritual states and deeds; is not this a sign of his exclusion and the evilness of his end? Surely there is no success in this, which is why it is said: "Whoever says to his shaykh, 'Why?' will never succeed." In other words, when his shaykh of spiritual seeking (*sulūk*) and training (*tarbiya*) has decided on a matter, the aspirant should put himself in his hands like a corpse in the hands of its washer. This is to the point that if the aspirant should have knowledge (*ʿulūm*), designs (*rusūm*), or works (*ʿamāl*), he should cast them aside and pay no attention to them. The fire of truth (*ḥaqq*) of the gnostic teacher makes manifest the filth in order that you may abandon it. The goodness remains, and the purity of the shaykh's essence and the preciousness of his kind is clarified. The purpose of volition (*irāda*) and the appointment of an arbitrator (*taḥkīm*) and their relationship is that whoever wants to journey to Allah (*al-sulūk ilā*

Allāh) does so at the hand of one of the arrived saints (*al-wāṣilīn*), and Allah makes it easy for him to know who is the shaykh. The aspirant thereby may obligate his ego-self to obey him, and subject himself to his commands and prohibitions.

The result of this commitment (*irtibāṭ*) differs according to the spiritual master involved. Some of them command the disciple with the remembrance of Allah. Some of them dress him in the Sufi's tattered gown (*khirqa*). Some of them do other things depending on their ways, which are very many indeed, to the extent it has been said that the paths (*ṭuruq*) to Allah are as many as the breaths of all the created beings.

The disciple should refrain from entering under the providential care of a shaykh until his spiritual state has overwhelmed him, or he has come to know of his understanding of the sciences of the sacred law (*al-sharīʿa*) and the divine Reality (*al-ḥaqīqa*). This is because the liars and pretenders are many in this path (*ṭarīqa*), although they have nothing to do with it. They are betaking themselves to the Fire on account of their evil deeds, the corruption of their conditions and words, and their rabid pursuit of the ephemeral world and their rejection of the everlasting Hereafter. Their only aim in calling to the spiritual path is to gather the vanities of the world, to obtain the tasty treats of the forbidden, and to waste away life in pagan ignorance and sin. So beware of their like and the deceit of their words and deeds. Whoever follows them loses his footing, finds regret, and is prevented from arriving at the slightest degree of divine perfection. Allah will bring him the greatest ruin, an exemplary punishment as warning to others.

You must yearn for the truth to be shown to you. Adorn yourself with truthfulness and sincerity by making diligent study of the *Iḥyāʾ* (*ʿulūm al-dīn*) of Ghazālī, may Allah have mercy on him. Study also the *Risāla* of Qushayrī, the *ʿAwārif al-maʿārif* of Suhrawardī[73] and the *Qūt* (*al-qulūb*) of Abū Ṭālib al-Makkī.[74] These works are useful in explaining the states of the sincere, truthful ones; as well as the deceits of the liars. They contain the recipe for exalted character traits, the love for poverty, the devotion to obedience, and the perseverence in religious devotions, not only those in congregation. They contain the means to remove oneself from the trivialities of people over whom Satan has become

73 This book has been translated by Qamar-Ul Huda, *Knowledge for Encountering God: al-Suhrawardi's ʿAwarif al-Maʿarif* (Fons Vitae, forthcoming). In this work, Abū Ḥafṣ al-Suhrawardī (d. 1234, Persia) explains various Sufi doctrines and practices with frequent reference to the Qurʾān and the Sunna.

74 The *Qūt al-qulūb fī muʿāmalāt al-maḥbūb wa waṣf ṭarīq al-murīd ilā maqām al-tawḥīd* by Abū Ṭālib al-Makkī (d. 996, Baghdad) is considered a foundational work of Sufi practice and doctrine. Ghazālī used it as a source for his *Iḥyāʾ*.

victorious, seducing them from the beautiful to the ugly, from the known right way to abomination, from what is praiseworthy to what is blameworthy. Such peoples have been drowned in the seas of lusts, of disgusting doctrines, of wishful desires. And with all of this, they believe they are doing good. What a fabrication they have invented!

May Allah provide us with the knowledge of the imperfections of ourselves, and grant us sanctuary from the lusts of the ego-self. May He sustain us with His good pleasure and peace through every tribulation and affliction until we meet with Him. Surely, He is the Bountiful, the Generous, the Kind, the Merciful.

The Friday Congregational Remembrance *(haylala)*

The remembrance of "There is no god but Allah" (*al-haylala*) following the afternoon prayer on Friday takes the following form: The plea for refuge in Allah the Exalted (*istiʿādha*), the utterance of "In the Name of Allah, the Compassionate, the Merciful" (*basmala*), and the opening chapter of the Qurʾān (*al-fātiḥa*), each recited once; the plea for forgiveness (*istighfār*) in the fashion of the daily office (*waẓīfa*), and the Invocation of the Opener (*ṣalāt al-fātiḥ*), both recited three times; the supplication beginning with, "Surely Allah and His angels send blessings on the Prophet," recited once; and the remembrance, "There is no god but Allah," to be repeated until the setting of the sun. This is the case if done in congregation; if performed alone, the individual should recite a total of 1000, 1200, 1500—this being the ideal amount—or 1600—this being the last of acceptable numbers. On the subject of Friday, the Day of Congregration, Allah the Exalted said: *And when the ritual prayer is finished, scatter in the land, and seek the gracious favor of Allah and remember Allah frequently, for then you may prosper* (62:10).

Supererogatory Tijānī Litanies and Remembrances

As for the non-obligatory Tijānī litanies (*awrād*) and remembrances (*adhkār*), which are innumerable, they are not excluded from the principles of authentication that we have established. Their source may be found in a text of the sacred law, or a supplication (*duʿāʾ*) in the Arabic language, the meaning of which is clearly in accordance with an unambiguous legal rule. The prayer also may have been discovered through a saint's spiritual insight or unveiling. The remembrances of the Sufi people cannot be discredited, therefore, except by an ignorant fool or stubborn critic. Allah the Exalted has said: *And since they will not be guided by it, they say: "This is an ancient lie!"* (46:11).

They envied the young man only because they could not match his efforts
Surely the Sufi people have enemies and adversaries

> Just as the co-wives of a beautiful woman speak to her face
> In open jealousy and loathing; O how reprehensible a deed!

Another has said:

> You can look forward to reconciling with every enemy
> Except the one who is your enemy out of envy

Indeed, the blame of the critic is evidence of perfection. As it has been said:

> If I should show you the censure of my critic
> It is surely a testimony to my perfection.

Appendix III

The Ecstatic Utterances of the Enraptured Ones

In the *Laṭāʾif al-minan*, Shaʿrānī, the saintly pole and scholarly gnostic who combined the sacred law and the divine Reality, quoted the following saying from the Shaykh of the Sufi group, Abū al-Qāsim al-Junayd ﷺ: "One of the enraptured ones said that he who remembers Allah the Exalted will attain a state such that, even if his face were struck with a sword, he would not feel it. I was not convinced of this for some time, until I finally experienced the matter to be just as he said." Shaʿrānī also said:

> The majority of those who fall into error concerning this subject are the authors of books of esoteric subtleties (*kutub al-riqāʾiq*) among the (would-be) Sufis who have not tasted the stations of the spiritual path. They relate everything they have come to know about a saint, without understanding the difference between his initial stage, his middle stage, and his final stage of development. They call everything they have not experienced on the spiritual path a station of the perfected ones. But if one so perfected were to study the books of these authors, he would recognize their ignorance. If these writers had experienced the stations of the spiritual path, they would only mention the saint's exploits in the final stage of his development.
>
> I once heard my master ʿAlī al-Khawwāṣ ﷺ say, "Since Allah's Messenger ﷺ was commanded to ask his Lord to increase him in knowledge, what do you think of everyone else?" Indeed, the Prophet ﷺ said of himself that he had been given the knowledge of all the people of the earlier and the later generations. So it is our firm conviction that Allah granted his prayer, and gave him more knowledge than those of former and those of later times.

This is to say, then, that the ultimate spiritual station belongs to no one except the Prophet ﷺ. If you have understood this, you will understand that the spiritual pauper who says, "I am Allah's servant now, (but) not for fear of His Fire, nor in hope of His reward," is simply a novice of the spiritual path, not one of those who have attained perfection. So you should avoid finding fault with him.

If the disciple devotes himself assiduously to the remembrance (of Allah), making it his usual practice by night and day, he certainly will recognize his veil. Then when his veil becomes threadbare, he will recognize that the remembrance is for Allah's sake, not for the servant's sake. He will hear the call of the Real, expressed in some form that conveys the meaning: "Who is more wretched than someone who worships Me for the sake of a Garden, or a Fire? If I had not created a Garden of Paradise and a Fire of Hell, would I not still be worthy of being worshipped?" Thus the servant will feel ashamed in Allah's Presence; ashamed to be worshiping Allah for fear of the Fire or for hope of a reward. Indeed, no one should expect to receive wages for another's work, only for his own work.

The disciple whose veil becomes thin will recognize therefore that he has no involvement in the performance of deeds. He is only fulfilling his duty in accordance with the pure sacred law. He will recognize, with clarity and certitude, that he is like the instrument with which the Mover sets the immobile in motion. Just as Allah is the Creator of the servant's essential being, He likewise is the Creator of his actions. This is similar to the statement you hear, "There is no Owner except Allah, and no one shares ownership with Him in anything!" This is a station experienced by the disciple in the beginning of his journey on the spiritual path. The person who says it is not laying claim to this as the final station, as others may suspect. Rather this is the first step on the spiritual path, in which the disciple acknowledges that ownership belongs to Allah, since He is the Creator of everything.

In *ʿIbāra al-minhāj*, Nawawī said: "Understand that the servant renounces all claim to ownership in the transference of ownership to his Master. When the servant has properly acknowledged that ownership belongs to Allah alone, his appropriate station becomes abstinence from the world and refraining from stinginess toward any of his fellow creatures, except for a purpose prescribed by the sacred law."

The servant's conduct in this station would be like a person who had a pile of gold stolen from him, but not one of his hairs turned gray because of it. He would actually feel pleased with the person who took it, for fear of the reckoning in store for him on the Day of Resurrection (as to how he spent the gold). For one at this station, Allah's giving and His withholding are the same in substance. The difference is only what is incumbent on the servant himself, like contentment, for example.

> He does not see himself sharing with his Lord in owning anything in this world or the next. Even if the Lord gave him everything, he does not imagine he owns it, except to the extent that the gift was only given to him for the sake of evoking thankfulness. So he detaches himself from the gift and attributes it to the Lord, the One who owns the gift and himself.

Shaʿrānī also said on this subject:

> Sarī al-Saqaṭī used to say, "There is no difference between the servant's saying, 'Allah has created me, sustained me, shaped me, taught me knowledge and the Qurʾān, and made me a blessed being,' and his saying, 'I am a saintly friend of Allah, and I am of the scholars who put their knowledge into practice,' and similar statements. Indeed, every true believer is a saintly friend of Allah the Exalted: *Allah is the protecting friend of those who believe. He brings them out of darkness into the light* (Qurʾān, 2:257). The scholar never stops putting his knowledge into practice, and he thanks Allah the Exalted for including him among those able to do so. If someone finds himself absolutely excluded from sainthood and knowledge, his thankfulness to Allah must have been very negligable indeed."
>
> Imam al-Layth b. Saʿd[1] used to say: "I know a shaykh who has never disobeyed his Lord from the moment when he became conscious of himself." His companions used to say to each other, "He must be referring to himself, because no one knows that about another except by inspiration from Allah the Exalted."
>
> A man once touched the foot of Abū al-ʿAbbās al-Sayyārī—one of the men mentioned in Qushayrī's *Risāla*—so Abū al-ʿAbbās said, "Are you touching a foot that has never walked in disobedience to Allah?"
>
> Shaykh Abū al-Ḥasan al-Shādhilī would often say to his companions: "You must publicize your devotion as a demonstration of your servitude, just as other people make a public display of sinful acts of disobedience. You should also inform the people of the sciences and gnostic understandings bestowed on you by Allah. These are some of the fruits from the righteous early believers. The scholars and the righteous did not applaud themselves boastfully or ostentatiously, far be that from them! Their conduct (in publicizing what Allah bestowed on them) was based entirely on valid principles and purposes consistent with the sacred law. So beware, my brother, of hurried disapproval of anyone among the gnostic sages when he commends himself. Do not accuse him of egocentric purposes, now that you have studied these proofs and fruits we have mentioned. Think well of their conduct, for

1 Layth b. Saʿd (d. 791, Cairo) was a renowned scholar also famous for his charitable giving and asceticism.

Allah has commended those who hear advice and follow the best of it, in His saying: *Those who hear advice and follow the best thereof, such are those whom Allah has guided, and such are men of understanding* (Qurʾān, 39:18)."

I once heard Sīdī ʿAlī al-Khawwāṣ, may Allah have mercy on him, say, "Disapproval (of enraptured ones) is not in accordance with the sacred law, except when the matter is not open to positive interpretation." He also used to say, "One aspect of the spiritual pauper's perfection is that he has a favorable interpretation of the speech of the spiritual dignitaries, recognizing their exclusion from deceit and egocentric frivolities. Even if he is incapable of responding in their defense by providing a plausible explanation for a statement or action issuing from them, he must submit to them and refrain from disapproval. In truth, the aims of the spiritual dignitaries are beyond our minds. This is especially the case with the imams of independent legal reasoning (*mujtahidūn*) and their followers. For example, how can you dare to refute the doctrine of Imam Abū Ḥanīfa? ﵁"

He also had this to say on the subject: "The reason for the critic's disapproval is sometimes due to his ignorance of the technical terminology of the Sufis, ﵃, and the lack of his experience of their stations. This was explained in the poem, *Tāʾiyya*, by Sīdī ʿUmar b. al-Fāriḍ, as well as in other poems. An intelligent person refrains from disapproval, and assigns what he does not understand to the general category of unknown things. Indeed, we have not received any evidence that one of the saints, ﵃, ever commanded people to omit the ritual ablution, the ritual prayer or fast, or commit any other violation of the sacred law. The fact is that their books are overflowing in obligating strict adherence to the Qurʾān and the Sunna. These books speak of remedying people's moral characters and their actions, on cleansing them of the machinations and maladies that distract a person from sincere devotion. They speak of enduring suffering and leaving aside the infliction of suffering. They speak of abstinence and piety, and on the fear and dread (of offending Allah).

"But it may be that this description (of ignorance of Sufi terminology) does not apply to the negative critic. The gnostic sage sometimes may speak, in his poetry for instance, in the language of the Real, Blessed and Exalted is He. He may sometimes speak in the language of Allah's Messenger ﷺ. He may sometimes speak in the language of the saintly pole (*quṭb*). A critic thus may assume that he is speaking on behalf of himself, so will rush to express his disaproval. You must understand this well."

Shaʿrānī also had this to say on the subject:

> The Sufi spiritual path has a special characteristic: when a genuine seeker enters this path, he comes to understand the technical terminology in every detail, from the first step [without lengthy study]. It is almost as if he himself is the creator of this terminology. This applies only to the genuine seekers on the spiritual path, not to the people in the other sciences. In other sciences, the student cannot do without a shaykh to acquaint him with the terminology of that science. This is the case, for example, for theology, logic, and mathematics.
>
> As for certain statements of which some critics disapprove, it often happens that some of these are inserted into the books of saints or othewise fabricated to discredit him. According to Shaykh Badr al-Dīn b. Jamāʾa[2] and others, this happened in the case of Shaykh Muḥyī al-Dīn b. al-ʿArabī ﵁. His books, primarily *Futūḥāt al-Makkiyya* and *Fuṣūṣ* (*al-ḥikam*), were inserted with a host of statements contrary to the literal meaning of the sacred law. This also happened to me in some of my books.

Here is a relevant passage from the (book of) legal opinions (*Fatāwā*) of the erudite scholar al-Ḥāfiẓ Ibn Ḥajar, may Allah have mercy on him:

> Question: What is the proper response to criticism of the ecstatic utterances of the saints? For example, the saying of Abū Yazīd (al-Bisṭāmī): "Glory be to me, in whose garment there is nothing but Allah;" or the statement of Ḥallāj: "I am the Real!" Or any such statement, where the words and gestures are subject to disapproval in their outer form, but the inner meaning is true, except in the opinion of those addicted to loathing and stubbornness?
>
> Answer: As for the ecstatic utterances experienced by the learned gnostic sages, may Allah be pleased with them, protect them from denial, and grant them acceptance, let the best light be put on that which issues from them. The most effective response to the critic is the one that silences and astounds him. None will be guided to accept such responses except those blessed with success, and none will turn away from them except those doomed to failure. So beware of becoming one of those who sip from the poisoned cup of disapproval and thereby instantly perish. Make haste toward salvation from Allah's wrath, His hostility, and His loathing, for the Prophet ﷺ has related Allah's words, "If someone treats a saint of Mine as an enemy, I have declared war on him!"[3] And the leading scholars have explained, "Allah the Exalted has not declared war on anybody, even those guilty of grave sins: except

---

2 Badr al-Dīn b. al-Jamaʿa (d. 1333) was a Shāfiʿī judge and *ḥadīth* scholar.

3 This is a sacred tradition (*ḥadīth qudsī*) reported by Bukhārī and Ibn Māja.

those who criticize His saints and those who consume usurious interest (*ribā*). And when Allah declares war on a person, he can never prosper."

Among the favorable interpretations (to give an esctatic utterance), the best is that these words constitute an inspiration from the Presence of the Real, an appropriate expression of the lights of Allah's presence they have witnessed. One of the stations of love, worshipful servitude, and divine proximity includes the prevalence of metaphorical expressions. So the speakers are exonerated, relieved of the burden of sin.

Those who have relied on this way of interpretation include Shihāb (al-Dīn) al-Suhrawardī, the acknowledged leader of the exoteric and esoteric sciences. He said in *ʿAwārif al-maʿārif*: "Concerning Abū Yazīd's ☙ statement, 'Glory be to me,' may Allah forbid that anyone should believe Abū Yazīd would say that except in the sense of a literal quotation from Allah the Exalted. This explanation also applies to Ḥallāj, may Allah have mercy on him, with regard to his saying, 'I am the Real.'"

He went on to say: "The saints may sometimes be commanded (to utter a declaration) in order to identify an ignoramus, or to give thanks and speak openly of Allah's beneficient grace. This latter happened to Shaykh ʿAbd al-Qādir (al-Jilānī). In the middle of dispensing wise counsel, he suddenly exclaimed, 'This foot of mine is on the neck of every saint of Allah!' He received an immediate response from the saints of this world—as well as the saints of the jinn, according to some—all of whom bowed their heads, submitted to him with humility and acknowledged what he said. The sole exception was a man of Isfahan, who refused and thus was deprived of his spiritual state.

"One of those who bowed their heads was Abū al-Najīb al-Suhrawardī, who said, 'Upon my head, upon my head!' Another was Aḥmad al-Rifāʿī. Ḥamīd was also among them; he said, 'When Shaykh ʿAbd al-Qādir said what he said, Abū Madyan in the Maghrib and I were both among them (who obeyed). By Allah (I said at the moment of the pronouncement), bear witness with the angels that I have heard and obeyed.' In response to further questions, he reported what the Shaykh said and recorded it in a chronicle. Shaykh ʿAbd al-Raḥīm al-Qināwī also stretched out his neck, saying, 'The truthful one whose word is trusted has spoken the truth.' He was asked about his statement, so he also reported what the Shaykh said.

"According to many of the gnostic sages mentioned, Shaykh ʿAbd al-Qādir did not speak except in obedience to a (divine) command that he should proclaim his saintly poleship so that no one could disagree. It has even been reported, with numerous chains of transmission from many respected authorities, that the saints were informed, up to one hundred years before his birth, that there would be born in Persia a child of splendid appearance who would say these very words, so that the saints of his time would be assembled beneath his foot."

The following account was related by the Imam of the Shāfiʿī school of jurisprudence of his time, Abū Saʿīd ʿAbd-Allāh b. Abī ʿAṣrūn:[4]

> I entered Baghdad in the quest for knowledge, and there I met Ibn al-Saqqā. I joined him seeking knowledge at the Niẓāmiyya college. We used to visit the righteous. There was in Baghdad a man called the Succor (*al-Ghawth*), who only appeared in public when he wished, and kept himself from view when he wished. Ibn al-Saqqā and I went to visit him, together with Shaykh ʿAbd al-Qādir (al-Jilānī), who was a young man at the time. While we were on the way, Ibn al-Saqqā said, "I am determined to ask him a question for which he will have no answer." I said, "I am determined to ask him a question, then see what he has to say about it." Shaykh ʿAbd al-Qādir said, "Let us take refuge with Allah from asking him anything! When I enter his presence, the blessing of seeing him will be my only expectation."
>
> We entered his place, but an hour went by before we saw him. Then the Shaykh (came and) looked at Ibn al-Saqqā with an angry glare, and said, "Woe unto you, O Ibn al-Saqqā! You have come to ask me a question for which I have no answer. This question is such-and-such, and the answer to it is such-and-such. I see the hellfire of unbelief blazing inside of you!" Then he looked at me and said, "O ʿAbd-Allāh, have you come to ask me a question, just to see what I have to say about it? This question is such-and-such and the answer to it is such-and-such. This world will surely immerse you in grief up to your ears because of your ill-mannered behavior." Then he looked at Shaykh ʿAbd al-Qādir, drew him close and treated him with respect. He said, "O Shaykh ʿAbd al-Qādir, you have pleased Allah and His Messenger with your well-mannered behavior. I seem to see you in Baghdad, where you have mounted the lectern and are addressing the public, and you have said, 'This foot of mine is on the neck of every saint of Allah!' And it is as if I can see the saints of your time, and they have bowed their necks in your honor." He then disappeared from sight.
>
> As for Shaykh ʿAbd al-Qādir, the signs of his nearness to Allah became clearly apparent, and both the elite and the common folk assembled in his presence. When he said, "this foot of mine," the saints of the time confirmed that for him.
>
> As for Ibn al-Saqqā, he devoted himself to the sciences of the sacred law until he excelled in them. He surpassed many of the people of his time, and achieved great renown by outstripping his competitors in all the sciences. He was gifted with an eloquent tongue and a brilliant style. The caliph regarded him as a master of arts, eloquence and style, so drew him close to himself, and sent him as an ambassador to the

4 Abū Saʿīd ʿAbd-Allāh b. Abī ʿAṣrūn (d. 1189) was a prominent jurist who settled in Syria. This story is related in Haytami's *Faṭāwa*.

> Byzantine emperor. The emperor also came to admire him greatly, and he introduced him to the priests and scholars of Christianity. He debated with them and left them dumbfounded and incapacitated. So he acquired tremendous prestige in the presence of the emperor, and the temptation he faced became increasingly seductive. When the emperor's daughter presented herself to him, he became excited and enchanted by her, so he asked her father to give her to him in marriage. The emperor said, "Not unless you become a Christian." So he became a Christian and married her. Then he contracted a disease, so they threw him into the marketplace, where he begged for his sustenance but nobody listened. Gloom and melancholy overwhelmed him, until someone who knew him came and said to him, "What has happened?" He replied, "An affliction has befallen me, the cause of which you can see." The man then asked him, "Do you have anything of the Qurʾān in your heart?" He said, "No, not apart from Allah's saying, *It may be that those who disbelieve will dearly wish that they were Muslims* (15:2)." So I myself went to see him one day, and found him as if he had been burned. He was in the agony of death, so I turned him toward the direction of Mecca, but he turned toward the East. I turned him back and he turned away again, and we continued like this until, when his spirit departed, his face was turned toward the East. He had been recalling the words of the saintly Succor, and had realized that he was being afflicted because of his actions.
>
> As for myself, I came to Damascus. There Sultan Nūr al-Dīn compelled me to take charge of the charitable public endowments (*awqāf*). I undertook their administration, and this world thrust itself upon me with considerable pressure. Thus what the saintly Succor said about each of us had turned out to be true.

This story, which we have mentioned before, contains a very stern reprimand and emphatic warning to refrain from negative criticism of the saints of Allah the Exalted. The negative critic is in danger of succumbing to this eternally destructive temptation to which Ibn al-Saqqā succumbed, a temptation (the end of which) is unparalleled in repulsiveness and gruesomeness. We take refuge from that with Allah! We beseech Him, by virtue of His noble countenance, and for the sake of his kind and compassionate beloved (Muḥammad ﷺ), to keep us safe from that and from every tribulation, by His gracious favor and noble generosity. The story also contains an incentive for believing in the saints, treating them decently and thinking well of them to the fullest possible extent.

Appendix IV

The Aspirant who Becomes Extinct to Himself

He who has not attained gnosis should beware of rejecting the words of an aspirant (*murīd*) who, annihilated in Allah, becomes intoxicated and absent to himself, and says such things as, "I have seen Allah!" or "I saw nothing but Allah!" Rather this matter should be entrusted to the consummate shaykh, for he is the one to test the aspirant. Indeed, expression of the spiritual vision (of Allah) has become frequent among the Sufi people ever since the time of the companions of the Prophet ﷺ. So let not the blind man deny (the sight of) one who can see.

The greatest shaykh, rare like red sulfur, Muḥyī al-Dīn b. al-ʿArabī al-Ḥātimī said in *Futūḥāt al-Makkiyya* , chapter 351, page 227:

> The various delineations (*ḥudūd*) of the divine Essence that distinguish the Real from the creation are only known by the people of direct spiritual vision (*ruʾya*), not by those of metaphorical witnessing (*mushāhada*) or others. They are also not known by reported information (*khabar*). But they can become known as consequential knowledge, beyond the need for proof (*ʿilm ḍurūrī*), as a favor Allah bestows on whom He wills among His servants. Otherwise this knowledge is not found in the divine revelations (*al-khabar al-ilahī*); and indeed, there is nothing a person cannot understand from scriptural revelation except this knowledge. So a person can gain real knowledge only through divine revelation or the bestowal of basic, indispensable knowledge (*ʿilm ḍurūrī*).
>
> The delineations of existing things of all sorts are directed according to the potentialities (of existence) within the essential reality of being (*al-ʿayn al-wujūdiyya*). As for the delineation of the essential reality of Allah's Essence (*al-ʿayn al-wujūdiyya al-dhātī*), the reality

of its being is existence itself, and its existence is the essence of reality, for there is nothing else in existence to be known.

The goal of the gnostics (*ʿārifīn*) is to delineate the boundaries between the whole of creation and Allah's Essence, the Compulsory Existent Being (*wājib al-wujūd*). But the real knowledgeable ones of Allah (*al-ʿulamāʾ bi-Llāh*) are above this illumination (*kashf*), for what is metaphorically witnessed (*mashhad*) is as previously mentioned (being inferior to the direct vision). So the knowledgeable ones, ﷺ, guard themselves in this station, for (the direct vision) may quickly leave their hearts. Whoever does not continuously possess this direct vision (*ruʾya*), with each breath, he cannot be one of the distinguished folk (*rijāl*).

This is the station of the one who says, "I have not seen anything except Allah." If he is asked, "And who is the seer?" he will reply, "It is He." And if he is asked, "Who is the one saying this?" he will say, "It is He." If he is asked, "Then who is the one asking you now?" he will respond, "It is He." If he is asked, "And how can this be?" he will say: "Affinities (*nisab*) appear in Him, from Him, and for Him; and there is nothing anywhere except Him, for He is the essence of 'anywhere' (*ʿayn thamma*)." So this was the doctrine (*madhhab*) of Abū Yazīd al-Bisṭāmī, may Allah be pleased with him for his spiritual state.

He also said in *Futūḥāt al-Makkiyya*, chapter 374, page 464:

> Allah has not made all His creation equal in knowledge of Him, so disparity in this regard is inevitable among Allah's servants. The Muʿtazila deny the possibility of seeing (Allah). The Ashʿarī consider seeing Allah intellectually conceivable and thus valid from the perspective of the sacred law. The philosophers reject the possibility on purely rational grounds, since they attach no importance to the sacred law and faith. But the people of Allah confirm the vision of Allah based on spiritual unveiling (*kashf*) and experience (*dhawq*).

The author adds to this precious statement in chapter 331 of the same text, where he discusses the spiritual vision, its possibility, means of approach, and advancement within it. After some discussion, he said:

> Do not suppose that Moses' request for the vision of his Lord was an appeal for the vision of Abū Bakr al-Ṣiddīq ﷺ, described in his saying, "I did not see anything without having seen Allah before it." Moses was not seeking this vision from his Lord, for this type of vision was already bestowed on him (Moses) because of the loftiness of his degree. Indeed, the spiritual experience of the truthful person (*ṣādiq*) is not the same as that of Truth's champion (*ṣiddīq*).
>
> In any case, the vision (of Allah) has been established beyond doubt; and this on the basis of spiritual experience and traditional

> report, not logic. The vision of Allah is one of those subjects that perplex the mental capacities.

After more discussion in this chapter, he said:

> Some claim (the vision of Allah)—with clear intention, sobriety, and perfect awareness—in a public gathering, but only because there is a need for them to say this in that particular gathering. This occurs when they see that the Real has empowered them to say what they say, and they have no power except His empowering of them. By His empowerment, they are not the speakers, for this power is the reality of the Real (*ʿayn al-Ḥaqq*). He provides information through their words, similar to the way that He provides a servant with a witnessing that defies the ordinary. So they say things like, *I am Allah* (Qurʾān, 27:9), and *Verily I am Allah* (20:14), and, *There is no god but I, so worship Me* (21:25).
>
> Abū Yazīd was among those reported as saying things like this in a state of full sobriety and establishment; knowing that the Real is the One manifesting in the servant's actions within the substance of potentialities. So in some of his states, he spoke as He, and in some states, he did not mention that he was (speaking) as He.
>
> Some of the gnostics said in regards to the disciple (of Abū Yazīd) who considers Allah sufficient for him in his claim (to have witnessed Him), thereby disregarding seeing Abū Yazīd, that seeing Abū Yazīd one time is better than seeing Allah one thousand times. (After the disciple was informed of this) Abū Yazīd passed in front of him, and he was told, "That is Abū Yazīd." When his eyes fell on the Shaykh, the disciple died. When Abū Yazīd was informed of his death, he said, "He saw what he could not bear, for Allah manifested Himself to him in me. He could not bear it, just as Moses could not bear it (when Allah manifested Himself to him on the mountain). Allah's manifestation in me was greater than the divine manifestation the disciple used to witness in himself."

Concerning the extraordinary claim (of seeing the unseen) by the man with a reputation for righteousness, the author of *al-Miʿyār*, the erudite scholar Wānsharīsī, had this to say:

> In his commentary on the traditions concerning the conceivability of the extraordinary, al-Māzinī related the following story of a man of Qarawiyyin[1] known for his righteousness.
>
> That man said, "I have seen such-and-such and such-and-such a thing from which the mental capacities recoil (from describing)." When this was mentioned to Ibn Abī Zayd (al-Qayrawānī), he said,

1 The famous Islamic university in Tunisia, which has the same name as the major university in Fes.

"Yes, his seeing this in his sleep in admissible, for the sleeper may see even more than this in his sleep."

He was told one day that the man said, "I have seen the Creator, Glorious and Exalted is He." The Shaykh said, "This is extraordinary indeed, but it is admissible for the human being to see the Lord of Might in his sleep."

When the righteous man heard that, he said, "I have not seen Him except in the state of wakefulness." When this statement came to the notice of Abū Muḥammad (Ibn Abī Zayd), he rejected it and composed a treatise criticizing the man. But the scholars of Qayrawān discouraged him, saying, "This treatise is a denial of the saintly miracles (*karāmāt*), and it constitutes Muʿtazila doctrine."

My dear brother, contemplate the splendor of Ibn Abī Zayd's mastery of the Islamic sciences, to the point that the people of the Mālikī school of jurisprudence gave him the name, "the Junior Mālik." When he was questioned for denying the saint's vision of the Creator, Glorious and Exalted is He, he retracted his denial. And when the matter was referred to the Judge Abū Bakr b. al-Ṭayyib, the latter composed a two-volume work in support of the righteous man, entitled, "the difference between the miracles of the prophets and the miracles of the saints." He prefaced the work by saying, "Given the extent of his knowledge of both the branches and roots of the Islamic sciences, our Shaykh Abū Muḥammad would certainly not deny the saintly miracles and espouse the doctrine of the Muʿtazila. All that his statement meant was such-and-such." So he proceeded to interpret his statement, providing suitable explanations to solve his problem.

It is strange that the vision of the Creator, the Glorious and Exalted, in a waking state is sometimes considered less admissible than the vision of the angels. This is more so the case given the report authenticated by ʿĪyāḍ in *Kitāb al-shifāʾ*, according to which Allah's Messenger ﷺ saw Him in person, and with his actual eyes. Since it has been established that every prophetic miracle could also be a saintly miracle, there should be no controversy (about seeing Allah).

When commenting on Allah's saying, *Allah! There is no god but He* (Qurʾān, 4:87, 20:8, 64:13), the author of *Rūḥ al-bayān* explained, "This is a sentence in which, grammatically speaking, the predicate belongs to the subject, which is the Mighty Name (Allah). The meaning is that only He has the right to be worshipped, none other." It has been related that the glorification of the pole of the saintly poles (*quṭb al-aqṭāb*) consists of saying, "O He!" (*yā Hū*), and, "O He who is He!" (*yā man Huwa Hū*), and "O who there is no God but He!" (*yā man lā ilāha illā Hū*). When he says this through the spiritual state, he is invested with the capacities of divine disposal. And there are three degrees belonging to the affirmation of divine Oneness (*tawḥīd*). The first is the *tawḥīd* of the beginner on the path, consisting of the realization of, "there is no god but Allah" (*lā ilāha ill-Allāh*). The second is the *tawḥīd* of the intermediate aspirant, consisting of realizing, "there is no god but You" (*lā ilāha illā Anta*), for he is in a stage of witnessing, so personal address is appropriate. The last is the *tawḥīd* of the perfected one, who hears of the Oneness from the One who affirms His Oneness, thus realizing, "there is no god but I!" (*lā ilāha illā Anā*). This perfected one is in the station of total annihilation, so nothing emerges (from his mouth) on his own behalf. The Shaykh's son said in the marginal commentary of the Qurʾān, on the Chapter of Sincerity (*Sūra al-ikhlāṣ*):

> The word "He" (*Hū*) is an allusion to the station of those drawn near (to the divine Presence), those who have considered the essential nature of things and their realities wherever they are. So they have reached the inevitable conclusion that nothing exists apart from Allah, because the Real is the One whose existence is essential for His own sake. As for anything else, it is a potential existent; so that if it is examined from the perspective of "He," this potential existent is in fact nonexistent. These people thus do not consider anything as existing apart from the Real, Glorious is He.

The following is a quotation from Ibn ʿAjība's *al-Futūḥāt al-ilāhiyya ʿala sharḥ al-mabāḥith al-aṣliyya*:[2]

> This reality of the soul is linked to the holy Presence
> It is only the receptacle that restrains it, from this (realization), the ascension begins.

The "reality of the soul" here refers to the subtle spirit (*rūḥ*) that permeates the physical bodies containing it. The "Holy Presence" is the eternal, ancient, subtle and hidden sublimity, which is given expression by the angelic world (*ʿālam al-jabarūt*). This was explained by Ibn al-Fāriḍ ☙ in his wine-ode (*khamriyya*) when he said:

> They said to me: describe it for us, for you are informed of its attributes
> Of course, for I do have knowledge of its descriptions:
>
> It is the purity of the purest water, but without water
> The wind's subtle grace, but without air
>
> Light without fire, spirit without body
> Its beginning preceded all existent beings

---

2   A translation of this complete work exists under the title, *The Basic Research Shaykh Ahmad ibn Ajiba*, by Abdalkhabir al-Munawwarah and Haj Abdassabur al-Ustadh (Madinah Press, 1998). The book of Ibn ʿAjība is a commentary on a poem by Ibn al-Banna Saragossa.

It is ancient without shape, present without form
All things began by it, but then because of divine wisdom
It was veiled from whoever lacks understanding.

What emerged from the eternal wine was the (created) objects (*mawḍūʿāt*) that became unveiled and apparent, which Allah made receptacles carrying meanings. Among these receptacles are the Adamic bodies, for they are the objects of the Lordly secret, which is the spirit (*rūḥ*). So the spirit is connected to this eternal wine, but it is prevented from rejoining its origin by the receptacle in which Allah put it to reside. The receptacles are dense (*kathīf*), while the spirits are light (*laṭīf*).

Whoever allows his denseness to prevail over his lightness—meaning his physical nature over his spiritual nature—he will remain imprisoned by the things surrounding him, limited to the confines of his body. Whoever gives victory to his lightness over his denseness—that is his spiritual nature over his physical nature—his spirit becomes joined to the holy Presence, returning to its origins. Neither the earth nor the heavens, nor even the Throne (*ʿarsh*) nor the Footstool (*kursī*), can veil it from its source. Indeed, one of the Sufi people said, "The Throne and Stool are among my armor." Another said, "If the Throne was in one of the corners of the gnostic's heart, he would not feel it."

Ibn ʿAṭāʾ Allāh said in *Kitāb al-ḥikam*: "If the realms of the unseen are not opened for a human being in this world, he will remain imprisoned by what surrounds him, bound in the confines of his body." In other words, once the realms of the unseen are opened for a person, neither the confines of the body nor the existent entities can bind him. He will ascend to the vast expanse of witnessing the divine, and his spirit will be united with the worshipped King. This communion (*ittiṣāl*) is known by the people of spiritual experience (*adhwāq*), and denied by the people of papers (*awrāq*).

ʿIzz al-Dīn b. ʿAbd al-Salām[3] provided an example to clarify the matter, to open its treasures for the one who has not experienced what the spiritually distinguished folk have tasted: "Know that the heart is unseen, and the Lord is unseen. So the Unseen (Lord) appears to the unseen (heart), by descending (on it), and not by incarnation (*ḥulūl*)." The wisdom in this (focus on the heart) is that the heart is a perfect creation possessed of both an apparent and a hidden aspect. The apparent side is earthly, lowly, and bound by nature and physicality. It is dense because it is turned toward the force of human nature. The hidden side is heavenly, exalted, luminous, and spiritual. It is light because it is turned toward the exalted, spiritual, divine, heavenly realms.

---

3 ʿIzz b. ʿAbd al-Salām al-Sulāmī (d. 1262) was known as the "Sultan of the Scholars" of his time. He was a student of Abū Ḥasan al-Shādhilī and Abū ʿAbbās al-Mursī.

Rays of light are reflected in the heart in accordance to the completeness of its facing the heavenly realms. The secrets of the heavenly realms thus become manifested in the inner realities of the heart. Such a person will see by the lights that have flooded into his heart, and he will understand by the secrets that have been revealed to him. So this is the meaning of "reflection": he sees the beauty of his Beloved in the mirror of his heart; and this without limit or partialness, without incarnation, and without separation or joining.

An example of this is a mirror with two sides. The back of the mirror is opaque, and the front reflects light. The front of the mirror reflects whatever is in front of it. Small or large, any created being will find its image in the mirror, even though the mirror is small and the object large. Whether a camel or a mountain, the mirror will show all of the object's parts. The object is not thereby incarnated in the mirror, connected to or part of the mirror.

Likewise, when the Real, Glorious and Exalted is He, manifests in the heart of the His believing servant, the servant will see Him with the eye of his heart. He will witness Him with his sight, without incarnation, partialness, connection, or separation. A clear indication of this is provided in the following poem:

> My Beloved graciously manifested Himself
> What a great honor He has shown me
>
> Making Himself known to me, until I became certain
> That I am seeing Him overtly, without illusion
>
> And in every state I see Him continuously
> On the mountain of my heart, where He speaks to me
>
> In this embrace, there is no union
> And no separation, exalted is He from either of these
>
> How is it possible for the like of me to contain the like of Him?
> How can the tiny star be compared to the full moon?
>
> But it happened that I saw Him in the purity of my inner being
> There I saw Perfection, too mighty and exalted to be partitioned
>
> Just as the full moon shows its face
> In the still pond, although it shines high in the heavens.

The saintly pole, our Shaykh al-Tijānī, Seal of the Saints ﵁, was recorded as saying in the *Jawāhir al-maʿānī*:

> As for the (divine) affiliation mentioned about the spiritually distinguished, surely it is the closest of affiliations. Indeed, the holy Presence is the loftiest purity, which does not accept contamination in any shape or form. If someone enters it, the whole of existence vanishes from him,

including his own self, so that nothing remains except sheer Divinity (*ulūhiyya*). In this spiritual state (*ḥāl*), the servant has no speech, no thought, no illusion, no movement, no rest, no designation (*rasm*), no explanation (*kayf*), no direction (*ayn*), no boundary, and no characteristic (*ʿalam*). If the servant were to speak in this state, he would say, "There is no god but I, glory be to Me! How exalted is My affair!" for he is only speaking on behalf of Allah, Almighty and Glorious is He.

It was in this context that Abū Yazīd uttered his pronouncement while his companions were circled around him: "Glory be to Me! How exalted is My affair!" His companions were afraid of speaking to him, for they knew that he himself was not there. Then, when he recovered from his intoxication, and they were thoroughly convinced of his sobriety, they told him what they had heard from him. He said, "I was not aware of anything of this. Why did you not kill me in that condition? If you had killed me, you would have been warriors in Allah's way, and I would have died a martyr." They responded, "But we could not have done that!"

As we have said, the divine Presence is the height of purity. It does not accept any other, or any otherness. When Allah the Exalted manifests Himself to the servant in the perfection of His majesty, He causes him to die to all beings. The servant comprehends no other and no otherness, so this is the utmost extent of purity. When our master the Messenger ﷺ of Allah reported the vision of his Lord during the Night Journey (*layla al-isrāʾ*), he reported: "I did not see in the vision of my Lord a single part of the creation, so I assumed that everything in the heavens and the earth had passed away."

This is the meaning of purity and nearness to the Lord. Nearness (*qurb*) means to forget everything other, and all otherness. In the first stage of nearness, all existence is at the farthest distance from the divine Presence. The one from whom Allah has removed the veil of existing things, so that he sees Allah's nearness with his own eye, is the sole exception. He becomes one of those witnessing Allah, while the rest of humans are distracted from Him. People are distracted from the Creator, Glorious and Exalted is He, because the development of their natural inclinations (*dhawāt*) causes them to forget Him. Indeed their natures are only dedicated to pursuing self-interests and avoiding harm, so they become distant from Allah.

According to Ibn ʿAbbās ﷺ: "That which keeps creatures distracted from Allah the Exalted is nothing but their preoccupation with themselves. If only they would abandon this preoccupation with themselves and distance themselves far from it, all of them would behold Allah with their own eyes."

The following citation is also taken from the *Jawāhir al-maʿānī*:

> Shādhilī ☙ was asked about the saying (*ḥadīth*) transmitted in some
> of the traditional reports: "If someone abandons everything for My
> sake, by detaching himself from everything, I shall manifest Myself
> to him in everything, so that he will see Me in everything." Shādhilī
> said, "This is the method of the common people, not the method of
> the distinguished spiritual elite. As for the method of the elite, it is as
> if Allah says, 'Whoever devotes himself to Me in everything, approv-
> ing My choice in everything, I shall detach him from everything, so
> that he will see Me nearer to him than everything.'" The former case
> is the description of the gnostics (*ʿārifīn*), while the latter is that of
> the unique individuals (*afrād*). May Allah, by His gracious favor and
> noble generosity, include us among them. Amen.

The following passage also occurs in the *Jawāhir al-maʿānī*, on the
subject of the ecstatic utterances (*shaṭḥiyyāt*):

> Self-extinction (*fanāʾ*) and total immersion (*istighrāq*) in the divine
> sometimes happen to the gnostic unexpectedly, so that he departs
> from the sphere of his sensory perception and consciousness, indeed
> from all of his faculties and personal existence. But sometimes, this
> passing away from the self results from his devotion to the Essence
> of the Real, Glorious and Exalted is He. An overflowing abundance
> of secrets descends on him from the holiness of the spiritual realm
> (*qudūs al-lāhūt*), requiring him to witness his own essential being as
> the eye (*ʿayn*) of the Real's Essence because of his utter effacement and
> obliteration in Him. It is in such a condition that the statement of the
> Glorious One comes to be declared, "There is no god but I Alone!"
> and other such glorifications, including, "Splendid is My Majesty and
> Sanctified is My Grandeur!"
>
> The ecstatic is excused for such statements, because his mind—
> which enables him to distinguish proofs and benefits and to classify
> the attributes of individual things—has absented itself from him. It
> has vanished, disappeared, and become obliterated. Due to this loss
> of the mind and the abundance of the holy Secret bestowed on him,
> the ecstatic speaks the way he speaks. The speech that occurs to him is
> created in him by the Real as His delegation of authority to him. So he
> speaks with the tongue of the Real, not with his own tongue, articulat-
> ing the Identity (*dhāt*) of the Real, not his own identity.
>
> Relevant in this context is the statement of Abū Yazīd al-Bisṭāmī:
> "Glory be to Me! How Sublime is My Majesty!" Likewise relevant is
> the statement of Ḥallāj, "And I am the Real, there is nothing in this
> robe except Allah!" Another has said, "For the earth is My earth, and
> the heaven is My heaven." Tustarī ☙ similarly said: "Behold! What a
> wondrous thing am I for the one who sees Me: I am the Lover and the

> Beloved. There is nothing comparable to Me." There is also his saying, "I am from Love, and Love is from Me." Many statements of this kind are attributed to Ibn al-Fāriḍ.
>
> So this is what is conferred on a person by way of self-annihilation and total immersion in the Essence of the Real. But this is a matter beyond the scope of verbal description, and understood only by means of spiritual experience and purified spiritual states. Indeed, it is a reality known only to the one who has tasted it.
>
> Sometimes the gnostic will experience annihilation and immersion in the person (*dhāt*) of the Prophet ﷺ. He passes away from his own self into the self (*dhāt*) of the Prophet ﷺ, becoming privy to one of his secrets ﷺ. When his essence becomes clothed in that secret, it experiences nothing but the essence (*dhāt*) of the Prophet ﷺ. In this way, Allah informs him of some of the unique, special qualities with which He has distinguished His Prophet ﷺ. So the servant comes to speak with the tongue of the Prophet ﷺ, because some of these qualities, which distinguish the Prophet ﷺ and endow him with sublimity, honor, and superiority in rank over all the other prophets and messengers, have been delegated to the servant. Thus the servant furnishes information with the authority that the Allah has granted His Prophet ﷺ, although it appears that he informs only on his own authority. The person who hears him thinks he is attributing the information to himself, but he is only attributing it to the Prophet ﷺ: the servant has absented himself from his own person.
>
> When the servant returns to himself after his annihilation and immersion (in the Prophet), he remains innocent of his statements because his knowledge proceeds from the Prophet's rank. You must apply this standard to any of the shaykhs when you hear from them what amounts to a claim of superiority over the prophets and messengers.

Whoever studies this carefully, with fair judgment and the light of truth, will know for certain that the vision of the divine (*ruʾya*) is not a heretical innovation among this Sufi group. Indeed, the most serious heretical innovation is denying a person's claim to the vision. The vision of Allah was never denied until after the first three centuries of Islam, when heretical innovations emerged with the sects of the Muʿtazila and philosophers, astray themselves and leading others astray. The erring sects have previously been discussed. I have embarked on the composition of a book entitled, *Tabṣira al-anām fī jawāz ruʾyat Allah fī yaqẓa wa al-manām* [The enlightenment of mankind, concerning the permissibility of seeing Allah in wakefulness and sleep]. Perhaps it will provide a fuller explanation of the subject of seeing Allah.

Connected with this subject is the poem of our Shaykh, our means of access to our Lord, the divine saintly pole, the eternal inheritor, the Ḥassān (b. Thābit) of our spiritual path, Sayyid Muḥamd b. al-Sayyid al-ᶜAllāma b. al-ᶜAlawī, in response to the misguided and misguiding deniers, for the poem has not left anything unsaid:

The Visitor returned to me, silently, at the time of sleeping
The heart was seized, ceaselessly

By the lover's remembrance of the Beloved, then He left
I spent the night after His departure without sleeping

I do not taste sleep, except a little
The bird of *thamād* drank the water of antimony

I spent the night prattling to myself that the destination should be close
But alas! How far it is!

The distance and the fatigue cause me doubt
Since I had thought it was no further than the next campsite

Or is it the wind blowing from the South that makes me sad?
Surely the southern winds sadden the heart

Rather it is the fragrance blowing from the Beloved
With the Spring's fresh air, air which can even quench the thirst

Reminding us of the dwellings of beautiful maidens
And meetings and appointments that have been held there

I will never forget the way these maidens pass in front of my eyes
As if they have no purpose but to haunt me

Toward me with great slowness they come, taking their time
They are discussing the highlands.

Indeed knowledge has become dead in these lands!
This epoch has donned robes of mourning

Its maidens of knowledge, before protected and veiled
Have fallen in the hands of the enemies

They have been humiliated, where before they were worthy of fabulous dowries
Expensive, difficult to possess

Their deflowering has been licensed unjustly
By every depraved reprobate, even though they are decent women

So knowledge became, after having been glorious and sublime
A toy in the hands of ignoramuses and scoundrels

Now the bald woman starts to demand

Expensive dowries of fine horses

Oh this sighing! How weak I have become!
Now my frailty is clear to everyone.

Among the ignorant you will find every dumb and blind person
Those who cannot survive without a dog to guide them

Clinging to the earth, unable to stand
Devoid of consciousness, deaf, like an inanimate object

And despite his incapacity and blindness, such a person denies
The vision of he who sees, the hearing of he who hears, the direction of he who guides

How strange the criticism of this blind man for the holy person!
How can those who are asleep challenge those who are awake?

Is the sight of the afflicted the same as the sight of the liberated one?
Surely the afflicted one is strained by perpetual chains

So they have denied out of ignorance
Things whose rules are clear for the people of principle

So the blind man denies the sun in broad daylight
Only because of his blindness, just as the sick man knows not the taste of cream

By my soul! How distant are the veiled ones, those full of lust
From those excellent, distinguished beings

The one who gets wet by the seaside
Then claims to be the ocean—

He is nothing but a laughingstock
An example of idiocy paraded in the villages and towns

So they conceive of knowledge as the state they find themselves in;
For all eternity, how great a lie is their illusion!

Knowledge for them is boasting and slander
Stubborn arguing

What sort of knowledge is this! Woe to your knowledge!
Leading naught but to slander of the saintly poles (*aqṭāb*) and cardinal supports (*awtād*)

Knowledge is not simply literature or rhetoric (*ʿilm al-lisān*)
Knowledge is having the fear of Allah in the heart

Indeed, the knowledge of rhetoric contributes nothing
To its possessors on the Day we shall stand witness (before Allah)

A parable is of a donkey carrying books
No benefit do they bring, only suffering

If it is really knowledge you are seeking,
Come to our spiritual masters (*ashyākh*), like shining stars they are

In them you will find numerous oceans
Each filled, undulating with precious gems

Such masters have left aside beautiful virgins to seek knowledge
They have left behind carpets and pillows

So they have returned with profound knowledge
Flabbergasting their critics

Rich meadows of knowledge have they traversed
Untouched by the greatest of researchers

At first, they took knowledge from fellow servants
Then directly from Allah, Lord of all servants

They have come to witness the Real openly, with their eyes
So they are elevated with every passing moment

Whenever they desire, they expand on any science at hand
With continuous overflowing bounty and spiritual support

Such expansion cannot be contained by the seven continents
Measured out, nor can it be contained in the seven heavens

Each of their nights is like the Night of Power
And their days are like festivals of celebration (*ʿĪd*) for Allah

Were they to walk with their full presence on the earth
Whole lands would have been destroyed, mountains crushed

And against such people some dare to mount criticism?
What delinquent ignoramuses!

Surely the Lord of such saints has promised to wage war against their enemies
And this is sufficient as a defense against the arrows of any enemy

Therefore, beware of criticizing others as long as you live
Except for disbelievers, since you will face them with strong proofs

O my Lord! Surely I am innocent from what has come from people
Importing from other religions the evil of criticism

When the misguided mount their criticisms (against the Shaykhs)
Witness that my own heart is filled with reverence!

And when the miserable ones cast doubt on them

Surely our love for the Sufi people has remained pure

Indeed! They are my family, and the carrier of my strength
My refuge against dismay on the Day of Reckoning.

Appendix V

The Vision of Allah within the Realm of Possibility

The substance of the issue is that the vision of Allah with the eyes, today in this world, is conceivable, even if it has not been legally demonstrated. As for the vision by means of spiritual insight (*baṣīra*), experience (*dhawq*), and unveiling (*kashf*), its occurrence is an indisputable fact. The expressions of the Sufi people differ concerning the vision of Allah. Some express it as not seeing any existence (*wujūd*) aside from the Real. Others say it means self-annihilation (*fanāʾ*), or others express it as the arrival in the divine Presence (*wuṣūl*). Some say it means union with the divine (*jamʿ*). In the words of a poet:

> Our expressions are diverse, but You have one meaning
> And everything points to this Perfection.

Imam al-Shaʿrānī said in (*al-Jawāhir wa*) *al-Durar*:

> I asked my brother Afḍal al-Dīn[1] ﷺ about the words of Allah the Exalted concerning Moses ﷺ: *He said, "My Lord, show (Yourself) to me, so that I may look at You"* (Qurʾān, 7:143). I asked, how could Moses ask to see Allah in this world, when Allah's Messenger ﷺ said, "No one will see his Lord until he dies"[2]? I asked, is there a stage in the mission of prophethood (*risāla*) in which a messenger requests to see Allah in

1 Afḍal al-Dīn was a prominent Sufi in the time of Shaʿrānī, whom the latter believed was one of the *arbāb al-aḥwāl* ("masters of spiritual states"). See Michael Winter, *Society & Religion in Early Ottoman Egypt: Studies in the Writings of ʿAbd al-Wahhāb al-Shaʿrānī* (New Brunswick, NJ: Transaction Publishers, 2006), p. 90.

2 Reported by Muslim in his *Ṣaḥīḥ*, and by Tirmidhī in his *Sunan*.

this world? If there is no such request, is the saying of the Prophet ﷺ, "No one will see his Lord until he dies," a general or a limited negation?

To this, he ؓ replied: "When Shaykh Muḥyī al-Dīn (Ibn al-ʿArabī) ؓ was asked such questions, he said, 'No Messenger is ignorant of this (matter).' Nothing remains to be said, therefore, except that there is indeed a stage in the mission of prophethood in which the messenger asks to see Allah in this world. The saying of the Prophet ﷺ is thus a general negation. Indeed, Moses ﷺ did not see Allah the Exalted until he fell down in a swoon, lifeless. Then he saw Him in his swoon."

I asked, "In a state of death?" He replied, "Yes, in a state of death, as he ﷺ was informed when he met with Him by means of spiritual unveiling (al-kashf al-rūḥānī).

Then I said to him, "Our Prophet ﷺ was uncertain about the spiritual state of Moses, for he said: 'I am the first of those from over whom the earth will be split asunder (at the Day of Resurrection), so I shall look out, and there will be Moses, clinging to the foot of the Heavenly Throne. But I do not know if this immunity from being stunned by the blast of the trumpet will be his reward for having swooned on the mountain, or whether he is simply one of those to whom Allah gave exemption (from the blast)."[3]

To this, Afḍal al-Dīn ؓ replied, "This saying of his ﷺ was uttered before Allah the Exalted informed him that Moses ﷺ was rewarded for the swooning he experienced when the mountain collapsed. Moses did not see Allah until he passed away and then, when he recovered from consciousness, he recognized (the One) whom he had seen and the sight of Him caused him to live for all eternity. That is why he said, *I turn to You in repentance* (Qurʾān, 7:143), for there was nothing for him to return to except Allah.

"He used to see Allah before he experienced this special vision of Him, but without realizing that it was Allah he was seeing. When the situation changed, Moses saw Him, while recognizing who he was seeing. This is what distinguished him from others, since others see Him without realizing that they are seeing Him. If it is in your heart to meet someone that you do not know with your eyes, when he meets you and greets you, you will not recognize him. So you have seen this person, but you did not see him."

I then said to him, "Allah the Exalted transformed Moses ﷺ with the experience on the mountain, but he said that He revealed Himself to the mountain and not to Moses." Afḍal ؓ replied, "He did reveal Himself to the mountain; and since nothing (in the vicinity)

---

3   Reported by Bukhārī in his *Ṣaḥīḥ*, and by Ibn Ḥanbal in his *Musnad*. The version in Bukhārī is contextualized by an argument between a Muslim and a Jew concerning the relative merits of Muḥammad and Moses. A similar version of the above was Muḥammad's answer.

could withstand His revelation, transformation was inevitable. So the mountain crumbled and Moses swooned. The One who caused the mountain to crumble for Moses was the One who caused him to swoon."

I then asked him, "Why was Moses returned to his natural form, but the mountain did not return to its original form after being crumbled to dust?" He ﷺ said, 'The identity of the mountain ceased to exist because it was devoid of the spirit (*rūḥ*). In the case of Moses ﷺ, on the other hand, his natural form and his identity did not cease to exist, even when he fell down swooning, because he was endowed with a spirit. His spirit clung to his form as it had been, whereas the mountain did not return to being a mountain because it did not have a spirit to cling to its form."

I then asked him, "What about the witnessing (*shuhūd*) of which the Sufis speak? Is it synonymous with seeing (*ruʾya*), or does it imply something else?"

To this, he ﷺ replied, "Witnessing is not the same as seeing. The difference between them is that seeing (*ruʾya*) is not preceeded by knowledge of that which is seen, whereas witnessing (*shuhūd*) is preceded by knowledge of that which is witnessed (*mashhūd*), meaning that which is designated by the articles of faith (*ʿaqāʾid*). This is why both confirmation and negation apply to witnessing of the otherworldly manifestation. But the vision is subject only to confirmation. One who witnesses is not called a witness unless he witnesses what he sees with belief and soundness."

I said to him, "With what did Moses hear the words of Allah?"

He said, "With his hearing."

I asked, "What did he hear then?"

He said, "In this regard, he was with the generality of people experiencing spiritual unveiling."

I asked him, "Then with what was he accorded special privilege?"

He said, "With the spiritual experience (*dhawq*) in this (hearing), which no one knows except the one who experiences it."

I asked him, "Are all the possessors of spiritual experience like this?"

He said: "Yes, but the spiritual experience is according to degrees; and from this perspective, Moses was specially honored. It was to him that the Prophet Muḥammad ﷺ returned during the Night Journey to discuss the affair of the ritual prayer;[4] and this was on account of the spiritual experience of Moses. So this (sort of spiritual experience) was among the tribe of Israel before our Prophet ﷺ. Surely the spiritual experience is a state not realized except through the experience itself;

---

4 According to the traditional account of the Prophet Muḥammad's Night Journey and Ascension, Allah commissioned the Prophet with fifty prayers for his community each day. It was successive discussions with Moses that convinced the Prophet to return to Allah and ask Him to decrease the amount, eventually to five.

and this simply emerges from the hearts of those endowed with spiritual experience."

I said to him, "The leading figures of the Muʿtazila have denied the possibility of seeing Allah the Exalted in this world and the Hereafter, apart from what has been related in the Qurʾānic verses and the traditional reports (*aḥādīth*)." He ﷺ then said, "Their denial is correct, because no one ever sees the Lord of Truth except from behind the cloak of supreme Greatness (*kibriyāʾ*), as related in the saying of the Prophet ﷺ concerning the manifestation of the Lord of Truth in the Gardens of Eden, 'There is nothing over the Face of Allah the Exalted except the cloak of supreme Greatness (*kibriyāʾ*).' The 'face' (*wajh*) of a thing is its essence (*dhāt*), so the meaning is that a veil is always present between you and Him, preventing the sight from reaching Him. Allah the Exalted spoke the truth in His saying to Moses: *You will not see Me* (Qurʾān, 7:143). The eyes reach only as far as the cloak. This is the standpoint of the leading figures of the Muʿtazila. As for the majority of their followers, they have adopted the superficial view of the matter, and denied the possibility of seeing Allah absolutely, so they have contravened the sacred law (*sharīʿa*) and been mistaken."

Ibn al-Zayātī said in *Farāʾid al-fawāʾid:*[5]

> There are two types of sainthood: minor and major. Where the minor type is concerned, it means that the servant devotes himself to his Lord by making a dedicated practice of obedience to Him, abstinence from the causes of His displeasure, compliance with the commandments, avoidance of the prohibitions, striving to control the senses, and endeavouring to regulate the breathing. As for the major type, it means that Allah the Exalted befriends His servant by ridding his heart of everything apart from Himself, and holding him so close to Him that he sees nothing but Allah. If he tried to direct his attention toward anything other than Him, he would find it impossible to do so. It is inconceivable, of course, that he would ever attempt to do so; taking notice of something would cause awareness to be divided, and he has no awareness of anything other than the One who is the object of his quest and ardent yearning. This (state) will be attained by all of those endowed with the major sainthood, if Allah wills. As for those endowed with the minor sainthood, (this state) may be attained by some of them, but not by all.

By all of this, you should know that the opinion of those who maintain that seeing Allah (*ruʾya*) is impossible, except in the case of the Seal of

---

5 This may be the *Farāʾid al-fawāʾid fī bayān al-ʿaqāʾid* (first published in Istanbul, 1804), by Aḥmad b. Muḥammad al-Amīn Istanbuli. The book concerns the basic tenets of Islam.

the prophets ﷺ, is a false opinion. It can only be held by someone who is ignorant of the formulations of words and their meanings. If something is impossible, it can never come into existence; it cannot happen to anyone, because the occurrence of the impossible is an absurdity that necessarily requires the distortion of the facts of reality. Know that nothing is impossible for Allah the Glorious, except any form of partnership with Him. He is tremendously Exalted far beyond such an ascription. Other than that, the impossibilities discussed by the scholars of theology include an accidental or non-essential impossibility (*mustaḥīl ʿaraḍī*). For example, it was not impossible for Allah to send another messenger after Muḥammad ﷺ, either like him or better than him, but His Will was not joined to this, so it became an accidental impossibility. According to *al-Miʿyār*:

> The grand judge in Tunis, Abū ʿAbd-Allāh Muḥammad b. ʿAbd al-Salām, was asked: "Is it possible, in terms of capability, for Allah the Exalted to create someone more excellent than our Prophet Muḥammad ﷺ?" To this, he replied, "It is possible in terms of capability, but it did not happen." That came to the attention of one of his contemporaries among the scholars of Tunis, the righteous jurist Shaykh Abū al-Ḥasan b. al-Muntaṣir, may Allah bestow His mercy upon him. So he wrote to Ibn ʿAbd al-Salām, "O Muḥammad, if only your mother had not given birth to you! Since she did give birth to you, if only you had not acquired knowledge! Since you did acquire knowledge, if only you had not spoken!" It is said that Ibn ʿAbd al-Salām withdrew from this discussion, saying, "What have the Sufi recluses (*murābiṭūn*) to do with meddling in this unnecessary issue," as the question had been attributed to the righteous Shaykh Abū Muḥammad ʿAbd al-Hādī al-Ṣūfī, may Allah bestow His mercy upon him."

According to al-Khaṭīb Abū Saʿīd al-Shilwī:

> The correct response (to the question mentioned above) is this: "Capacity is relevant only to possibilities. As for the inconceivable, it cannot be defined in terms of capability or incapacity. Since Allah created the Prophet ﷺ as the most excellent of human beings, it is inconceivable that anyone might be more excellent than him."

According to Wānsharīsī,[6]

> One of the scholars has said, "The protest of the remonstrator against Ibn ʿAbd al-Salām is a shortcoming, an unjust assault against him, and a criticism of his answer that has been made without careful consideration, because the matter is controversial."

---

6 Aḥmad b. Yaḥyā al-Wānsharīsī al-Tilimsānī, also pronounced Wānsharīshī (d. 1508), was a North African scholar of the Mālikī school. He is the author of *Kitāb al-Miʿyār*, a collection of legal rulings.

The erudite scholar, the judge, Shaykh Abū ʿUthmān Saʿīd al-ʿAqabānī said in his commentary of *al-ʿAqīda al-burhāniyya*:[7]

> Know that something that has been possible in itself, should the command appear (to the contrary), may become inconceivable (*muḥāl*). For example: the belief of Abū Jahl[8] was possible in itself, but once Allah's decree concerning its nonexistence became known, from this perspective, it became inconceivable. So in cases such as these: does the capacity (*qudra*) hinge on the possibility in itself, or not; since preordained knowledge (*al-ʿilm al-qadīm*) decided on that particular thing's inconceivability? There is difference of opinion concerning this issue. Ghazālī answered the two statements in the affirmative, that the meaning of the first statement was that something's occurrence, in its essence, hinged on its capacity. The meaning of the second statement has to do with something's occurrence hinging on the knowledge that it will not happen. But the condition that something will not occur does not remove it from the realm of capacity. The explanation of this is that capacity does not hinge on what is inconceivable, nor does it hinge on what is necessary. It is as if Allah knows that something will not happen, so from this perspective its occurrence is impossible. So too, when Allah knows something will happen, its occurrence becomes obligatory from this perspective. But if His knowledge of something's non-occurrence should remove it from the realm of possibility, everything would become an obligated occurrence (and therefore removed from the realm of capacity). So something's occurrence thus depends on its occurrence or lack of occurrence in Allah's knowledge (not on capacity alone). So it is necessary that capacity not remain bound by the final decision, far Exalted is Allah from that!

It is apparent from the words of the Shaykh there there is dispute and difference of opinion on this issue between the theologians. The Shaykh considered it more beneficial to consider the capacity of an occurrence, and this was also the answer of Shaykh Ibn ʿAbd al-Salām, may Allah have mercy on him. If you contemplate all of this, it will become apparent to you the correctness of his answer, may Allah have mercy on him, as well as the accuracy of the response of Ghazālī to the two statements and his confirmation thereof, as brought forth by ʿAqabānī, may Allah have mercy on him. In this is perspective and searching for those who ponder, for the words here concern the permissible possibility. This possibility does not

7 This is *al-ʿAqīda al-burhāniyya* by the Moroccan scholar Abū Amr Salajī al-Uṣūlī (d. 1149, Fes).

8 Abū Jahl (the "father of ignorance") was the nickname for Amr b. Hishām (d. 624), one the Meccan leaders foremost in torturing and humiliating early converts to Islam in Mecca. At one point, the Prophet had prayed that Allah strengthen Islam with the conversion of either ʿUmar b. al-Khaṭṭāb or Abū Jahl.

necessitate the existence or nonexistence of an inconceivability. Such was the faith of Abū Jahl, at the same time both possible and intellectually inconceivable. So ponder this well.

Appendix VI

Racial Discrimination in the Spiritual Path

My dear brother, may Allah have mercy on you: know that Allah the Exalted said to the Prophet ﷺ in a sacred tradition (*ḥadīth qudsī*), "If My servant draws near to Me by a hand's breadth, I draw nearer to him by an arm's length." Allah did not limit this promise to the ancients only, nor the contemporary folk; nor the red or the black. Indeed, blackness of the skin does not prevent entry among the rank of those drawn near (to their Lord). The Prophet ﷺ said of the Abyssinians (al-Ḥabasha), they being black people (*al-sūdān*), "Even if the true faith had been in the Pleiades (*thurayya*),[1] they would have attained it!" He ﷺ also said, "Salmān[2] is one of us, the people of the Prophet's house (*ahl al-bayt*)." In connection with the saying of Allah, *And others among them who have not yet joined them, and He is the Omnipotent, the Wise* (Qurʾān, 62:3),[3] it is reported in *al-Jawāhir al-ḥisān* that Allah's Messenger ﷺ was asked, "Who are the others?" So he took hold of Salmān's hand and said, "Even if the true faith had been in the Pleiades, men such as these would

1 The Pleiades are a group of seven stars in the constellation Taurus.

2 Salmān al-Farsi was a Persian companion of the Prophet Muḥammad, who had been enslaved for many years before his emancipation at the hands of the Prophet. Due to his high merit, the companions of the Prophet were once arguing whether Salmān was one of the Ansar ("helpers" from Medina) or the Muhajirun ("emigrants" from Mecca). The matter was referred to the Prophet, who solved the issue by saying, "Salmān is one of us, the people of the house." See Majlisī, *Bihar al-anwār.*

3 Here are the relevant verses in full (Qurʾān, 62:2–3): *It is He who has sent among the illiterate folk a Messenger from among themselves to rehearse to them His Signs, to purify them, and to instruct them in Scripture and wisdom—although they had previously been in clear error—as well as others of them who have not yet joined them. And He is the Omnipotent, the All-Wise.*

have attained it!"[4] This narration is found in the collections of Muslim and Bukhārī.

Notice, may Allah have mercy on you, how the Prophet ﷺ applied this distinction to Salmān's people in particular, when there was no other black person present at the gathering.[5] So you must realize that black people may be endowed with goodness. May Allah furnish us with understanding of the secrets of His speech and the speech of His Prophet, for He is the Custodian thereof and the One who is Capable of it! You should also study the twenty-ninth chapter of *al-Futūḥāt al-Makkiyya*, by the Greatest Shaykh Ibn al-ᶜArabī al-Ḥātimī, concerning knowledge of the secret that linked Salmān to the people of the Prophet's family and the saintly poles (*al-aqṭāb*) whose secret knowledge he inherited. Here you will discover the cure for burning thirst and sickness. This matter is also mentioned in *Rūḥ al-bayān*, in connection with the Qurʾānic verse mentioned above.

Sahl b. Saᶜd al-Sāʾidī reported that the Prophet ﷺ once said, "In a dream, I saw myself watering black sheep, then white sheep next in turn. What is your interpretation, O Abū Bakr?" So Abū Bakr said, "O Prophet of Allah, as for the black sheep, they represent the Arabs; and as for the white sheep, they represent the non-Arabs who will follow you after the Arabs." The Prophet ﷺ then told him, "That is just how the angel Gabriel explained it to me."[6]

You should also study chapter 366 of *al-Futūḥāt al-Makkiyya*, where the author speaks about the prophetic inheritor (*khalīfa*) in the fourth generation (*qarn*) after three.[7] He explains that his distinguished followers (*rijāl*) will follow in the footsteps of the Prophet's companions, may Allah be well pleased with them. Ibn al-ᶜArabī says:

> Allah will appoint as his viziers a party whom Allah has concealed in the secrecy of His unseen realm. Through unveiling and spiritual witnessing, He has made them privy to the realities and the command of Allah among His servants. Affairs will be decided through their mutual consultation, for they are the gnostics, aware of things as they are. As for the *khalīfa*, he bears a sword of truth and civilized government. He has from Allah what his rank and status require, for he is the *khalīfa* of settlement (*musaddad*). He will understand the speech of the animals. His justice flows among the human beings and the jinn, by the secrets of his viziers' knowledge appointed by Allah

---

4 Reported by Bukhārī in his *Ṣaḥīḥ*, Muslim in his *Ṣaḥīḥ*, by Tirmidhī in his *Sunan*, and Ibn Ḥanbal in his *Musnad*.

5 In explaining this section, Shaykh Ḥasan Cisse (Medina-Baye, Kaolack, 2000) said that Salmān, although not of African descent, was dark skinned.

6 Reported by Ibn Ḥanbal in his *Musnad*.

7 The word *qarn*, here translated as "generation," may also mean "summit" or "mountain peak."

for him. Allah said, "It is incumbent upon Us to assist the believers" (Qur'ān 30:47). So they (the viziers) will follow in the footsteps of the distinguished ones (*rijāl*) among the Prophet's Companions, for *They are true to what they covenanted with Allah* (Qur'ān 33:23). And they will be from among the non-Arabs.

Concerning the verse, "Surely the noblest among you in the sight of Allah is the one of you who is most righteous" (Qur'ān 49:13), the author of *Rūḥ al-bayān* said:

> This divine statement contains a reason for the prohibition of racial prejudice, for it is said that the noblest in the sight of Allah is the one who is most righteous (who has *taqwā*), even if he is a black Abyssinian slave like Bilāl ﷺ. If you would compare yourself to others, therefore, you must compete with them in true devotion (*taqwā*); and in Allah's gracious favor and mercy; indeed, in Allah Himself. Consider the saying of the Prophet ﷺ, "I am the master (*sayyid*) of the children of Adam, and I say this without boasting."[8] In other words, "I do not take pride in the mastery (*siyāda*) or in messengership, but rather in worshipful servitude, for this is the honor, and what an honor it is!" Sufficient as a mark of honor is the precedence given to the servant over the messenger in the tesimony, "I bear witness that Muḥammad is His servant and His messenger."

It has been related that Allah's Messenger ﷺ once passed through the market of Medina, and he noticed that a young black man was saying, "If someone buys me as a slave, he must do so on the condition that he will not prevent me from performing the five daily prayers behind Allah's Messenger ﷺ." A man purchased him, and Allah's Messenger ﷺ used to see the black man at every prayer. Then he noticed that he was missing, so he asked his owner about him. The owner said, "He has a fever." So he ﷺ paid him a visit, then asked about him some days later. The owner told him, "His energy is spent and he is preparing for the death that is overtaking him." He ﷺ came and found him making his last movement and breathing his last breath, so he took charge of his funeral washing and burial. A matter of tremendous importance then came to the attention of the Emigrants (Muhājirīn) and the Helpers (Anṣār), through the revelation of the Qur'ānic verse (49:13), *Surely Allah is All-Knowing,* meaning of all of you and your deeds, and "*All-Aware*, meaning of the secrets of your spiritual states.

In his marginal notes, the Shaykh's son said: "Lineage is taken into account in customary usage and in Islamic law, so that a female descendant of the Prophet ﷺ (*sharīfa*) may not marry a Nabataean (Nabatī)." According to the dictionary, the Nabataeans (al-Anbāt) were a tribe with obscure origins, inhabiting the regions between the Euphrates and the

8 Reported by Muslim in his *Ṣaḥīḥ* and by Tirmidhī in his *Sunan.*

Syria. But lineage ceases to be of any consequence in the face of belief and true devotion (*taqwā*), which are greater and dearer than lineage. Lineage in the face of *taqwā* is as the stars that disappear when the sun rises. The disobedient sinner, even if he belongs to the Prophet's tribe of the Quraysh or is wealthy like a king, has no worth compared to the righteous believer, whether he is a black Abyssinian [or another race].

People pride themselves on many things in this world, but genealogy is most insidious. Unlike money, offspring, and property, genealogy is unattainable by someone who does not already possess it. The poor man may become rich, to the chagrin of the one who used to flaunt his wealth in front of him. For this reason, Allah made a particular point of declaring genealogy insignificant in the face of true devotion (*taqwā*). As genealogy is the greatest source of pride, the irrelevance of other things may easily be deduced by the irrelevance of genealogy in the face of *taqwā*. According to prophetic tradition, "Your Lord is One, and your father (Adam) is one. The Arab has no superiority over the non-Arab, or the non-Arab over the Arab; nor the red over the black, or the black over the red, except by virtue of righteousness (*taqwā*)."[9] On this (nobility due to *taqwā*), the religious scholars are in unanimous agreement, as has been attested to in *Baḥr al-ʿulūm*.[10]

One of the distinguished scholars has said, "The rivalry among creatures for precedence in the sight of Allah is due to their lineage, not their point of origin. With respect to the point of origin they are one, but where lineage is concerned they are rivals. According to the Qurʾān, *Surely the noblest among you in the sight of Allah is the one of you who is most righteous* (49:13). The contest for precedence is not resolved by deeds, since he who follows may outstrip the one who came before. And if nobility belonged to things because of their inherent prestige or their abodes, nobility would belong to the Devil (Iblīs) over Adam ﷺ, which is why he said, *I am better than him (Adam). You created me from fire, while You created him from clay* (Qurʾān, 7:12). But Iblīs was foolish in his assertion, for nobility is a divine prerogative, conferred only by Allah the Exalted. So nobility truly belonged to Adam ﷺ."

Jesus ﷺ the son of Mary was asked, "Who is the noblest of human beings?" He grasped two handfuls of dust, and he asked, "Which of these two is the more noble?" Then he put them together and threw them away. He said, "All human beings come from dust, and the noblest of them in the sight of Allah is the one who is most righteous." Salmān al-Fārsī ﷺ said, "My father is Islam; I have no father apart from it, while they boast of descent from Qays or Tamīm." The Prophet ﷺ said, "Allah does not take

9 Reported by Ibn Ḥanbal in his *Musnad* and by Abū Nuʿaym in *Ḥilya al-awliyāʾ*.

10 This could be the *Kitāb baḥr al-ʿulūm* by Abū Layth al-Samarqandī, a prominent work of Qurʾānic exegesis.

notice of your outer forms or your possessions, but He does take notice of your hearts and your intentions."[11] He is also recorded as having said, "O people, humankind consists of only two types: a righteous believer, noble in the sight of Allah, or a wretched corruptor, despised by Allah."[12] According to a report from Ibn ʿAbbās ♦, the Prophet ﷺ said: "The nobility of this world is wealth, and the nobility of the Hereafter is *taqwā*." Another *ḥadīth* is related from Abū Hurayra ♦, as recorded in *Kashf al-asrār*:[13]

> The people will be assembled on the Day of Resurrection; then they will be made to stand. Allah the Exalted will say to them, "Often you used to speak while I was silent, but today you will be silent and I will speak! I exalted My spiritual relationship, but you acknowledged only your genealogies. I said: 'Surely the noblest among you in the sight of Allah is the one of you who is most righteous.' But you were scornful, and said, 'No, the noblest are so-and-so, the son of so-and-so, and so-and-so the son of so-and-so.' So you exalted your genealogies and disparaged My spiritual relationship. But today I shall exalt My spiritual relationship and disparage your geneaolgies. On this day, the people assembled will surely come to know who are the holders of nobility. So where are the righteous folk?"

Imam al-Shāfiʿī said, "Allah will pay no attention to four things on the Day of Resurrection: the abstinence of the eunuch, the righteousness of a soldier, the fidelity of a woman, and the worship of a young boy." And this is explained as referring to the majority (within each group), as has been mentioned in *Maqāṣid al-ḥasana*.[14]

In *al-Taʾwīlāt al-najmiyya*,[15] the saying of Allah the Exalted, *O human-kind, We created you from a male and a female* (Qurʾān, 49:13), is said to refer to the creation of the hearts. This is meant to indicate that every human has been created from a male, meaning the spirit (*rūḥ*), and a female, meaning the soul (*nafs*). The verse continues: *And We have made*

---

11 Reported by Ibn Ḥanbal in his *Musnad*, Muslim in his *Ṣaḥīḥ*, and by Ibn Māja in his *Sunan*.

12 Reported by Tirmidhī in his *Sunan*.

13 The *Kashf al-asrār* by Ruzbihan al-Baqlī (d. 1209, Persia) describes the author's visionary experiences in the unseen world. It has been translated by Carl Ernst as *The Unveiling of Secrets: Diary of a Sufi Master* (N.p.: Parvardigar Press, 1997).

14 *Al-Maqāṣid al-ḥasana* is a work on *ḥadīth* by Muḥammad al-Sakhāwī (d. 1497), an Egyptian scholar of Shāfiʿī jurisprudence and prophetic traditions.

15 *Al-Taʾwīlāt al-najmiyya* is the comprehensive work of Qurʾānic exegesis written by the Persian Sufi ʿAlāʾ al-Dawla al-Simnānī at the end of the thirteenth century. Simnānī was a disciple of Najm al-Dīn al-Kubrā (of the Kubrāwiyya Sufi order), and claims that his own text records the beginning of his Shaykh's own exegesis. See Jamal Elias, *The Throne Carrier of God: The Life and Thought of ʿAla ad-Dawla As-Simnani* (Albany: State University of New York Press, 1995), p. 203–204.

you races and tribes. In other words, "We have made you into two types, those of races (*shuʿūb*), inclined toward their mother, she being the soul (*nafs*); and those of tribes (*qabāʾil*), inclined toward their father, he being characterized by the attributes of the spirit (*rūḥ*). The Qurʾānic verse concludes: *So that you may become mutually acquainted*. That is to say: "So that you may become acquainted with one another as masters of the hearts and lords of the souls." It is not meant to imply "that you may compete for numerological superiority, put each other down, or rival one another in boastfulness, taking pride in mental faculties and natural psychological characteristics." Such an interpretation (of the verse) lends itself to obscurity and murky darkness, from which no benefit can be derived. The only solution is to join (the verse) to faith and righteousness. Actions thereby remain untainted by hypocritical ostentation. Moral virtues remain free from passionate desires. Permitted desires are not related to self-conceit. Only in this case can benefit be derived from competition and rivalry.

Allah the Exalted said, *Surely the noblest among you in the sight of Allah is the most righteous*. The Prophet ﷺ added, "Nobility is righteousness (*taqwā*)."[16] The righteous one is he who is furthest from human characteristics and closest to divine characteristics. *Taqwā* means being cautiously on guard, and the one with *taqwā* is he who guards against his ego-self (*nafs*) by taking refuge in his Lord. Such a person is nobler in the sight of Allah than anyone else.

---

16 Cited in the *Iḥyāʾ ʿulūm al-dīn* of Imam al-Ghazālī.

Femininity and Sainthood

Know that femininity does not prevent inclusion among the best of Allah's chosen servants. Allah did not mention men's achievement of spiritual stations without also mentioning women's achievement. The Most High said:

Muslim men and Muslim women
Men who believe and women who believe
Men who speak the truth and women who speak the truth
Patient men and patient women
Humble men and humble women
Men who give in charity and women who give in charity
Men who keep the fast and women who keep the fast
Chaste men and chaste women
And men who remember Allah frequently and women who remember—
Allah has prepared for them forgiveness and a vast reward (Qurʾān, 33:35).

Of all the spiritual stations attained by men—other than bearing revelation (*risāla*), prophecy (*nubuwwa*), or the axis of sainthood (*quṭbāniyya*)—there is not one that is not teeming with women who are true believers, devoutly pious, pure, righteous, humble, and filled with good. Consider what has come in the Qurʾān concerning Mary in praise of her condition (*amr*): *Falsehood cannot approach it from in front or behind* (41:42). Allah's praise of Mary reached the extent of His mentioning her thirty times in the Qurʾān, resulting in scholarly disagreement as to whether or not she was actually a prophet. The truth of the matter was that she was a champion of truth (*ṣiddīqa*), for prophecy only comes through men. The proof is Allah's statement, *The Messiah, son of Mary, was only a Messenger ... and his mother was a champion of the Truth* (*ṣiddīqa*) (5:75).

So it has been made known that women are not denied access to the station of Truth's champions, nor to any of the other spiritual stations. There have been women who attained to spiritual stations attained only by very few men. Examples include Rābiʿa al-ʿAdawiyya[1] and those who have followed in her footsteps to the present day, like Lālla Manāna[2] in the time of our Shaykh (al-Tijānī), and others such as Amina bint al-Khāl. There is no end to the mention of such women. A poet has said:

> If women were as we have mentioned
> Women must surely be superior to men
> For femininity is no disgrace for the noun, "sun" (*shams*)
> And masculinity is no pride for the "crescent moon" (*hilāl*).[3]

It is related in the *Jawāhir al-maʿānī*[4] that ʿAlī Harāzim once asked Shaykh al-Tijānī ☙ the meaning of Allah's saying, *And when the angels said, "O Mary, Allah has chosen you and made you pure, and has preferred you above the women of all the worlds"* (Qurʾān, 3:42); and His saying, *And We inspired the mother of Moses, saying: "Suckle him, and when you fear for him, cast him into the river and do not be afraid, and do not grieve, for We shall bring him back to you, and We shall make him one of the Messengers"* (28:7). He asked him, "Does the speech of the angels to Mary mean that she was a prophet? And does the inspiration (*waḥy*) to the mother of Moses

---

1   Rābiʿa al-ʿAdawiyya al-Qaysiyya (717-801), of Basra (Iraq), was a famous ascetic and disciple of Ḥasan al-Baṣrī. Many of her statements have passed into the canon of Sufi aphorisms, such as, "O Allah! If I worship You out of fear for the Hellfire, throw me in it. If I worship You out of desire for Paradise, prevent me from it. But if I worship You for Your own sake, do not deny me Your everlasting Beauty." She died in Jerusalem. For more, see Farīd al-Dīn ʿAṭṭar, "Rabeʿa al-Adawiya," in *Muslim Saints and Mystics*, trans. Arberry (London: Routledge & Kegan Paul, 1983); and Margaret Smith, *Rābiʿa the Mystic & Her Fellow-saints in Islām: Being the Life and Teachings of Rābiʿa al-ʿAdawiyya al-Qaysiyya of Basra, Together with Some Account of the Place of the Women Saints in Islām* (Cambridge: Cambridge University Press, 1984).

2   Lālla Manāna was a companion of Shaykh Aḥmad al-Tijānī known for her spiritual unveilings. She was on good terms with the Moroccan Sultan, Mawlay Sulayman, and was influential in directing others to take the Tijānī Path, such as Aḥmad al-Banānī. She used to refer to Shaykh Tijānī as "the Sultan." On her first meeting with him, he informed her of an impending plague descending on Fes and asked her to pray for Allah to lift the calamity from the Muslims. This she did, and the plague was averted. See Aḥmad Sukayrij, *Kashf al-ḥijāb*. Sukayrij also mentions another prominent female enraptured mystic (*majdhūba*) of Fes who was Shaykh al-Tijānī's follower, Ṣafiyya Labbada, also famous for her spiritual unveilings.

3   Arabic nouns are endowed with either masculine or feminine genders that determine verbs and adjectives relating to them. Unlike many European languages, the Arabic word for sun is feminine while the word for moon is masculine.

4   The lengthy citation that follows is excerpted from the last chapter of the first volume of *Jawāhir al-maʿānī*, concerning Shaykh al-Tijānī's explanation of various verses of the Qurʾān put to him by his disciples.

likewise mean she was a prophet? And concerning the matron (*sayyida*) Mary and our matron Fāṭima (daughter of Muḥammad), which of them is superior? What about the (other) women of the worlds? What about (the merit of) Asiya bint Muzāhim, or Khadīja, or ʿĀʾisha, or Fāṭima, may Allah be pleased with them all?" The Shaykh replied:

> Here is the answer to your question, and with Allah is the success by His blessing and generosity:
>
> Know that the prophecy attributed to the matron Mary, and the argument of those who maintain it, is indeed based on Allah's saying, *And when the angels said, O Mary, Allah has chosen you and made you pure, and has preferred you above the women of all the worlds.* And the attribution of prophecy to the mother of Moses is likewise related to His saying, *And We inspired the mother of Moses.* These assertions are unreliable, however. The definitive opinion on the subject is that prophecy is not possible for women.
>
> As for Mary and Asiya, the Prophet ﷺ said about them: "Among men are many who have been perfected. But no women have achieved perfection except Asiya, the daughter of Muzāhim, and Mary, the daughter of ʿImrān."[5] The meaning here is that Asiya and Mary attained the rank of sincere truthfulness (*ṣiddīqiyya*), which is the highest degree in knowledge and gnosis of Allah—a knowledge permeating the whole being. There is nothing beyond this rank except that of that of the saintly poles (*quṭbaniyya*) and prophets (*nubuwwa*). So this is the height to which these women attained.
>
> As for Khadīja, the Prophet ﷺ spoke openly of her superior merit. This caused ʿĀʾisha to say, "I was never jealous of any woman among his wives with the exception of Khadīja, for he so often mentioned and venerated her."[6] Ibn Sabʿ[7] reported in his *Shifāʾ* that the Prophet one day told the people, "My favorite among my women would surely be ʿĀʾisha the daughter of (Abū Bakr) al-Ṣiddīq, were it not for the superior merit Allah bestowed on Khadīja, the daughter of Khuwaylid." Thus the Prophet proclaimed the superiority of Khadīja over ʿĀʾisha.
>
> (As for the superiority of Fāṭima) It has also been reported in the *Shifāʾ* of Ibn Sabʿ that the Prophet once said to Fāṭima, "You are the matron (*sayyida*) of the women of all the worlds." She put her hand on her head in modesty and asked, "But what of Asiya the daughter of Muzāhim, Mary the daughter of ʿImrān, and Khadīja the daughter

5 A *ḥadīth* reported in Bukhārī, Muslim, Tirmidhī, and Ibn Māja.

6 Narration found in Bukhārī, Muslim, Tirmidhī, Ibn Māja, and Ibn Ḥanbal.

7 Ibn Sabʿ was a scholar of prophetic traditions who was cited by Jalāl al-Dīn al-Suyūṭī in support of the idea that the Prophet Muḥammad's being was light, so that he did not caste a shadow.

of Khuwaylid?" He told her, "Asiya bint Muzāhim is the matron of the women of her world, Mary bint Imrān is the matron of the women of her world, Khadīja bint Khuwaylid is the matron of the women of her world, and you are the matron of the women of your world."[8] And he told ʿAlī on the day of his marriage to Fāṭima, "I have given the matron of the women of all the worlds to you in marriage."

As for ʿĀʾisha, the Prophet once said, "The superiority of ʿĀʾisha over all other women is like the superiority of meat and broth over all other food."[9]

The scholars have differed in regard to relative superiority of Fāṭima and ʿĀʾisha. Each side favoring one or the other has based its argument on the relevant prophetic tradition cited above. Mālik said, "As for myself, I do not consider anyone superior to her whom he described as a part of him ﷺ."[10]

The gnostic sages have arrived at a similar conclusion, but by way of spiritual unveiling, not by listening to reports. They have generally concluded that after the death of her father ﷺ, Fāṭima attained the exalted station of the saintly poles (*quṭbaniyya*). This being the case, there is no comparison between Fāṭima and ʿĀʾisha. Allah says, *Surely the noblest among you in the sight of Allah is the one of you who is most truly devout* (Qurʾān, 49:13). And after the prophets, none of Allah's creation, whether among humans or angels, whatever they may achieve, can realize one tenth of one percent of the true devotion (*taqwā*) realized by the pole of the saintly poles (*quṭb al-aqṭāb*). This saintly pole is the most excellent Muslim in each age, apart from the "keys of the treasures" (*mafātīḥ al-kunūz*) that may exist. The *quṭb* is superior to them in some respects, and they are superior to him in some respects.

If you have understood this, you will know that Fāṭima's excellence surpasses that of ʿĀʾisha, Mary, and Asiya. Her attainment to the station of the saintly pole, from which other women are excluded, was due to the fact she did not menstruate. Also, she received from her father a degree of perfection to which other women could not aspire. So this explains (in part) how she became the saintly pole, and the saintly pole (*quṭb*) is the master of existence (*sayyid al-wujūd*) in every time, apart from the Keys of the Treasuries (*mafātīḥ kunūz*) that may exist. The lack of her menstruation was due to her formation (in the womb of Khadīja) from the Prophet's seed after he had eaten one of the apples from the Garden of Paradise. For this reason, the Prophet ﷺ said of her,

8 A *ḥadīth* cited by Zabīdī in *Ittiḥāf al-sāda al-muttaqīn fī sharḥ Iḥyāʾ ʿulūm al-dīn* and by Haythamī in *Majmaʿ al-zawāʾid*.

9 A *ḥadīth* on the authority of Abū Mūsā al-Ashʿarī found in the *Sunan* of Ibn Māja.

10 The Prophet once said, "Fāṭima is a part of me. Whatever upsets her upsets me. Whatever harms her harms me" (*ḥadīth* in Muslim, with similar wording in Tirmidhī).

"She is a human houri." Her being a houri was due to the fact that she was not created from the specks of dust transmitted from the body of Adam, peace be upon him, to the rest of his offspring. The seed that created her was formed from the mysteries and secrets of the Garden, from which Allah created the houris. This resulted in the perfection of her purity, for she was untouched by (some of) the conditions of human nature that other women experience. So she became a human houri, and she attained to the highest degree in the presence of the Real, above which there is no degree except prophethood. ʿĀʾisha and the others could never aspire to this, so it must be clear to you that Fāṭima is more excellent than all excellent women.

We said that the attribution of prophecy to Mary is an invalid hypothesis, and this is based on (her inability to attain) the degree of the saintly pole (implicit in prophethood). In every time, the saintly pole has a mandate (*wijha*) for every atom among the existing entities, thus assisting and improving everything in existence, atom by atom. Whenever a worshipper prostrates himself for the sake of Allah, or bows for Him, or stands erect for Him, or remembers Allah, the saintly pole is the one who makes this possible for him (*muqīm lahu*). It is through the saintly pole that the spiritual master (*shaykh*) performs his glorification, and it is through him that the worshipper performs his worship, through him that one who prostrates before Allah prostrates. And it is through him that the other design (*wijha*), which cannot be described, is realized.

The essence of the matter is that the saintly pole is to the whole of existence as the spirit (*rūḥ*) is to the body. The body has no vitality, no sense and no movement without the spirit. All faculties of the physical body, external and internal, are made possible by the living spirit linked to the body. If the spirit departs from the physical body, all of its faculties cease to function, and it becomes a corpse.

The same applies to all the elements in existence, with regard to their relationship to the saintly pole. He is for them like the spirit for the physical body. If his spirituality (*rūḥāniyya*) departed from them, the whole of existence would pass into extinction. He is the spirit of existence, and the entirety of its properties. He is responsible for their grouping and their separation, their commonality and their particularity, their liberation and their confinement. None of the elements of existence can survive unless the spirituality of the saintly pole exists within them. If the saintly pole's spirituality was removed from them, the whole of existence would cease, becoming a featureless corpse.

This power of his comes from his bearing the burden of the supreme secret, and his traveling in the entirety of its domains. By means of the secret of the Greatest Name, he has come to be steadfast in the presence of Allah, perfectly observing the modes of conduct prescribed by the divine Presence. He perfectly fulfills Allah's rightful dues, whether pertaining to the manifestation of His Names, His Attributes, or His Essence; and this at all times and in every instant measured by the blink of an eye.

There is no limit to the ways in which our Lord is constantly manifesting Himself in every instant measured by the blink of an eye, through His Names, His Attributes, His Essence, and the revolving of His affairs. Throughout all of this, the saintly pole remains steadfast in the presence of Allah, according to each manifestation what it rightfully deserves in terms of proper conduct, duties, and service; in every instant measured by the blink of an eye. Even while Allah's manifestations keep multiplying endlessly, he fulfills all their rightful dues and treats them each with proper conduct.

There is no one in existence apart from the saintly pole who can bear the burden of all of these manifestations of the Real. And he is engaged in this throughout his life, in every instant measured by the blink of an eye. If all the sincerely truthful (*ṣiddīqīn*) stood together in Allah's presence to fulfill these terms, they would become extinct in less than the blink of an eye. But this is the saintly pole's regular habit.

If you have understood this well, you will realize that women do not have the strength to bear this burden, because menstruation precludes them from the performance of devotions. If a woman assumed the station of saintly polehood (*quṭbaniyya*), surely she would neglect some of the rights due to Allah on certain days of her life, namely the days of her menstruation. And if she did neglect the obligations due to Allah, the office of saintly polehood would be annihilated, and this would result in the extinction of the whole of existence.

So you have understood why women cannot assume the office of saintly polehood. And since this is true of the saintly polehood, it is even more logical in regards to the office of prophethood. Indeed, prophethood is a weightier task than axial sainthood (*quṭbaniyya*). As for Fāṭima, may Allah be pleased with her, she attained to the rank of the saintly pole because she acquired certain divine perfections, so she could bear the burden of the secret of the Greatest Name.

Appendix VIII

Ecstasy and the Spiritual Concert

As for the ecstasies of the enraptured ones and the lovers, and their infatuation with the remembrance of Allah, or the recitation of the poems of the lovers, they have a firm basis and a strong support. The Prophet ﷺ was once passionately affected, so that his cloak fell off. He then presented it to those who remembered the Beloved, and he said something that was interpreted as, "If someone is not moved by the rememberance of the Beloved, he is not one of the noble-hearted."

In *al-Futūḥāt al-Makkiyya*, at the end of one of his wise counsels, the author (Ibn al-ʿArabī) relates:

> We were informed, in the city of Mosul in the year 601 A.H. (1204 C.E.), by Aḥmad b. Masʿūd b. Shaddād al-Muqriʾ al-Mawṣilī, he being a reliable source; that he was informed by Abū Jaʿfar b. al-Qāḍī; on the authority of Yūsuf b. al-Qāsim al-Diyābakrī; on the authority of Jamāl al-Islām Abū al-Ḥasan ʿAlī b. Aḥmad al-Qurayshī al-Hakkārī; on the authority of Abū al-Ḥasan al-Karkhī; that Abū al-ʿAbbās Aḥmad b. Muḥammad b. al-Faḍl al-Nihāwandī said that his Shaykh, Jaʿfar b. Muḥammad al-Khuldī, said:
>
> "I traveled with Junayd, may Allah bestow His mercy upon him, on the road to the Hijaz, until we reached Mount Sinai. Junayd climbed the mountain, and we along with him. When we stood upon the spot upon which Moses ﷺ had once stood, we were overcome by the awesome dignity of the place. We were accompanied by an eloquent speaker; so Junayd urged him to say something. He said:
>
> There appeared to him, after the passion had subsided,
> A lightning flash that shimmered, with a scintillating glow
>
> It appeared like the hem of a cloak, and beneath it

Shelter was hard to find, its columns unapproachable.

So he tried to see how it shined, but he could not look at it
And He, the Exalted, turned him away,

For its scimitars consisted of fire
And its scabbards were streaming with rain.

"Junayd then fell into ecstasy, and we along with him. None of us knew whether we were in heaven or on earth.

"There was a monastery in our vicinity, and in it was a monk. The monk cried, 'O community of Muḥammad! For the sake of Allah, respond to me!' However no one paid him any attention because of the pleasure of the moment. The monk cried out a second time, 'For the sake of the true religion, you must respond to me!' But still no one answered him, so he appealed a third time, 'For the sake of the One whom you worship…' and yet still no one gave him a response. Then when we retired from the spiritual concert (*samāʾ*), and Junayd was about to descend from the mountain, we said, 'This monk appealed to us and entreated us, but we paid him no heed.' Junayd then said, 'Let us return to him, for perhaps Allah will guide him to Islam.'

"So we called out to him and he came to join us. He saluted us with the greeting of peace (*salām*), and he asked, 'Which of you is the teacher?' Junayd replied, 'All of them are masters and teachers.' He said, 'Surely, one of them must be the most distinguished,' and we all pointed to Junayd. The monk said, 'Tell me about this knowledge that you have acquired. Is it particular to your religion or is it universal?' Junayd replied, 'It is surely particular.' The monk then proceeded to ask, 'Is it for special groups of people, or for people in general?' Junayd said, 'It is surely for special groups of people.' The monk inquired, 'With what intention do they stand up (in the spiritual concert)?' Junayd said, 'With the intention of hope and delight in Allah the Exalted.' He asked, 'With what intention do you listen?' Junayd replied, 'With the intention of hearing from Allah the Exalted.' The monk then asked, 'With what intention do you cry aloud?' Junayd responded, 'With the intention of compliance with Lordly service, as when Allah the Exalted said to the spirits: *"Am I not your Lord?" They said, "Yes indeed, we testify"* (Qurʾān 7:172). The monk then asked, 'What is this voice?' Junayd said, 'A pre-eternal call.' The monk asked, 'With what intention do you sit down?' Junayd said, 'Out of fear of offending Allah the Exalted.' The monk exclaimed, 'You have spoken the truth!'

"He then said, 'Stretch out your hand! I bear witness that there is no god but Allah, One without partners, and that Muḥammad ﷺ is Allah's servant and messenger.' The monk embraced Islam and maintained its excellence. Junayd asked him, 'How did you know I was telling the truth?' He replied, 'Because I read in the Gospel (*Injīl*), which had been revealed to the Messiah, son of Mary:

> The elite members of the community of Muḥammad will wear a tattered gown (*khirqa*). They will eat a piece of bread, and they will be satisfied with a mouthful. In Allah they will rejoice, for Him they will yearn with ardent longing, and in Him they will become passionately affected. They will both love and fear Him.

"The monk stayed with us for three days and then died, may Allah bestow His mercy upon him."

For more on the subject of the spiritual concert (*samāʿ*), the reader should refer to the section pertaining to congregational remembrance (Section I, Chapter 3).

Appendix IX

Concerning Spiritual Retreat, the Qurʾān and the Spiritual Path

Shaykh Sīdī Mukhtār al-Kuntī was once asked, "What is the reason for prohibiting the recitation of the Qurʾān in the spiritual retreat (*khalwa*)?" To this, he replied:

> The recitation of the Qurʾān is not forbidden under any circumstances, except in cases of a legal prohibition. The spiritual retreat is a special case, for the simple reason that its purpose is confined to the concentration on the Name. In this way, the divine manifestation may be singular, and this singular manifestation is imprinted on the mirror of the seeker's insightful perception. For when one illumination (*fatḥ*) is opened, it becomes a doorway to all illuminations.
>
> The manifestations of the Qurʾān are manifold, and when they are numerous, the seeker's aspiration (*himma*) is correspondingly fragmented and the journey becomes protracted for the seeker. His aim is the shortening of the journey, for he is intent on spiritual elevation (*tarqiya*) and not engaged in the quest for rewards. Otherwise, those who draw near to their Lord will not draw near in the manner described (in a *ḥadīth qudsī*) in which Allah the Exalted says, "If My servant draws nearer to Me by a hand's breadth, I draw near to him by an arm's length."

Shaykh al-Kuntī was also asked, "Is it permissible for someone to enter the spiritual path (*ṭarīqa*) before he has finished acquiring all the knowledge he may need, or is it not?" The Shaykh replied:

> It is permissible, and it is not far-fetched if we maintain its necessity. Entry into the spiritual path will only increase him in knowledge by virtue of his affiliation with the chain (*silsila*) of the spiritual masters (*shuyūkh*). However, it is not appropriate to enter isolation or pious seclusion before he has acquired the knowledge he needs, for these practices are not accompanied by learning and teaching."

Concluding Supplication

It has occurred to me that I ought to refrain from including too much in this Appendix, for fear of becoming tediously long-winded.

I ask Allah to provide us with the perfection of approval and acceptance, just as I beg Him for pardon, well-being, and everlasting dispensation in the religion, in this world and in the Hereafter. I ask Him to resurrect us in the company of Shaykh al-Tijānī, the Seal of the Saints. Allah is the Custodian of my supplication and the One who is Capable of it. I ask Him to grant us enough of what concerns us and what does not concern us in the business of this world and the Hereafter.

I ask Him to benefit us, and to make us a source of benefit to all of His servants, the believing men and the believing women, the Muslim men and the Muslim women, those of them who are still alive and those who have died. Amen, O Lord of all the worlds!

This work was concluded on the eighth day of Muḥarram, in the year 1351 A.H. (1932 C.E.) in the village of Kossi.

Glory be to your Lord, the Lord of Majesty,
Far from what they attribute!
And peace be upon those sent as Messengers,
And praise be to Allah, Lord of all the worlds!
(Qurʾān, 37:180–182)

Glossary of Arabic Terms

ʿAdnān	Adnān was a descendent of the Prophet Ismāʿil through his son Kedar. The Banū, or tribe, or people, of ʿAdnān are the ʿAdnānī Arabs tracing descent through the Prophet Ibrāhīm. The "best of the Banū ʿAdnān" refers to the Prophet Muḥammad.
ʿālim / ʿulamāʾ	Scholar of the classical Islamic sciences.
ʿārif	Knowledgeable person of God, one who has attained gnosis (*maʿrifa*); a gnostic.
Ashʿariyya	The school of Islamic theology that emerged in opposition to the Muʿtazila, thus holding to the primacy of revelation over reason. It became the dominant school of theology after the ninth century of the common era.
Banū Muḍar	The Banū Muḍar, one of two branches of the ʿAdānī tribe of northern Arabia, trace descent from Muḍar, who descended from Niẓār, a son of ʿAdnān.
basmala	The name for the phrase, "In the Name of Allah the Compassionate the Merciful."
dhāt	The essence or essential being (of Allah).
dhawq	Literally "taste," in the context of Sufism meaning the taste or experience of divine realities and spiritual states.
dhikr / adhkār	The remembrance or recollection of God.
fatḥ	Literally "opening" or "victory;" in Sufism, this refers to spiritual illumination.
fayḍa	Flood, overflowing grace or bounty.
fiqh	Literally "understanding," this has come to mean the understanding of the sacred law by Muslim jurists, thus jurisprudence.

ghawth	Savior or succor. In Sufism the word is often used interchangeably with pole (*quṭb*).
ḥadīth	Traditions or sayings reported from the Prophet Muḥammad.
ḥaḍra	Spiritual presence; similar to a divine Reality (*ḥaqīqa*). Thus *al-Ḥaḍra al-Muḥammadiyya*, the spiritual presence of Muḥammad, is similar in meaning to the Muḥammadan spiritual reality (*al-Ḥaqīqa al-Muḥammadiyya*).
Ḥājj	The pilgrimage to Mecca compulsory for all Muslims with means.
ḥāl	Spiritual state, considered a gift bestowed by God; usually an ephemeral experience, as opposed to the spiritual station (*maqām*).
ḥaqīqa	Reality, in the context of Sufism, the Reality of divine Being.
haylala	The congregational remembrance of *La ilaha ill-Allāh*
himma	Spiritual or devotional zeal, aspiration. An individual's *himma* is not always limited to himself; the *himma* of the spiritual guide is considered an important inspiration for the disciple, sometimes likened to a magnetic force or rope pulling the disciple into the divine Presence.
ʿilm / ʿulūm	Knowledge, science, religious learning; sometimes connoting knowledge gained by exercise of the mind, rather than gnosis (*maʿrifa*) obtained directly from God.
Imām	Technically the leader of the prayer in the mosque, but more generally the head or leader of a community.
ism / asmāʾ	A name; one of the ninety-nine Names of God.
jadhb	The attraction or rapture the Sufi aspirant feels for God
jinn	Beings or "spirits" of free will, created from fire and thus unseen by most humans.

Khārij	The Khārij, or khawārij, get their name from "going out" of the community by rejecting the authority of ᶜAlī b. Abī Ṭālib, and any later imam who they believed went against the commandment of Allah. They were responsible for the assassination of ᶜAlī.
maᶜrifa	The experiential knowledge of God, gnosis; as opposed to rational speculation.
madhhab	A school of Islamic jurisprudence, usually referring to one of four: the Ḥanafī, Mālikī, Shāfiᶜī, or Ḥanbalī schools.
Mahdi	The "rightly guided one"; in Islamic eschatology, he is the expected savior who will usher in a period of peace prior to the coming of the Antichrist and the subsequent return of Jesus.
majdhūb	One who has been attracted or enraptured by the divine.
Malāmatiyya	The Malāmatiyya were Sufis that invited public reproach by pretending to be engaged in reprehensible behavior. This was a means of hiding their real spiritual position and purifying their ego-selves. Later Sufis justified the appellation "Malāmatī" for a person of high spiritual state who blended with the ordinary Muslims, not distinguishing himself by public displays of piety beyond that normally practiced by the Muslim community.
maqām	Spiritual station; an enduring state of spiritual elevation that the aspirant acquires in his progress towards God; as opposed to *ḥāl*, the temporary spiritual state.
Muᶜtazila	The Muᶜtazila originated in the eighth century and strove to reconcile Islamic doctrines with the Hellenistic framework of reason.
mujaddid	"Renewer"; according to *ḥadīth*, one will come every hundred years to renew the faith of Islam.
mujtahid	Scholar of independent legal reasoning, not bound by a particular school of jurisprudence (*madhhab*).
murīd	Literally "one who desires"; thus an aspirant or Sufi disciple.
nafs	The self, soul, or ego of the human being.

quṭb / aqṭāb	According to Sufis, the saintly "pole" through whom Allah maintains the universe through his exemplary consciousness of God.
rūḥ	The spirit or "eternal soul" of the human being.
sharīʿa	The Islamic sacred law based on the texts of the Qurʾān and the Sunna.
Shaykh	A general term for an Islamic scholar, but in Sufism the word also carries the meaning of a spiritual master or guide capable of training aspirants.
ṣifāt	The attributes or descriptions (of Allah).
sulūk	The act of traveling the path to God
Sunna	The model of sayings and actions left by the Prophet Muḥammad and his Companions.
tahlīl	The act of declaring God's Oneness, saying *La ilaha ill-Allāh.*
taḥmīd	The act of praising or thanking God, saying *Alḥamdu-li-Llāh.*
takbīr	The act of magnifying God, saying *Allahu-Akbar.*
tarbiya	In the context of Sufism, the spiritual training or education leading to gnosis.
ṭarīqa / ṭuruq	Spiritual path, way, or Sufi order.
taṣawwuf	The science of the soul's purification, thus Sufism.
tasbīḥ	The act of glorifying God, saying *Subḥān-Allāh.*
walī / awliyāʾ	A friend of God; thus saint.
waẓīfa	Literally an "office" or "duty"; in the context of Sufism a daily practice of remembrance similar to the *wird.* Within the Tijāniyya, the *waẓīfa* is recited aloud and in congregation, as opposed to the *wird*, which is recited silently and individually.
wird / awrād	The liturgical arrangement of remembrance practiced by a particular Sufi order.
zakāt	Official alms-tax, calculated at 2.5% of a Muslim's wealth.

Sources for the *Kāshif*

The following sources are cited most frequently by Shaykh Ibrāhīm. They do not include *ḥadīth* collections such as *Ṣaḥīḥ* Bukhārī or the *Muwaṭṭāʾ* of Imam Mālik. Works which are only cited once or twice are not included here.

Baqlī, Ruzbihan al-, *Arāʾis al-bayān.*
Baqlī (d. 1209) was a famous Sufi of Shiraz, Persia. The *Arāʾis* is a Sufi commentary on the Qurʾān. He is also the author of *Kashf al-asrār*, which has been translated by Carl Ernst as *The Unveiling of Secrets: Diary of a Sufi Master* (Chapel Hill, NC: Parvardigar Press, 1997).

Barūsī, Ismāʿīl al-Ḥaqqī, *Rūḥ al-bayān.*
The ten-volume Qurʾānic exegesis of Ismaʿīl al-Ḥaqqī Barūsī (or Burūsāwī or Bursāwī, d. 1724, Anatolia), *Rūḥ al-bayān*, is one of the most comprehensive Sufi exegeses of the Qurʾān.

Ghazālī, Abū Ḥamīd al-, *Iḥyāʾ ʿulūm al-dīn.*
Ghazālī (d. 1111, Baghdad), was known the "Proof (Ḥujja) of Islam," and is credited with the most comprehensive reconciliation of Sufism with the Islamic legal tradition. His primary work is the *Iḥyāʾ ʿulūm al-dīn*, translated as *The Revival of the Religious Sciences*, comprising four volumes of ten chapters (or books) each. The most reliable translations are the "Ghazālī series" published by the Islamic Texts Society, which has completed books 9, 11–13, 15, 32, 34, and 37. The website www.ghazali.org has collected primary sources and translations of most of the *Iḥyāʾ*'s forty chapters from various sources and has made them available online.

Harāzim al-Barāda, ʿAlī al-, *Jawāhir al-maʿānī wa bulūgh al-amānī fī fayḍ Sīdī Abī al-ʿAbbās al-Tijānī.*

The *Jawāhir al-maʿānī*, written in 1799 by Shaykh Aḥmad al-Tijānī's closest disciple, is considered the most important primary source for the Tijāniyya.

Ibn ʿAbbād al-Rundī, Abū ʿAbd-Allāh, *Ghayth al-mawāhib al-ʿalīyya* (known as *al-Tanbīh*)

Ibn ʿAbbād (d. 1390) was born in Ronda, Andalusia, and later settled in Fes, Morocco, where he led the Friday prayer in the Qarawiyyin mosque. He was a renowned shaykh of the Shādhiliyya order, and his book, *al-Tanbīh* is the first commentary on the *Ḥikam* of Ibn ʿAṭāʾ Allāh. He also authored two collections of letters. For more on his life and works, see John Renard, trans., *Ibn ʿAbbad of Ronda: Letters on the Sufi Path* (New York: Paulist Press, 1986).

Ibn ʿAjība, Aḥmad, *Īqāẓ al-himam fī sharḥ Kitāb al-ḥikam.*

Ibn ʿAjība (d. 1809) was a prominent scholar of the Shādhiliyya Sufi order in Morocco. His commentary on the *Kitāb al-ḥikam* by Ibn ʿAṭāʾ Allāh (d. 1309, Alexandria) is considered one of the best of many such commentaries, and it is widely known in West Africa. His autobiography has been translated: *The Autobiography (Fahrasa) of a Moroccan Sufi: Aḥmad ibn ʿAjiba*, by Jean-Louis Michon and David Streight (Louisville, KY: Fons Vitae, 1999).

Ibn al-ʿArabī al-Ḥātimī, Muḥyī al-Dīn, *al-Futūḥāt al-Makkiyya*

Ibn al-ʿArabī (d. 1240) was born in Andalusia and later settled in Syria. He was known as "the Greatest Shaykh," and his writings have influenced later Sufi scholars, including those of the Tijāniyya. His most comprehensive work is the multi-volume *al-Futūḥāt al-Makkiyya*, translated as *Meccan Illuminations*. This latter work speaks about the Seal of the Saints that will be found in Fes, Morocco. Numerous studies have appeared on the Shaykh and his writings. Noteworthy among these are the works of Henry Corbin, Michel Chodkiewicz, William Chittick, Titus Burckhardt, Claude Addas, Michael Sells, and Alexander Knysh.

Ibn al-ʿArabī al-Ḥātimī, Muḥyī al-Dīn, *ʿAnqāʾ mughrib fī maʿrifat khatm al-awliyāʾ wa shams al-maghrib.*

This work concerns the saintly hierarchy and the concept of the Seal of the Saints. It has been translated by Gerald Elmore, *Islamic Sainthood in the Fullness of Time: Ibn ʿArabi's book 'The Fabulous Gryphon'* (Leiden: Brill, 1999).

Ibn ʿAṭāʾ Allāh al-Iskandarī, *Kitāb al-tanwīr fī isāt al-tadbīr.*

This work has been described as the "basic training manual for Sufis in North Africa." It has been translated by Scott Kugle, *The Book of Illumination* (Louisville, KY: Fons Vitae, 2005). Ibn ʿAṭāʾ Allāh (d.

1309) was the second successor to Abū Ḥasan al-Shādhilī after Abū ʿAbbās al-Mursī.

Ibn ʿAṭāʾ Allāh al-Iskandarī, *Kitāb al-ḥikam*
The "Book of Aphorisms," is the most famous work of Ibn ʿAṭāʾ Allāh. It has been translated by Victor Danner, *The Book of Wisdoms* (New York: Paulist Press, 1979).

Ibn Ḥajar al-ʿAsqalānī, *Fatḥ al-Bārī.*
Ibn Ḥajar (d. 1448) was a prominent Egypt *ḥadīth* scholar who wrote numerous works, the most widely known being *Fatḥ al-Bārī*, a commentary on the *ḥadīth* collection of Bukhārī.

Ibn Ḥajar al-Haytamī al-Makkī, *al-Fatawa al-ḥadīthiyya*
Haytamī (d. 1556) was a prominent scholar of Mālikī jurisprudence and Sufism.

Ibn al-Ḥājj al-Abdārī al-Fāsī, Muḥammad, *Madkhal al-sharʿ al-sharīf ʿala al-madhāhib.*
The *Madkhal* is a four volume work discussing various points of Islamic law, mostly from the perspective of Mālikī jurisprudence. Ibn al-Ḥājj (d. 1336) taught at the Qarawiyyin University in Fes, Morocco, but traveled throughout North Africa, and is buried in Egypt.

Ibn al-Mishrī, Muḥammad, *Kitāb al-jāmiʿ li al-ʿulūm al-fāʾida min biḥār al-quṭb al-maktūm*
The *Kitāb al-jāmiʿ* is one of the primary sources of the Tijānī order, written during the founder's lifetime in 1808. Its author was Muḥammad b. al-Mishrī (d. 1809), a prominent Sufi and scholar from Constantine, Algeria. Unlike the *Jawāhir al-maʿānī*, the work has never been published.

Ibn al-Mubārak al-Lamaṭī, Aḥmad, *al-Dhahab al-ibrīz min kalām Sayyid ʿAbd al-ʿAzīz al-Dabbāgh.*
Ibn al-Mubārak was the disciple of Shaykh ʿAbd al-ʿAzīz al-Dabbāgh (d. 1717, Fes), a renowned master of the Shādhilī order who articulated ideas later associated with the *Ṭarīqa Muḥammadiyya* movements of Shaykh Aḥmad al-Tijānī and Aḥmad b. Idrīs. For a recent translation, see: John O'Kane and Bernd Radtke, *Pure Gold from the Words of Sayyidī ʿAbd al-ʿAzīz al-Dabbāgh: Al-Dhahab al-Ibrīz min Kalām Sayyidī ʿAbd al-ʿAzīz al-Dabbāgh* (Leiden: Brill, 2007).

Ibn al-Sāʾiḥ, Muḥammad al-ʿArabī, *Bughya al-mustafīd.*
Ibn al-Sāʾiḥ (d. 1892, Rabat) was one of the most celebrated Tijānī scholars of the nineteenth century. His work *Bughya al-mustafīd,* a commentary on a poem called *Munya al-murīd* written by the Mauritanian Shaykh Aḥmad al-Tijānī Sīdī Bābā al-ʿAlawī al-Shinqīṭī, is one of the primary works of the Tijāniyya. For more on his life and

work, see Abdelaziz Benabdallah, *Le Soufisme Afro-Maghrebin aux XIX et XXème Siècles* (Rabat, 1995).

Khafājī, Shihāb al-Dīn al-, *Nasīm al-riyāḍ fī sharḥ Shifāʾ al-Qāḍī ʿIyād*
This work by the Egyptian Ḥanafī scholar al-Khafājī (d. 1659) is a commentary on the *Shifāʾ* of Qāḍī Īyād, the renowned book of *ḥadīth* and prophetic biography from the twelfth century.

Kuntī, al-Mukhtār al-, *al-Kawkab al-waqqād fī faḍl dhikr al-mashāʾikh wa ḥaqāʾiq*.
Kuntī (d. 1811), described by Shaykh Ibrāhīm as "the shaykh of shaykhs, the renowned scholar and divine gnostic," was one of the most important Qādiri shaykhs and scholars in eighteenth-century West Africa. He lived in Timbuktu, Mali, but revived the Qādiriyya Sufi order throughout West Africa, becoming the shaykh of Usmane dan Fodio (d. 1817), the founder of the Sokoto Caliphate based in northern Nigeria, as well as several Mauritanian branches of the Qādiriyya. For more on Kuntī, see Aziz Batran, *The Qadiryya brotherhood in West Africa and the Western Sahara: The life and times of Shaykh al-Mukhtar al-Kunti, (1729–1811)* (Rabat: Université Mohammed V, 2001).

Nawawī, Yaḥyā b. Sharaf al-, *Kitāb al-adhkār*
Nawawī (d. 1278) was an eminent *ḥadīth* scholar and Shāfiʿī jurist in Damascus. He wrote numerous books, including *ḥadīth* compilations such as *Riyāḍ al-ṣālihīn*, works on jurisprudence such as *Minhaj al-ṭālibīn*, a book on prophetic supplications and remembrances called *Kitāb al-adhkār*, and a work on inner sincerity, *Bustān al-ʿārifīn*.

Qushayrī, Abū al-Qāsim al-, *Risāla ilā al-ṣūfiyya*.
Qushayrī (d. 1072) was an important Persian scholar, famous for *ḥadīth* transmission, Qurʾān exegesis and his Sufi teachings. His *Risāla* [Epistle to the Sufis] has been most influential work. For a translation of al-Qushayrī's *Risāla*, see Barbara Von Schlegell, trans., *Principals of Sufism by al-Qushayri* (Berkeley, CA: Mizan Press, 1990), or Alexander Knysh, trans., *al-Qushayri's Epistle on Sufism: al-Risala al-Qushayriyya fī ʿilm al-Tasawwuf* (Reading, UK: Garnet Publishing, 2007).

Rāzī, Muḥammad b. ʿUmar Fakhr al-Dīn al-, *Tafsīr al-kabīr*.
Rāzī (d. 1210, Herat, Persia) was a great theologian, philosopher, and scientist. His multi-volume *Tafsīr al-kabīr*, also known as *Mafātiḥ al-ghayb*, is a comprehensive exegesis of the Qurʾān.

Ṣāwī, Aḥmad al-, *Ḥāshiya al-Ṣāwī ʿala al-Jalālayn*
Ṣāwī (d. 1825) was a Mālikī scholar from India who wrote a commentary on the margins (*ḥāshiya*) of the *Tafsīr al-Jalālayn* of Jalāl al-Dīn al-Suyūṭī and Jalāl al-Dīn al-Maḥallī. Ṣāwī's *ḥāshiya* became popular among West African scholars, for whom the *Tafsīr al-Jalālayn* has been

one of the most important works of exegesis for centuries. Ṣāwī was an early critic of the Wahhabi movement in Saudi Arabia, and accused it of being a contemporary manifestation of the Khawārij.

Shaʿrānī, ʿAbd al-Wahhāb al-, *Baḥr al-mawrūd fī al-mawāthiq wa al-ʿuhūd.*
Shaʿrānī (d. 1565) was a renowned Egyptian Shādhilī Sufi shaykh and jurist of the Ḥanafī school. He was the disciple of ʿAlī Khawwāṣ, and emerged as one of the primary interpreters of Ibn al-ʿArabī.

Shaʿrānī, ʿAbd al-Wahhāb al-, *Kitāb al-jawāhir wa al-durar min-mā istafādu Sayyid ʿAbd al-Wahhāb al-Shaʿrānī min Shaykhihi Sayyidi ʿAlī al-Khawwāṣ.*
The *Kitāb al-jawāhir* is a collection of teachings of Shaʿrānī's Shaykh ʿAlī al-Khawwāṣ.

Shaʿrānī, ʿAbd al-Wahhāb al-, *Laṭāʾif al-minan wa al-akhlāq.*
This work may be considered Shaʿrānī's spiritual autobiography. It should not be confused with the *Laṭāʾif al-minan* of Ibn ʿAṭāʾ Allāh.

Shaʿrānī, ʿAbd al-Wahhāb al-, *al-Ṭabaqāt al-kubrā al-musamma bi Lawāqiḥ al-anwār fī ṭabaqāt al-akhyār.*
The *Ṭabaqāt* is a collection of 430 biographies of righteous Sufis, from the time of the Prophet's companions to Shaʿrānī's s own time.

Suyūṭī, Jalāl al-Dīn al-, *Tafsīr al-Jalālayn*
Suyūṭī (d. 1505) was famous Egyptian scholar known as the renewer (*mujaddid*) of the faith in his century. He was also an accomplished Sufi. He authored numerous works, many of which quickly became widespread in West Africa. Most significant in this regard has been the work of Qurʾānic exegesis, *Tafsīr al-Jalālayn*, co-authored by Jalāl al-Dīn al-Maḥallī.

Thaʿālibī, ʿAbd al-Raḥmān al-, *Jawāhir al-ḥisān fī tafsīr al-Qurʾān.*
Thaʿalibī's (d. 1471) *Jawāhir al-ḥisān* is a multi-volume exegesis of the Qurʾān.

ʿUbayda b. Muḥammad al-Ṣaghīr, *Mīzāb al-raḥma fī al-tarbiya bi al-ṭarīqa al-Tijāniyya.*
ʿUbayda was a nineteenth-century Mauritanian scholar of the Ḥāfiẓiyya Tijānī legacy. His primary work is considered a synthesis of the teachings of Muḥammad al-Ḥāfiẓ al-Shinqīṭī. The book, written in 1851, details a process of spiritual training (*tarbiya*) based on the principle of gratitude (*shukr*) passing through the three stations of *islām*, *īmān*, and *iḥsān*.

ʿUmar al-Fūtī Tāl, *Kitāb al-rimāḥ hizb al-Raḥīm ʿala nuhūr ḥizb al-rajīm.*
Ḥājj ʿUmar (d. 1864) was originally from Futa Toro, Senegal, but died in Mali fighting a *jihād* against the pagan Bambara kingdoms

and encroaching French influence. He briefly established an Islamic state in what is now part of Mali, Senegal, and Guinea. The *Kitāb al-rimāḥ* established Ḥājj ʿUmar as one of the nineteenth century's most renowned Tijānī scholars. For more on his social and political activities, see David Robinson, *The Holy War of Umar Tal* (New York: Oxford University Press, 1985).

Wāḥidī, Abū al-Ḥasan al-, *Kitāb asbāb nuzūl al-Qurʾān.*
Wāḥidī (d. 1076) was a famous interpreter of the Qurʾān from Persia whose work *Asbāb nuzūl* concerns the circumstances of revelation of various verses of the Qurʾān.

Wānsharīsī, Aḥmad b. Yaḥyā al-, *Kitāb al-miʿyār.*
Wānsharīsī, also pronounced Wānsharīshī (d. 1508), was a North African scholar of the Mālikī school. His *Kitāb al-miʿyār* is a comprehensive collection of legal rulings and is considered an important historical and legal source. This work was the central source for David Powers, *Law, Society and Culture in the Maghrib, 1300–1500* (Cambridge: Cambridge University Press, 2002).

Yadālī, Muḥammad al-, *Sharḥ khātima al-taṣawwuf.*
Yadālī (d. 1753) was a famous Mauritanian jurist and Shādhilī Sufi of the Daymanī tribe. Besides the works on Sufism, *Sharḥ shahiyya al-samāʾ*, and *Sharḥ khātima al-taṣawwuf*, he also wrote an exegesis of the Qurʾān called *al-Dhahab.*

Zabīdi, Murtaḍā al-, *Tāj al-ʿarūs min jawāhir al-qāmūs.*
Shaykh Muḥammad al-Ḥusayni, known as Murtaḍā al-Zabīdi (originally from India, d. 1790, Egypt) was one of the most famous *ḥadīth* scholars of his time; he was a Ḥanafi jurist, and lexicographer. *Tāj al-ʿarūs min jawāhir al-qāmūs* is one of the largest Arabic dictionaries, originally meant as a commentary on *al-Qāmūs al-muḥīt.* For more on Zabīdī, see Stefan Reichumuth, *The World of Murtada al-Zabidi* (Cambridge: Gibb Memorial Trust, 2009).

Zarrūq, Aḥmad, al-Burnūsī al-Fāsī, *Taʾsīs al-qawāʾid wa al-uṣūl wa taḥṣīl al-fawāʾid li-dhawī al-wuṣūl fī al-taṣawwuf.*
Zarrūq (d. 1493) was a scholar and Sufi from North Africa who stressed the proper balance between the sacred law (*sharīʿa*) and Sufism. He spent many years in Cairo, where he studied under Muḥammad al-Sakhāwī, the student of Ibn Ḥajar al-ʿAsqalānī. His primary spiritual guide in Cairo was Aḥmad b. ʿUqba al-Ḥaḍramī (d. 1489), a saint with both Shādhili and Qādirī Sufi affiliations, originally from Yemen, he settled in Cairo. Zarrūq himself eventually settled in Libya. Like his Shaykh Ḥaḍramī, Zarrūq's exact Sufi affliliations are ambiguous, seemingly a mixture of the Shādhiliyya, Qādiriyya, and Suhrawardiyya lines of transmission and practices. He wrote numerous works on juris-

prudence, prophetic traditions, supplications, and Sufism. For more on Shaykh Aḥmad Zarrūq, see Scott Kugle, *Rebel between Spirit and Law: Ahmad Zarruq, Sainthood, and Authority in Islam* (Bloomington: Indiana University Press, 2006); and Ali Fahmi Khashim, *Zarruq, the Sufi: A guide in the Way and a Leader to the Truth, a Biographical and Critical Study of a Mystic from North Africa* (Tripoli: General Company for Publication, 1976); and Zainab Istrabadi, "The Principles of Sufism (Qawāʾid al-Taṣawwuf)": An Annotated Translation with Introduction (Ph.D. diss., Indiana University, 1988).

Prominent Personalities

The following list of personalities is meant as a reference for figures mentioned frequently by Shaykh Ibrāhīm in the *Kāshif*.

Abū Madyan Shuʿayb

Abū Madyan (d. 1198) was born in Andalusia and died in Tlemcen (Algeria). He was the teacher of ʿAbd al-Salām b. Mashīsh and thus an important figure in the development of the Shādhiliyya order. He had begun teaching in Bougie (Algeria) after returning from pilgrimage, influencing the likes of Ibn al-ʿArabī, Ibn Mashīsh and Shādhili. For more on his life and thinking, see Vincent Cornell, *The Way of Abu Madyan: Doctrinal and Poetic Works of Abu Madyan Shuʿayb ibn al-Husayn al-Ansari* (Cambridge: Islamic Texts Society, 1996).

Abū Yazīd al-Bisṭāmī

Abū Yazīd (d. 874) was a prominent Sufi from Bisṭām, Persia. He is credited with numerous ecstatic utterances.

ʿAlī al-Khawwāṣ

ʿAlī al-Khawwāṣ (d. 1532) was a shaykh of the Shādhiliyya Sufi order under whom Shaʿrānī studied in Egypt.

Dhū al-Nūn al-Miṣrī

Dhū al-Nūn (d. 859) was an early Sufi of Egypt. He was arrested in 829 on charges of heresy and sent to prison in Baghdad. He later returned to Cairo, where he is buried.

Ḥājj ʿAbd-Allāh b. al-Ḥājj al-ʿAlawī

ʿAbd-Allāh wuld al-Ḥājj (d. 1927) was a renowned scholar and gnostic from Mauritania who traveled widely in the Senegambian region, frequently visiting al-Ḥājj ʿAbd-Allāh Niasse. His *silsila* passes through Shaykh Aḥmad b. Baddi (known as "Abba," d. 1905), to his father Shaykh Muhamdi "Baddi" (d. 1855), the most prominent disciple of Shaykh Muḥammad al-Ḥāfiẓ b. al-Mukhtār (d. 1830). Al-Ḥājj ʿAbd-Allāh wuld al-Ḥājj was the father of Muḥammad (known as "al-Mishri"), the father of the current Shaykh of Matamawlana (Mauritania), al-Ḥājj ʿAbd-Allāh Mishrī.

Ḥākim al-Tirmidhī
Tirmidhī (d. 905 or 910) lived in Tirmidh, near Balkh, in modern-day Afghanistan. He is the first known Sufi or expound on the concept of the Seal of Saints.

Ḥasan al-Baṣrī
Ḥasan al-Baṣrī (d. 737) became a student of ʿAlī b. Abī Ṭālib at a young age. He moved from Medina to Iraq, where he formed a school and taught both juristic and ascetic sciences. Most lines of Sufi knowledge transmission pass through him to ʿAlī.

Imam al-Ḥaramayn
ʿAbd al-Mālik Abū al-Maʿali al-Juwaynī al-Shāfiʿī (d. 1085, Hijaz), known as Imam al-Ḥaramayn, was one of the most famous scholars of the Ashʿarī school of theology. He was also the teacher of Abū Ḥāmid al-Ghazālī.

ʿIzz al-Dīn al-Sulamī
ʿIzz al-Dīn (d. 1261) was a famous Shāfiʿī jurist and Shādhilī Sufi who spent most of his life in Syria and wrote *Aqāʾid ahl al-Islām*.

Junayd b. Muḥammad Abū Qāsim al-Khazzāz
Junayd (d. 910, Baghdad) was perhaps the most famous of the early Sufis within Islam, articulating ideas of sobriety in mysticism and the annihilation (*fanāʾ*) of the ego in Allah. See Michael Sells, *Early Islamic Mysticism: Sufi, Qurʾān, Miʿraj, Poetic and Theological Writings* (New Jersey: Paulist Press, 1996), p. 21–22. Nearly all the Sufi orders, except the Tijāniyya (whose *silsila* goes directly from the Prophet to Shaykh Aḥmad al-Tijānī), provide their followers with a chain of spiritual transmission (*silsila*) passing through Junayd.

Khiḍr
Khiḍr is the name given for the mystical guide of Moses mentioned in the Qurʾān (18:66).

Makhzūmī, ʿUmar b. Mūsā al-
"Sirāj al-Dīn" al-Makhzūmī (fifteenth century) was head judge of his time in Damascus. He was the student of Sirāj al-Dīn al-Bulqinī, a famous *ḥadīth* specialist. Both Bulqinī and Makhzūmī came to defend Ibn al-ʿArabī, Bulqinī after originally criticizing him. Jalāl al-Dīn Suyūṭī listed al-Makhzūmī as one of his teachers.

Mālik b. Anas
Imam Mālik (d. 795) is the eponym for the Mālikī school of jurisprudence. He lived in Medina, the city of the Prophet, and authored the *Muwaṭṭāʾ*, an early collection of traditions, mostly with legal bearing. For more on Imam Mālik's role in the development of Islamic juris-

prudence, see Yasin Dutton, *The Origins of Islamic Law: The Qurʾān, the Muwaṭṭāʾ and the Madinan ʿAmal* (London: Routledge, 2002).

Mawlūd Fāl

Shaykh Mawlūd Fāl was initiated into the Tijāniyya by Muḥammad al- Ḥāfiẓ, and later traveled to Fes, Morocco to have his initiation renewed at the main *zāwiya* there just after the passing of Shaykh Aḥmad al-Tijānī (1815). Mawlūd Fāl traveled widely throughout West Africa and left many propagators of the Order in regions such as Futa Jallon, northern Nigeria, and Sudan.

Muḥammad al-Ḥāfiẓ b. al-Mukhtār b. al-Ḥabīb al-Shinqīṭī

Shaykh Muḥammad al-Ḥāfiẓ (1759–1830), mentioned in the text as "our Shaykh and our means of access to Allah ... by whose hand the Ṭarīqa has spread in the lands of the far west." Shaykh al-Ḥāfiẓ was of the Idaw ʿAlī people in Mauritania. He visited Shaykh Aḥmad al-Tijānī in Fes in from 1800–1804/5 and was the first to bring the Tijāniyya Order into Mauritania, from where it later spread to the rest of West Africa.

Sahl al-Tustarī

Tustarī (d. 896) was an influential figure in the early development of Sufism. Qushayrī said of him, "He had no peer in his time for correct transactions and fearing Allah, and he was a man of miraculous occurrences."

Shādhilī, Abū Ḥasan al-

Shādhilī (d. 1258) was a renowned Sufi scholar of Moroccan origin who settled in Egypt and became the eponym for the Shādhiliyya Sufi order, found primarily in North Africa.

Tijānī, Abū al-ʿAbbās Aḥmad al-

Shaykh Aḥmad al-Tijānī (b. 1737, Algeria; d. 1815, Fes) was a descendent of the Prophet Muḥammad ﷺ who founded the Ṭarīqa Muḥammadiyya Tijāniyya by order of the Prophet in a waking vision. His followers consider him the "Hidden Pole" (*al-quṭb al-maktūm*) and the "Seal of the Saints" (*khatm al-ʿawliyāʾ*), based on his unprecedented proximity to the Prophet.

Lightning Source UK Ltd.
Milton Keynes UK
UKHW02f1955070918
328515UK00013B/269/P

9 781891 785474